Qualitative Research with Socio-Technical Grounded Theory

Rashina Hoda

Qualitative Research with Socio-Technical Grounded Theory

A Practical Guide to Qualitative Data Analysis and Theory Development in the Digital World

Springer

Rashina Hoda
Faculty of Information Technology
Monash University
Melbourne, VIC, Australia

ISBN 978-3-031-60532-1 ISBN 978-3-031-60533-8 (eBook)
https://doi.org/10.1007/978-3-031-60533-8

Cover illustration: iStock.com/antoniokhr

This Springer imprint is published by the registered company Springer Nature Switzerland AG
The registered company address is: Gewerbestrasse 11, 6330 Cham, Switzerland

Dedicated to my parents, Mrs Sabiha Hoda, retired Professor of English Literature, and Dr Najmul Hoda, retired Professor of Pedodontics and WHO Fellow—the original socio-technical influences in my life.

Foreword

Software engineering (SE) has, during its more than half a century of research and practice, gradually been accepted as a socio-technical endeavour. Populated by software engineers and computer scientists, research and development projects have, to a large degree, been staffed mostly by people based on their skills in numbers, algorithms, and structured logic. Consequently, they observed and interpreted the world primarily in terms of numbers, algorithms, and formal structures.

With the emerging insight that not all SE issues can be deduced from mathematical foundations, empirical approaches started to emerge under the label of experimental software engineering during the 1970s and 1980s. Still, the pioneering work was dominantly quantitative, applying hypothesis testing to experimental setups, with humans conducting limited SE tasks in highly controlled environments. While these efforts were groundbreaking in adding rigour to the knowledge creation process, they mostly treated social factors equal to technical factors, trying to control and sample their variation—which due to the huge number and variation of factors is a Sisyphean task.

Caroline Seaman's landmark paper from 1999 on qualitative methods in empirical SE—a silver jubilee this year—broke the ice to acknowledge the social side of SE and consequently to methods emerging from Social Sciences. In the related research area of Information Systems, qualitative methods, including grounded theory (GT), were more commonly received, while the engineering community remained quite sceptical. However, SE researchers gradually adapted and adopted methods from the qualitative tool-box, including my own and colleagues' work on case studies. Still, grounded theory studies were considered somewhat strange birds by many, including myself. Maybe the cult-like character of language in professing oneself to the Glaserian, Strauss-Corbinian, or Constructivist faction was a deterrent? Most probable, ignorance played a bigger role in the scepticism, at least in my own case, where embracement has come with increasing knowledge and understanding of grounded theory principles and practices.

It is therefore highly appreciated that Prof. Rashina Hoda now presents a comprehensive book on Qualitative Research with Socio-Technical Grounded Theory, where she adapts general grounded theory methods to the specific context and audience of socio-technical SE, based on her own extensive research practice. The book has a potential to reduce the ignorance among SE researchers and set a standard for research practice—not the least in the hands of supervisors and peer reviewers. The book extends and deepens her TSE paper on the same topic, framing it in the research philosophy context, adding detailed guidance and examples of data collection and analysis, as well as of theory development. My only concern is its sheer volume. Few senior researchers allow themselves to read a book from cover to cover. However, they do not have to since the book is well structured and written, allowing the reader to find guidance when needs appear.

In these days of "nulla dies sine AI",[1] when ML and LLM models are thrown at various data sets for research purposes, what relevance do these technologies have for socio-technical grounded theory? In the concluding chapter, Hoda opens up for a balanced discussion through examples about both technical and social implications of using LLMs, like ChatGPT, in the research process. She concludes that the experienced human analyst still is at the core of grounded theory research, and my hypothesis and hope is that it will remain so even when more powerful tools assist the process.

This book is a valuable and timely contribution to the SE community. It is a gold mine for PhD students who may learn by examples and be empowered to teach their supervisors to adopt socio-technical grounded theory to further advance SE research. It is published at the right time, when the acceptance for qualitative research is growing, and before new attempts to quantify it—for example, by requesting inter-rater statistics in the coding process—have taken ground, and before ChatGPT's successors have taken over.

Lund, Sweden
March, 2024

Per Runeson

[1] Paraphrase of the Latin phrase "Nulla dies sine linea" meaning "no day without a line", often read as "no day without a line of writing". The idea was originated by Pliny the Elder in the first century AD.

Preface

I first caught the qualitative research "bug" as I embarked on my PhD journey around the mid-2000s at Victoria University of Wellington, New Zealand. Agile software development had just started proliferating across the software industry. It placed people at the heart of software engineering (SE), validating my own experiences as a software developer. I became motivated to study agile software teams. Borrowing a qualitative research method from Sociology was a natural choice for this purpose. However, piecing together an understanding of the traditional grounded theory (GT) methods from the many different books written by and for sociologists did not come easy. Subsequently, I wrote several papers elucidating GT steps and procedures and sharing my experiences with the wider SE research community.

Through my own research experience and that of supervising and reviewing others over time, I was convinced of two things. First, it did not have to be that difficult for SE researchers to excel in qualitative research and theory development. Second, there was something unique about the SE research context that meant GT had to be adapted, but that had not been systematically addressed. Motivated by these concerns, I decided to write a book that would serve as a practical guide to ease GT adoption and practice in SE research. By the time I had expanded on how SE researchers could go about charting their paths to qualitative data analysis and theory development, I realised it was no longer Glaserian, Strauss-Corbinian, or Constructivist GT that I was writing about. What I had ended up formulating was a modern socio-technical version of traditional GT. I defined the socio-technical research framework that underpinned my version and called it socio-technical grounded theory (STGT). While traditional GT methods enable the study of social phenomena, STGT enables the study of socio-technical phenomena that abound in SE and related disciplines. Traditional GT methods subscribe to specific research paradigms. In contrast, STGT can be applied with different paradigms depending on physical, virtual, and extended realities and researcher worldviews. Traditional GT methods focus exclusively on enabling theory development. STGT, on the other hand, can be applied as a full method for theory development and in a limited capacity for data analysis within qualitative and mixed-methods research studies. STGT was formally introduced in my TSE article (early access 2021, published 2022) while I continued to write this book.

The book is structured into five parts. Part I—Introduction includes three chapters that serve to provide an overview of the book in Chap. 1 About This Book; a brief history of the origins and evolution of the grounded theory methods in Chap. 2

Traditional Grounded Theory Methods; and an introduction to STGT in Chap. 3 Socio-Technical Grounded Theory: An Overview. Part II—Foundations of Research includes three chapters that serve to cover the foundational building blocks of empirical research through a simple yet powerful approach to designing research methods in Chap. 4 Research Design Canvas; the fundamental concepts of philosophy in Chap. 5 Research Philosophy; and the myriad of literature review methods including those suited to STGT in Chap. 6 Literature Reviews

Part III—Qualitative Data Collection and Analysis includes four chapters that serve to explain the key concepts related to collecting qualitative data in Chap. 7 Basics of Qualitative Data Collection; a wide range of techniques used for collecting qualitative data in Chap. 8 Techniques of Qualitative Data Collection; how to go about preparing and filtering qualitative data in Chap. 9 Qualitative Data Preparation and Filtering; and the data analysis procedures of open coding, constant comparison, and memoing in Chap. 10 STGT for Qualitative Data Analysis.

Part IV—Theory Development includes two chapters that explain what is considered theory (or theoretical outcomes) in Chap. 11 What Is Theory?; and the advanced STGT steps of theory development in Chap. 12 Theory Development. Part V—Evaluation and Future Directions includes two chapters that present the evaluation guidelines for assessing STGT applications and outcomes in Chap. 13 Evaluation Guidelines; and explore new opportunities in qualitative research using large language models in Chap. 14 Future Directions in Qualitative Research.

If you are new to qualitative research or research in general, you will benefit from reading all the chapters, preferably in sequence. If you are considering a *full STGT study*, the book will take you through a full research journey, from an interest in a topic to developing mature theoretical outcomes. If you are considering a limited application of *STGT for data analysis* as part of a qualitative or mixed-methods research study, you will find the chapters in Parts II and III especially valuable.

If you are an experienced researcher who is time-poor, you can select specific chapters to browse (or download in the digital format) based on what piques your interest or addresses your doubts and challenges (see Chap. 1 About This Book for a detailed overview). If you are a reviewer, you will find the foundational research concepts in Part II and evaluation guidelines in Part V particularly illustrative and handy. If you are curious about how the future of qualitative research may be transformed with the advent of large language models powering Generative AI, you will enjoy my interactions with ChatGPT in the last chapter.

Writing this book has been a transformational journey across time, space, and disciplines. The manuscript travelled and transformed with me as I crossed the "ditch" from the University of Auckland, New Zealand, to Monash University, Australia. Even as the global pandemic took much away from us, I found refuge in writing, pouring my passion and experiences into words. It lured me down the rabbit holes of Philosophy and Ethics and into the AI wonderland.

Like most research method guide books, this is a labour of love—my love for qualitative research and confidence in STGT to enable rich studies on socio-technical topics. Simply put, this is the book I wish I had at the start of my research journey. I hope it makes yours easier, enriching, and enjoyable.

Melbourne, VIC, Australia
March, 2024

Rashina Hoda

Acknowledgements

Then which of the favours of your Lord will you deny?
– repeated 31 times, Chapter Ar-Rahmaan (The Compassionate), The Holy Qur'an

All praise be to Allah (Arabic for God), who blessed me with knowledge and patience and surrounded me with supportive and kind people who inspire me.

Narrated Abu Huraira: The Prophet (peace be upon him) said: *He who does not thank the people is not thankful to Allah* (Source: Sunan Abi Dawud 4811)

This book would not have been possible without the unwavering support of my loving family and friends. I am forever indebted to my late grandma—Mrs Qamrun Nisa Begum, a fearless champion of girls education, light-years ahead of her times—whom I will always aspire to emulate; my parents, retired Professors Najmul Hoda and Sabiha Hoda, who gifted me my wings; my husband, Mohammed Asif, who added the wind beneath those wings so I could fly; my elder son, Atif, who was my sounding board and creative guide for many design ideas; and my younger son, Imran, I love you. I am grateful to my brother and *guru*, Asif Hoda, for our numerous discussions on theories during the writing of this book and to my eldest brother, Shariq Hoda, for always expecting the very best from me. I thank my best friend, Amaara Rehmaan, for her faith in me. I lovingly thank my cat, Noorie, who made some serious attempts at contributing to the book by walking across the keyboard and whose antics provided much-needed comic relief.

There are a number of incredible people I need to thank on the professional front. I am sincerely grateful to Barney Glaser and Anselm Strauss for their invaluable contributions to the qualitative research community through the introduction of the original grounded theory research method, and to Juliet Corbin, Anselm Strauss, and Kathy Charmaz for the evolution of the method. My editor at Springer, Ralf Gerstner, for his encouragement, patience, and support through the writing of this book, including some challenging times during the global pandemic. I thank my long-term mentor, John Grundy. When I expressed concern about people being accustomed to reading research guide books authored by men with Anglo-Saxon names and questioned whether anyone would read one written by an usually named woman of colour, he simply replied "it's about time." My Dean, Ann Nicholson, the mentor I didn't know I needed, for always encouraging me to keep going. My lovely colleagues and students at the HumaniSE lab, Software Engineering group, and the wider Faculty of Information Technology.

I am especially grateful to Per Runeson for his wonderful foreword and support of the book. I am highly indebted to Christoph Treude, Philippe Kruchten, Mark Swillus, and John Grundy for their invaluable and in-depth feedback for improvements. I express my sincere gratitude to Margaret-Anne Storey, Klaas-Jan Stol, Zainab Masood, Johannes Berlind Soderqist, Steve Adolph, Burak Turhan, Dulaji Hidellaarachchi, Bran Selic, Ingo Mueller, Kla Tantithamthavorn, and Arty Starr for providing their inputs and thoughtful feedback. I thank Associate Editor Ana Monero and the anonymous reviewers of my Socio-Technical Grounded Theory (STGT) article in the *IEEE Transactions on Software Engineering*.

There are several acts of kindness I need to acknowledge that have become stepping stones in my book-writing journey. I thank Helen Sharp, Yvonne Dittrich, Alex Sloley, and all the participants of the open space session I hosted at XP2018, who enthusiastically cheered me on as I nervously announced my book writing in a public setting for the first time. I am grateful to Xavier Franch for his excellent chairing of my first STGT technical briefing at ICSE 2021 and all the participants of the technical briefings at ICSE 2021, ICSE 2023, ICSE 2024, and various talks and seminars on STGT. I am grateful to Margaret-Anne Storey, Evan Leybourn, Alessandro Garcia and Wesley K. G. Assunção, and Zerina Tomkins for inviting me to present to the empirical research methods class, the Business Agility Institute's research group, the PUC-Rio graduate course, and the Digital Health Week 2023, respectively—all of these experiences helped me address a wide range of needs and audiences. I am grateful to Rachel Slattery for allowing me to use her talk and article as an example of visual notes-taking and open coding, and to Paul McIntosh whose pro tip for proof reading proved highly effective towards the end of my book-writing journey.

I am extremely grateful to those who guided me at the beginning of my research journey, my PhD supervisors, James Noble for believing in me when I doubted myself, and Stuart Marshall, for our numerous debates on qualitative research. I thank George Allan for planting the seed of adapting traditional GT in my mind many years ago. I thank Angela Martin and Michael Waterman with whom I exchanged tips and tricks of the trade as we navigated our PhD journeys. I am blessed to have been able to guide the PhD journeys of Zainab Maṡood, Yogeshwar Shastri, Yanti Andriyani, and Latha Murugesan at the University of Auckland, New Zealand, and Kashumi Madapme, Aastha Pant, Dulaji Hidellaarachchi, Hashini Gunatilake, Ulrike Maria Graetsch, and Harsha Perera at Monash University, Melbourne.

I express my sincere gratitude to all the industry practitioners worldwide who have participated in my research studies and those run by my students over the years—your generously shared experiences make our research grounded. I thank all those people who have ever asked me a question or two, and expressed their curiosity, interests, concerns, confusion, or frustration with qualitative data analysis and theory development—I have tried to address them in the book. I humbly acknowledge all those new and seasoned researchers who are using STGT in their research in expected and unexpected domains, including software engineering, requirements engineering, artificial intelligence, human robot interaction, human computer interaction, digital health, blockchain, and other emerging and interdisciplinary areas.

Finally, I thank you, the reader, who has picked up this book, for being interested in learning about qualitative research, producing robust qualitative findings, and possibly even developing theories—this is for *you*, I hope it helps!

Contents

About the Author

Rashina Hoda is a Professor of Software Engineering in the Faculty of Information Technology at Monash University, Australia, where she researches the human and socio-technical aspects of software engineering (SE) and artificial intelligence. She is passionate about helping people improve processes and outcomes—reflected in her empirical research on agile methods, mentoring of early career researchers on the use of research methods, and her educating of the next generation of software engineers. She is a passionate champion of marginalised girls and women in STEM and serves as the Associate Dean (Equity Diversity and Inclusion).

Rashina has been immersed in empirical research for two decades, practising, supervising, reviewing, and editing qualitative and mixed methods SE research. She has published over 130 peer-reviewed papers in premier SE venues, many being outcomes of Grounded Theory (GT) research. Two of her GT papers appear in the five "most comprehensive and detailed" of the nearly hundred papers reviewed in a critical review of GT in SE research by Stol et al. (2016). She received a distinguished paper award at the International Conference on Software Engineering (ICSE 2017).

Based on years of learning and reflections, she adapted the traditional GT methods to suit the unique socio-technical context of SE research projects and developed socio-technical grounded theory (STGT). She first introduced STGT in a TSE paper (early access 2021, published 2022) and has since presented it as a journal first talk at ICSE 2022 and as technical briefings at ICSE 2021, ICSE 2023, and ICSE 2024.

She is an active member of the international SE research community, serving as an Associate Editor of IEEE Transactions on Software Engineering and on the organising and programme committees for ICSE, International Conference on the Cooperative and Human Aspects of Software Engineering (CHASE), Foundations of Software Engineering (FSE), International Conference on Information Systems (ICIS), and International Conference on Agile Software Development (XP). She is a public speaker, presenting her research at TEDxAuckland, Agile conferences, industry and public events, and in news, print, and media.

Previously, she was a Senior Lecturer at the University of Auckland, New Zealand. She holds a PhD in Computer Science from Victoria University of Wellington, New Zealand, and a Bachelors (Honours) degree in Computer Science from Louisiana State University, USA. She has also had a short experience in the industry as a software developer. Rashina is often described as having a knack for presenting complex ideas in simple, clear, and engaging ways, a skill liberally applied in this book. In her free time, she enjoys sketching, reading, writing poems and short stories, walking in nature, and spending time with family and friends.

PART I

Introduction

1 About This Book

Abstract This chapter explains the motivations behind writing this book, who the book is for, how to use the book, and the role of the book in relation to research practice.

1.1 Why This Book? Why Now?

Socio-technical grounded theory (STGT) was first introduced in a paper published in the IEEE Transactions on Software Engineering (Hoda, 2022). Since then, STGT has been applied to study a range of topics across the domains of software engineering (SE), requirements engineering, artificial intelligence, human–robot interaction, human–computer interaction, digital health, blockchain, and other emerging and interdisciplinary areas. Some topics investigated using STGT include:

- Understanding and supporting neuro-diverse software developers (Gama & Lacerda, 2023)
- Human aspects in requirements engineering (Hidellaarachchi et al., 2023)
- Emotion-oriented requirements change handling (Madampe et al., 2023)
- Data challenges in data-intensive software systems (Graetsch et al., 2023)
- Ethics in artificial intelligence (Pant et al., 2023)

R. Hoda, *Qualitative Research with Socio-Technical Grounded Theory*,
https://doi.org/10.1007/978-3-031-60533-8_1

- Empathy in software developer and user interactions (Gunatilake et al., 2024)
- Enhancing block chain adoption (Li et al., 2023)
- Adapting user interfaces for software supporting chronic diseases (Wang et al., 2023)
- Understanding human–robot encounters (Chan & Hauser, 2023)

One of the motivations for writing this book was to describe in depth the procedures and techniques of qualitative research using STGT and to share relevant tips and examples in a way that a journal form can simply not afford.

Besides this, there are several other motivations behind writing this book. Some are common across disciplines, such as the need to address the changing landscape of qualitative research in an increasingly digital world. This is also the prime motivation for introducing a socio-technical research framework (described in Chap. 3 Socio-Technical Grounded Theory: An Overview.) Other motivations are more specific to software engineering and related disciplines, such as the rise of human aspects research, growing interest in inductive theory development, and challenges faced by researchers from non-social science backgrounds with qualitative research, especially when using traditional grounded theory methods. These are explored below.

1.1.1 Qualitative Research in a Digital World

Qualitative research has long been popular in traditional disciplines such as social sciences, health and nursing, business, and management. At the same time, qualitative research is becoming increasingly popular in relatively newer disciplines such as software engineering, human–computer interaction, artificial intelligence, and information systems (Seaman, 1999; Easterbrook et al., 2008; Bano et al., 2024). Qualitative research methods such as case studies, ethnography, survey research, and grounded theory typically originate from the social sciences and have been enabling researchers to investigate social topics for the past few decades.

Modern disciplines such as software engineering, however, are full of topics that are predominantly *socio-technical—where the social and technical aspects are interwoven in such a way that studying one without due consideration of the other makes for an incomplete investigation and understanding* (Hoda, 2022). For example, topics such as the impact of developers' well-being on code quality, the role of emotions in software testing activities, and ethical AI dilemmas faced by AI practitioners in everyday software practice demand a thorough investigation of both the social and the technical aspects involved, and how they interact with each other.

At the same time, most traditional disciplines today are undergoing digital transformations, where digitisation and technological innovations are fundamentally redefining them into socio-technical fields. Consider e-commerce, digital health, and digital marketing as examples. Research topics in these areas can no longer be adequately and comprehensively addressed using a purely social science approach. For example, topics such as the role of collaborative healthcare robots in aged care facilities, child development in the digital world, and project management using artificial intelligence tools demand a socio-technical approach to qualitative research, one that considers both the social and the technical aspects and how they interact with each other.

This book aims to be a timely and practical guide to conducting qualitative research with a socio-technical approach. This approach is captured in the form of a *socio-technical research framework*, described later in the book. The book covers the foundations of research including research design, research philosophy, and literature review. It covers qualitative data collection, qualitative data preparation, and filtering. It explains qualitative data analysis using the techniques of socio-technical grounded theory (STGT), such as open coding, constant comparison, and memoing. It also covers the advanced techniques of qualitative theory development using the emergent or structured modes. Finally, it presents evaluation guidelines for research studies applying STGT's techniques and procedures and a vision for future directions including the role of large language models in qualitative research.

This book will help researchers in modern as well as traditional disciplines to conduct rigorous qualitative research on socio-technical topics in the digital world. Applying the guidance available in its chapters, researchers will be able to approach qualitative research with confidence and produce valuable research outcomes in the form of rich descriptive findings, taxonomies, theoretical models, theoretical frameworks, preliminary and mature theories, recommendations, and guidelines, all grounded in empirical evidence.

1.1.2 Rise of Human Aspects Research

In the last few decades, there has been a clear shift from a worldview of software engineering (SE) as a primarily technical domain to a socio-technical domain, that includes not only technical but also human and social aspects at its very core. Research communities such as human–computer interaction (HCI),[1] computer-supported cooperative work and social computing (CSCW),[2] and the cooperative and human aspects of software engineering (CHASE)[3] have been at the forefront of driving this change. This shift in perspective is not orthogonal to the meteoric rise of agile methods (Hoda et al., 2018) that place "*people and interactions*" at the heart of all SE endeavours (Beck et al., 2001). The agile software development research community has also contributed as a catalyst for the increasing focus on human and social aspects in SE through publications in the dedicated XP[4] conferences but also generally in quality SE conferences and journals.

[1] https://chi2021.acm.org/

[2] https://cscw.acm.org/2021/

[3] https://conf.researchr.org/home/chase-2021

[4] https://www.agilealliance.org/xp2021/

SE researchers have investigated the social aspects of SE teams such as *team organisation* (Hoda et al., 2010, 2012) and *customer collaboration* (Martin et al., 2004; Hoda et al., 2011), but also individual roles and practices such as *the role of the project manager in agile teams* (Shastri et al., 2021), *daily standup* (Stray et al., 2016), *retrospectives* (Andriyani et al., 2017), and *self-assignment* (Masood et al., 2020). SE researchers continue to explore diverse human aspects (Grundy et al., 2023) such as *age* (McIntosh et al., 2021), *gender* (Burnett et al., 2016), *personality* (Salleh et al., 2010), *motivation* (Beecham et al., 2008; Hidellaarachchi et al., 2023), *values* (Hussain et al., 2022), *emotions* (Novielli & Serebrenik, 2019; Madampe et al., 2021, 2023), and *empathy* (Gunatilake et al., 2023, 2024) of the people involved in SE, such as developers, users, and stakeholders (Hidellaarachchi et al., 2021). STGT is well placed to support qualitative and mixed-methods research into such human and socio-technical aspects of SE and related areas.

Furthermore, the latest resurgence of artificial intelligence is accompanied by an increasing focus on deeper understanding of humans and the socio-technical context of technology development and use, including their ethical aspects (Pant et al., 2023) and data related challenges (Graetsch et al., 2023). STGT has the potential to play a key role in this context, enabling researchers to deeply understand the problem space before proceeding to develop solutions in the form of tools, technologies, and platforms.

1.1.3 Growing Interest in Theory Development

Another significant motivation for detailing STGT in this book is its ability to support theory generation. Theories have been acknowledged to be useful to both research and industry (Sjøberg et al., 2008; Herbsleb, 2018; Stray et al., 2022). Theory development can also be seen as a sign of discipline maturity. Theories of psychological and cognitive development in psychology and sociological theories, such as *attachment theory* and *conflict theory*, have not only informed our general understanding of human behaviour and society but also helped establish and progress these research disciplines. Similarly, theories in natural sciences, such as the *theory of relativity* in physics and the *theory of evolution* in biology, have defined and redefined fundamental knowledge in these disciplines and guided practical applications.

Relative to classic disciplines, theory development in SE is in its infancy. I find this is to do with the nature and maturity of SE as a discipline. SE is not only the youngest engineering discipline, only over half a century old (Ebert, 2018), but also one strongly driven by rapid changes and innovations in practice. As a young and dynamic discipline, SE abounds with phenomena that typically originate and find wide-scale success in industrial practice well before they are empirically researched and theoretically understood. *Agile software development*, *DevOps*, *cybersecurity*, the influence of *social media*, the resurgence of *artificial intelligence*, and *developers working from home* are some examples of contemporary phenomena that have originated in practice first and have then been followed up in research to explain what, how, when, where, and why they work, and may vary in practice.

Recent years have registered a growing interest in theory development in SE, in tandem with an increasing use of the grounded theory (GT) methods (Stray et al., 2022). Researchers are exploring STGT as a rigorous method to systematically generate evidence-based theories to capture, explain, and possibly predict various practical SE phenomena, helping establish theoretical foundations and guide practical solutions and innovations (Graetsch et al., 2023; Chan & Hauser, 2023). As more technology developers seek theoretical foundations to guide their solutions and tools development, STGT has a key role to play in enabling theory development for those interested.

1.1.4 Challenges of Traditional Grounded Theory Methods

Finally, a strong motivation for writing this book is to help researchers access and apply qualitative research well and achieve quality outcomes. Software engineering researchers have faced numerous challenges in applying traditional GT methods from the social sciences—*Glaserian GT* (Glaser & Strauss, 2017, first published 1967), *Strauss-Corbinian GT* (Corbin & Strauss, 1990), *Constructivist GT* (Charmaz, 2006)—to studying socio-technical topics. These include difficulties in parsing the traditional GT texts that are written by and for sociologists and social science researchers, confusion over the three social GT methods and what to use when, confusion over how to apply traditional GT methods, methodological issues arising from adapting traditional GT methods to suit SE research studies without any explicit guidance, claims of applying GT when it is not done well, poor presentation of GT findings, and extremely lenient or harsh reviews of traditional GT studies in SE research (Hoda, 2022). These challenges are summarised in Chap. 2 Traditional Grounded Theory Methods. STGT has been designed to address these challenges and provide interested researchers with a fair chance to perform robust qualitative data analysis and theory development on socio-technical topics, no matter what their discipline.

1.2 Who Is This Book For?

This book is for anyone who wants or needs to analyse qualitative data to produce robust research findings. They may be interested in qualitative data analysis only (using *STGT for data analysis*) or they may want to progress to theory development (using the *full STGT method*).

Application of *STGT for data analysis* involves the *basic* data analysis procedures of open coding, constant comparison, and memoing, and can be used to generate rich, nuanced, and layered descriptive findings, emerging taxonomies, theoretical models, frameworks, and in some cases emerging hypotheses and preliminary theories. Application of the *full STGT method* involves interleaved rounds of *basic* data collection and analysis and *advanced* theory development, and can be used to generate novel, useful, parsimonious, and modifiable theories and other theoretical outcomes.

People who will most benefit from reading the book as a whole, or its individual chapters, include novice researchers such as Masters and PhD students, early career researchers, experienced researchers looking to improve their practice, and new and experienced supervisors who wish to guide their students in producing quality research findings from qualitative data. They may be researchers from various modern disciplines, such as SE, artificial intelligence, human–computer interaction, human–robot interaction, requirements engineering, information systems, and blockchain. They may be researchers from digitised versions of traditional disciplines such as digital health, e-commerce, digital marketing, and other interdisciplinary areas. They may be looking to conduct exclusively qualitative research or qualitative work within mixed-methods research, in a professional academic, industrial context, or in a personal capacity.

Who this Book is for

People who will benefit from reading the book as a whole, or its individual chapters, include novice and experienced researchers—from academia and industry—aiming to achieve any of the following:

- Investigate and explain socio-technical topics in various domains
- Learn about the socio-technical research framework
- Learn how to set up a research project using the *research design canvas*
- Learn about the basics of research philosophy
- Learn about various forms of literature reviews, such as lean and targeted reviews
- Learn how to collect qualitative data using various techniques, such as interviews, surveys, and data mining
- Learn how to analyse qualitative data through basic *STGT for data analysis* techniques to develop and present descriptive findings, key categories, and *emerging* relationships, hypotheses, propositions, theoretical models, frameworks, taxonomies, and theories
- Learn how to apply the *full STGT method* to develop and present *mature* theoretical outcomes such as mature theoretical models, frameworks, taxonomies, and theories
- Self-evaluate the quality of the research application and findings

And reviewers and examiners who have to:

- Evaluate the quality of qualitative research application and findings

1.3 How to Use This Book?

How to Use this Book

This book is structured into five main parts: Part I: Introduction, Part II: Foundations of Research, Part III: Qualitative Data Collection and Analysis, Part IV: Theory Development, and Part V: Evaluation and Future Directions.

If you are new to qualitative research or research in general, you will benefit from reading all the chapters of the book, preferably in sequence. However, the chapters of this book are purposefully designed to be standalone, so they can be read in non-linear sequence, as selected chapters for specific needs, or in combination with other chapters.

Part I: Introduction

- To learn about the traditional grounded theory methods as they originated in sociology and how they have been applied in software engineering, including the challenges associated with applying them in socio-technical contexts, read Chap. 2 Traditional Grounded Theory Methods.
- To gain an understanding of the *socio-technical research framework* and an overview of socio-technical grounded theory (STGT) and how it differs from the traditional GT methods, read Chap. 3 Socio-Technical Grounded Theory: An Overview.

Part II: Foundations of Research

- To learn how to design and set up a research project using the *research design canvas*, not only for STGT research but for empirical research generally, read Chap. 4 Research Design Canvas.
- To learn about foundational concepts of research philosophy, including reasoning, ontology, epistemology, research paradigms, and other perspectives, read Chap. 5 Research Philosophy. It provides simple introductions to these foundational concepts in general that will be beneficial for any research, and also includes details of how they are specifically manifested when applying STGT.
- To learn about the different types of literature reviews relevant for STGT research, including *lean literature review* as applied in the basic stage and *targeted literature review* as applied in the advanced stage, read Chap. 6 Literature Reviews. It also covers the role of *grounded theory literature review*, *informal* and *systematic reviews*, and a selection guide to help decide what literature review approach to apply when.

Part III: Qualitative Data Collection and Analysis

- To learn about qualitative data collection, including different types of sampling, read Chap. 7 Basics of Qualitative Data Collection.
- To learn about traditional data collection techniques used in qualitative research such as observations, pre-interview questionnaires, interviews, surveys, and modern techniques such as data mining and immersive experiences, and dealing with data ethics, quality, saturation and more, read Chap. 8 Techniques of Qualitative Data Collection.
- To learn how to filter and prepare qualitative data for analysis, including filtering into key information, contextual information, and noise, read Chap. 9 Qualitative Data Preparation and Filtering.
- To learn how to perform qualitative data analysis using STGT procedures such as open coding with hashtags, constant comparison, memoing, and tips for robust qualitative data analysis, read Chap. 10 Socio-Technical Grounded Theory for Qualitative Data Analysis.

The key procedures and techniques covered from Chap. 7 up to Chap. 10 make up the STGT's *basic stage* of qualitative data collection and analysis.

Part IV: Theory Development

- To understand what is meant by theory and the four genres of theory generated from applying STGT, read Chap. 11 What is Theory?
- To understand how to perform theory development using one of two modes (emergent or structured) and the differences between them with examples, read Chap. 12 Theory Development. It includes an *Is Theory Development for Me? Quiz* to self-assess your appetite for theory development and understand what traits and skills that requires from individuals.

The key procedures and techniques covered in Chap. 12 along with the Targeted Literature Review from Chap. 6 make up the STGT's *Advanced Stage* for those interested in developing theory.

Part V: Evaluation and Future Directions

- To learn about the quality criteria to consider when applying STGT applications for qualitative data analysis only as well as when applying the full STGT method for theory development, read Chap. 13 Evaluation Guidelines. The same guidelines can be used by reviewers and examiners to assess the quality of STGT applications and outcomes.
- To learn more about possible future directions in qualitative research and STGT, especially with the advent of large language models, read Chap. 14 Future Directions in Qualitative Research.

In line with the design of the book and its chapters, ideas from the book can be used and cited directly, such as by referring to the chapters in which they appear.[5]

Example

The full citation for the book is:
Hoda, R. (2024). Qualitative Research with Socio-Technical Grounded Theory, Springer.

To cite the *socio-technical research framework* as the "sweet spot" or motivation for using STGT in text, use:
(Hoda, 2024, Chap. 3).

To cite the *research design canvas* in text, use:
(Hoda, 2024, Chap. 4).

To cite the application of STGT for qualitative data analysis in text, use:
(Hoda, 2024, Chap. 10).

To cite the application of the full STGT method for theory development in text, use:
(Hoda, 2024).

1.4 Role of This Book

> "Learning how to apply a research method from reading a book is like learning how to ride a bike from reading the instruction manual. The instruction manual only prepares us to a certain extent. A lot of the actual learning comes from practice. The concepts covered in the book will make a lot more sense with practice as the researcher reflects on the book in light of their real-world research experiences and vice versa."

As with any book on research methods, this book covers some basic and advanced topics. It introduces several foundational aspects of what makes good research that apply generously to qualitative research but some apply more broadly to empirical research whether qualitative, quantitative, or mixed methods; for example, see Chaps. 4 Research Design, 5 Research Philosophy, and 6 Literature Reviews.

Some of the chapters focus on what makes for good qualitative research, e.g., see Chaps. 7 Basics of Qualitative Data Collection, 8 Techniques of Qualitative Data Collection, 9 Qualitative Data Preparation and Filtering, and 10 STGT for Qualitative

[5] Individual chapters can be downloaded separately in the online format.

Data Analysis. These chapters will benefit not only STGT researchers but also those applying other qualitative research methods.

Some chapters are dedicated to theory development, e.g., see Chaps. 11 What is Theory? and 12 Theory Development.

Finally, the last two chapters are focused on evaluation and future directions in qualitative research, including the role of large language models; see Chaps. 13 Evaluation Guidelines and 14 Future Directions in Qualitative Research.

References

Andriyani, Y., Hoda, R., & Amor, R. (2017). Reflection in agile retrospectives. In *Agile Processes in Software Engineering and Extreme Programming: 18th International Conference, XP 2017, Cologne, Germany, May 22–26, 2017, Proceedings 18* (pp. 3–19). Springer International Publishing.

Bano, M., Hoda, R., Zowghi, D., & Treude, C. (2024). Large language models for qualitative research in software engineering: Exploring opportunities and challenges. *Automated Software Engineering, 31*(1), 8.

Beck, K., Beedle, M., Van Bennekum, A., Cockburn, A., Cunningham, W., Fowler, M., Grenning, J., Highsmith, J., Hunt, A., Jeffries, R. et al. (2001). *Manifesto for agile software development.* https://agilemanifesto.org/

Beecham, S., Baddoo, N., Hall, T., Robinson, H., & Sharp, H. (2008). Motivation in software engineering: A systematic literature review. *Information and Software Technology, 50*(9–10), 860–878.

Burnett, M., Stumpf, S., Macbeth, J., Makri, S., Beckwith, L., Kwan, I., Peters, A., & Jernigan, W. (2016). Gendermag: A method for evaluating software's gender inclusiveness. *Interacting with Computers, 28*(6), 760–787.

Chan, Y.-C., & Hauser, E. (2023). Understanding reactions in human-robot encounters with autonomous quadruped robots. *Proceedings of the Association for Information Science and Technology, 60*(1), 86–97.

Charmaz, K. (2006). *Constructing grounded theory: A practical guide through qualitative analysis*. Sage.

Corbin, J. M., & Strauss, A. (1990). Grounded theory research: Procedures, canons, and evaluative criteria, *Qualitative Sociology, 13*(1), 3–21.

Easterbrook, S., Singer, J., Storey, M.-A., & Damian, D. (2008). Selecting empirical methods for software engineering research. In *Guide to advanced empirical software engineering* (pp. 285–311). Springer.

Ebert, C. (2018). 50 years of software engineering: Progress and perils. *IEEE Software, 35*(5), 94–101.

Gama, K., & Lacerda, A. (2023). Understanding and supporting neurodiverse software developers in agile teams. In *Proceedings of the XXXVII Brazilian Symposium on Software Engineering* (pp. 497–502).

Glaser, B. G., & Strauss, A. L. (2017). *Discovery of grounded theory: Strategies for qualitative research*. Routledge (First Published 1967).

Graetsch, U. M., Khalajzadeh, H., Shahin, M., Hoda, R., & Grundy, J. (2023). Dealing with data challenges when delivering data-intensive software solutions. *IEEE Transactions on Software Engineering* . https://doi.org/10.1109/TSE.2023.3291003

Grundy, J., Kanij, T., Hoda, R., Khalajzadeh, H., Madugalla, A., & McIntosh, J. (2023). ED&I and SE: Challenges, progress and lessons. In *Equity, diversity, and inclusion in software engineering: Best practices and insights*. APress.

Gunatilake, H., Grundy, J., Hoda, R., & Mueller, I. (2024). Enablers and barriers of empathy in software developer and user interactions: A mixed methods case study, *ACM Transactions on Software Engineering and Methodology* . https://dl.acm.org/doi/pdf/10.1145/3641849

Gunatilake, H., Grundy, J., Mueller, I., & Hoda, R. (2023). Empathy models and software engineering—A preliminary analysis and taxonomy. *Journal of Systems and Software, 203*, 111747.

Herbsleb, J. (2018). What would a science of software engineering look like?. In *Keynote address delivered jointly to the Cooperative and Human Aspects of Software Engineering (CHASE) and Crowd Sourcing in Software Engineering (CSI-SE) Workshops (ICSE 2018)*. https://herbsleb.org/web-pres/slides/crowd-chase-2018-final-dist.pdf

Hidellaarachchi, D., Grundy, J., Hoda, R., & Madampe, K. (2021). The effects of human aspects on the requirements engineering process: A systematic literature review. *IEEE Transactions on Software Engineering, 48*(6), 2105–2127.

Hidellaarachchi, D., Grundy, J., Hoda, R., & Mueller, I. (2023). The influence of human aspects on requirements engineering-related activities: Software practitioners' perspective. *ACM Transactions on Software Engineering and Methodology, 32*(5), 1–37.

Hoda, R. (2022). Socio-technical grounded theory for software engineering. *IEEE Transactions on Software Engineering, 48*(10), 3808–3832.

Hoda, R., Noble, J., & Marshall, S. (2010). Organizing self-organizing teams. In *Proceedings of the 32nd ACM/IEEE International Conference on Software Engineering-Volume 1* (pp. 285–294).

Hoda, R., Noble, J., & Marshall, S. (2011). The impact of inadequate customer collaboration on self-organizing agile teams. *Information and Software Technology, 53*(5), 521–534.

Hoda, R., Noble, J., & Marshall, S. (2012). Self-organizing roles on agile software development teams. *IEEE Transactions on Software Engineering, 39*(3), 422–444.

Hoda, R., Salleh, N., & Grundy, J. (2018). The rise and evolution of agile software development. *IEEE software, 35*(5), 58–63.

Hussain, W., Shahin, M., Hoda, R., Whittle, J., Perera, H., Nurwidyantoro, A., Shams, R. A., & Oliver, G. (2022). How can human values be addressed in agile methods? A case study on safe. *IEEE Transactions on Software Engineering, 48*(12), 5158–5175.

Li, Z. Z., Wang, H., Gasevic, D., Yu, J., & Liu, J. K. (2023). Enhancing blockchain adoption through tailored software engineering: An industrial-grounded study in education credentialing. *Distributed Ledger Technologies: Research and Practice, 2*(4), 1–24.

Madampe, K., Hoda, R., & Grundy, J. (2021). A faceted taxonomy of requirements changes in agile contexts. *IEEE Transactions on Software Engineering, 48*(10), 3737–3752.

Madampe, K., Hoda, R., & Grundy, J. (2023). A framework for emotion-oriented requirements change handling in agile software engineering. *IEEE Transactions on Software Engineering*. https://doi.org/10.1109/TSE.2023.3253145

Martin, A., Biddle, R., & Noble, J. (2004). The XP customer role in practice: Three studies. In *Agile Development Conference* (pp. 42–54). IEEE.

Masood, Z., Hoda, R., & Blincoe, K. (2020). How agile teams make self-assignment work: A grounded theory study. *Empirical Software Engineering, 25*, 4962–5005. https://doi.org/10.1007/s10664-020-09876-x

McIntosh, J., Du, X., Wu, Z., Truong, G., Ly, Q., How, R., Viswanathan, S., & Kanij, T. (2021). Evaluating age bias in e-commerce. In *2021 IEEE/ACM 13th International Workshop on Cooperative and Human Aspects of Software Engineering (CHASE)* (pp. 31–40). IEEE.

Novielli, N., & Serebrenik, A. (2019). Sentiment and emotion in software engineering. *IEEE Software, 36*(5), 6–23.

Pant, A., Hoda, R., Spiegler, S. V., Tantithamthavorn, C., & Turhan, B. (2023). Ethics in the age of AI: An analysis of AI practitioners' awareness and challenges. *ACM Transactions on Software Engineering and Methodology* . https://doi.org/10.1145/3635715

Salleh, N., Mendes, E., & Grundy, J. (2010). Empirical studies of pair programming for CS/SE teaching in higher education: A systematic literature review. *IEEE Transactions on Software Engineering, 37*(4), 509–525.

Seaman, C. B. (1999). Qualitative methods in empirical studies of software engineering. *IEEE Transactions on Software Engineering, 25*(4), 557–572.

Shastri, Y., Hoda, R., & Amor, R. (2021). The role of the project manager in agile software development projects. *Journal of Systems and Software, 173*, 110871.

Sjøberg, D. I., Dybå, T., Anda, B. C., & Hannay, J. E. (2008). Building theories in software engineering. In *Guide to advanced empirical software engineering* (pp. 312–336). Springer.

Stray, V., Hoda, R., Paasivaara, M., Lenarduzzi, V., & Mendez, D. (2022). Theories in agile software development: Past, present, and future introduction to the XP 2020 special section. *Information and Software Technology, 152*, 107058.

Stray, V., Sjøberg, D. I., & Dybå, T. (2016). The daily stand-up meeting: A grounded theory study. *Journal of Systems and Software, 114*, 101–124.

Wang, W., Khalajzadeh, H., Grundy, J., & Madugalla, A. (2023). Adaptive user interfaces for software supporting chronic diseases. In *2023 IEEE Symposium on Visual Languages and Human-Centric Computing (VL/HCC)* (pp. 215–218). IEEE.

2

Traditional Grounded Theory Methods

Abstract This chapter provides an overview of the suite of traditional grounded theory research methods. First, the ideas of *research and research methods* is introduced. This is followed by presenting the *origin* of grounded theory from sociology including its *overviews* and *evolution* into three versions: *Glaserian GT*, *Strauss-Corbinian GT*, and *Constructivist GT*. Next, the key *reasons* propelling the use of *traditional grounded theory methods in Software Engineering* are presented including when it makes most sense to apply traditional GT methods. Next, a set of common *challenges* of practising traditional GT methods in software engineering contexts are described as patterns. The chapter concludes with a discussion of how to *address* these common challenges, motivating the need for an updated and contextualised set of guidelines in the form of a new version called socio-technical grounded theory (STGT) for conducting, presenting, and evaluating qualitative research in today's modern digital world.

R. Hoda, *Qualitative Research with Socio-Technical Grounded Theory*,
https://doi.org/10.1007/978-3-031-60533-8_2

2.1 Research Methods

Definition

Research is the process of systematically investigating a phenomenon using multiple evidences, ideally from a variety of sources, to understand, explain, and potentially make predictions about the studied phenomenon, in ways that confirm, refute, or expand existing knowledge and/or create new knowledge. **Research method** is a coherent encapsulation of the steps and procedures needed to conduct research.

Formal use of the term research goes well beyond the layperson's reference to "*googling it*" and includes established approaches and methods. Conducting research professionally or as part of a formal degree programme, such as a Masters or doctoral study, typically requires the use of established research methods. Beyond such practical necessities, using research methods is desirable because applying a well-defined process improves the chances of producing high-quality outcomes. Research outcomes can be in the form of *descriptive* knowledge (e.g., concepts, theoretical models, theories), *solutions* (e.g., software tools, techniques, and artefacts), or *combinations* of these (Storey et al., 2020).

Research methods represent the culmination of human trials and experiments, knowledge and experience of conducting research, codified into a set of principles and guidelines, aimed at making future research journeys simple, focused, effective, and simply the best they can be.

> "Research methods can be thought of as paths charted by previous voyagers who have painstakingly mapped the research world. Illuminating the paths that lead, warning of those that mislead. These maps and directions are available to use but the research journey and its trials and triumphs remain personal, unique. Occasionally, new topology and uncharted territories are discovered that require new paths, workarounds, and updates to old maps. Timely updates to the repertoire of research methods serves to collectively progress the research community."

Depending on the nature of the data predominantly being used, research methods are often classified as *quantitative*, *qualitative*, or *mixed*, that is, working with a combination of quantitative and qualitative data. Quantitative data is numeric data while qualitative data is text-based or data in other non-numeric forms that can be effectively transcribed or summarised into text forms (e.g., videos, photographs, artefacts). A spreadsheet containing the demographic information of a population such as age, gender, and ethnicity is quantitative data and can be analysed using statistical and quantitative analysis methods to identify traits such as averages, mean, median, trend-lines, and outliers. On the other hand, the text contained in the document describing the constitution of a country is qualitative data. Qualitative data is best analysed using qualitative data analysis methods to identify key patterns such as strengths, weaknesses, gaps, and biases.

Popular research methods typically classified as quantitative methods include *experiments, quasi-experiments, and randomised control trials*. Popular research methods classified as qualitative methods typically originate from the social sciences and include *case studies, ethnography, grounded theory (GT), and action research. Survey research* is typically used as a quantitative research method but is also employed as a mixed or qualitative method. Much like tools for a job, there are no right or wrong research methods. One can be selected based on the research aims, needs, preferences, and constraints.

To understand and compare empirical, and particularly qualitative, research methods, consult the guides to research methods listed in Table 2.1. Some of them address grounded theory (GT) as a full qualitative research method while others position it as a data analysis technique to be used within other methods (Wohlin & Aurum, 2015)—an approach not compliant with the intended use of the traditional sociological GT methods (described later in this chapter) that focus on full method application to develop theory.

> “Research methods are in many ways like software development methods. They capture processes to perform research and software development respectively. Software development methods comprise of activities such as requirements elicitation, analysis, design, implementation, testing, deployment, and maintenance. Similarly, research methods comprise of a set activities research design, data collection, analysis, synthesis, write-up, and publication.
>
> Software development methods help ensure that not only the right product is being built but also that it is being built right. Similarly, research methods help ensure not only that quality outcomes are derived from the research activities but also that they are derived using the most appropriate and robust steps and procedures.
>
> There are a variety of linear and iterative software development methods to choose from such as waterfall, spiral, and agile. Similarly, there are a variety of research methods such as case studies, survey research, ethnography, and socio-technical grounded theory. Methods can be selected based on the aim, needs, preferences, and constraints.”

Reference	Research methods guide
Seaman (1999)	Qualitative methods in empirical studies of software engineering
Myers and Avison (2002)	Qualitative research methods in information systems
Shull et al. (2007)	Guide to Advanced Empirical Software Engineering
Easterbrook et al. (2008)	Selecting empirical methods for software engineering research
Wohlin and Aurum (2015)	Towards a decision-making structure for selecting a research design in empirical software engineering

Table 2.1 Empirical research methods guides (between 1999 and 2015)

2.2 Origin of Grounded Theory

Grounded theory (GT) finds its origins in sociology. It was introduced by two American sociologists, Barney G. Glaser and Anselm L. Strauss, based on their joint research on the awareness of dying patients and the role of their social status in the level of nursing care received. Strauss received an MA and PhD in Sociology from the University of Chicago in 1942 and 1945 respectively. Glaser received his MA from Stanford University in 1952 and a PhD from Columbia University in 1961 (Kenny & Fourie, 2014).

Findings from their research were interspersed across three texts, *Awareness of Dying* (Glaser & Strauss, 1966), *Time for Dying* (Glaser & Strauss, 2017, first published 1967), and *Status Passage* (Glaser & Strauss, 2011). The steps and procedures applied in their research were formalised into a new research method, *grounded theory*, described in their 1967 book *The Discovery of Grounded Theory: Strategies for Qualitative Research* (Glaser & Strauss, 2017, first published 1967). Since its introduction, GT has evolved into three versions:

- *Glaserian or Classic GT* by Barney Glaser, who continued to support the original version (Glaser, 1992; Glaser & Strauss, 2017, first published 1967)
- *Strauss-Corbinian GT* introduced in 1990 by the other founding father, Anselm Strauss, with Juliet Corbin (Strauss & Corbin, 1990)
- *Constructivist GT* introduced by Kathy Charmaz in (2006)

These are collectively referred to as *traditional GT methods*[1] in this book. Differences among the three versions have been a subject of much debate and can be challenging for novice researchers to understand and select from. We will discuss them in the upcoming section, *Evolution of Grounded Theory*.

GT emerged in sociology at a time when quantitative research methods were dominating the research scene, both in the social and natural sciences. With their focus on traits such as objectivity, accuracy, verifiability, and generalisability, quantitative research methods had become synonymous with the very idea of scientific research. On the other hand, qualitative research was being seen as relying on anecdotal evidence and lacking rigour.

The introduction of GT challenged the status quo and marked a strong resurgence of qualitative research. Its systematic nature, attention to nuance, and rigorous analysis techniques propelled GT towards being accepted as a powerful research method for scientific inquiry. Where quantitative methods seemed to over-emphasise *theory verification*, GT argued for *theory generation* as an equally, if not more, fundamental research objective. In introducing GT, Glaser and Strauss seem to go out of their way to emphasise the role of theory development through a bottom-up *inductive* approach. Their strongly defensive stance is discernible in most of their writing and accounts introducing and describing the GT method. It can be understood in terms of

[1] Traditional here refers to the original grounded theory methods arising from sociology and subsequent versions created by other sociologists to develop theories on social topics.

making a bold statement against the then popular view of what constituted valuable, and therefore funded, sociological research.

Since its origin in 1967, GT has not only become popular in its native field of sociology, but has also been adopted widely to study social phenomena in nursing (Schreiber et al., 2001), medical education (Kennedy & Lingard, 2006; Watling & Lingard, 2012), and psychology (Rennie et al., 1988; Fassinger, 2005).

2.3 The Traditional Grounded Theory Methods

Definition

Traditional GT methods are a suite of systematic research methods designed by and for sociologists that enable evidence-based theory development on social phenomena. *Iterative* and *interleaved* rounds of data collection and analysis are a hallmark feature of GT methods, as is *theory* development *grounded* in real-world evidence, lending GT its name. There are three versions of traditional GT: *Glaserian GT* (Glaser & Strauss, 2017, first published 1967), *Strauss-Corbinian GT* by Anselm Strauss and Juliet Corbin (1990), and *Constructivist GT* by Kathy Charmaz (2006).

Traditional GT methods cover the full research life cycle, including basic steps of data collection and data analysis as well as the more advanced steps of theory development. Originating from sociology, the traditional GT methods are social science methods that apply a social lens to understanding and explaining social phenomena. GT derives its name from generating a *theory* outcome that is *grounded* in real-world evidence.

A popular misconception about GT is that literature review is entirely forbidden. This is not true. Review of literature in the same field is discouraged with the view to avoid biasing theory development. However, review of literature in an "unrelated field" is encouraged (Glaser, 1992, page 35) to improve the researcher's propensity for theory development in general, also known as *theoretical sensitivity* (Glaser, 1978; Strauss & Corbin, 1990).

Traditional GT methods typically begin with collecting evidence from the real world about the phenomenon of interest. Glaserian GT accepts a variety of data, as famously captured in Glaser's dictum "*all is data*". Semi-structured interviews and observations remain the two most popular data collection mechanisms applied across the three traditional GT methods. Data gathered is saved in a textual form, e.g., through transcribing audio recordings or manual note taking, ready for analysis. Traditional GT methods are acknowledged to support and encourage both qualitative and quantitative data but their rigorous and robust textual data analysis procedures mean they excel when applied as qualitative methods (Glaser & Strauss, 2017, first published 1967).

All GT methods include a common set of data analysis procedures—*open coding* and *constant comparison*—that enable the inductive extraction of key patterns from the data. These patterns are grouped together at increasing levels of abstraction, raising the analysis from *codes* to *concepts* to *categories*. Once the most significant categories are established (also known as core categories), data analysis is applied in a more selective capacity on the core and related categories, referred to as *selective coding* in Glaserian GT and *focused coding* in Constructivist GT. Strauss-Corbinian GT features a different analytical procedure called *axial coding* that is more structured in its approach (Strauss & Corbin, 1990). It also features the idea of subcategories and uses the term selective coding differently, referring to forming relationships between subcategories and categories.

A distinguishing feature of the GT suite of methods is the *iterative* and *interleaved* application of data collection and analysis, such that one feeds into the other. Their iterative and incremental approach stands in contrast to other qualitative methods that are mostly linear in nature, completing data collection and then following up with analysis as a sequential next step towards reporting findings. Methods such as case studies and ethnography do not overrule iterative data collection and analysis, and indeed some iterations are inevitable in practice. However, GT emphasises this interplay as a key method feature, guiding rounds of data sampling and collection to respond to the theoretical concepts emerging from the analysis rounds, referred to as *theoretical sampling*. Guided by the theoretical gaps, the researcher can refine research protocols and decide what to collect next, from whom, when, where, and how.

Theory development in Glaserian GT is propelled by procedures such as theoretical sampling, *memoing*, *sorting*, and *theoretical coding*. Memoing is the procedure of capturing researchers' reflections on the emerging concepts and patterns, potential relationships between them, and questions to ask of the data, and identifying gaps in the emerging theory to guide the next rounds of data collection and analysis. Sorting is the process of arranging theoretical memos in a conceptually coherent structure, forming the outline of the theory. In Glaserian GT, the theory can optionally be further structured into a best matching theoretical template, a procedure called *theoretical coding*. When data analysis reaches a point of diminishing results, where collecting more data does not yield any new patterns or insights, the process is said to have reached *theoretical saturation* and data collection can stop at this point.

The outcome of a well-applied traditional GT method is a mid-range *theory* which encapsulates a set of key patterns and relationships between them. Because the theory is grounded in evidence, it does not necessitate further validation. The application of the theory is limited to the contexts studied and is not claimed to be universally generalisable (Glaser & Strauss, 2017). However, the resulting theory remains open to "*inevitable modification and reformulation*" in light of new evidences, data, and contexts (Glaser & Strauss, 2017).

Further details of these traditional GT procedures can be found in the traditional texts (Glaser & Strauss, 2017; Glaser, 1978, 1998; Strauss & Corbin, 1990, 1994; Charmaz, 2006, 2014).

2.4 Evolution of Traditional Grounded Theory

As with most methods, GT has been adapted, and has evolved over the years into three versions. Barney Glaser remained aligned with the original version introduced in 1967, which became known as *Glaserian GT*. Glaserian GT continued to support an emergent approach of theory development, where theory is generated bottom up from the evidence grounded in practice. It is seen as an open and emergent approach to theory development (Glaser, 1978). Applying Glaserian GT typically involves extended periods of uncertainty about the emerging theory followed by "*eureka*" moments of discovery where the various concepts, categories, and emerging relationships start to firm up and become cohesive, typically later in the study. Structuring of the theory into predefined theoretical templates, or *theoretical coding*, is considered as an optional last step in Glaserian GT.

About two decades later, in 1990, the other founding father, Anselm Strauss, introduced a new version of GT in collaboration with Juliet Corbin in their book *Basics of Qualitative Research*, which came to be known as *Strauss-Corbinian GT* (Strauss & Corbin, 1990). Their version is seen as a more prescriptive and structured approach to theory development compared to Glaserian GT. A distinguishing feature of the Strauss-Corbinian version is the analytical procedure of *axial coding*—a "*process of systematically relating categories and sub-categories*". In practice, this involves the use of analytical tools such as *coding paradigm*, a template that allows the researcher to investigate and explain specific aspects of the phenomenon such as the context, causal conditions, intervening conditions, consequences, and action-interaction strategies. *Conditional matrix* is another such analytical technique to help structure the theory as it develops. Applying Strauss-Corbinian GT typically results in identifying a theoretical structure early and subsequently developing and deductively verifying it in the later stages of the study.

The structured approach of Strauss-Corbinian GT was met with strong objections from Glaser, who labelled it as a "*whole different method*" rather than a version of GT. Glaser published his rejoinder *Basics of Grounded Theory Analysis: Emergence vs. Forcing* (Glaser, 1992), where he retorted to what he saw as a "*forced*" approach to theory development. After the passing away of Anselm Strauss in 1996, Juliet Corbin continued publishing their co-written second edition and a third edition, maintaining their joint position.

Fifteen years after the second version, Kathy Charmaz introduced the third version, *Constructivist GT*, in her book *Constructing Grounded Theory* (Charmaz, 2006). Charmaz characterised Glaserian GT as applying a primarily positivist research paradigm and Strauss-Corbinian GT as positivist with pragmatic influences.

A positivist approach is one where the role of the researcher is to remain neutral and "discover" the objective reality of the phenomenon. A pragmatic approach is one where the researcher is concerned with capturing reality that is of practical value to those involved in the phenomenon. With her version, Charmaz introduced a constructivist approach to theory development, where the researcher acknowledges the subjective nature of reality and "constructs" it through their investigation and interactions with the participants (Charmaz, 2014). An introduction to these fundamental philosophical considerations such as ontology, epistemology, and research paradigms as applicable to GT practice is presented in Chap. 5 Research Philosophy.

Charmaz emphasised the application of "*flexible guidelines*" in her approach as opposed to "*methodological rules, recipes, and requirements*" and acknowledged building on pragmatist underpinnings and advancing interpretive analysis in her approach. The initial response to Charmaz's version was divided along gender lines, with mainly women supporting the constructivist approach. Her plenary presentation "*caused quite a stir*" in 1993 (Charmaz, 2014). Subsequently, Constructivist GT became a prominent GT version with many applications.

Overall, the evolution of GT over the years has pivoted around two focal points: the approach to theory development, e.g., emergent versus structured, and differences in research paradigms, e.g., positivist, interpretivist, and constructivist. Differences between the different GT versions have been discussed at length in Babchuk (1996); Heath and Cowley (2004) and Kenny and Fourie (2014). Other aspects of GT such as types and sources of data, collection, analysis, research tools, and techniques have remained largely unchanged in the last half century.

Collectively, the three GT versions represent the traditional social science approach to theory development in the context of studying social phenomena. But what happened when traditional GT, a social sciences research method, met software engineering (SE), a socio-technical domain? We will explore this next.

2.5 Traditional Grounded Theory in Software Engineering

The use of *traditional* grounded theory (GT) methods—*Glaserian GT*, *Strauss-Corbinian GT*, and *Constructivist GT*—originating from sociology has gained steady acceptance in software engineering (SE) research over the years. Some exemplar traditional GT studies in SE that present theories and describe their method application in detail are listed in Table 2.2. In addition to these exemplars, dedicated papers that present guidelines on applying traditional GT methods to SE research can also be consulted (Hoda et al., 2011b; Adolph et al., 2011; Stol et al., 2016), including a humorous account of a "hypothetical" PhD student's experiences with practising GT presented as a patterns paper (Hoda et al., 2011a).

Table 2.2 Exemplar studies applying traditional GT methods in software engineering (*distinguished paper award)

Reference	Title and venue
Coleman and O'Connor (2007)	*Using grounded theory to understand software process improvement: A study of Irish software product companies*, Information and Software Technology
Hoda et al. (2010)	*Organizing self-organizing teams*, IEEE International Conference on Software Engineering
Dagenais et al. (2010)	*Moving into a new software project landscape*, IEEE International Conference on Software Engineering
Hoda et al. (2011b)	*The impact of inadequate customer collaboration on self-organizing agile teams*, Information and Software Technology
Hoda et al. (2012b)	*Self-organizing roles on agile software development teams*, IEEE Transactions on Software Engineering
Adolph et al. (2012)	*Reconciling perspectives: A grounded theory of how people manage the process of software development, Journal of Systems and Software*
Maglyas et al. (2013)	*What are the roles of software product managers? An empirical investigation, Journal of Systems and Software*
Jantunen and Gause (2014)	*Using a grounded theory approach for exploring software product management challenges, Journal of Systems and Software*
*Waterman et al. (2015)	*How much up-front? A grounded theory of agile architecture*, IEEE International Conference on Software Engineering
Stray et al. (2016)	*The daily stand-up meeting: A grounded theory study, Journal of Systems and Software*
*Hoda and Noble (2017)	*Becoming agile: A grounded theory of agile transitions in practice*, IEEE International Conference on Software Engineering
Sedano et al. (2017)	*Software development waste*, IEEE International Conference on Software Engineering
*Sousa et al. (2018)	*Identifying design problems in the source code: A grounded theory*, IEEE International Conference on Software Engineering
Masood et al. (2020a)	*How agile teams make self-assignment work: a grounded theory study*, Empirical Software Engineering
Masood et al. (2020b)	*Real world scrum a grounded theory of variations in practice*, IEEE Transactions on Software Engineering
Shastri et al. (2021a)	*The role of the project manager in agile software development projects, Journal of Systems and Software*
Shastri et al. (2021b)	*Spearheading agile: the role of the scrum master in agile projects*, Empirical Software Engineering

Example

The **Theory of Becoming Agile** (Hoda & Noble, 2017) is an example of a grounded theory generated using the traditional *Glaserian GT* method in the SE research context. It explains the phenomenon of SE teams becoming agile as a process of transitions across five dimensions, representing the key categories identified in the study. It presents four hypotheses that explain and predict the relationships between these key categories.

Five Dimensions of Transition

- Software development practices dimension transitions from tradition to hybrid to agile
- Team practices dimension transitions from manager-driven to manager-assisted to team-driven

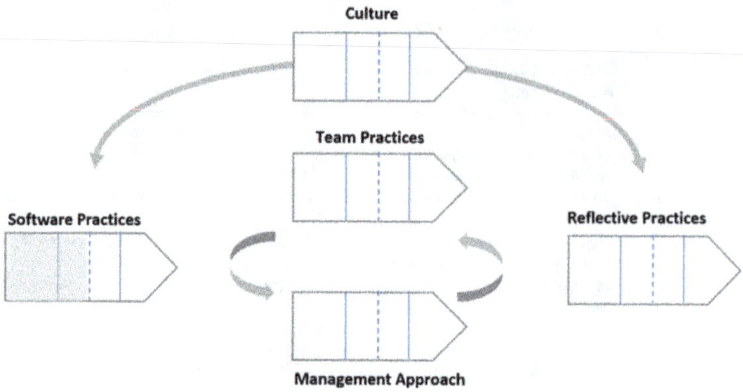

Fig. 2.1 Grounded theory of becoming agile (Hoda & Noble, 2017)

- Management approach dimension transitions from driving to adapting to empowering
- Reflective practice dimension transitions from limited to open to embedded
- Culture dimension transitions from hierarchical to evolving to open

Four Hypotheses

- The transition of a team's software development practices from traditional towards agile is necessary (though not sufficient) for the changes in the team practices and the management approach to occur.
- The transition in the team practices and the management approach tend to reflect and adapt to each other.
- Transitions in team practices and management practices are necessary (though not sufficient) for changes in the team's reflective practices.
- All changes are influenced by a combination of the organisational, team, and individual culture.

The core components of the theory, the five categories, and the relationships among them are visualised in a theory diagram, captured in Fig. 2.1.

2.6 When to Use Traditional Grounded Theory?

Traditional GT methods are best employed to study topics and contexts that are social in nature. For studying socio-technical topics and contexts such as those common in software engineering and related disciplines, socio-technical grounded theory

(STGT), introduced in the next chapter, is better suited. Additionally, traditional GT methods are focused on full theory development. If you are looking to apply the qualitative data analysis procedures such as open coding and constant comparison without aiming for full theory development, you can use *STGT for data analysis*. Similarly, if you are unsure whether you would like to eventually proceed to theory development, *STGT for data analysis* is a good place to start.

2.7 Traditional Grounded Theory Challenges

GT is one of the most misunderstood, misused, and poorly presented and evaluated research methods in SE. SE researchers are generally appreciative of its theory development capabilities and acknowledge its strength and rigour, but at the same time, most also consider it as an advanced and complex method that is extremely difficult to apply effectively in practice.

A critical review of the use of traditional GT methods in SE confirmed its growing popularity while raising serious quality concerns (Stol et al., 2016). The review analysed 98 journal papers and identified that about half of them explicitly claimed to be performing traditional GT. Only one-third of the papers provided details of the method application, applying primarily either the *Glaserian* or *Strauss-Corbinian* version. Others were seen to combine guidelines without providing rationales and several were found to apply GT practice *à la carte* without reference to any particular method guidelines. Only five of the 98 papers were found to be comprehensive, providing sufficient details of their GT application, and serving as exemplars: Coleman and O'Connor (2007), Hoda et al. (2011b), Adolph et al. (2012), Hoda et al. (2012b), and Jantunen and Gause (2014). These and other exemplar traditional GT studies in SE, including distinguished paper award winners, are listed in Table 2.2.

Over 15 years of experience in practising, supervising, reviewing, and editing traditional GT studies in SE has led me to believe this poor-quality show can be traced back to a number of reasons. These include, but are not limited to, *method slurring* or false claims of applying method guidelines (Baker et al., 1992). Other reasons are to do with researcher apprehensions, misunderstandings, poor presentation of method application and findings, and extreme evaluations. I have captured these common challenges of applying traditional GT methods in SE research in a set of eight patterns, listed in Hoda (2022) and described next.

2.7.1 Eager But Not Equipped

Definition

The **#EagerButNotEquipped** pattern captures one of the first hurdles to effective GT practice where SE researchers are interested in using GT but struggle to understand and apply it.

Traditional GT methods—*Glaserian GT*, *Strauss-Corbinian GT*, and *Constructivist GT*—were written by and for sociologists, using language, style, and examples native to social scientists. Naturally, these texts are challenging for SE researchers to parse and understand, especially given that most of them have little background or experience in sociological or qualitative research methods. For example, SE researchers are often missing fundamental knowledge and skills that sociologists often naturally possess, such as concepts from philosophy (e.g., ontology, epistemology, research paradigms) and qualitative research (e.g., effective survey design, conducting interviews, textual data analysis). Unfortunately, many SE researchers are never exposed to this fundamental knowledge and these skills. Those who are introduced to them, e.g., as part of a research method course, are still typically missing an introduction to GT, which is not covered because of its assumed complexity and time requirements.

While exemplar studies (Table 2.2) provide useful examples of quality GT outcomes and contain details of method application, they do not serve as method guidelines, comprehensive enough to guide all aspects of a GT application from scratch and in full detail.

Currently, achieving high-quality GT applications in SE demands that the SE researcher first understand the three traditional GT methods introduced in their native sociological context, select one of them to apply, then effectively abstract out their practices and procedures, and finally, translate and apply them to their own native SE context without losing its full capabilities and nuances. That's a lot to expect from novice SE researchers, creating a high entry barrier into GT.

2.7.2 No Version Control

Definition

The **#NoVersionControl** pattern captures another early challenge where SE researchers are unaware or unclear about the different versions of traditional GT methods and how to apply them in practice.

Traditional GT comes in three different versions—*Glaserian*, *Strauss-Corbinian*, and *Constructivist GT*. It is already challenging for SE researchers to understand the basics of GT because of its native sociology flavour (as captured in the #EagerBut-NotEquipped pattern above). Having to understand three different versions upfront and then select one of them to apply raises the entry barrier to GT even higher.

Existing guidelines for GT in SE research focus on a particular version of GT, e.g., both Hoda et al. (2012a) and Adolph et al. (2011) cover *Glaserian GT*, or provide a high-level comparison of the three versions (Stol et al., 2016). And although in-depth comparisons of the different GT versions exist outside of SE literature, e.g., Heath and Cowley (2004); Babchuk (1996) and Kenny and Fourie (2014), it becomes an extended task for novice SE researchers to compare these versions, especially when many of the actual differences only start making sense after the researcher has gained some experience with the various GT procedures. Swapping versions at a later stage typically demands extensive rework and can risk methodologically unsound applications.

2.7.3 Scope Confusion

Definition

The **#ScopeConfusion** pattern captures the challenge where SE researchers find it difficult to distinguish between conducting a full GT study and using GT data analysis techniques alone.

Traditional GT methods' common data analysis procedures such as open coding and constant comparison are popular in qualitative studies. However, applying their data analysis procedures alone, without their other core features and procedures such as iterative and interleaved data collection and analysis, theoretical sampling, and memoing, does not comply with the intentions of the traditional GT methods that instead focus on full application. SE researchers often mislabel their GT application, claiming to have done "*a GT study*" when only using some of the procedures in a limited capacity for data analysis. Such claims are inevitably met with harsh reviews.

2.7.4 DIY Gone Wrong

Definition

The **#DIYGoneWrong** pattern captures the challenge where SE researchers attempt to adapt traditional GT methods but lack guidelines to do so.

Despite their best attempts, SE researchers experience the need to adapt traditional GT to suit their native SE research contexts. However, by introducing a seemingly simple adaptation to one procedure, researchers can unknowingly and easily diminish or break some overarching GT principle or introduce weaknesses in other complementary procedures. For example, a novice SE researcher applying a *Glaserian GT* approach may be asked to present a literature review as a part of their PhD degree requirements at their university or institution to establish how their topic is sufficiently novel and different to what has been done before. While *Glaserian GT* does not prohibit literature review *per se*, it discourages reviews of existing theories in the same substantive area of research (Glaser & Strauss, 2017, first published 1967). Adapting *Glaserian GT* to accommodate a comprehensive literature review may satisfy the internal panel but can land the researcher in trouble later when external reviewers evaluate their manuscripts in accordance with their expectations of a *Glaserian GT* study. For example, reviewers can demand an explanation of how the literature review findings were handled by the research team and how they avoided their original theory development becoming 'biased' by the literature review findings. Implementing and justifying adaptations in practice without full consideration for the potential philosophical and methodological dissonance created as a result is difficult to say the least. Combining practices from multiple traditional GT versions can pose similar risks.

2.7.5 Evidence Gate Keeping

Definition

The **#EvidenceGateKeeping** pattern captures a presentation-related challenge where SE researchers find it difficult to support their GT findings with adequate evidence without compromising ethics.

There is an increasing push towards replicability and reproducibility as key quality criteria for SE research, leading to researchers making their full datasets and analysis publicly available. While this works well for studies working with open-source datasets and typically quantitative studies that can share their underlying numerical data with ease, it is particularly challenging for qualitative researchers because of the confidentiality and anonymity clauses binding their research. Many practitioners agree to share their professional experiences and stories only once researchers guarantee that access to their data will be limited to the immediate research team and not shared publicly. In the spirit of maintaining their ethics obligations, many GT researchers err on the side of not sharing any evidence of their underlying data whatsoever. This makes it virtually impossible for reviewers and examiners to ascertain the credibility and quality of the research.

2.7.6 The Facade

Definition

#TheFacade captures scenarios where SE researchers do not apply GT carefully but claim to do so.

Sometimes it is easy to see from the method and/or findings descriptions of a manuscript that the GT method was not applied as well as it was claimed. Addressing challenging and complex research questions demands meticulous and rigorous application of research methods. With the ever increasing pressure to publish, quasi-gamification of researcher profiles based on mono-dimensional metrics (e.g., h-index that does not account for variations in disciplines or career stages), and the advent of large language models-based research, it is not uncommon to see SE researchers focusing on simple (or even trivial) research questions and presenting rushed, shallow, or poor applications of research methods. System-permeated pressures such as tenure tracks, peer pressure, and international rankings add to the problem. This is not a GT-specific issue and plagues SE and other research communities at large. Nonetheless, until a focus on deep scholarly work and quality outcomes (over quantity) is restored, poor GT applications, misuse, and abuse will likely continue to be seen.

2.7.7 Poor Presentation

Definition

The **#PoorPresentation** pattern captures contexts where SE researchers struggle to present GT studies to a high standard.

This pattern captures a scenario that is opposite to #TheFacade. Here, there are typically indications in the manuscript that the researchers applied the traditional GT method effectively but the poor presentation of the research outcomes detracts from the contributions. Poor presentation often includes an extraneously succinct findings section, without sufficient description of the key findings and pertinent quotes to back them, and an overall sense of reading *walls of text*, without useful sign-posting and cross-referencing, and lack or ineffective use of figures, tables, or icons to provide visual links and summaries. Unlike #TheFacade, manuscripts suffering from #PoorPresentation can usually be salvaged and improved with diligent revisions.

2.7.8 Extreme Reviews

Definition

The **#ExtremeReviews** pattern captures the scenarios where SE reviewers are extreme, overly trusting, or harsh in their review of GT studies.

Sometimes SE reviewers are easily impressed by GT studies that are successful in satisfying some checklist of GT practices, e.g., studies that claim theoretical sampling was applied, theoretical saturation was reached, and so on, without providing details of how the practices were applied. Similarly, a reasonable-looking theory, where the key concepts look relevant to the topic and seem to be related in the way they are claimed, can also pass under the radar without due scrutiny of how the theory was developed from the evidence chain. Such a naïve approach to reviewing can accept #TheFacade as credible GT research, leading to widespread quality issues.

On the other hand, an extremely harsh approach to reviewing GT research can also be seen in the SE community. One of the most common manifestations of this problem occurs when a reviewer who is primarily a quantitative researcher themselves reviews qualitative GT research using quantitative evaluation criteria, e.g., reproducibility, replicability, and generalisability, instead of the relevant GT criteria. Some reviewers tend to hold GT studies to exceptionally high standards and expect textbook applications of the method. They are not accepting of any practical adaptations, no matter how well reasoned. Rejecting manuscripts with statements such as "*this is not GT!*" and recommending a post facto rebranding of GT studies as mixed methods, case studies, or interview-based studies to "*solve the problem*" can be counterproductive and crushing to the morale and confidence of SE researchers making genuine attempts to apply GT, many of whom are PhD students. Additionally, it does not address the underlying issues, which may be some of the other patterns.

2.8 Addressing the Challenges

It can be seen from the various challenges faced by SE researchers in practising and evaluating GT studies that there is a fundamental misalignment between the traditional GT guidelines written for social science research and the socio-technical context of SE research. These challenges need to be addressed.

In order to address the **#EagerButNotEquipped** challenge, the steps and procedures of the GT method need to be written for SE researchers, using a language, style, and examples native to them. In other words, simple, comprehensive, and contextualised GT guidelines for conducting and evaluating SE research are required. While SE-specific GT guidelines will make traditional GT more accessible to SE researchers, there are still a number of aspects which need to be addressed to help SE researchers achieve high-quality outcomes. One such aspect is explicitly defining the fundamental knowledge and skills that SE researchers need to possess in order to conduct quality GT studies, including those from philosophy and qualitative research.

One way to address the **#NoVersionControl** challenge is to have a unified GT method that is also flexible enough to accommodate the differences between the three traditional GT versions: *Glaserian GT*, *Strauss-Corbinian GT*, and *Constructivist GT*. In order to address the **#ScopeConfusion** challenge, the new SE-specific guidelines need to distinguish between applying GT's data analysis techniques, e.g., within other methods such as case studies or survey research, and conducting a full GT study where the full gamut of GT steps and procedures is applied. They also need to include corresponding evaluation guidelines for each application scope to avoid the scenarios associated with **#ExtremeReviews**.

#DIYGoneWrong is a challenge that occurs as SE researchers attempt to adapt traditional GT methods to suit their socio-technical SE research context. In the absence of adaptation guidelines, most adaptation attempts fail to maintain the philosophical and methodological integrity of the method. The new SE-specific GT guidelines also need to include adaptations to suit SE's unique research contexts. For example, updated guidelines may include and describe the use of modern data sources and types, beyond the typical interviews and observations covered in traditional GT methods.

In order to address the **#EvidenceGateKeeping** challenge, the new guidelines need to clearly describe how sufficient underlying evidence can be shared with the reviewers and public to establish research credibility and rigour while also maintaining ethical considerations. Challenges such as **#TheFacade**, **#PoorPresentation**, and **#ExtremeReviews** can be addressed by presenting clear and practical application, presentation, and evaluation guidelines that are comprehensive, nuanced, and thoroughly quality focused.

Overall, addressing the common challenges of applying traditional GT methods in SE research contexts requires a set of updated and contextualised guidelines for SE's modern and socio-technical research context. Given its unique focus on socio-technical research contexts, this new version is called **socio-technical grounded theory** or STGT for short. Table 2.3 presents an overview of the common challenges associated with SE researchers attempting traditional GT research, labelled as patterns, and approaches to addressing these challenges using STGT. The STGT method is introduced in Chap. 3 Socio-Technical Grounded Theory Overview.

Table 2.3 Traditional GT context and limitations, associated SE challenges presented as #patterns, and approaches to addressing them through the introduction of socio-technical grounded theory (STGT)

Traditional GT context and limitations	Associated SE challenges	Addressing challenges using STGT
Traditional GT guidelines were written by and for sociologists	#EagerButNotEquipped	STGT method is written by and for ST researchers using format, language, and examples native to SE
Traditional GT guidelines are spread across multiple books and three versions—*Glaserian, Strauss-Corbinian, Constructivist*	#NoVersionControl	STGT guidelines present one research method, offering flexibility in its application
Traditional GT guidelines expect the researcher to understand all three versions and select one upfront	#NoVersionControl	STGT delays the decision about theory development modes, *emergent* or *structured*, after some experience is gained
Traditional GT guidelines assume that the researcher is aware of and possesses the prerequisite knowledge and skills for conducting successful GT studies	#EagerButNotEquipped #PoorPresentations #ExtremeReviews	STGT guidelines explicitly spell out the fundamental knowledge and skills for conducting successful STGT studies
Traditional GT guidelines focus on theory generation	#ScopeConfusion #ExtremeReviews	A *full STGT study* can be used to generate theories and *STGT for Data Analysis* can be used for a data analysis only within other research frameworks, e.g., case study
Traditional GT methods were designed to study social phenomena	#DIYGoneWrong #ExtremeReviews	STGT method enables the investigation of socio-technical phenomena and domains
Traditional GT guidelines were designed to use traditional data types, sources, and collection techniques	#DIYGoneWrong #ExtremeReviews	STGT method is designed to leverage traditional and modern data types, sources, and collection techniques
Glaserian and Strauss-Corbinian GT were designed to be standalone methods	#DIYGoneWrong #ExtremeReviews	STGT method can be applied standalone or in combination with other methods and techniques
Traditional GT guidelines did not have to consider the need to share detailed evidence	#EvidenceGateKeeping	STGT method provides guidelines on presenting sufficient sanitised evidence and examples to establish credibility and enable proper evaluation

2.9 Summary

In this chapter, we learned the definition of *research* and why we need *research methods*, including references to some useful guidelines to empirical research methods. Next, we learned about the *origin* of traditional grounded theory (GT) from sociology and its overview including its distinguishing features and procedures. Then, we learned about the *evolution* of the GT method over the years into three different versions. Next, we learned about the use of *traditional GT in software engineering (SE)*, including an example of a theory generated using traditional GT, a list of exemplar studies, and existing traditional method guidelines. Next, we learned about the reasons *why* GT adoption progressed in SE research and contexts where traditional GT has been successfully applied in SE research. Then, we learned about the common *challenges* faced by SE researchers in conducting, presenting, and evaluating GT studies, presented as patterns. Finally, we learned about possible approaches to *addressing* these challenges, which in turn requires a set of updated and contextualised guidelines for conducting qualitative research in today's modern digital world—called socio-technical grounded theory (STGT). An overview of STGT is presented in the next chapter and is detailed in the remaining chapters of the book.

References

Adolph, S., Hall, W., & Kruchten, P. (2011). Using grounded theory to study the experience of software development. *Empirical Software Engineering, 16*(4), 487–513.

Adolph, S., Kruchten, P., & Hall, W. (2012). Reconciling perspectives: A grounded theory of how people manage the process of software development. *Journal of Systems and Software, 85*(6), 1269–1286.

Babchuk, W. A. (1996). Glaser or Strauss? Grounded theory and adult education. In *Proceedings of the 15th Annual Midwest Research-to-Practice Conference in Adult, Continuing, and Community Education* (pp. 1–6). ERIC.

Baker, C., Wuest, J., & Stern, P. N. (1992). Method slurring: The grounded theory/phenomenology example. *Journal of Advanced Nursing, 17*(11), 1355–1360.

Charmaz, K. (2006). *Constructing grounded theory: A practical guide through qualitative analysis*. Sage.

Charmaz, K. (2014). *Constructing grounded theory*. Sage.

Coleman, G., & O'Connor, R. (2007). Using grounded theory to understand software process improvement: A study of irish software product companies. *Information and Software Technology, 49*(6), 654–667.

Dagenais, B., Ossher, H., Bellamy, R. K., Robillard, M. P., & De Vries, J. P. (2010). Moving into a new software project landscape. In *Proceedings of the 32nd ACM/IEEE International Conference on Software Engineering-Volume 1* (pp. 275–284).

Easterbrook, S., Singer, J., Storey, M.-A., & Damian, D. (2008). Selecting empirical methods for software engineering research. In *Guide to advanced empirical software engineering* (pp. 285–311). Springer .

Fassinger, R. E. (2005). Paradigms, praxis, problems, and promise: Grounded theory in counseling psychology research. *Journal of Counseling Psychology, 52*(2), 156.

Glaser, B. (1978). *Theoretical sensitivity: Advances in the methodology of grounded theory*. Sociology Press.

Glaser, B. G. (1992). *Basics of grounded theory analysis: Emergence vs forcing*. Sociology Press.

Glaser, B. G. (1998). *Doing grounded theory: Issues and discussions*. Sociology Press.

Glaser, B. G., & Strauss, A. L. (1966). *Awareness of dying*. Transaction Publishers.

Glaser, B. G., & Strauss, A. L. (2011). *Status passage*. Transaction Publishers.

Glaser, B. G., & Strauss, A. L. (2017). *Discovery of grounded theory: Strategies for qualitative research*. Routledge (First Published 1967).

Glaser, B. G., & Strauss, A. L. (2017, first published 1968). *Time for dying*. Routledge (First Published 1968).

Heath, H., & Cowley, S. (2004). Developing a grounded theory approach: a comparison of Glaser and Strauss. *International Journal of Nursing Studies, 41*(2), 141–150.

Hoda, R. (2022). Socio-technical grounded theory for software engineering. *IEEE Transactions on Software Engineering, 48*(10), 3808–3832.

Hoda, R., & Noble, J. (2017). Becoming agile: A grounded theory of agile transitions in practice. In *2017 IEEE/ACM 39th International Conference on Software Engineering (ICSE)* (pp. 141–151). IEEE.

Hoda, R., Noble, J., & Marshall, S. (2010). Organizing self-organizing teams. In *Proceedings of the 32nd ACM/IEEE International Conference on Software Engineering-Volume 1* (pp. 285–294).

Hoda, R., Noble, J., & Marshall, S. (2011a). Grounded theory for geeks. In *Proceedings of the 18th Conference on Pattern Languages of Programs (PLoP)* (pp. 1–17).

Hoda, R., Noble, J., & Marshall, S. (2011b). The impact of inadequate customer collaboration on self-organizing agile teams. *Information and Software Technology, 53*(5), 521–534.

Hoda, R., Noble, J., & Marshall, S. (2012a). Developing a grounded theory to explain the practices of self-organizing agile teams. *Empirical Software Engineering, 17*(6), 609–639.

Hoda, R., Noble, J., & Marshall, S. (2012b). Self-organizing roles on agile software development teams. *IEEE Transactions on Software Engineering, 39*(3), 422–444.

Jantunen, S., & Gause, D. C. (2014). Using a grounded theory approach for exploring software product management challenges. *Journal of Systems and Software, 95*, 32–51.

Kennedy, T. J., & Lingard, L. A. (2006). Making sense of grounded theory in medical education. *Medical Education, 40*(2), 101–108.

Kenny, M., & Fourie, R. (2014). Tracing the history of grounded theory methodology: From formation to fragmentation. *The Qualitative Report, 19*(52), 1.

Maglyas, A., Nikula, U., & Smolander, K. (2013). What are the roles of software product managers? An empirical investigation. *Journal of Systems and Software, 86*(12), 3071–3090.

Masood, Z., Hoda, R., & Blincoe, K. (2020a). How agile teams make self-assignment work: A grounded theory study, *Empirical Software Engineering, 25*, 4962–5005. https://doi.org/10.1007/s10664-020-09876-x

Masood, Z., Hoda, R., & Blincoe, K. (2020b). Real world Scrum: A grounded theory of variations in practice. *IEEE Transactions on Software Engineering, 48*(5), 1579–1591.

Myers, M. D., & Avison, D. (2002). *Qualitative research in information systems: a reader*. Sage.

Rennie, D. L., Phillips, J. R., & Quartaro, G. K. (1988). Grounded theory: A promising approach to conceptualization in psychology?. *Canadian Psychology/Psychologie Canadienne, 29*(2), 139.

Schreiber, R. S., Stern, P. N. et al. (2001). *Using grounded theory in nursing*. Springer.

Seaman, C. B. (1999). Qualitative methods in empirical studies of software engineering. *IEEE Transactions on Software Engineering, 25*(4), 557–572.

Sedano, T., Ralph, P., & Péraire, C. (2017). Software development waste. In *2017 IEEE/ACM 39th International Conference on Software Engineering (ICSE)* (pp. 130–140). IEEE.

Shastri, Y., Hoda, R., & Amor, R. (2021a). The role of the project manager in agile software development projects. *Journal of Systems and Software, 173*, 110871.

Shastri, Y., Hoda, R., & Amor, R. (2021b). Spearheading agile: the role of the scrum master in agile projects. *Empirical Software Engineering, 26*(1), 1–31.

Shull, F., Singer, J., & Sjøberg, D. I. (2007). *Guide to advanced empirical software engineering*. Springer.

Sousa, L., Oliveira, A., Oizumi, W., Barbosa, S., Garcia, A., Lee, J., Kalinowski, M., de Mello, R., Fonseca, B., Oliveira, R. et al. (2018). Identifying design problems in the source code: A grounded theory. In *Proceedings of the 40th International Conference on Software Engineering* (pp. 921–931).

Stol, K.-J., Ralph, P., & Fitzgerald, B. (2016). Grounded theory in software engineering research: A critical review and guidelines. In *Proceedings of the 38th International Conference on Software Engineering* (pp. 120–131).

Storey, M.-A., Ernst, N. A., Williams, C., & Kalliamvakou, E. (2020). The who, what, how of software engineering research: A socio-technical framework. *Empirical Software Engineering, 25*(5), 4097–4129.

Strauss, A., & Corbin, J. (1990). *Basics of qualitative research*. Sage publications.

Strauss, A., & Corbin, J. (1994). Grounded theory methodology. *Handbook of Qualitative Research, 17*(1), 273–285.

Stray, V., Sjøberg, D. I., & Dybå, T. (2016). The daily stand-up meeting: A grounded theory study. *Journal of Systems and Software, 114*, 101–124.

Waterman, M., Noble, J., & Allan, G. (2015). How much up-front? A grounded theory of agile architecture. In *2015 IEEE/ACM 37th IEEE International Conference on Software Engineering* (Vol. 1, pp. 347–357). IEEE.

Watling, C. J., & Lingard, L. (2012). Grounded theory in medical education research: Amee guide no. 70, *Medical Teacher, 34*(10), 850–861.

Wohlin, C., & Aurum, A. (2015). Towards a decision-making structure for selecting a research design in empirical software engineering. *Empirical Software Engineering, 20*, 1427–1455.

3 Socio-Technical Grounded Theory: An Overview

Abstract This chapter provides an overview of socio-technical grounded theory (STGT) for conducting qualitative research within qualitative and mixed-methods research studies. First, we will learn about the underlying *socio-technical research framework* which acts as the sweet spot for applying STGT and more generally for conducting qualitative empirical research in the modern digital world. Next, we will be introduced to STGT including an *overview* of its philosophical foundations, methodological steps and procedures for qualitative research, and published examples. We will learn about the possible applications of the *full STGT method* or in a limited capacity as *STGT for data analysis*. We will also learn about an application selection guide to help us decide how best to apply STGT and when possibly not to. Finally, we will be introduced to the evaluation guidelines. This chapter serves to provide a birds-eye view of STGT, encouraging further exploration in the remaining chapters.

R. Hoda, *Qualitative Research with Socio-Technical Grounded Theory*,
https://doi.org/10.1007/978-3-031-60533-8_3

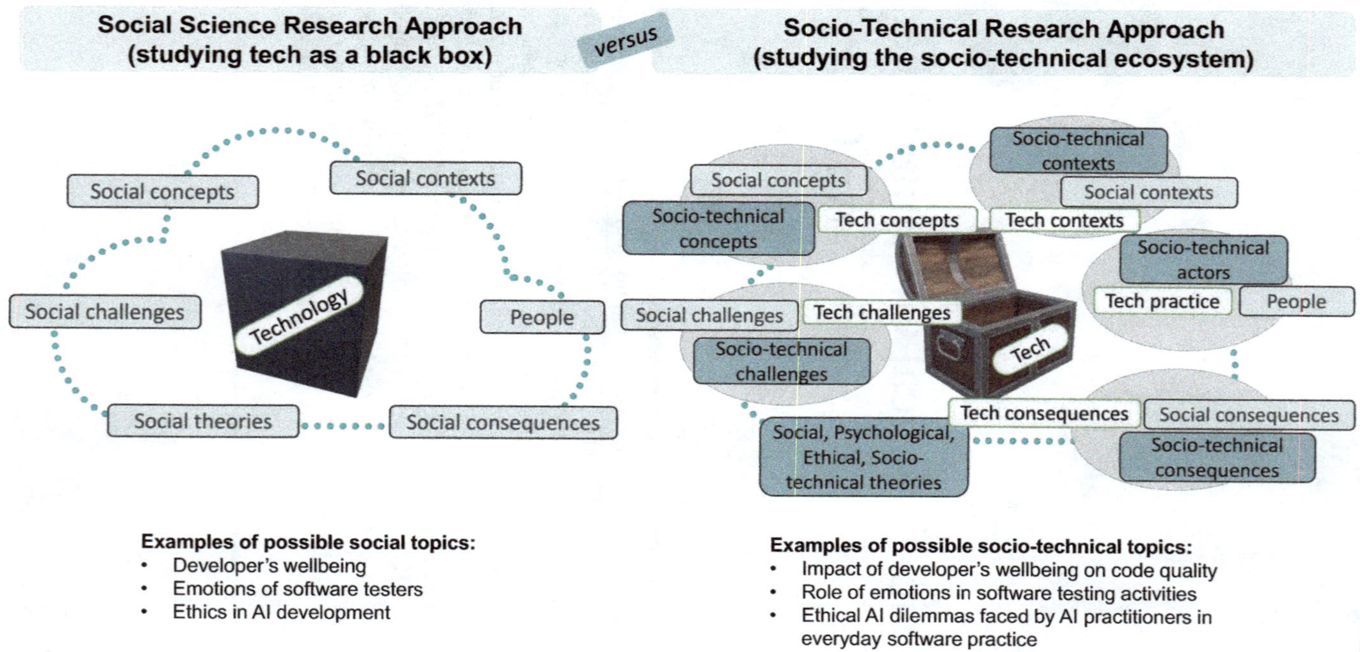

Fig. 3.1 Social science research approach that focuses on social aspects and treats technology as a black box (left-hand side) versus socio-technical research approach that considers the full socio-technical ecosystem including the technological aspects and how they interact with the social aspects (right-hand side)

3.1 What Is Socio-Technical Research?

Qualitative research in software engineering (SE) borrows heavily from the social sciences. Research methods such as case studies, ethnography, survey research, and grounded theory are all examples of research methods originating from the social sciences that have been applied over the decades mainly to conduct empirical qualitative research and study the human and social aspects of SE. Informal adaptations to the traditional qualitative methods have been made by researchers to ease their application in software engineering and related disciplines. Contextualised guidelines by methodology experts such as Runeson and Höst (2009) for case studies and Sharp et al. (2016) for ethnography as well as modern adaptations such as Schwartz (1989) and Pink (2020) for visual ethnography have helped researchers navigate the differences between the original contexts these methods were designed for and more modern application contexts. The latter are characterised by both social and technological aspects and their interplay, i.e., a *socio-technical ecosystem.* Let us consider these differences to understand why method adaptations and contextualised guidelines are required.

3.1.1 Social Science Research Approach

A social science approach to research focuses on the social aspects of the topic under study while mostly treating any existing technical aspects as a black box (see left-hand side of Fig. 3.1). This may be adequate and even desirable if the study aims to focus purely on social aspects and constructs. For example, topics that focus on studying social constructs in SE settings such as *well-being of software developers*, *emotions of software testers*, and *ethics in AI development* can be studied with a social science approach focusing on studying the core social/psychological/ethical constructs of well-being, emotions, and ethics respectively. In this case, the application domain (i.e., software engineering) is usually considered a context where the social aspects manifest themselves. A primarily social science approach tends to disregard the technical nuances of the context and focuses mostly on studying the social aspects themselves.

An extreme version of this observation has been captured in what is termed as the *football test for human and social studies in software engineering*, first raised by Michael Jackson and later addressed by Lionel Briand in his ACM SIGSOFT outstanding researcher keynote. The test suggests replacing the term *software engineering* with the term *football* in the research paper to see whether the paper still makes sense. In other words, what difference does the context make to the research? And following that logic, can it still be considered software engineering research?

Ideas such as the *football test* represent an interesting, albeit rather reductionist and perhaps somewhat harsh, outlook on what constitutes social science research in software engineering. Those of us who engage more deeply with human and social aspects research in software engineering know and will agree that the application domain has a significant impact on human and social aspects. But how do we demonstrate this? My experience suggests that most studies do so implicitly through sharing the details of the context as part of the findings. However, the onus of piecing the social and the technical aspects together and understanding their interplay is often left to the reader for the most part.

One way to more explicitly explain the true nature of research that studies both social and technical aspects in software engineering is to first acknowledge that it is *socio-technical* research, rather than social science research. Figure 3.2 shows a visual representation of the spectrum of research in software engineering and related disciplines. This spectrum spans from primarily technical research, such as research on programming languages and formal methods, to primarily social science based, such as social aspects of software engineering and collaborative software engineering. The area in the middle constitutes socio-technical research, which concerns itself with studying and explaining both the social and technical aspects and their interplay in a given research topic, such as human and socio-technical aspects of SE and interdisciplinary areas such as robot– human interaction, ethics in AI, digital health, and so on.[1]

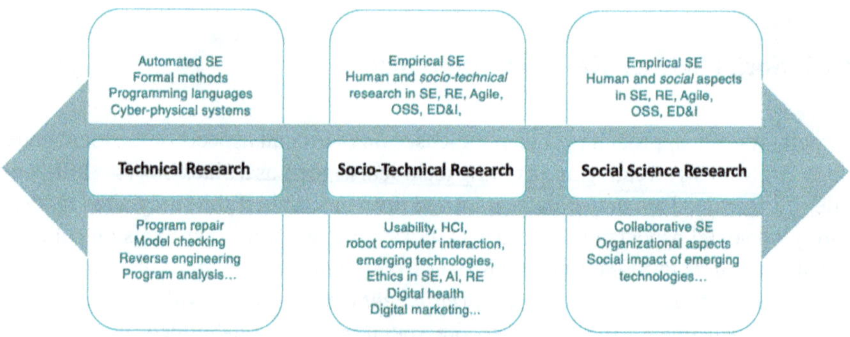

Fig. 3.2 The research spectrum spanning primarily technical to socio-technical to social science-based research with some example areas of application

I attempt to define the socio-technical research approach more explicitly through the idea of a *socio-technical research framework*, presented in my TSE paper (Hoda, 2022), and summarized next.

[1] An acknowledgement of the variety of research conducted in SE is reflected in the recent change in the name of the International Conference on Software Engineering (ICSE)'s main track from the *technical* track to the *research* track, where ICSE is the flagship conference in software engineering.

3.1.2 Socio-Technical Research Framework

The modern digital world abounds with research topics that are predominantly *socio-technical—where the social and technical aspects are interwoven in such a way that studying one without due consideration of the other makes for an incomplete investigation and understanding* (Hoda, 2022).

A traditional social science approach tends to be neither adequate nor comprehensive for studying most increasingly socio-technical topics in the modern digital world. Almost all software engineering practices are socio-technical in nature. For example, customer collaboration, requirement elicitation, software project management, software architecture and prototype design, pair/mob/group programming, daily standups, functional and acceptance testing, software deployment, maintenance, and multi-team coordination are all socio-technical activities, with varying levels of human–human and human–technology interaction.

In modern disciplines such as software engineering and artificial intelligence, topics such as the *impact of developers' well-being on code quality*, *role of emotions in software testing activities*, and *ethical AI dilemmas faced by AI practitioners in everyday software practice* demand a socio-technical approach to research (see right-hand side of Fig. 3.1), which tends to be typically empirical and qualitative.

With increasing digitilisation, most phenomena in our contemporary world are also socio-technical. For example, consider how the domains of digital health, online education, digital banking, e-commerce, online retail, remote work, and social networking are fundamentally transforming how we approach and operate with these domains in the material and virtual worlds. In these modern versions of traditional disciplines such as digital health, digital marketing, and e-commerce, topics such the *role of collaborative healthcare robots in aged care facilities*, *child development in the digital world*, and *project management using artificial intelligence tools* demand a socio-technical approach.

Similarly, classic theories in sociology and psychology may need to be re-examined to account for their new socio-technical implications. For example, consider the study that led to the formulation of the original GT research method, on the role of the social status of dying hospital patients in the level of nursing care received and the awareness of dying (Glaser & Strauss, 2017, first published 1967). When considered in contemporary times, these can no longer be considered strictly social processes. Today, an investigation of *social status* without due consideration of the patient's online and social media profile and an *awareness of dying* without investigating the impact of readily available credible and scrupulous online medical information will be considered incomplete. Similarly, consider Piaget's classic *theory of cognitive development* that explained the four stages of children's cognitive development as sensorimotor, pre-operational, concrete operational, and formal operational. The theory may well need to be re-calibrated for the digital natives who are known to be able to operate complex digital devices as early as a few months old. Approaching these as the socio-technical topics that they are will enable more comprehensive and effective investigations and theory development.

I designed the *socio-technical research framework* to explicitly explain the socio-technical nature of most modern research topics. The framework captures and explains four dimensions of socio-technical research: *socio-technical phenomenon*, *domain and actors*, *researcher(s)*, and *data, tools, and techniques*. It combines social science knowledge and skills with an understanding of technology and the relevant application domains. Applying a socio-technical approach to research will enable the researcher to open the metaphorical black box and investigate how the technology (and the related domain constructs) interact with the social aspects in practice. Figure 3.1 shows a visual representation of the differences between the social and socio-technical research approaches.

The socio-technical research framework (Fig. 3.3) can be used as a litmus test to ascertain when STGT is a viable option for a research study. When the proposed study mostly fits the four dimensions of the socio-technical research framework, it is a good indicator that the study will benefit from applying STGT. In other words, the proposed research study fits the STGT *sweet spot*. Examples of how a socio-technical research framework fit has been used to motivate the use of STGT in qualitative and mixed-methods studies can be found in Graetsch et al. (2023), Hidellaarachchi et al. (2023), and Madampe et al. (2022).

Definition

Socio-technical research topics are those *where the social and technical aspects are interwoven in such a way that studying one without due consideration of the other makes for an incomplete investigation and understanding* (Hoda, 2022).

The **socio-technical research framework** is composed of four dimensions:

- **Socio-technical Phenomenon** refers to a phenomenon (or topic) where the social and technical aspects are interwoven in such a way that studying one without the other leads to an incomplete or shallow investigation. Increasingly, most research phenomena or topics are socio-technical, not purely social or technical in nature.

- **Socio-technical Domain and Actors** refers to relatively newer domains (or disciplines) such as SE, artificial intelligence, computer science, information systems, human–computer interaction, and human–robot interaction, as well as modern variations of traditional domains such as digital health, digital marketing, and e-commerce. *ST actors* refer to people who act in these domains, e.g., software engineers, data scientists, business analysts, managers, software users, digital healthcare practitioners, robots, AI agents, and others.

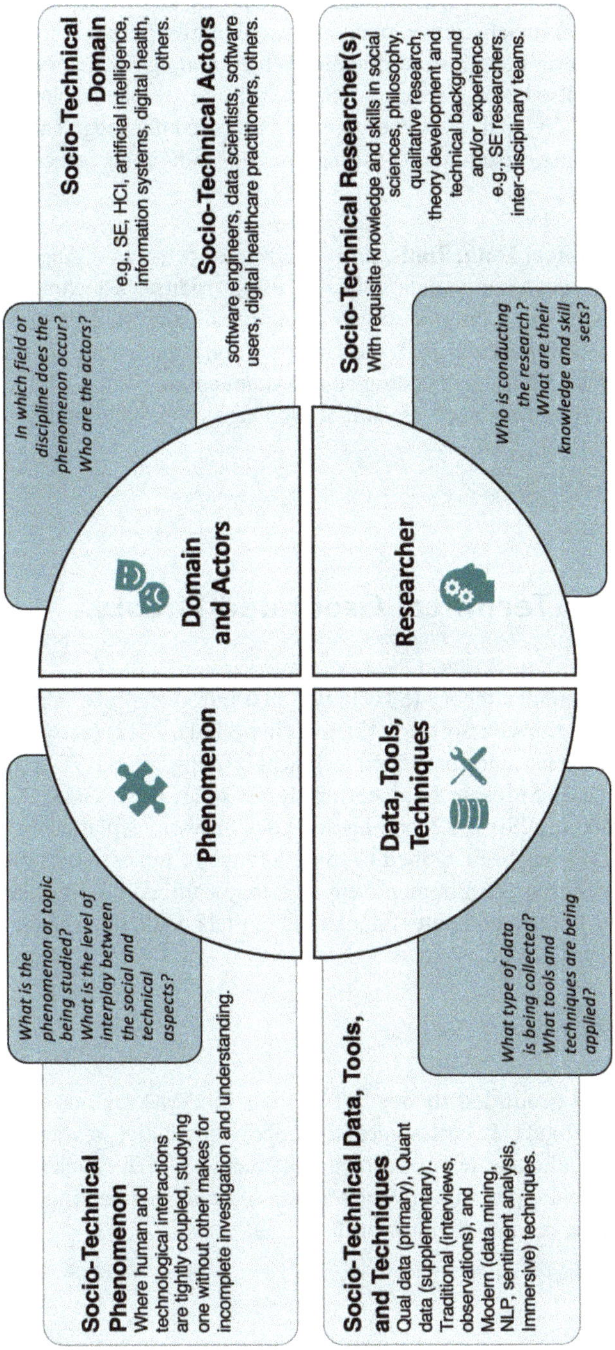

Fig. 3.3 The socio-technical research framework (Hoda, 2022)

- **Socio-technical Researcher(s)** refers to researchers who are (or are committed to becoming) equipped with the requisite knowledge and skills in areas such as social science, philosophy, qualitative research, technology, and the relevant application domain. Where aiming for theory development, they also have, or are committed to gaining, relevant expertise. They can be an individual researcher with all requisite knowledge and skills or a team of inter-disciplinary researchers with individuals specialising in different areas.

- **Socio-technical Data, Tools, and Techniques** refers to a range of qualitative and quantitative data collected using traditional techniques such as semi-structured interviews and observations and modern techniques such as data mining and analysis using traditional qualitative data analysis procedures such as open coding and constant comparison combined with modern procedures such as natural language processing and sentiment analysis.

3.2 Socio-Technical Grounded Theory

Socio-technical grounded theory (STGT) was first introduced in a paper published in the IEEE Transactions on Software Engineering (Hoda, 2022) (early access 2021, published 2022). I have since presented technical briefings on STGT at the International Conference on Software Engineering (ICSE 2021, ICSE 2023, ICSE 2024), a journal first talk at ICSE 2022, and invited talks on various platforms.[2] Since its introduction, STGT has been applied to study a range of topics across the domains of software engineering, requirements engineering, artificial intelligence, human–robot interaction, human–computer interaction, digital health, blockchain, and other emerging and interdisciplinary areas.

Definition

Socio-technical grounded theory (STGT) is a modern variation of the traditional GT methods. It is designed to support qualitative research within either purely qualitative or mixed-methods studies. STGT enables research on socio-technical topics that are abundant in software engineering and other disciplines in the modern digital world.

[2] Videos and slides of these talks are available at www.rashina.com.

STGT applies the socio-technical research framework to adapt and expand traditional GT's social science context, philosophical foundations, methodological steps and procedures, application, and evaluation guidelines for socio-technical research contexts.

Unlike traditional GT methods that focus on theory development, STGT can be applied in two ways:

- **Full STGT study** that involves interleaved rounds of *basic* data collection and analysis and *advanced* theory development through either an *emergent* or *structured* mode to generate novel, useful, parsimonious, and modifiable theories and other theoretical outcomes.
- **STGT for data analysis** that involves the *basic* data analysis techniques of open coding, constant comparison, and memoing. It is used to generate rich, nuanced, and layered descriptive findings, emerging taxonomies, theoretical models, frameworks, and in some cases emerging hypotheses and preliminary theories.

The rest of this section provides an overview of the key components of STGT, including suitable research topics and questions, philosophical foundations, methodological steps and procedures, scope and application, an application selection guide, and evaluation guidelines. In summarising these, the key points of difference to the traditional sociological GT methods are also highlighted.

3.2.1 Research Topics and Questions

STGT is suited to studying a range of research topics and questions. It is best suited to studying topics that are socio-technical in nature and where the research team wishes to produce rich and layered qualitative findings and possibly even theories. Table 3.1 presents examples of published journal articles and conference papers that report on their application of the *full STGT method* or *STGT for data analysis* in qualitative and mixed-methods studies across various domains (up to early 2024). Table 3.2 presents a list of other possible research topics, overarching research questions, and associated sub-questions that are well suited to studying with STGT. These are meant to be suggestions and are by no means exhaustive or limiting.

3.2.2 Philosophical Foundations

Conducting quality STGT studies requires a set of requisite knowledge and skills, including fundamental concepts from philosophy such as types of reasoning, ontol-

Table 3.1 Examples of studies applying socio-technical grounded theory (STGT) as a *full method* and in limited capacity *for data analysis*

Reference	Title	Research domains	Publication venue	STGT application	Study type	Reported outcome
Graetsch et al. (2023)	*Dealing with data challenges when delivering data-intensive software solutions*	Artificial Intelligence, Software Engineering	IEEE Transactions on Software Engineering	Full STGT method *(basic & advanced stages)*	Qualitative	Theory
Pant et al. (2023)	*Ethics in the age of AI: An analysis of AI practitioners' awareness and challenges*	Artificial Intelligence, Software Engineering	ACM Transactions on Software Engineering and Methodology	STGT for data analysis	Mixed methods	Descriptive findings
Gama and Lacerda (2023)	*Understanding and supporting neurodiverse software developers in agile teams*	Psychology, Software Engineering	Proceedings of the XXXVII Brazilian Symposium on Software Engineering	Full STGT method *(basic stage)*	Qualitative	Descriptive findings
Hidellaarachchi et al. (2023)	*The influence of human aspects on requirements engineering-related activities: Software practitioners' perspective*	Requirements Engineering	ACM Transactions on Software Engineering and Methodology	STGT for data analysis	Mixed methods	Descriptive findings
Gunatilake et al. (2024)	*Enablers and barriers of empathy in software developer and user interactions: A mixed methods case study*	Human aspects, Software Engineering	ACM Transactions on Software Engineering and Methodology	STGT for data analysis	Mixed methods	Descriptive findings
Madampe et al. (2023)	*A framework for emotion-oriented requirements change handling in agile software engineering*	Requirements Engineering, Software Engineering	IEEE Transactions on Software Engineering	STGT for data analysis	Mixed methods	Descriptive findings
Madampe et al. (2022)	*The emotional roller coaster of responding to requirements changes in software engineering*	Requirements Engineering, Software Engineering	IEEE Transactions on Software Engineering	STGT for data analysis	Mixed methods	Descriptive findings
Li et al. (2023)	*Enhancing blockchain adoption through tailored software engineering: An industrial-grounded study in education credentialing*	Blockchain, Software Engineering	Distributed Ledger Technologies: Research and Practice	STGT for data analysis	Mixed methods	Descriptive findings
Wang et al. (2023)	*Adapting user interfaces for software supporting chronic diseases*	Digital Health, Human–Computer Interaction	IEEE Symposium on Visual Languages and Human-Centric Computing	STGT for data analysis	Mixed methods	Descriptive findings
Chan and Hauser (2023)	*Understanding human-robot encounters*	Human–Robot Interaction	Proceedings of the Association for Information Science and Technology	Full STGT method	Mixed methods	Emerging theory

Table 3.2 Some prospective research topics and questions suited for studying with STGT

Research topic	Overarching research question	Research sub-questions
Code review practice	How do software developers practise and use code reviews?	*What code review practices and approaches are used by developers?* *How do developers practise code reviews?* *Who uses the results of code reviews and how?*
Role of DevOps engineers	What is the role of the DevOps engineers?	*What do DevOps engineers do on an everyday basis?* *What are the challenges faced by DevOps engineers?* *How do DevOps engineers overcome these challenges?*

ogy, epistemology, and research paradigm. These are summarised briefly below and detailed in Chap. 5 Research Philosophy.

- **Reasoning** refers to the approach to drawing inferences from data. The full STGT method explains how theories can be generated from large amounts of raw qualitative data through a predominantly and overarching *inductive* approach while also acknowledging and explaining the role of *deductive* and *abductive* reasoning in the process.

- **Ontology** refers to "*what we believe exists or what we perceive as reality*" (Hoda, 2022). STGT expands the *ontological frame* of traditional GT methods by acknowledging and being flexible to studying *extended realities* beyond the physical world, such as virtual, augmented, and combined realities.

- **Epistemology** refers to "*what we treat as knowledge and how we can know about what we perceive as reality*" (Hoda, 2022). STGT expands the *epistemological positions* of traditional GT methods by being flexible to applying *objective* (knowledge is discovered objectively by a neutral observer), *interpretive* (knowledge is interpreted by the observer), and *subjective* (knowledge is constructed by a subjective and reflexive observer) positions best fit for the realities being studied.

- **Research Paradigm** refers to "*the combination of ontological and epistemological stances that informs the researcher's worldview*" (Hoda, 2022). Traditional GT methods have a one-on-one mapping with research paradigms. For example, Glaserian GT is widely seen to align to positivism, Strauss-Corbinian GT is aligned to symbolic interactionism, and Charmaz' GT is aligned to Constructivism. STGT, on the other hand, is flexible to applying one of many research paradigms, e.g., positivism or constructivism, and different perspectives, e.g., critical theory or feminism, depending on the research context.

3.2.3 Methodological Steps and Procedures

Figure 3.4 shows a diagrammatic representation of the STGT method, including its *basic* data collection and analysis stage and *advanced* theory development stage. The steps and procedures of the STGT method are summarised briefly below and detailed in the remaining chapters of this book.

- **Literature Reviews.** The STGT method offers two types of literature reviews: *lean literature review*, a lightweight, high-level review performed in the early stages to identify research gaps, and *targeted literature review*, an in-depth focused review of literature relevant to emerging categories and hypotheses performed periodically and toward the later stages of theory development to compare and situate new findings in the wider research landscape. Details of these and other literature review methods can be found in Chap. 6 Literature Review.

- **Basic Stage—STGT for Qualitative Data Analysis.** The basic stage includes (theoretical) sampling, basic qualitative data collection, qualitative data analysis (open coding and constant comparison), and basic memoing, and generates key concepts and (sub)categories, along with possible preliminary hypotheses. Details of the steps and procedures of the basic stage can be found in Chaps. 7 Basics of Qualitative Data Collection, 8 Techniques of Qualitative Data Collection, 9 Qualitative Data Preparation and Filtering, and 10 STGT for Qualitative Data Analysis.

- **Advanced Stage—Theory Development.** STGT offers a choice of two modes of theory development in the advanced stage, *emergent* and *structured*. It delays this decision making to a point where the researcher has experience of the basic stage and is able to select a best fit for their needs. *Glaserian* and *Strauss-Corbinian* GT, on the other hand, demand a firm choice between the two at the very beginning of the project, with no room for easy switching or combining of procedures later. Similarly, *Constructivist GT* demands the use of the constructivist research paradigm. In case of STGT, the choice of research paradigm is open positivist, constructivist, interpretivist, and so on. Details of the steps and procedures of the advanced stage can be found in Chaps. 11 What is Theory? and 12 Theory Development.

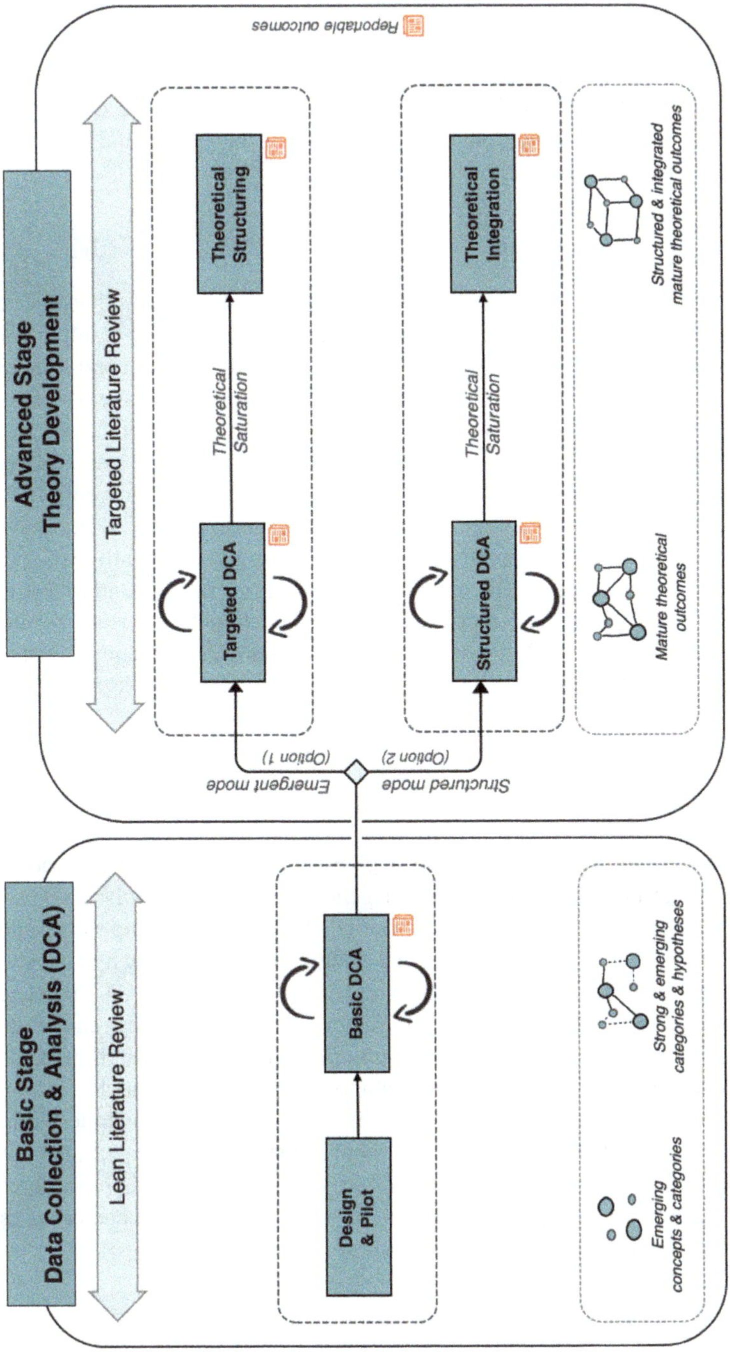

Fig. 3.4 The socio-technical grounded theory method (adapted from Hoda, 2022)

3.2.4 Two Application Levels

STGT offers two possible application levels: first, as the *full STGT method* for theory[3] development; and second, as STGT *for data analysis*, where a limited set of STGT steps and procedures are applied for data analysis, typically using other research techniques or methods. Traditional GT methods, on the other hand, assume full method application for the purpose of theory development.

Definition

Full STGT Method refers to the application of both the basic and advanced stages of STGT. Application of the full STGT method is likely to result in one or more mature theoretical outcomes. Full STGT studies can be conducted as *standalone studies*, using only steps and procedures from within the STGT research method and not in combination with other full research methods such as case studies, survey research, or ethnography. However, survey questionnaires or ethnographically inspired observations can be applied as data collection techniques within a standalone STGT study. A standalone STGT can make use of qualitative data or combinations of qualitative and quantitative (mixed) data, based on the nature of the phenomenon being investigated and access to different types of data. When applied well, a standalone STGT study results in rich findings grounded in empirical evidence and does not require further validation, e.g., through a survey.

Definition

STGT for Data Analysis refers to applying STGT in a limited capacity, harnessing its data analysis procedures to generate findings. It involves STGT's basic data analysis procedures such as open coding, constant comparison, and memoing, likely resulting in some strong categories and emerging hypotheses. It is ideal for research projects where conducting a standalone STGT study and developing a theory is not the aim, but rather where STGT is desired mainly for its data analysis procedures, in *combination* with other research methods such as case studies, survey research, ethnography, action research, (quasi-) experiments, and user experience research. Practically, this is manifested in teams specialising in one or the other research method (e.g., experiments or case studies) that wish to harness STGT's rigorous data analysis procedures to extract rich and in-depth findings in terms of concepts, (sub)categories, as well as present preliminary hypotheses or propositions.

[3] Theory here refers to mature theoretical outcomes such as mature theoretical models, frameworks, taxonomies, and theories.

3.2.5 Application Selection Guide

Selecting when and how to apply STGT requires considering some key points. Figure 3.5 summarises the selection process in the form of an *application selection guide*.

One of the first things you may consider is whether you have qualitative data to analyse, as part of either a purely qualitative or a mixed-methods research study. If yes, you can consider STGT as an option among other qualitative data analysis methods. If there is no qualitative data involved, i.e., it is a purely quantitative study, applying STGT will make little sense.

Next, you want to consider whether the qualitative data is mostly of non-trivial amounts. For example, if the qualitative data is limited to a few words' worth of text-based responses to an open-ended question in a survey, it may not require a rigorous data analysis method. Having said that, sometimes even responses from one open-ended question can be so detailed and deep that applying STGT's data analysis procedures will yield rich findings worth reporting. Indeed, much of the sense to understand these nuances comes with experience of dealing with many different types and numbers of datasets.

The next aspect to consider is whether the data is unstructured, semi-structured, or structured. If the data is finely structured, there will be little scope for emergence to work its magic through inductive reasoning. STGT data analysis works best on semi-structured and unstructured data.

At this point, you may consider whether you would like to develop a theory. This seems like a massive question. However, I have met several researchers for whom the driving motivation for conducting qualitative research is to develop theory. There may be other ways of developing theory that I will not get into here, but few are as systematic and rigorous as STGT. If theory development is a motivation, I would argue that applying the **full STGT method** is a natural choice.

On the other hand, many researchers do not have the faintest idea of what is involved in developing theory. I was one of them when I first started my PhD study. If your answer is in the negative or if you are unsure about developing theory, the next and final aspect to consider is whether you are interested in generating rich and layered qualitative findings. If your answer is no, you may be better off applying other data analysis techniques such as content analysis, discourse analysis, narrative analysis, and topic modelling. That is not to say that rich findings are not possible through these methods, but experience suggests the data analysis procedures of STGT have an advantage in terms of the depth they can help achieve. If your answer is yes, **STGT for data analysis** is a robust choice.

Thematic analysis is one of those methods that can be applied in a lightweight way to produce lightweight descriptive findings but can also be applied with more rigour to produce deeper findings. Researcher skills notwithstanding, my experience suggests that *STGT for data analysis* with its open coding, constant comparison, and memoing procedures will still yield richer, more layered, and nuanced findings than thematic analysis can yield. This is because STGT data analysis procedures raise the raw data through multiple levels of abstraction from codes to concepts to categories

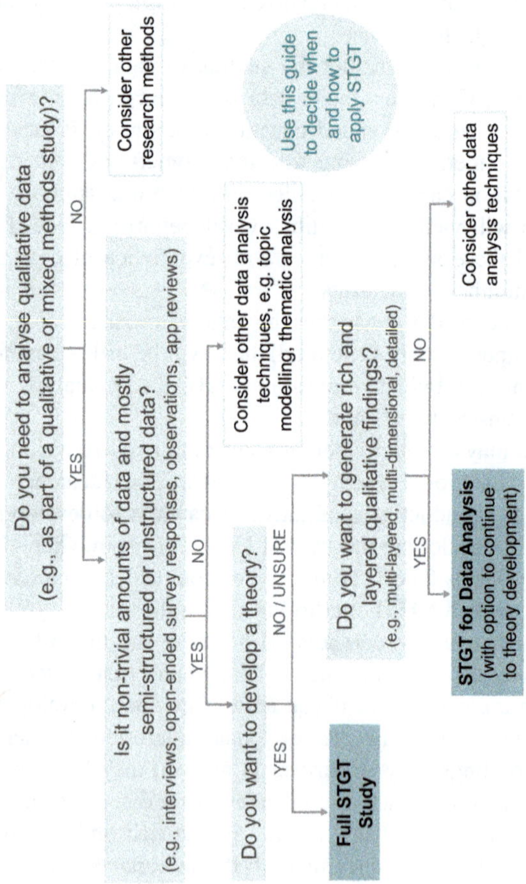

Fig. 3.5 Socio-technical grounded theory—application selection guide

(and sometimes subcategories or super categories), which in turn creates layers and depth.

3.2.6 Application Scope

STGT studies can vary in size and scope, from small-scale to large-scale studies, and can be conducted in standalone or combined capacities. STGT practitioners need to be careful to select and apply the application level that fits their research needs. Similarly, reviewers should apply the evaluation criteria commensurate to the application level, as explained later in this chapter. Figure 3.6 depicts possible scope and application, and they are described in detail below.

- **Small-scale STGT studies** (Fig. 3.6 bottom left) typically focus on a narrow topic, lasting between 6 and 18 months. Small-scale STGT studies can be conducted by a primary researcher with guidance from experts, a team of researchers, or a single STGT researcher. They tend to result in one mature theory that is presented in a single, in-depth publication. However, interim results and the preliminary theory can be reported along the way.

- **Large-scale STGT studies** (Fig. 3.6 bottom right) typically focus on a broad topic, lasting between 3 and 4 years, e.g., as a PhD study. Large-scale STGT studies can be conducted by a primary researcher with guidance from experts (e.g., a PhD student with supervisors and/or advisors) or a team of researchers. A single researcher is not recommended to perform a large-scale STGT study on their own, primarily because of lack of internal validation and potential loss of motivation along the way. Large-scale STGT studies typically result in multiple theories that are presented in individual publications, with periodic reporting of interim and partial findings (e.g., concepts and categories) and preliminary theories. Examples can be seen in Hoda et al. (2011, 2012) and Masood et al. (2020, 2021). It is recommended that publications resulting from the same overarching large STGT study cross-reference one another, explaining their individual focus and potentially complementary nature. When conducted as a part of a PhD study, the PhD thesis usually captures how multiple theories resulting from a large STGT study make sense together as a comprehensive whole (e.g., see Hoda, 2011).

- **STGT in Mixed-Methods studies** (Fig. 3.6 top left) captures the scenario where an STGT study is conducted as part of mixed-methods[4] studies, typically as a first step to deeply investigating and understanding the problem space before proceeding to solutions development (e.g., tools, techniques, platforms, and guidelines) or broad validation (e.g., through surveys or data mining). Examples of the use

[4] Mixed methods here refers to applying a combination of research methods.

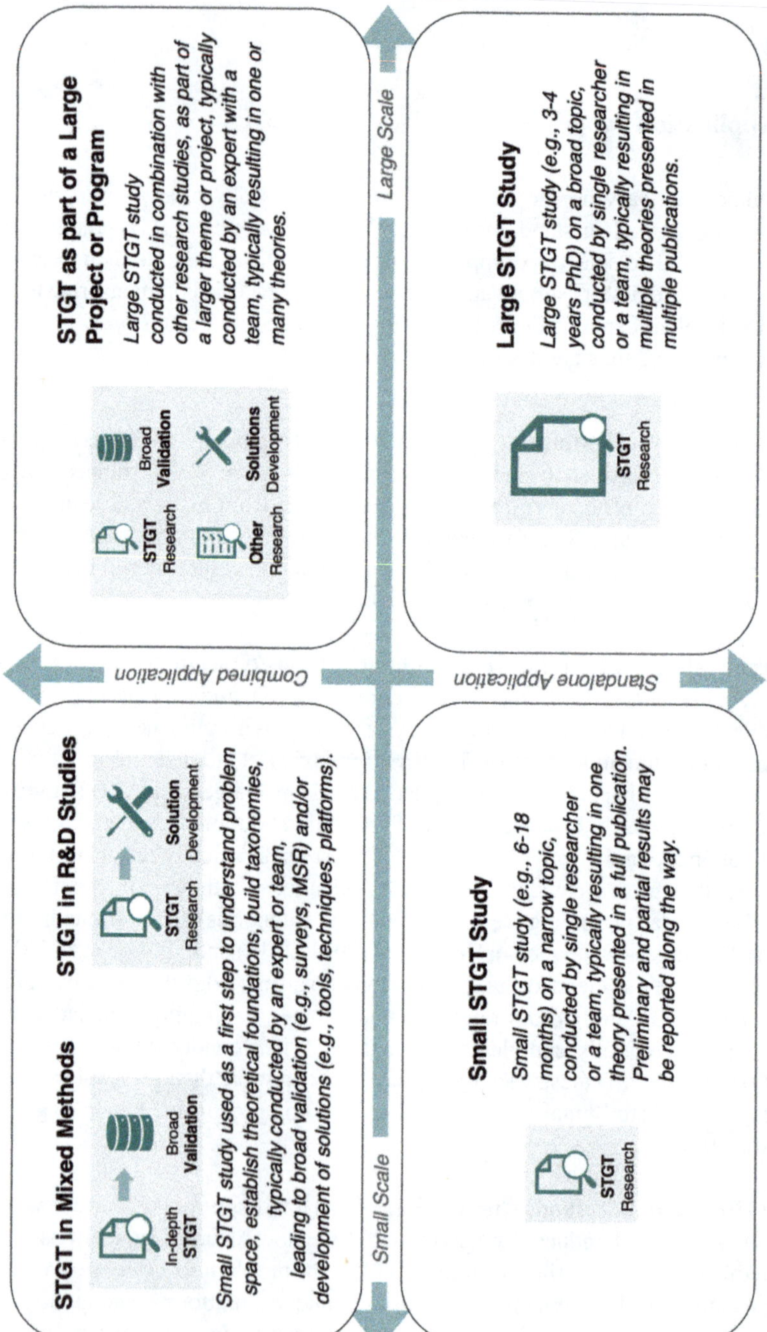

Fig. 3.6 Scope and application of socio-technical grounded theory

of STGT in mixed-methods research include studies on the role of emotions in requirements engineering (Madampe et al., 2022, 2023) and understanding the influence of human aspects in requirements engineering (Hidellaarachchi et al., 2021).

- **STGT in R&D studies** (Fig. 3.6 top right) captures the scenario where an STGT study is conducted as part of a large research program, typically spanning several years, with multiple sub-teams focusing on various, typically complementary, objectives. For example, the STGT team may be responsible for establishing a deep understanding of the problem space. Results of the STGT study can guide other project objectives such as those developing software tools and those conducting evaluation of those tools.

3.2.7 Evaluation Guidelines

Evaluating STGT outcomes extends beyond using a simple checklist approach. The STGT evaluation guidelines are deliberately nuanced to differentiate between evaluating the method application and the outcomes of that application. They are further nuanced to distinguish between evaluating preliminary, partial, and interim findings on the one hand and evaluating mature outcomes on the other.

The criteria for evaluating STGT method application are *credibility* and *rigour*. The criteria for evaluating preliminary outcomes are *originality*, *relevance*, and *density*, while those for evaluating mature theories are *novelty*, *usefulness*, *parsimony*, and *modifiability*. Details of the STGT evaluation guidelines can be found in Chap. 13 Evaluation Guidelines.

3.3 Summary

In this chapter, we learned about the research spectrum that spans from technical to socio-technical and social science research and what that means for researchers in the modern digital world. Next, we gained an understanding of the socio-technical research framework and an overview of socio-technical grounded theory (STGT). We learned about its characteristic socio-technical research context, its relevant philosophical foundations, its methodological steps and procedures, and possible ways of applying STGT—as a *full STGT method* or, in a limited capacity, as *STGT for data analysis*, including an application selection guide. Finally, we learned about what is covered in the STGT's evaluation guidelines. This chapter served to provide a birds-eye view of STGT, encouraging further exploration in the remaining chapters.

References

Chan, Y.-C., & Hauser, E. (2023). Understanding reactions in human-robot encounters with autonomous quadruped robots. *Proceedings of the Association for Information Science and Technology, 60*(1), 86–97.

Gama, K., & Lacerda, A. (2023). Understanding and supporting neurodiverse software developers in agile teams. In *Proceedings of the XXXVII Brazilian Symposium on Software Engineering* (pp. 497–502).

Glaser, B. G., & Strauss, A. L. (2017). *Discovery of grounded theory: Strategies for qualitative research.* Routledge (First Published 1967).

Graetsch, U. M., Khalajzadeh, H., Shahin, M., Hoda, R., & Grundy, J. (2023). Dealing with data challenges when delivering data-intensive software solutions. *IEEE Transactions on Software Engineering, 49*, 4349–4370 . https://doi.org/10.1109/TSE.2023.3291003

Gunatilake, H., Grundy, J., Hoda, R., & Mueller, I. (2024). Enablers and barriers of empathy in software developer and user interactions: A mixed methods case study. *ACM Transactions on Software Engineering and Methodology* . https://dl.acm.org/doi/pdf/10.1145/3641849

Hidellaarachchi, D., Grundy, J., Hoda, R., & Madampe, K. (2021). The effects of human aspects on the requirements engineering process: A systematic literature review. *IEEE Transactions on Software Engineering, 48*(6), 2105–2127.

Hidellaarachchi, D., Grundy, J., Hoda, R., & Mueller, I. (2023). The influence of human aspects on requirements engineering-related activities: Software practitioners' perspective. *ACM Transactions on Software Engineering and Methodology, 32*(5), 1–37.

Hoda, R. (2011). *Self-organizing agile teams: A grounded theory*, PhD Thesis, Open Access Te Herenga Waka-Victoria University of Wellington.

Hoda, R. (2022). Socio-technical grounded theory for software engineering. *IEEE Transactions on Software Engineering, 48*(10), 3808–3832.

Hoda, R., Noble, J., & Marshall, S. (2011). The impact of inadequate customer collaboration on self-organizing agile teams. *Information and Software Technology, 53*(5), 521–534.

Hoda, R., Noble, J., & Marshall, S. (2012). Self-organizing roles on agile software development teams. *IEEE Transactions on Software Engineering, 39*(3), 422–444.

Li, Z. Z., Wang, H., Gasevic, D., Yu, J., & Liu, J. K. (2023). Enhancing blockchain adoption through tailored software engineering: An industrial-grounded study in education credentialing. *Distributed Ledger Technologies: Research and Practice, 2*(4), 1–24.

Madampe, K., Hoda, R., & Grundy, J. (2022). The emotional roller coaster of responding to requirements changes in software engineering. *IEEE Transactions on Software Engineering, 49*(3), 1171–1187.

Madampe, K., Hoda, R., & Grundy, J. (2023). A framework for emotion-oriented requirements change handling in agile software engineering. *IEEE Transactions on Software Engineering, 49*, 3325–3343. https://doi.org/10.1109/TSE.2023.3253145

Masood, Z., Hoda, R., & Blincoe, K. (2020). How agile teams make self-assignment work: A grounded theory study, *Empirical Software Engineering, 25*, 4962–5005. https://doi.org/10.1007/s10664-020-09876-x

Masood, Z., Hoda, R., & Blincoe, K. (2021). What drives and sustains self-assignment in agile teams. *IEEE Transactions on Software Engineering, 48*(9), 3626–3639.

Pant, A., Hoda, R., Spiegler, S. V., Tantithamthavorn, C., & Turhan, B. (2023). Ethics in the age of AI: An analysis of AI practitioners' awareness and challenges. *ACM Transactions on Software Engineering and Methodology, 33*, 1–35. https://doi.org/10.1145/3635715

Pink, S. (2020). *Doing visual ethnography*. Sage.

Runeson, P., & Höst, M. (2009). Guidelines for conducting and reporting case study research in software engineering. *Empirical Software Engineering, 14*(2), 131–164.

Schwartz, D. (1989). Visual ethnography: Using photography in qualitative research. *Qualitative Sociology, 12*(2), 119–154.

Sharp, H., Dittrich, Y., & De Souza, C. R. (2016). The role of ethnographic studies in empirical software engineering, *IEEE Transactions on Software Engineering, 42*(8), 786–804.

Wang, W., Khalajzadeh, H., Grundy, J., & Madugalla, A. (2023). Adaptive user interfaces for software supporting chronic diseases. In *2023 IEEE Symposium on Visual Languages and Human-Centric Computing (VL/HCC)* (pp. 215–218). IEEE.

PART II

Foundations of Research

4 Research Design Canvas

Abstract This chapter focuses on describing how to go about designing a research project. First, we will learn about framing the research study as a *project*. Then, we will be introduced to the *research design canvas*. While the details are specific to socio-technical grounded theory (STGT) studies, the research design canvas or template can be used for research project design in general. Next, we will learn about the 10 elements of the research design canvas, including the forming of the *research team*, identifying the *domain and actors*, selecting the *phenomenon* and *topic* to investigate, carefully assessing *research ethics* and considering the *research values*, formulating the guiding *research questions*, acknowledging the team's *research philosophy*, deciding on the initial *research protocols* including data, techniques, and tools, and listing the desirable *research impact*. The chapter concludes by describing a *pilot study* to apply and refine the above elements of the research project design.

4.1 The Research Project

A project is defined as "*a temporary endeavor undertaken to create a unique project service or result*" by the PMBOK® Guide—fourth edition (Institute, 2008). In simple terms, a project is a finite entity with a defined beginning and end within which the

R. Hoda, *Qualitative Research with Socio-Technical Grounded Theory*,
https://doi.org/10.1007/978-3-031-60533-8_4

key aims and objectives are achieved and progress is actively tracked and risks managed. A research project is no different. Designing a research project involves designing the research context in which the study will occur as well as the project management aspects to monitor and accomplish.

Defining and treating our socio-technical grounded theory (STGT) research study as a *project* is desirable as it helps us to be professional in our approach and ensure overall success. It gives us a common vocabulary to refer to associated aspects, such as the aims, objectives, and timeline, the milestones to mark and track progress, the budget, the roles of people involved and expected to benefit, and the expected outputs. It enables us to be aware of and manage them well. It also prepares us for future projects, so we can apply our learning and optimise processes.

When designing an STGT research project, we also need to consider the scope of the study in terms of its length and expected outcomes, as well as the most appropriate application of STGT in the project. For example, a research study aimed at developing a theory can be designed as a small-scale full STGT study spanning between 6 and18 months or as a large-scale full STGT study lasting for up to three to 4 years. The latter is likely to result in multiple theories. STGT can also be applied in a limited capacity, as *STGT for data analysis*, to analyse qualitative data as part of a research study conducted using another overall research method, such as case study, ethnography, or survey research. The *STGT Application Selection Guide* in Chap. 3 STGT—An Overview can be consulted to make an appropriate selection.

4.2 The Research Design Canvas

Designing a research project requires thinking about and planning for a number of aspects. To ease this task for novice and experienced researchers, I present the *research design canvas*,[1] a template for designing research projects, depicted in Fig. 4.1. There are 10 elements of the research design canvas: *research team*, *domain and actors*, *research topic*, *research ethics*, *research values*, *research questions*, *research philosophy*, *research protocols*, *research impact*, and *pilot study*. The template includes examples of what goes under each element of the canvas.

To use the research design canvas, researchers can fill each element with details specific to their project. The order of filling in the elements is likely to vary from project to project, typically starting with the elements that are clear and come easiest to the researchers. In some cases, the research team is the first element to be finalised followed by selecting a research topic and questions. In other cases, the research domain and topic may have been established early as part of an advertised research project and the team may be built up subsequently.

[1] The format of the Research Design Template is inspired by the Business Model Canvas that provides a template for designing new business models (Osterwalder & Pigneur, 2010).

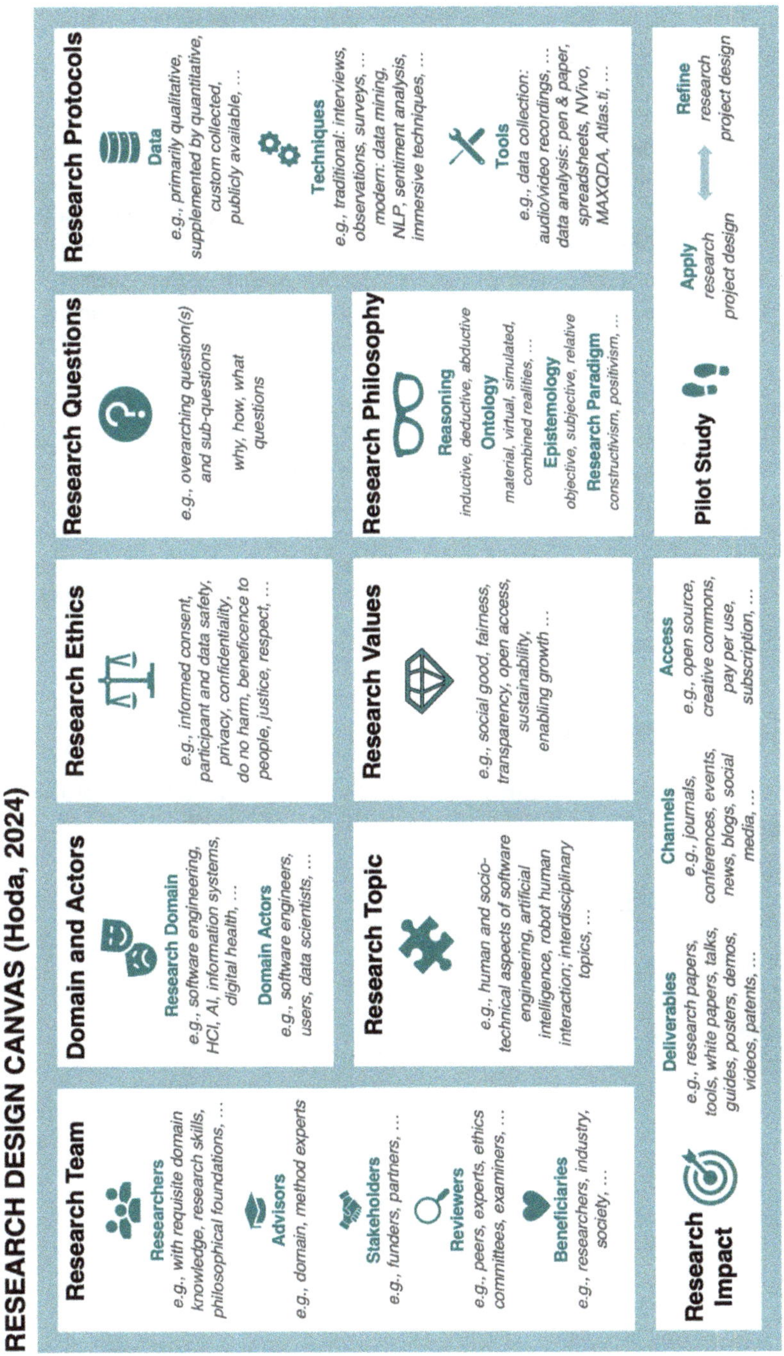

Fig. 4.1 Research design canvas—A template for designing research projects

Some elements might require discussions amongst the research team. Novice researchers such as PhD students can fill the template in consultation with their advisors/supervisors and seek feedback from other research stakeholders.

Regardless of the order, these are key elements of designing and setting up a research project. Most of the elements need to be selected initially with room for refinement later. It is recommended that the research design be trialled in a pilot study. This can be followed by any refinements as required. Significant changes to the research team, domain, topic, ethics, values, and philosophy later in the project are rare and usually forced by constraints. Other elements such as the research questions, parts of the research protocol, and desired research impact are more likely to be refined over the course of the project to adapt to the emerging focus and findings. For example, parts of the protocol, such as interview questions, are expected to continue to be refined regularly to align with emerging findings from the iterative and interleaved data collection and analysis cycles in an STGT study applying theoretical sampling. Similarly, research tools and data sources can be reconsidered during the course of the research project and revised based on needs and potential challenges and constraints faced during execution. However, it is important to have these formulated initially so the project can start off smoothly and refinements can be made to the plans as needed.

Each of these elements of the research design template is described in the rest of the chapter. Researchers may also wish to consider other approaches to research design (Saunders & Tosey, 2013; Creswell & Poth, 2016; Wohlin & Aurum, 2015).

Tips

Tips for Research Project Design and Start-Up Checklist

Use the **research design canvas** (Fig. 4.1) to guide your research project design. Make sure you have addressed each of its 10 elements:

- The research team
- The research domain and actors
- The research topic
- The research ethics
- The research values
- The research questions
- The research philosophy
- The research protocols
- The research impact
- The pilot study

You can present your research design using the research design canvas in your research proposals and reports (e.g., thesis, papers, project and grant reports), and describe each of its elements as specific to your own project, in as much detail as the proposal/report format allows. Completing a research design canvas (or template) is also a useful exercise to share these details with the research ethics committee for ethics approval.

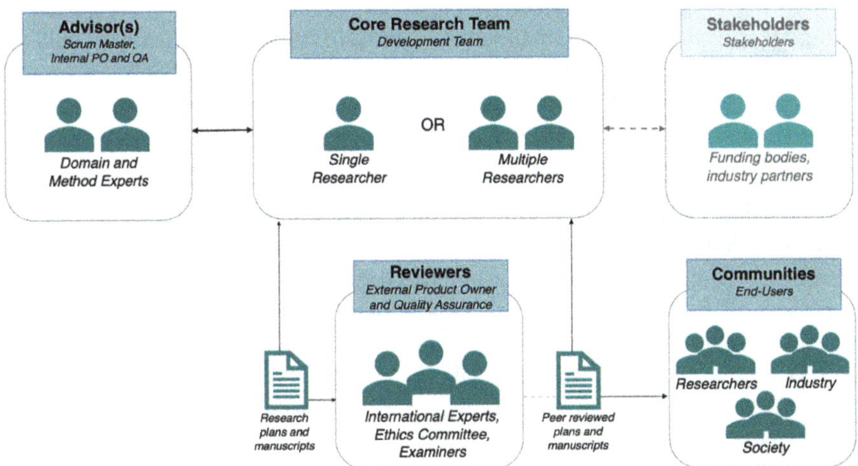

Fig. 4.2 The agile research team and related roles

4.3 The Research Team

For software engineering (SE) researchers and others familiar with agile methods, using an agile software team model can be a useful way to think about and organise research teams. The roles defined for a Scrum project provide a good mapping, as shown in Fig. 4.2 and described below using an STGT research team as an example.

Research Team (as the "Development Team"). This includes all those executing the project in a hands-on manner. The research team can be as large as several researchers collaborating on a project and as small as one person carrying out most of the core research activities, e.g., a higher degree research (HDR) scholar such as a Masters or PhD scholar.

Definition

Socio-Technical Researchers refer to *researchers who have "the requisite knowledge and skills from social sciences, philosophy, qualitative research, and theory development as well as technical background and/or experience applicable to the domain" (Hoda, 2022).*

To conduct an effective STGT study, the project team needs to be composed of socio-technical researchers. However, this does not imply that they need to be experts in each knowledge area and skill. Nor does it mean a single researcher needs to possess all the knowledge and skills. An interdisciplinary, multidisciplinary, or transdisciplinary team of researchers from software engineering and sociology as well as necessary domain experts make for an effective socio-technical research team. A socio-technical researcher or team collectively possesses a "*core repertoire of knowledge and skills*" (Hoda, 2022), as depicted in Fig. 4.3.

- *Domain knowledge* is a reasonable, and preferably in-depth, understanding of the research domain. The lead researchers may be from within the research domain. For example, an SE researcher studying phenomena that occur in the SE domain possesses the requite domain knowledge. In other contexts, domain knowledge is typically provided by a subject matter expert. For example, a medical doctor

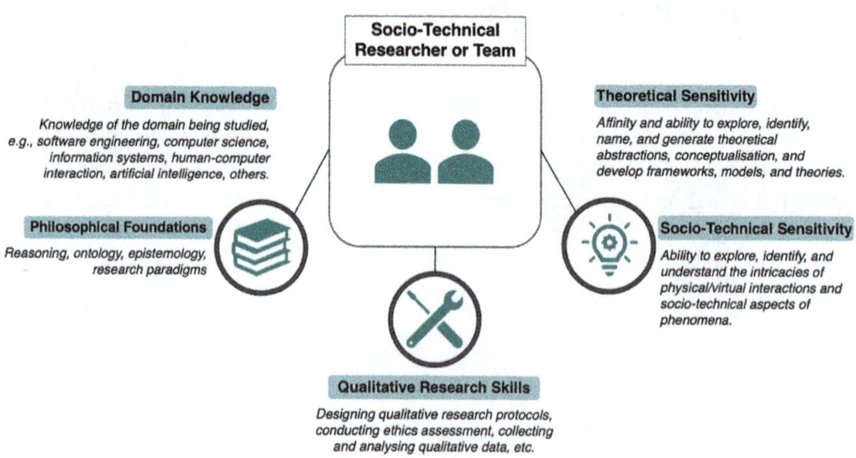

Fig. 4.3 Socio-technical researcher (or team) with their core repertoire of knowledge and skills

or nurse can provide an in-depth understanding of the medical domain where the research team, including SE researchers, is studying the use of technology.
- *Socio-technical sensitivity* is the researcher's affinity and ability to explore, identify, and understand the intricacies of human interactions and socio-technical aspects of phenomena.
- *Theoretical sensitivity* is the researcher's affinity and ability to explore, identify, name, and generate theoretical abstractions and conceptualisations, and develop frameworks, models, and theories.
- *Qualitative research skills* include designing qualitative research protocols, conducting ethics assessment, and collecting and analysing qualitative data.
- *Philosophical foundations* include types of reasoning, ontology, epistemology, and research paradigms.

In addition to the diversity of skills, the research team will ideally be composed of both novice and experienced researchers to promote learning and enable growth while ensuring the project objectives are successfully achieved in a timely manner. For example, a PhD scholar with their supervisors is a common research team configuration. A team of early career and experienced researchers is another. Similarly, a group of researchers from complementary disciplines can make for a good interdisciplinary research team.

Definition

Advisors (as the "Scrum Master" and *internal* "Product Owner" and "Quality Assurance") refer *to those who may set the vision of the project, guide the team, perform internal quality evaluations, and provide feedback for improvements.*

While some HDR scholars may consider their supervisors as part of the research team, typically most supervisors/advisors are not as intimately involved in the everyday research activities such as data collection and analysis. Rather, they tend to play the dual roles of scrum master and product owner as needed. When they mentor and guide the team on the research domain, topic, method, and overall research life cycle and its various steps such as publications, they effectively play a scrum master role in a research context. When they set the vision of the project, guide the team on desired outcomes, perform internal evaluations, and provide feedback on incremental outputs, they effectively play a product owner role that is internal to the research team.

In the Australasian context, typically, there are between one and three co-supervisors on each HDR project, with one being the primary supervisor. The research team can also include external advisors, who provide feedback and guidance to the team from time to time. Even when there is no student involved and the research project is being conducted collaboratively by a team of professional researchers, typically there is at least one expert or most experienced researcher who can take on the dual roles of scrum master and internal product owner for the rest of the team. These supervisors, advisors, and experts, much like scrum masters and product owners on industrial software projects, have their own individual styles and approaches to interacting with the research team.

Quality assurance is enforced by the advisors and experts, and for most HDR projects, by an internal review panel typically composed of other researchers in the faculty or university not directly involved in the project.

Definition

Stakeholders (also called "Stakeholders" in an agile team) refer *to those who have a vested interest in the research project. These can include industry partners, government partners, and funding bodies.*

Oftentimes, research projects are conducted in partnership with industry or are funded by specific funding bodies, such as through government-based funding schemes, direct industry funding, or cooperatives. Where there is an industry partner or funding involved, they can be considered stakeholders, similar to how an industrial software project has stakeholders who are invested in its success. Depending on the set-up of the funding, the stakeholders may be more or less involved in following the research progress and outcomes. Where the governing policies of the funding lay out special conditions, the research team is obliged to manage them in addition to the core research activities and keep their stakeholders well informed, as well as seek regular feedback from them. Sometimes, reconciling priorities and perspectives of the stakeholders with those emerging from empirical evidence can be a challenge. In such cases, careful stakeholder expectations management is key to staying true to research. An additional consideration on funded research projects is to declare the funding sources in the research project outputs in order to manage potential conflicts of interest in the peer review process.

Definition

Reviewers (as *external* "Product Owners" and "Quality Assurance") refer *to those who evaluate the quality of the research and provide constructive feedback to steer its direction.*

Reviewers external to the research team, such as a university review committee, the ethics committee, and international peer reviewers in conferences and journals, can be considered the external product owners or customers in a research project. Their role is to evaluate the quality and acceptability of the product increments and the final product. Reviewers of journals, conferences, and workshops to which the research team submits their work typically assess the product increments, e.g., individual research papers, posters, code, presentations, etc. Reviewers or examiners of the HDR thesis can be considered as assessing the complete project output or the final product, e.g., the thesis, software, tools, guidelines, patents, etc. Often reviewers act as gatekeepers, recommending improvements. Incorporating their feedback on incremental outputs will undoubtedly improve the quality of both those outputs and the overall project.

Definition

Beneficiaries (as the "End users") refer to *those who will "use" the research and stand to ultimately benefit from it. Depending on the nature of the research project and outcomes, the wider research community, relevant industry practitioners, and general society can be the beneficiaries or end users of research.*

If the research topic is applied, i.e., industry relevant, industry practitioners in that area can be the primary end users and the potential for the research project's impact on practice is high. For more theoretical topics, the research community will be the primary user, citing and building upon the work to achieve research impact. Some research topics lend themselves well to both sets of users. Increasingly, there is focus on making research accessible to society at large so it can achieve societal impact. In this case, the general society can be considered one of the end users.

4.4 The Research Domain and Actors

Definition

Research domain refers to *the discipline in which the phenomenon takes place and/or is studied.* **Actors** refer to *the key people involved in enacting the phenomenon being studied and who are well placed to share their experiences about it.*

Consider an example. The phenomenon of *software testers conducting quality assurance* plays out in the SE domain and the actors are software testers and related software practitioners, such as developers, customers, and managers that the testers interact with. Discerning the domain and actors is straightforward in this case. Another example is the phenomenon of *the use of digital health software services* which plays out primarily in the medical and health domain. In this case, which is interdisciplinary across software engineering and medical domains, the primary domain can be identified as the context from where most research data is collected. For example, if the focus is on the *use* of digital health software, the primary domain is expected to be medical and health and the key actors are clinicians, patients, and caregivers. If the focus is on the *design* of digital health software, the primary domain would be software engineering and the key actors are the software development team and end users of the software where accessible. Identifying the primary domain enables effective research project design, including recruiting subject matter experts to the research team as needed.

Domains such as software engineering, computer science, human–computer interaction, artificial intelligence, and information systems are inherently socio-technical domains, where the social and technical aspects are tightly coupled. In these domains, technology is not only a platform or enabler, but also the very raison d'être for organisations. Actors in these domains such as software engineers, computer scientists, and data scientists are often described as "geeks" and represent a unique cultural group with their own norms, language, interactions, and worldviews. Software engineers are both the producers and users of technology. Using a combination of material and digital tools such as GitHub, Trello, JIRA, Slack, and Zoom, they are constantly involved in enacting socio-technical phenomena. For example, picture a software developer at Google, "googling" for APIs and libraries. In some sense, this is the *real* "metaverse",[2] a world where technology is created using technology and where phenomena and interactions are deeply socio-technical. STGT can be employed to effectively study such domains that play out in multiple realities and actors, who may be human, AI agents such as chatbots, or virtual avatars.

Another interesting and extremely important set of actors to consider are the software users. Depending on the domain, they can be clinicians, educators, pharmacists, artists, and government officials. In some cases, such as the statewide or nationwide Covid-19 tracing and service apps, the "general public" is the ultimate end user and represents one of the broadest varieties of diverse users.

4.5 The Research Topic

Definition

Research topic refers to *the topic selected for the research. It can be a phenomenon that plays out involving a process, practice, tool, role, or artefact.*

[2] https://en.wikipedia.org/wiki/Metaverse.

Another key element of designing a research project is to select a research topic. In some cases, the research team will attempt to align the research topic to calls for funding. Once funding is received, a number of new research personnel are recruited, typically including HDR scholars and postdoctoral research fellows. For these members of the team, the research topic is effectively predefined.

In other cases, the research team may have more freedom in selecting the research topic and phenomenon. It is also common for research topics to be selected and finalised through discussions within the research team. For example, it is common for HDR candidates to approach prospective supervisors who are experts in a given research area, with a proposed research topic. The topic is then discussed, typically narrowed, and finalised to align with their mutual interests and trends in the industry and/or relevant research communities.

When selecting and narrowing research topics, three key aspects are important to consider: *interest*, *feasibility*, and *impact*. Ideally, the research topic falls within the sweet spot across these three aspects (see Fig. 4.4).

- **Interest**. Good research topics arouse curiosity and interest in the research team. Interest in the topic will boost the team's motivation to perform well over the course of the project. For example, a PhD project typically demands 3 to 4 years of focus and effort, so consider a topic that the team is interested in or is likely to grow into. The topic can be an extension of previous topics researched by the team or a fresh perspective on a well-studied topic, or can open doors to completely new research areas and disciplines. The opportunity to learn new methods, processes, tools, techniques, and even research areas or disciplines can be a strong driver of interest in a topic.

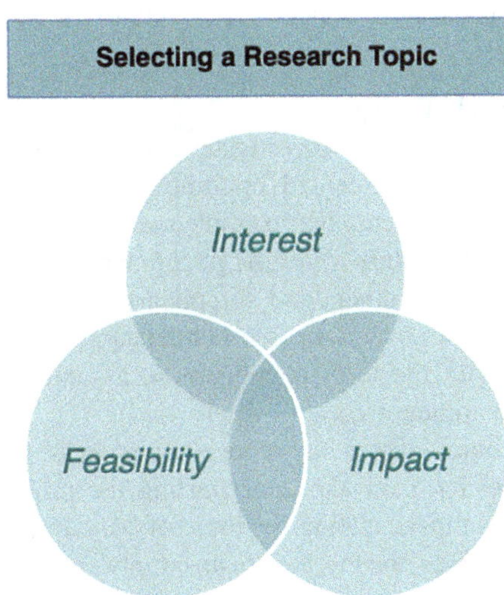

Fig. 4.4 Selecting a research topic based on interest, feasibility, and (potential for) impact

- **Feasibility**. The research project scope and approach needs to be practically feasible to achieve within the project duration. Estimating the project's scope and size demands experience. The research team can discuss the topic amongst themselves or, in the case of HDR scholars, with their supervisors and advisors to help estimate and refine the scope to fit within the project timeline, if necessary. Similarly, the research approach can be discussed and refined. Some questions to assess feasibility include: *What research tools and techniques are required and does the team have easy access to use them or to receive training to learn how to use them? What types of data sources are required and how will they be sourced? What are the expected costs and are there sufficient funds to cover them?* These questions can help assess feasibility and refine the research topic.

- **Impact**. Increasingly, research topics are expected to have a high potential to make an impact on practice and/or society, in addition to research impact. Practical impact refers to *the research project's ability to create a positive change in the lives of those being directly or indirectly studied, through its findings, which may be a theory, a set of guidelines, and/or policy and practical recommendations*. For example, a topic such as *the effect of individual personality on software team climate* is likely to produce practical recommendations for software teams and managers on how to form, organise, and reorganise teams to leverage personality traits, mitigate and manage interpersonal conflicts, and improve team climate. If a research topic is of interest to the research team and is practically feasible, but has little scope for real-world impact, it can be reconsidered or refined. In contrast, a full STGT study aims to produce theoretical outcomes that are typically empirical evidence-based, i.e., drawn from the investigation of real-world phenomena. Selecting a research topic that is practice-oriented will not only improve the project's chances of achieving impact but also improve its feasibility as it is easier to collect data about topics that focus on real-world phenomena.

Socio-Technical Research Topics

An STGT research project typically investigates a specific phenomenon which may occur in the material, virtual, augmented, or combined realities. Not not all research topics align to specific phenomena. For example, *automated testing tools* is a broad research topic but does not capture a specific phenomenon to study. The *adoption of automated testing tools*, on the other hand, is a phenomenon that can be investigated within this broader topic. However, for ease of understanding, I use the term research topic interchangeably with the term phenomenon, assuming the topic is narrow enough to capture a phenomenon.

In some cases, the topic—which can represent a process, practice, tool, artefact, role, etc.—is known to the team ahead of starting the project. For example, the team may be interested in investigating the topic of *onboarding data scientists into software teams*. In other cases, the research team simply begins with a broad research topic and allows the most important concern of the participants to emerge as the key focus. This is quite common with PhD students as they learn research skills and find their focus, typically in the first year. A professional research team on a tighter timeline may wish to decide on a relatively narrower topic to focus on earlier in the project.

For a discussion of socio-technical research topics suitable for STGT studies, see Chap. 3 Socio-Technical Grounded Theory—An Overview.

4.6 The Research Ethics

Definition

Research ethics refers to *the ethical considerations related to a research study such as data and participant privacy and confidentiality, safety, informed consent, and more.*

Empirical research studies typically involve collecting data from various sources. Qualitative research studies additionally involve interacting with humans or human-related data. The research team needs to conduct an assessment of the possible ethical considerations associated with their study design. There can be several ethical, and in some cases physical or medical, risks and questions associated with a research project. Most common among these are ethical concerns to do with participant and data privacy, confidentiality, safety, security, and ethical usage, in addition to informed consent, beneficence to individuals and organisations (Singer & Vinson, 2001), justice, respect for persons and law, and public interest (Dittrich et al., 2012).

There are a number of resources that provide guidelines for ethical research in empirical software engineering (Singer & Vinson, 2001), software engineering (Singer & Vinson, 2002), information and communication technology (Dittrich et al., 2012), social media (Townsend & Wallace, 2016), mining software repositories (Gold & Krinke, 2020), and the open-source community (El-Emam, 2001). Some key ethical concerns relevant to STGT studies are described below, along with guidance on how to address them.

4.6.1 Ethics for Custom Collected Data

Addressing ethical concerns for custom collected data, such as through surveys, interviews, and observations, is relatively straightforward. For example, an effective call for participation makes it clear who can participate and reaches out to as many relevant practitioners as possible. Once potential participants respond, they need to be provided with full details of the study, including a participant information sheet and consent form. Signing the form ensures informed consent and voluntary participation. Any reimbursements (e.g., parking, commute) or rewards (e.g., gift vouchers, place in a draw for a gift) for participants need to be clearly advertised and duly followed through. When reporting findings, any identifiable details of the individual or organisation can be obfuscated (e.g., blurring out faces in photographs). Similarly, sample raw data such as quotations presented in the paper and/or shared with reviewers need to be first sanitised to ensure participant confidentiality (e.g., using codes such as P1, P2 for participants instead of their real names).

4.6.2 Ethics for Public Data

Working with publicly available data, such as videos on YouTube, posts on Twitter and LinkedIn, and posts on developer forums such as Stack Overflow, can be tricky. This is because they are easily and freely accessible, which leads to the temptation to use them without much thought about ethical concerns. In fact, the same ethical concerns apply to publicly available data as do to custom collected data. Where possible, qualitative researchers can attempt to seek approval from the speaker, author, or account holder. Alternatively, they can obscure identifiable information in case there are chances of potential harm arising from its inclusion and presentation in the study. For instance, using a video on YouTube with identifiable information is an example of poor software engineering practices, unless the video was listed as such.

4.6.3 Ethics Approvals

In most research institutions or departments, conducting human-related studies requires the approval of an established ethics committee. Typically, the committee will want to review all relevant research protocols (plans, documents, and artefacts designed to conduct the study) such as the research call for participation, details of how the call for participation will be distributed, the participant information sheets, participant consent forms, and research instruments such as a list of potential interview questions, surveys or questionnaires, and more. The ethics requirements vary widely from one institution to the other. It is a good idea to explore the ethics requirements at your institutions upfront and apply for approval with the necessary documentation in advance as it can take some time and a few iterations before approval is granted. The research design canvas can be used for the purpose of sharing the research design with the ethics committee to seek approval.

4.7 The Research Values

Definition

Research values refer to *the concepts or beliefs considered important by the research team such as self-direction, creativity, achievement, and so on.*

Research is conducted by and for the people.[3] People have values. Values have been defined as "*concepts or beliefs that pertain to desirable end state or behaviours, transcend specific situations, guide selection or evaluation of behaviour and events, and are ordered by relative importance*" (Schwartz, 1992). Based on Schwartz's *Theory of Basic Human Values*, there are 10 near-universal basic human values: self-direction, stimulation, hedonism, achievement, power, security, tradition, conformity, benevolence, and universalism. Underneath these categories, there are 56 individual value items or motivational goals. For example, freedom, self-respect, creativity, and choosing own goals are some value items under the self-direction category.

Human values in software engineering have been investigated in literature (Perera et al., 2020) and empirically (Hussain et al., 2020, 2022). But what about values in research? What do researchers value and how might that impact the research they perform? This is worth investigating in the SE research context, especially as SE increasingly involves engineering of AI-based or smart software.

In the meantime, researchers can perform some values assessment and alignment exercises. The *Research Team Values Assessment and Alignment Exercise*, or simply the *Team Values Exercise*, can be performed as part of team building to identify what the wider team or lab collectively values in general, irrespective of specific projects. The research team values can help guide the type of projects, application domains, funding sources, stakeholders, and collaborators that the team considers and selects for their various projects. They may also unravel value differences between individuals in the team and provide them with an opportunity to be aware of their value differences, address them where possible, agree to disagree where not possible to reconcile, and agree on a combined set of values for the team irrespective of these differences. The Team Values Exercise can be conducted as a team workshop, typically lasting between half an hour and an hour, depending on the size of the team and extent of the discussions.

Exercise 1: Research Team Values Assessment and Alignment

- *Step 1. Identify Individual Values*
  As a first step, all the individuals in the team consider the values framework

[3] The possible role of artificial intelligence in assisting with research is explored in Chap. 14 Future Directions in Qualitative Research.

(Schwartz, 1992) individually in their own time prior to the workshop (asynchronously) or individually while in a group (synchronously). Each person identifies up to five value items from across the 10 value categories that speak the most to their personal values in the context of conducting research.

- *Step 2. Share and Combine*
  In this step, the team goes around the individual members, one at a time, and they share their own ranked list of values. Then one person creates a combined list of the unique values shared by everyone. At the same time, they note how many people identified each value, for example, *freedom* ($n = 6$) or *self-discipline* ($n = 4$).

- *Step 3. Discuss and Align*
  As the last step, the team discusses each of the values, in either ascending or descending order, considering questions such as: *Why is that value important to the team when conducting research? How may it impact the research that the team conducts?* Everyone is encouraged to provide their views, even if it was not a value they selected individually, addressing *why it is important to the research team.* As the team discusses these aspects, it is fine for people to change their selections. However, they may only swap values, not add more. The combined list can be updated accordingly. The top five values of the resulting combined list are the *Research Team Values*. The team may decide to have a top three or four instead, but no more than five values are recommended as it typically becomes difficult to consider them explicitly when conducting research if there are more than a handful.

The three steps and general flow of the Team Values Exercise are shown in Fig. 4.5. The same is followed in the *Research Project Values Assessment and Alignment Exercise*, or simply the *Project Values Exercise*, except it is performed for specific projects with the specific project team, which may be a subset of the wider research team or lab and may include collaborators from other research groups or organisations. The research project values can help guide the research questions, data collection and analysis methods, and results communication venues and strategies.

Fig. 4.5 Three steps and general flow of the Research Team Values and Research Project Values exercises

As with the Team Values Exercise, the Project Values Exercise can be conducted as a team workshop, typically lasting between half an hour and an hour, depending on the size of the team and extent of the discussions. The project values exercise has the same format as the Team Values Exercise, except it focuses on a specific research project and considers values in light of that project.

Exercise 2: Research Project Values Assessment and Alignment

- *Step 1. Identify Individual Values*
  As a first step, all the individuals in the team consider a wider set of values, individually in their own time prior to the workshop (asynchronously), or individually while in a group (synchronously). This set is ideally the whole values framework (Schwartz, 1992). Alternatively, a subset of the full framework or the research team values identified in Exercise 1 above can also be a starting point, with the opportunity to bring in new values from the wider Schwartz values framework. Each person identifies up to five value items from across the 10 value categories that they think speak the most to the particular research project they are about to conduct. In doing so, they can consider aspects such as research domain, topic, stakeholders, and the beneficiaries/end users.

- *Step 2. Share and Combine*
  In this step, the team goes around the individual members, one at a time, and shares their individual ranked list of values. Then one person creates a combined list of the unique values shared by everyone. At the same time, they note how many people identified each value, for example, *freedom* ($n = 6$) or *self-discipline* ($n = 4$).

- *Step 3. Discuss and Align*
  As the last step, the team discusses each of the values, in either ascending or descending order, considering questions such as: *Why is that value important when conducting the research project? How may it impact the research project?* Everyone is encouraged to provide their views, even if it was not a value they selected individually, addressing *why it is important to the research project.* As the team discusses these aspects, it is fine for people to change their selections. However, they may only swap values, not add more. The combined list can be updated accordingly. The top five values of the resulting combined list are the Research Project Values. The team may decide to have a top three or four values instead.

Value alignment is expected to not only influence how the research is conducted and presented but is also likely to improve its practical impact. For example, if one of the key values is *equality*, the team may consider making their research available freely to society through sharing preprints on their personal Web sites and archiving sites (e.g., Arxiv, TechArxiv, GitHub, Zenodo) as allowed by the publishers.

4.8 The Research Questions

Definition

Research questions refer to *questions that drive the research study and which the study aims to answer. A study can have a broad overarching research question and/or a number of focused ones.*

Formulating research questions can be a valuable exercise in focusing the research project and clarifying expectations around what is within scope and what is not. Research questions also help the stakeholders, such as funding bodies, ethics committees, potential participants, reviewers, and the end users, gain an understanding of the main focus of the research project.

What makes STGT different from most other research methods is that it does not strictly require that we formulate research questions. We can start off the project with a broad research area or topic. The iterative steps of the STGT process allow us to incrementally narrow the focus of the study as the key concerns of the participants start to emerge. An advantage of such an approach is that the research team will be able to form a broad knowledge base about the research topic and a number of related aspects on the one hand, while gaining in-depth knowledge about the key categories and concepts that emerge from the study on the other. A disadvantage of this approach is that it can considerably prolong the length of the study, which may not be desirable. Formulating research questions is not forbidden in an STGT study. In fact, there may have been some explicit or implicit research questions that sparked the team's interest in the topic in the first place.

4.8.1 Types of Research Questions

Full STGT studies will benefit from formulating an overarching research question that is sufficiently *deep* and *complex*. Different types of research questions can lead us to different results. For example, focused *what* type questions can be formulated to derive a *classification* or *taxonomy* as an end product, while *how* type questions can be formulated to typically result in *process-based* theories, and *why* type questions typically result in theoretical models and theories that explain the causes, consequences, possible strategies, and contingencies.

The overarching question can be broken down into sub-questions. Such a two-layered approach has several benefits. First, it allows the research team to break down the larger problem into smaller parts that can be addressed through multiple stages of the project, using different research techniques as suited to the sub-question. Second, it leaves room for the sub-questions to be derived later to focus on the key concepts and categories that emerge from the STGT study. Finally, it allows the research team to develop a publication plan where one or more papers can answer one, some, or all of the research sub-questions.

"How" and "Why" Questions

Full STGT studies are well suited to answering the *how* and *why* type overarching research questions. For example, "*How do developers approach ethics in AI development?*" is a sufficiently open, industry-relevant, and challenging question that is likely to benefit from being investigated using a full STGT study approach. Such deep and complex questions enable the exploration of the topic in a comprehensive manner, from various angles, and derive multifaceted findings and theories that justify the application of a full STGT study.

Because STGT is a relatively sophisticated research method, applying it simply for queries may not harness its full potential and may not be worth the time and effort invested. For example, "*What code review approaches are used by developers?*" is a relatively simple research question. By *simple*, I mean it can be answered using a straightforward research approach such as survey research, and is likely to result in listing a classification or a *taxonomy* of the different types of code review approaches. Applying a full STGT study to investigate such a straightforward overarching research question is akin to using a sledgehammer to crack a walnut.

"What" Questions

While the *how* and *why* type questions are well suited to a full STGT study, it does not necessarily eliminate the use of *what* type questions. There are of course exceptions depending on how broadly the questions are framed. For example, "*What does it take to become a self-organizing team?*" is phrased as a *what* type question but is broad enough to enable a comprehensive exploration and result in multidimensional findings (Hoda & Noble, 2017). However, it could have also been phrased as "*How do software teams become self-organising agile teams?*"

What type questions can make for good sub-questions. For example, the question "*What code review approaches are used by developers?*" can make for a useful sub-question within a wider, more complex overarching research question such as "*How do software developers practise and use code reviews?*" in a full STGT study on the topic of *code review practice in software engineering*.

There is yet another possibility for *what* type questions with an STGT approach. As explained in Chap. 3 Socio-Technical Grounded Theory—An Overview, STGT can also be applied in a limited manner, as *STGT for data analysis*, to analyse the data collected as part of a study driven by more *what* type questions and being conducted using another overarching research method, such as case study or survey research.

4.8.2 Evolving Questions

While changes to the research project's topic and overarching research question are rare, the sub-questions can be expected to evolve in an STGT study. For example, in an STGT study on the research topic *responding to changes in software engineering*, a viable overarching research question to guide the study is "*How do software developers respond to changes?*" Under normal circumstances, the topic and overarching question are likely to remain stable throughout the research project. However, the research sub-questions can be expected to evolve, and typically narrow down, to focus on specific changes. For example, the study may start by exploring the first research sub-question: "*What is the nature and frequency of changes that software developers have to respond to?*" This investigation can result in a classification or taxonomy of the main types of changes developers face, for example, changes in *requirements*, changes in *development tools and platforms*, changes in *target end users*, changes in *industry partners*, changes in *budget and time frame*, changes in *team personnel*, changes in *compliance and regulation*, changes in *work arrangements* (e.g., work from home during a pandemic), and so on.

The next part of the STGT study can aim to answer the sub-question "*What is the nature and frequency of changes in X?*" Based on the most prominent changes emerging from the analysis, X may be development tools and platforms or work arrangement. Such evolution of questions is to be expected as the study narrows down. Similarly, new sub-questions can be added later. For example, "*How do developers respond to changes in development tools and platforms?*" may be added to the study later in response to insights emerging about how developers are responding to such changes.

4.8.3 Research Questions vs Hypotheses

It is critical to make a distinction between research questions and hypotheses in the context of an STGT study. A hypothesis is not the same as a research question. A hypothesis refers to our reasonable guess at an answer to a research question and captures our expectations about the findings from a research study. It is stated as a statement to be proven right or wrong in the study through evidence collected and analysed from practice.

Example

For example, in a study on the *Role of DevOps Engineers*, we may have the following hypotheses:

- [H1]: "*DevOps engineers face significant coordination overheads as part of their role*".

- [H2]: "*DevOps engineers find it challenging to take ownership of the operations and maintenance parts of their role*".

In both hypotheses [H1] and [H2], the researcher is making an assumption or an educated guess about a particular challenge and aspect of the DevOps engineer's role that they expect to find in practice. Subsequent data collection and analysis can serve to prove or disprove these assumptions. Most quantitative and some qualitative research methods are guided by such a *hypothetico-deductive* approach, where hypotheses are formulated upfront and then tested through the research study to see if evidence supports or disproves them.

Hypothesis testing is not compatible with an STGT study approach since STGT focuses on evidence-based theory generation as opposed to hypothesis testing or verification. STGT is guided by an overarching inductive approach, where evidence-based hypotheses are generated as *outcomes* of the study, through applying its procedures and steps, rather than as *inputs* into the study.

Example

To address the same topic of the *Role of DevOps Engineers* as an STGT study, we can formulate the following overarching research questions and sub-questions:

Overarching research question: "*What is the role of DevOps engineers in software engineering?*"

- [RQ1]: "*What do DevOps engineers do on an everyday basis?*"
- [RQ2]: "*What are the challenges faced by DevOps engineers?*"
- [RQ3]: "*How do DevOps engineers overcome these challenges?*"

Such research questions are beneficial in guiding the focus of STGT studies. While formulating research questions is not strictly required, they can help guide and frame the study and guide data collection, such as what practices to observe, what questions to ask in interviews, what kind of project data to collect, and so on. Upfront hypotheses formulation and subsequent validation, on the other hand, is not compatible with an STGT study.

4.9 The Research Philosophy

Definition

Research philosophy refers to *the research team's beliefs about how research should be conducted. It includes considerations of reasoning, ontology, epistemology, and research paradigm.*

As part of setting up an STGT research project, it is recommended that the research team members acquaint themselves with fundamental philosophical concepts relevant to conducting their STGT study, if not already familiar with them. Chapter 5 Research Philosophy can be consulted for this purpose. It defines the fundamental philosophical concepts relevant to STGT studies and explains their role in the study, including:

- *Types of reasoning*, which refers to *how we reason about ideas and concepts in terms of the directionality of our thinking*. For example, an STGT study is expected to involve inductive, deductive, and abductive reasoning.
- *Ontology*, which refers to *what we believe exists or what we perceive as reality, in a research context*. For example, STGT studies can be designed to focus on material reality, societal reality, virtual reality, augmented reality, mixed reality, and combinations of these realities, depending on the phenomenon being studied.
- *Epistemology*, which refers to *what can be treated as knowledge and how that knowledge is gained, in a research context*. For example, an STGT study can select an epistemology suited to study the given phenomenon, such as objective or subjective.
- *Research paradigms*, which refers to *a combination of ontological and epistemological stances from a research worldview*. For example, an STGT study can be conducted using different paradigms, such as positivist, constructivist, and interpretivist. While STGT offers flexibility in applying research paradigms, it requires one to be applied consistently once selected.

The team can discuss and deliberate on the ontology and epistemology relevant to the socio-technical phenomenon they are studying and select an overall research paradigm to apply in the study. A *Research Philosophy Alignment Exercise*, similar to the values alignment exercise above, can be conducted to achieve this. As part of this discussion, the team can also carefully consider the role of the researcher. The research team can document their selections, including the rationales leading up to the decisions so they can be easily referenced to ensure the various steps of the STGT study are being conducted in alignment with the selected research philosophies.

4.10 The Research Protocols

As part of commencing a software development project, software teams consider and set up their *development environment* including deciding on the software development platforms, tools, techniques, programming languages, technology stacks, application programming interfaces (APIs), networking and hosting requirements, and much more. Similarly, the research team needs to design the research protocols, which include the types of data to collect, from which sources, using what techniques and instruments, and what research tools may be useful in the process. In both software engineering and research projects, careful design and selection of protocols initially facilitates a smooth-running project with plenty of room for later refinements as necessary.

4.10.1 Research Data

Definition

Research data refers to *the evidence that is required in the research study to draw conclusions about the topic being studied and to answer the research questions.*

An STGT study can be conducted using a variety of data sources and techniques. While it can include supplementary quantitative data, an STGT study is well suited to working with qualitative data, acquired from a variety of traditional and modern sources.

Tips

Tips for Deciding on the Data Type and Sources for a Research Project

- *What types of data are needed to conduct a rich investigation?*
- *What are the sources of the data? Is the data pre-existing or does it need to be custom collected?*
- *If pre-existing, is it publicly available and does it need permission to access? Who can provide access?*
- *If publicly available, what is the plan to gain consent (where possible) and ensure ethical use?*
- *How can we ensure the credibility and quality of pre-existing and publicly available data?*

- *If data has to be custom collected, what are the relevant sources? How will we gain access to or recruit the relevant participants?*
- *What will be our initial sampling technique?*
- *Who can help us gain access to relevant participants?*

Traditional Data Sources and Collection Techniques

Traditional GT studies have typically used traditional data sources and techniques such as interviewing the relevant people, conducting observations of practices, field trips to workplaces, diaries of practice and experience, and conducting surveys. These continue to be relevant for modern STGT studies in software engineering and other socio-technical domains. Data from such sources tend to be directly and custom collected for specific projects. For example, interviews allow the researchers to ask highly relevant and direct questions to elicit in-depth information about the participants' lived experiences related to the phenomenon or topic. They also enable follow-up questions and clarifications which are typically not possible from surveys and other sources. Similarly, observations enable the researchers to see relevant practices play out in their natural settings and capture many nuances from interactions between participants, their body language, and accompanying artefacts and cues. Recruiting participants for traditional data collection is non-trivial. Salleh et al. (2018) address a number of challenges faced in gathering empirical data, engaging practitioners, and managing feedback, and offer strategies to work around them.

Research literature can also be a source of data for traditional GT and STGT studies. Wolfswinkel et al. (2013) propose the grounded theory literature review (GTLR) method for applying GT principles to conduct literature reviews, applied by Pant et al. (2024) in software engineering (see Chap. 6 Literature Reviews.) Similarly, grey literature (Garousi et al., 2019) can also be leveraged as data in STGT studies.

In most cases, traditional data is typically custom collected, as opposed to pre-existing in some form, using manual techniques such as interviews and observations. While they offer unparalleled access and insights, these data sources and techniques are typically limited in scale because of the human effort involved. Large research teams can achieve more by distributing data collection and analysis responsibilities across their members.

Modern Data Sources and Collection Techniques

Modern research data include pre-existing data such as software repositories, source code, documentation, developer forums, and wikis (Hoda, 2022). Some of these may be publicly available, such as for open-source projects, while others may need permissions to access them. Other modern data sources such as social media platforms, app store reviews, and specific user group discussion forums provide large quantities of freely available data. While gaining access to pre-existing data may be relatively straightforward in most cases, filtering these datasets for relevant information is a well-known challenge (Hassan, 2008). Data from such repositories and forums can be extracted using modern techniques such as data mining.

Retrospective data analysis, simulation, and mathematical modelling have also been suggested as modern data sources (Perry et al., 2000). These can also be leveraged in STGT studies. With the increasing popularity of gaming and emerging technologies such as augmented and virtual reality, the complex new worlds they create can also make for interesting and rich sources of data. Data from these sources can be collected using immersive and experiential techniques where the researcher immerses in these complex reality worlds.

Modern data come with their own set of challenges in ascertaining quality and permissions. The *Data Quality Evaluation Guidelines* in Chap. 7 Basics of Qualitative Data Collection can be consulted to gain an understanding of these issues.

4.10.2 Research Analysis Techniques

DEFINITION

Research techniques refer to *procedures, mechanisms, and strategies used in the research study to collect and analyse data. In STGT, these include the open coding, constant comparison, and memoing in the basic stage and either targeted coding or structured coding in the advanced stage. They can also be combined with modern qualitative data techniques such as sentiment analysis and natural language processing.*

STGT offers open coding, constant comparison, and memoing as the basic data analysis techniques. It offers advanced memoing and a choice of two modes in the advanced stage of theory development listed below. To revisit these two modes and the differences between them, consult Chap. 3—STGT Overview.

- *Basic data analysis:* open coding, constant comparison, and memoing
- *Advanced data analysis:* advanced memoing and
  Option 1—targeted coding in the emergent theory development mode
  Option 2—structured coding in the structured theory development mode

Examples of STGT data analysis—presented in Chap. 10 STGT for Qualitative Data Analysis—demonstrate how to perform data analysis in order to extract the complete socio-technical codes, concepts, and (sub)categories from the data.

In addition to its native data analysis techniques, STGT offers the possibility to combine them with modern data analysis techniques such as natural language processing and sentiment analysis. While such combinations of modern data analysis techniques with traditional GT data analysis techniques are not forbidden in traditional GT methods, they do not explicitly acknowledge them or provide guidance on how they may be combined in practice. STGT studies offer examples of how these can be combined for effective research outcomes (Madampe et al., 2020, 2021).

4.10.3 Research Tools

Definition

Research tools refer to all the instruments and tools we need to perform and manage the various research activities. Table 4.1 presents some common research support and management tools.

There are various tools available to support research project management, organisation of the research artefacts, and coordination amongst team members. For example, Trello and JIRA boards can be used to track research tasks, ownership, and status in research teams that are relatively large and/or distributed. Similarly, research teams may employ a number of mechanisms and tools for communication, for example, meetings (physical, virtual, hybrid), emails, and communication platforms such as Slack and Whatsapp.

Google Drive, Microsoft OneDrive, and Dropbox are popular online data and document storage options. To ensure data privacy and security, they can be fortified by encryption tools such as Boxcryptor for Dropbox.

For collection of traditional data such as from interviews and observations, some common research instruments include semi-structured interview questions, structured surveys and questionnaires, observation protocols, and usability evaluation protocols. Such protocols are usually designed on text editors such as Microsoft Word and Google Docs. However, in order to use them to collect data, they need to be translated into data collection tools. Qualtrics, SurveyMonkey, LimeSurvey, and Google Forms[4] are some examples of research tools to operationalise survey questionnaires. Hardware such as audio or video recorders, cameras for photography, digital devices, and physical notebooks for taking field notes are tools used to execute interviews, observations, and focus groups. Many of these tools can be used in face-to-face, physical meetings, while video conferencing tools such as Zoom or Microsoft Teams can be used to conduct interviews and focus groups online.

For collection of modern data such as information in repositories, online forums, and app reviews, data mining tools such as Appbot,[5] Perceval,[6] and Pydriller[7]

[4] Google Forms may not be accessible everywhere in the world, causing researchers to miss certain geographic locations.

[5] https://appbot.co/.

[6] https://github.com/chaoss/grimoirelab-perceval.

[7] https://github.com/ishepard/pydriller.

are commonly used. Some of these offer sentiment analysis and natural language processing in addition to automated data collection and filtering abilities.

Table 4.1 Common research support and management tools

Research Activity	Common Tools
Research project management	Trello, JIRA
Research team communication	Meetings, emails, Slack, WhatsApp
Research data storage/sharing	OneDrive, Dropbox, Boxcryptor, Google Drive
Survey tools	Qualtrics, SurveyMonkey, LimeSurvey, Google Forms (where accessible)
Data recording	Audio/video recorders, video conferencing tools (Zoom, Microsoft Teams), digital cameras, other digital devices, physical notebooks
Data organisation and analysis	NVivo, MAXQDA, Atlas.ti, spreadsheets, pen and paper
Supplementary analysis	Weka, R, Python scikit-learn packages
Data mining	Appbot, Perceval, Pydriller
Research writing	Overleaf, Latex, Microsoft Word, Google Docs
Data visualisation	Canva, Tableau, Lucidchart, PowerPoint

Software tools such as NVivo, MAXQDA, and ATLAS.ti are popular for qualitative data organisation and analysis. Paper and pen as well as spreadsheets continue to be popular tools for *old-school* data analysis. Supplementary data analysis of modern data, such as from software repositories, can be conducted using Weka, R, and Python scikit-learn packages. Similarly, SentiStrengthSE and Job Emotion Scale can be used for analysing sentiments and emotions to support STGT qualitative data analysis (Madampe et al., 2020).

Design tools such as Microsoft PowerPoint, Canva, Tableau, and Lucidchart can be useful for visualising concepts, categories, and relationships between them. A number of tools are available for writing up research. For example, Overleaf and Google Docs provide ease of use and collaboration in synchronous and asynchronous modes. Latex and Microsoft Word also continue to be used by some researchers.

While most research support and management tools are easily available, the research instruments, such as interview questions, generally need to be designed. They are usually designed from scratch, modelled after existing instruments from other research projects, or tweaked to suit the unique research needs of each project. Some researchers share their research instruments in their reports and publications. Designing research instruments is non-trivial and requires careful drafting and revisions. We will consider the design and use of some common research instruments used in STGT studies in Chap. 8 Techniques of Qualitative Data Collection. The use of large language model based Generative AI tools is discussed in Chap. 14 Future Directions in Qualitative Research.

4.11 The Research Impact

Definition

Research impact refers to *the expected ripple effects caused as a result of the research outcomes. Research deliverables, access control (e.g., open access), and communication channels need to be considered in order to achieve impact.*

Instead of assuming that research will achieve some impact once it is completed, research impact can be carefully considered and impact goals can be set upfront. Often, this helps the research team stay motivated as they envision the difference their research is likely to make.

Tips

Tips to Design for Research Impact

- *What are the likely deliverables of the research project?*
- *What are the likely access controls? How can research be made widely accessible?*
- *What are the most appropriate channels for communicating the research findings?*

Research publications are one of the most common deliverables of a research project. Research publications typically take the shape of workshop papers, doctoral symposium papers, posters, new ideas papers, short conference papers, full conference papers, and journal articles presenting emerging and mature findings. Some publication venues are pitched at both academic and industry readers. *IEEE Software* is an example of a publication venue where both traditional research papers and practitioner-oriented articles are published . Research findings can also be published in other, non-academic venues. These can take the shape of white papers, personal and professional blogs, and popular practitioner news and information websites such as InfoQ, which is read by over 1.5 million developers worldwide.

Research publications are often accompanied by presentations. For example, invited presentations can be made for papers published in conferences and *journal first* presentations of selected journal articles at affiliated conferences. In addition to research venues, STGT researchers will benefit from sharing their research findings at non-academic, practitioner-led conferences and events, for example, agile conferences around the world, GoTo conferences focused on software engineers, or the TED and TEDx talks to reach the wider society. Similarly, research findings can be shared with the wider society through digital and social media platforms. This includes sharing links on social media platforms such as Twitter and LinkedIn.

Guidelines and recommendations are other possible research outputs. These can take the form of a set of recommendations listed within a research publication or white paper or as part of a standard or policy document. For example, recommendations arising from an STGT research study may be adopted by a relevant government department as part of their official policy on the subject, thereby achieving strong real-world impact.

Empirical research projects can be designed to use STGT for empirical grounding, and develop tools for addressing the challenges identified. For example, an empirical research project on understanding how software practitioners respond to requirements changes applied *STGT for data analysis* and produced a tool—*Emotimonitor*, as a Trello plugin—to enable practitioners to record and monitor emotions at work (El-Migid et al., 2022). Tools are often demoed at special *demo* or *tools* track of conferences and are published as conference or journal papers. The tool itself is either released into the market, e.g., through Apple or Google Playstores, or into specific marketplaces such as the Atlassian and Eclipse marketplaces.

Sometimes, the intellectual property associated with research outputs can be captured and protected through patents. This is usually done where the research team has plans for commercialising a research output. Patenting can be an expensive and long process. However, where the return on investment is expected to be worth it, research teams can apply for patents. If patenting is an option, the research team needs to be careful about what information they make available in the public domain about their research. Typically, research and academic organisations have a commercialisation and legal arm that can guide the research team on the dos and don'ts of patenting.

Depending on their research values discussion, the research team may decide to make all or most of their research deliverables freely accessible to the wider society. Sharing freely accessible author preprints on personal websites and archiving sites such as Arxiv, under various creative commons copyright options, is becoming increasingly popular. Similarly, tools can be released for free or using a pay per use or subscription model on selected marketplaces.

4.12 The Pilot Study

Definition

Pilot study refers to *a small trial conducted to test and refine the research process and protocols including data collection techniques and analysis procedures.*

Once ethics approval is received, it is recommended to conduct a pilot study. A pilot allows the research team to test out the research protocols and set-up. It involves using the actual data collection instruments to collect some sample data. For example, a pilot study can involve collecting data through interviews with typically two or three people. Preferably these people come from the targeted participant cohort. For example, in a study of the challenges faced by DevOps engineers, the pilot is ideally conducted with a few DevOps engineers. The key difference between a pilot study and actual data collection for the study lies in their purpose. In the latter case, the purpose is to collect data to include in the study. In the case of a pilot, the main purpose is to test the research instruments, tools, and approaches and refine them based on review and feedback. If the pilot is conducted using the same source or cohort as the actual study, the pilot data can be included in the study.

If it's difficult to find relevant participants or data sources for the pilot and the team wishes to save the few sources they have access to for the actual data collection, then the pilot can be conducted with the closest possible proxy sources. For example, undergraduate or graduate students learning DevOps would be a close proxy to professional DevOps engineers. Others, further removed from the real context, such as research supervisors/advisors, peers, friends, and family with some knowledge and experience of the research topic, can also make for potential proxies for the pilot. While this is not ideal, it can help to assess and refine the research protocols and tools prior to actual data collection. However, the data collected from proxy participants can be excluded from the STGT study data as it does not represent the same data sources as required for the study.

What can be done with the data collected in a pilot? If the pilot study uses relevant data and does not result in significant changes to the research instruments, tools, approach, or topic, we can include the pilot data in our research project. However, if the pilot results in extensive changes such that it is difficult to maintain the integrity of the research and integrate the data from the pilot with data from the subsequent collection cycles, then it can be excluded from the study. It will have served its purpose and is not a wasted effort. Neither will it be manipulation of data because the intent was to test our own process and tools rather than work towards the research findings. As a new researcher, the easiest way to be confident about this issue is to decide beforehand whether you will include the data or are using the data collection strictly for piloting purposes.

4.13 Summary

In this chapter, we learned about designing and finalising the key elements of a research project. These elements are captured in the *research design canvas* that the research team can use to set up their research project. Once the research design looks promising, researchers can proceed to STGT's basic stage, described over the next few chapters.

References

Creswell, J. W., & Poth, C. N. (2016). *Qualitative inquiry and research design: Choosing among five approaches*. Sage publications.

Dittrich, D., Kenneally, E., et al. (2012). The menlo report: Ethical principles guiding information and communication technology research. *Technical report*, US Department of Homeland Security.

El-Emam, K. (2001). Ethics and open source. *Empirical Software Engineering, 6*(4), 291.

El-Migid, M.-A. A., Cai, D., Niven, T., Vo, J., Madampe, K., Grundy, J., & Hoda, R. (2022). Emotimonitor: A trello power-up to capture and monitor emotions of agile teams. *Journal of Systems and Software, 186*, 111206. https://www.sciencedirect.com/science/article/pii/S016412122100279X

Garousi, V., Felderer, M., & Mäntylä, M. V. (2019). Guidelines for including grey literature and conducting multivocal literature reviews in software engineering. *Information and Software Technology, 106*, 101–121.

Gold, N. E., & Krinke, J. (2020). Ethical mining: A case study on MSR mining challenges. In *Proceedings of the 17th International Conference on Mining Software Repositories* (pp. 265–276).

Hassan, A. E. (2008). The road ahead for mining software repositories. *2008 Frontiers of Software Maintenance* (pp. 48–57). IEEE.

Hoda, R. (2022). Socio-technical grounded theory for software engineering. *IEEE Transactions on Software Engineering, 48*(10), 3808–3832.

Hoda, R., & Noble, J. (2017). Becoming agile: a grounded theory of agile transitions in practice. In *2017 IEEE/ACM 39th International Conference on Software Engineering (ICSE)* (pp. 141–151). IEEE.

Hussain, W., Perera, H., Whittle, J., Nurwidyantoro, A., Hoda, R., Shams, R. A., & Oliver, G. (2020). Human values in software engineering: Contrasting case studies of practice. *IEEE Transactions on Software Engineering, 48*(5), 1818–1833.

Hussain, W., Shahin, M., Hoda, R., Whittle, J., Perera, H., Nurwidyantoro, A., Shams, R. A., & Oliver, G. (2022). How can human values be addressed in agile methods? a case study on safe. *IEEE Transactions on Software Engineering, 48*(12), 5158–5175.

Institute, P. M. (2008). A guide to the project management body of knowledge (PMBOK® guide).

Madampe, K., Hoda, R., & Grundy, J. (2021). A faceted taxonomy of requirements changes in agile contexts. *IEEE Transactions on Software Engineering, 48*(10), 3737–3752.

Madampe, K., Hoda, R., & Singh, P. (2020). Towards understanding emotional response to requirements changes in agile teams. In *Proceedings of the ACM/IEEE 42nd International Conference on Software Engineering: New Ideas and Emerging Results* (pp. 37–40).

Osterwalder, A., & Pigneur, Y. (2010). *Business model generation: A handbook for visionaries, game changers, and challengers* (Vol. 1). Wiley.

Pant, A., Hoda, R., Tantithamthavorn, C., & Turhan, B. (2024). Ethics in AI through the developer's view: A grounded theory literature review and guidelines. *Empirical Software Engineering, 29*(3), 67.

Perera, H., Hussain, W., Whittle, J., Nurwidyantoro, A., Mougouei, D., Shams, R. A., & Oliver, G. (2020). A study on the prevalence of human values in software engineering publications, 2015-2018. In *2020 IEEE/ACM 42nd International Conference on Software Engineering (ICSE)* (pp. 409–420). IEEE.

Perry, D. E., Porter, A. A., & Votta, L. G. (2000). Empirical studies of software engineering: A roadmap. In *Proceedings of the Conference on The Future of Software Engineering* (pp. 345–355).

Salleh, N., Hoda, R., Su, M. T., Kanij, T., & Grundy, J. (2018). Recruitment, engagement and feedback in empirical software engineering studies in industrial contexts. *Information and Software Technology, 98*, 161–172.

Saunders, M., & Tosey, P. (2013). The layers of research design. *Rapport* (Winter), 58–59.

Schwartz, S. H. (1992). Universals in the content and structure of values: Theoretical advances and empirical tests in 20 countries. In *Advances in experimental social psychology* (Vol. 25, pp. 1–65). Elsevier.

Singer, J., & Vinson, N. G. (2001). Why and how research ethics matters to you, yes you!. *Empirical Software Engineering, 6*(4), 287–290.

Singer, J., & Vinson, N. G. (2002). Ethical issues in empirical studies of software engineering. *IEEE Transactions on Software Engineering, 28*(12), 1171–1180.

Townsend, L., & Wallace, C. (2016). Social media research: A guide to ethics. *University of Aberdeen, 1*(16), 1–16. https://www.gla.ac.uk/media/Media_487729_smxx.pdf

Wohlin, C., & Aurum, A. (2015). Towards a decision-making structure for selecting a research design in empirical software engineering. *Empirical Software Engineering, 20*, 1427–1455.

Wolfswinkel, J. F., Furtmueller, E., & Wilderom, C. P. (2013). Using grounded theory as a method for rigorously reviewing literature. *European Journal of Information Systems, 22*(1), 45–55.

5 Research Philosophy

Abstract This chapter covers the fundamentals of research philosophy in general and as applied to socio-technical grounded theory (STGT) studies. First, it addresses *why* being aware of research philosophy and its fundamental building blocks is important. Next, it presents simple definitions and descriptions of these fundamental philosophical concepts such as *reasoning*, which can be inductive, deductive, and abductive, and how each is manifested in STGT's different steps and procedures. After this, it covers *ontology*, and how STGT expands ontology. Then it covers *epistemology*, and how STGT offers a range of epistemological options. Finally, the chapter moves into discussing prominent *research paradigms* and their application in STGT studies. This includes a discussion of how mismatched research paradigms of reviewers and the study can lead to harsh and unfair reviewing.

R. Hoda, *Qualitative Research with Socio-Technical Grounded Theory*,
https://doi.org/10.1007/978-3-031-60533-8_5

5.1 Why Research Philosophy

Definition

Research philosophy, or philosophy as applied to research, deals with what constitutes reality for a research project, the role of the researcher, how the researcher goes about the research, and how they make sense of it all to develop new knowledge.

Research philosophy can be thought of as the meta level of research. While the study of philosophy has been central to social science disciplines, unfortunately, software engineering (SE) researchers and those in other socio-technical domains often do not have much training in, or even exposure to, philosophy. Much of what we know and apply is often based on reading exemplar studies in our domains, and only some of those expand on their philosophical assumptions.

The role of philosophy in research is undeniable and indispensable. Whether or not aware, everyone has a stance when it comes to research philosophy, and we consciously or unconsciously apply it. Researchers who are unaware of fundamental philosophical concepts such as epistemology, ontology, and research paradigms (e.g., positivism, constructivism, pragmatism) are likely to mix up approaches in ways that threaten the credibility of their methods and applicability of their outcomes. Researchers who are aware of their philosophical stance are able to consciously apply it in conducting studies, presenting findings, and evaluating research.

Critically, declaring the philosophical stance of the research will help editors and programme committee chairs select appropriate reviewers for the work. In turn, it will help the reviewers better evaluate the work. For example, a reviewer who predominantly conducts research aligned with a positivist stance may, consciously or unconsciously, expect the papers they review to demonstrate quality criteria typically expected from a posivitist research approach such as generalisability, reproducibility, and replicability. In this case, if the paper reports findings from research that (un)consciously used a constructivist stance, it can be rejected or receive very harsh reviews from this reviewer. The same fate may befall research papers that (un)consciously apply a positivist stance when reviewed by a reviewer who is (un)consciously aligned to a constructivist stance.

> “As someone once said, we should not judge a fish by its ability to climb a tree. In software engineering and other socio-technical domains, the dominance of a positivist stance and the lack of awareness of other research paradigms leads to unnecessary review cycles at best and unwarranted rejections of robust research at worst. A basic understanding of fundamental research philosophy will greatly benefit our community.”

Sometimes qualitative and quantitative research is used as proxy for research philosophy. For example, quantitative research is often aligned with positivism while qualitative research is often aligned with constructivism. This is possibly why we expect a reviewer who is well versed in quantitative research to review quantitative research papers well and vice versa. However, these are generalisations. In practice, reviewers may be mixed-methods researchers—conducting mixed studies that involve both qualitative and quantitative methods—and may be comfortable with both types of research. Also, technically, qualitative research can be conducted with a positivist approach and quantitative research can be conducted with a constructivist stance, although these combinations are rare.

Moreover, an individual researcher's general philosophy in life may be different to their research philosophy. For example, in their life outside research, the individual may be following a pragmatic approach, working within the realms of what is possible and beneficial. However, in their role as a researcher, they may choose to (or unknowingly tend to) apply a positivist approach, especially if they primarily conduct quantitative research, or a constructivist one if they primarily conduct qualitative research. The difference between their philosophical approach in life and in their research can lead to challenges, especially if they are unaware of these differences.

Finally, researchers tend to have their favourite or "go to" research philosophy which they apply to a majority of their research studies. However, we do not have to conduct all research using the same philosophical stance. Much like selecting research methods and tools, researchers can also consciously choose a philosophical stance that may differ from their usual one based on what suits the nature of the research study. Being unaware of, or agnostic to, research paradigms is not the same thing as consciously choosing to apply different paradigms in different scenarios. Philosophical flexibility requires a mature understanding of philosophical foundations and high levels of researcher self-awareness and reflection (Hoda, 2022).

The above discussion is not meant to scare researchers further away from research philosophy. Rather, it is aimed to describe how important it is for researchers to be aware of, and consciously apply, research philosophy in our research and reviewing practice. In the following sections, I describe some of the fundamental aspects of research philosophy with a conscious effort to make it as accessible to our SE and other socio-technical research communities as possible.

5.2 Reasoning

Definition

Reasoning, also referred to as logic or inference, is how we make sense of the world and develop knowledge. The three main types of reasoning approaches are *inductive*, *deductive*, and *abductive* reasoning.

Reasoning or logic is not only central to understanding our human experience, but is also at the heart of how artificial intelligence systems are developed to process data in order to derive information and insights. Here, we focus on reasoning in the context of human knowledge development.

There are different types of reasoning: a top-down approach called *deductive* reasoning, a bottom-up approach called *inductive* reasoning, and what I call a "detour" approach, *abductive* reasoning. Each has its own advantages and limitations. Understanding the different types of reasoning approaches is important in the research journey in general, and particularly in the systematically development of theoretical models, frameworks, taxonomies, and theories. Next, I explain these different types of reasoning in general, followed by their application in STGT's different stages and procedures.

> Socio-technical GT (STGT) considers *abductive* reasoning as a key part of theory development, in addition to its predominantly *inductive* reasoning approach and a manifestation of *deductive* reasoning in some of its procedures.

5.2.1 Inductive Reasoning

Definition

Inductive reasoning or induction is a bottom-up approach of drawing general conclusions from patterns evidenced across specific instances. Inductive reasoning aims to answer the question: *What do we see in the data?*

In the case of an inductive approach, the research does not start with hypotheses of what the researcher predicts may be true or false, nor does it try to test the validity of such hypotheses. Instead, the researcher observes specific instances of a phenomenon in practice, tries to find common patterns across them, and proposes more general conclusions based on those patterns. In other words, the findings of the research are developed "bottom up" from empirical evidence. For example, a researcher using an inductive approach may set out to explore what factors influence the perceived happiness of software developers and how that might, if at all, relate to the quality of the code they produce or impact other SE activities. Here the researcher has not set out to prove anything to be true or false; rather they are taking an exploratory approach to what they can find out about the perceived happiness of developers and its impact on SE activities, including potentially on code quality.

An advantage of using inductive reasoning is that the researcher can afford to be open and exploratory. In the above example, the research may not find any relationship between happiness and code quality. However, they are likely to find all sorts of interesting insights about what constitutes developer happiness in an SE context and its influence on a range of SE activities. A limitation of an inductive approach is that the findings apply to the contexts studied and by extension to similar contexts. Typically, the findings cannot be claimed to be more widely applicable.

Inductive Reasoning in STGT

STGT is guided by a predominantly and overarching inductive approach, the same as the traditional GT methods. When GT was introduced by Glaser and Strauss in 1967 (Glaser & Strauss, 2017, first published 1967), it challenged the then popular top-down approach of verifying existing theories, also known as a *hypothetico-deductive* approach. They challenged the status quo for what was considered robust and scientific social science research at the time by highlighting the importance of a bottom-up *inductive* approach to generating new and original theories. Other traditional versions of GT (Strauss & Corbin, 1990; Charmaz, 2006), as well as the socio-technical version presented in Hoda (2022) and detailed in this book, follow the same overarching inductive approach.

In STGT, inductive reasoning or induction is explicitly manifested in the procedures of *open coding* and *constant comparison* in the basic data collection and analysis stage. In open coding, evidence is collected and analysed bottom up. Using constant comparison, similar codes are combined to form a higher level of abstraction called concepts, and similar concepts are grouped to form a yet higher level of abstraction called subcategory or category. This movement from specific empirical evidence on the ground to common and abstract patterns at the theoretical level manifests an inductive approach, and gives grounded theory its name. If the researchers decide to proceed to STGT's advanced stage of theory development using an emergent mode, they apply another round of induction in the form of *targeted coding* and *constant comparison*, where the coding is limited and targeted to the most promising concepts and categories emerging from the basic stage.

5.2.2 Deductive Reasoning

Definition

Deductive reasoning or deduction is a top-down approach of drawing conclusions about specific instances from established facts or generally expected outcomes. Deductive reasoning aims to answer the question: *Do we see it in the data?*

In the case of a deductive approach, the research begins with a statement that makes a generalised claim about a known or assumed fact. For example, a researcher using a deductive approach may set out to verify the hypothesis that states: "*happy developers will produce better quality code*". Here, the researcher starts with a general statement about software developers that aims to establish a co-relation between their perceived happiness and code quality. They will then collect systematic evidence to test the hypothesis. This can be done through a range or combination of methods including experiments, point in time observations, longitudinal ethnography, happiness tests, and so on. Data will be collected and analysed to deduce whether the general relationship that is hypothesised is evidenced in practice. The research results may support or refute the hypothesis or it may remain inconclusive.

An advantage of using deductive reasoning is that the end goal is evident from the start, i.e., to prove a hypothesis as true or false, also known as the hypothetico-deductive approach (Glaser & Strauss, 2017, first published 1967). This typically makes it easier to chart and predict the research steps required. In other words, when using a deductive approach, the level of uncertainty in the research process is typically lower than that in an inductive approach. However, the uncertainty of outcome remains. A related limitation is that negative or inconclusive results or those that are statistically insignificant are often difficult to publish, as seen in trends evidenced across disciplines (Fanelli, 2012). However, this should not deter researchers from attempting deductive approaches or from attempting to publish their hard-earned results, whether positive, negative, or inconclusive.

Deductive Reasoning in STGT

In a bid to delineate its stance, grounded theory is often presented as an inductive method. However, classifying GT methods as purely inductive has been acknowledged to be naïve (Haig, 1995). For example, Glaserian Grounded Theory (GGT) acknowledges the role of *deduction* in guiding theoretical sampling (Glaser & Strauss, 2017, chapter II, first published 1967). *Strauss-Corbinian GT* (SCGT) demonstrates a strong role of deduction in the later stages of theory development (Strauss & Corbin, 1990). SCGT recommends systematically verifying the emergent theory against the data, which is indicative of a deductive approach. Glaser, on the other hand, is strongly opposed to the idea of verification, claiming it as "*forcing*" rather than emergence of theory (Glaser, 1992). This was one of several differences that arose between the two originators of traditional GT, leading to distinct versions: Glaserian GT and Strauss-Corbinian GT. Kathy Charmaz, who introduced a third version of GT in sociology (Charmaz, 2006), argued that an inductive approach lends GT its strength, rather than considering it as a limitation (Urquhart, 2012).

STGT acknowledges its predominantly inductive approach, like the traditional GT versions. STGT also acknowledges the use of deduction in specific procedures. For example, deduction is manifested in the procedure of *theoretical sampling*. Once some data is collected and data analysis begins, the sampling of further data can be driven by the perceived gaps in the emergent concepts and categories (and in the advanced stages, in the emergent theory). This involves assessing what we have identified so far in terms of findings and deciding what to collect next, how, and from where/whom. In applying theoretical sampling, the direction of the logic or inference flows from the general patterns (current established or emerging findings) to look for specific instances of data/evidence to further expand on them. However, this is not done to verify or validate the existing/emergent findings, although some new data may end up doing so. The main aim here is to achieve richness in concepts and categories, exploring as many of their nuances and facets as possible, and ultimately saturate them, i.e., when no new insight is discernible from further data collection within the defined research context.

Acknowledging the deductive nature of theoretical sampling helps present a more comprehensive view of the philosophical underpinnings of STGT, instead of making it appear as a purely inductive method, which most traditional sociological versions do. Practically, the awareness of the deductive nature of theoretical sampling will help us to more consciously and better apply the procedure to achieve desired outcomes. See Chaps. 7 Basics of Qualitative Data Collection and 12 Theory Development for more on theoretical sampling.

5.2.3 Abductive Reasoning

Definition

Abductive reasoning or abduction is a "detour" approach of proposing the best possible explanation based on all the evidence, albeit incomplete, available. Abductive reasoning aims to answer questions about the observations made in the data such as *How is this possible?* and *Why is this happening?* and to explore *what-if scenarios*. In theory development, abduction is often the process by which preliminary evidence-based hypotheses are born.

Most discourse on reasoning is dominated by a discussion of deductive and inductive reasoning, and differences between the two. Abductive reasoning or abduction is rarely acknowledged or explained but is an important part of research inquiry.

Charles Sanders Peirce defines abduction as "*a process of forming an explanatory hypothesis*" (Douven, 2017; Haig, 1995). Different modes of abductive reasoning include reason or hunch, clue, metaphor or analogy, symptom, pattern, and explanation (Shank, 1998). Abductive reasoning is known to drive diagnosis in medical sciences, where plausible hypotheses are explored for how well they fit the symptoms and conditions being observed and are then accepted or discarded accordingly. Similarly, criminal investigations, and the practice of law more generally, also offer examples of abductive reasoning where different lines of plausible action are investigated and inquiries are pursued with the help of available evidence to draw conclusions. The certainty of the conclusion, and therefore possible conviction, relies on the strength and chain of evidence and how convincing the retrospective explanations of the possible sequence of events are.

Some of the most entertaining examples of abductive reasoning, sometimes portrayed as deductive reasoning, can be found in the pursuit of the famous fictional character of the detective Sherlock Holmes. Peirce also refers to a personal detective experience often used to describe abduction (Reichertz, 2007).

Let us consider an example of abductive reasoning in software engineering. Suppose a researcher starts to notice a pattern around the extent to which daily standups or sprint planning is conducted by software teams. Based on her observations, she develops a hunch that this may be related to the presence of the scrum master in those meetings. Such ideas usually dawn on the researcher in a specific moment in time or may emerge gradually over the course of the research. The researcher decides to revisit their work to confirm if such a relationship can be seen in the existing evidence, and starts to keep an eye out for exploring this possible relationship as they proceed, either waiting for it to emerge or investigating it more explicitly. In either case, they may end up firming up the emerging hypothesis with further evidence or list it as a possible relationship for future research studies to explore.

Abductive Reasoning in STGT

Abductive reasoning plays an important role in theory development, but remains to be fully explained (Bruscaglioni, 2016; Martin, 2019). Understanding abduction and its various modes, e.g., hunch, clue, reason, metaphor, analogy, symptom, pattern, and explanation (Shank, 1998), enables the researcher to think creatively, which is considered key to theorising and theory development (Martin, 2019).

The traditional sociological GT methods do not cover the role of abduction in any detail, except for Charmaz (2006). For example, Glaser talks about sudden or slow-dawning "*sensitive insights of the observer*" as "*the root sources of all significant theorizing*" (Glaser & Strauss, 2017, chapter XI, first published 1967). This description aligns with the Peircean views on abduction but Glaser does not explicitly refer to abduction. *Strauss-Corbinian GT* is seen to be influenced by abduction as well but, as Charmaz points out, only refers to it in a footnote in Strauss' book (Strauss, 1987). Charmaz, on the other hand, acknowledges the role of abduction in theory development, describing it as a type of "inferential leap" required when chancing upon a surprising finding that does not fit the emergent patterns (Richardson & Kramer, 2006; Charmaz, 2014). She explains that this "imaginative way" of reasoning gives rise to useful explanations, also referred to as *theoretical conjectures* or *inferences*. In turn, it leads the researcher to re-examine or collect more data to check the conjectures.

STGT considers abductive reasoning or abduction as a key part of theory development. Abduction is often the process by which preliminary evidence-based hypotheses are born. In STGT, abduction is most strongly manifested during the procedures of memoing, theoretical structuring, and theoretical integration procedures described in Chap. 12 Theory Development. Memoing can be done at any time, and is recommended to be done as soon as the researcher feels the urge to capture or revisit an idea. The researcher is likely to come up with hunches about some concepts and categories, and more likely about possible relationships, during memoing. The opposite is also true, that is, the researcher may sense a hunch which urges them to record a memo. These hunches can be thought of as *educated guesses* based on all the evidence at hand, often triggered by *thought experiments*.

With evidence and saturation, preliminary hypotheses may become solidified and be reported as a set of hypotheses that make up a mature theory (or another theoretical outcome such as a theoretical model, framework, or taxonomy). In this sense, the reasoning process whereby Albert Einstein formulated the initial propositions for what became the theory of relativity (through his famous thought experiments) or Charles Darwin initially came up with his idea for what became the theory of evolution of species (through pondering on observed patterns in data) seems closer to abduction than anything else.

5.3 Ontology

Definition

Ontology refers to what we believe exists or what we perceive as reality.

As strange as it may sound at first, researchers can hold different views on what constitutes reality in the research context. For example, a researcher, say a physicist, may believe reality to be made up of only directly observable material bodies in the natural world. Another researcher, say an anthropologist, may believe reality is socially constructed based on concepts such as identity, culture, values, and their combinations. Neither is wrong: these are simply different approaches to defining reality that make most sense in a given research discipline or for a given phenomenon. This acceptance of what is "real" is referred to as ontology. While it applies to the human experience at large, the discussion here is limited to the research context.

Our ontological stance is often influenced by the training we receive in our research domain. For example, researchers in domains that are typically referred to as the "hard" sciences (e.g., maths and physics) often regard material and measurable concepts as reality. Phenomena studied in these domains are typically relatively stable in their expected behaviour under regular circumstances, e.g., acceleration or gravity in Newtonian physics. Such phenomena are often measured through interchangeable objects, e.g., dropping a ball to study gravity, where one ball can be replaced by another (of the same dimensions, mass, etc.) without any impact on the experiments (Hoda, 2022). Such directly observable, material reality is often studied using quantitative means such as numbers, focusing on accuracy and precision.

On the other hand, researchers in domains that are typically referred to as the "soft" sciences (e.g., psychology and sociology) often consider material, immaterial, and/or socially constructed concepts as part of reality. Phenomena studied in these domains are typically full of variations, e.g., people's competency in driving, cooking, or software programming (Hoda, 2022). Such phenomena are often measured through interactions with non-interchangeable subjects, e.g., one person replacing another in a study on programming competency will lead to multiple variations in the findings. Such phenomena are often studied using qualitative means such as text-based data, focusing on credibility and richness.

5.3.1 STGT Expands Ontology

> "STGT acknowledges that the traditional views on ontology are limited when it comes to socio-technical domains such as software engineering. It formally acknowledges a revised ontology composed of multiple and complex realities that are unique to the socio-technical world we live in today."

Using STGT, the researcher can not only investigate the traditional "physical" reality and associated socially constructed realities (as summarised above), but also approach modern *extended and socio-technical realities* with confidence.

For a start, STGT acknowledges that the traditional views on ontology are limited when it comes to socio-technical domains such as SE, artificial intelligence, and human–computer interaction. These domains are full of phenomena that often unfold in multiple new realities, such as virtual reality (VR), augmented reality (AR), mixed reality (MR), and their combinations with the physical reality (Hoda, 2022). These extended realities have only been created in the past 50 years or so, and have fundamentally redefined human societies and communication, and challenged the traditional sociological concepts of the human *mind*, *self*, and *society* (Mead, 1934; Wolfe, 1991).

Naturally, traditional GT methods developed in the mid-1960s (Glaser & Strauss, 2017, first published 1967, chapter XI; Strauss & Corbin, 1990) and updated in the mid-2000s (Charmaz, 2006) do not explicitly address these modern realities, or provide guidance on how to deal with them in the research context. Researchers who have attempted to study modern extended realities using traditional GT have done so by applying their own understanding and adaptations to the traditional methods, with little support from the traditional GT guidelines.

To understand how fundamentally different the realities of a socio-technical domain such as SE are, let us consider the "world" of a software development team. This world may consist of physical spaces (e.g., team meeting rooms), physical artefacts (e.g., Kanban boards), and physical interactions (e.g., physical project planning meetings). This world may also include virtual spaces (e.g., Zoom meetings and breakout rooms), virtual artefacts (e.g., Trello boards), and virtual interactions (e.g., emails, online chats, exchange on online forums). Teams in this world may also be working with simulated and augmented realities (e.g., those developing and testing software games) and combined realities (e.g., the team conducting an estimation session in hybrid mode using a virtual task board and their online avatars) (Hoda, 2022). Studying phenomena in such complex realities requires a revised ontology that extends beyond the traditional views.

STGT formally proposes a revised ontology composed of these multiple and complex realities that are unique to the socio-technical world we live in today. Accepting this *extended and socio-technical* ontological stance is important for researchers so they can consciously be aware of the unique opportunities, limitations, and threats posed when researching in such realities. For example, while it may have been difficult to directly observe phenomena unfold in the past (unless they were recorded or documented), having virtual spaces and artefacts affords the opportunity for researchers to directly observe phenomena unfold at length, in-depth, and in real-time, both synchronously and asynchronously. Studying a developing trend on LinkedIn is an example of such new research opportunities.

At the same time, these new realities pose several new limitations and threats. Faking identity in a traditional research context (e.g., a research participant posing as someone they are not) was a rare occurrence as physically verifying people's identities used to be relatively straightforward. With the advent of extended reality and research in these contexts (e.g., conducting research on social media trends), verifying the identity of people and/or authenticity of available information is no longer straightforward. Additional effort is required to establish the credibility and authenticity of the data available or elicited in modern extended realities (see *Data Quality Evaluation Guidelines* in Chap. 7 Basics of Qualitative Data Collection).

The revised ontology not only expands reality beyond the physical to extended realities. It also extends the idea of socially constructed realities into *socio-technically constructed* realities. For example, the traditional concept of *social identity* is mostly incomplete in the modern world without a comprehensive consideration of a person's *socio-technical identity*. To fully understand how a person sees themselves and which groups they feel a sense of belonging to, researchers will need to consider their relevant virtual identities and interactions (e.g., LinkedIn, Twitter, email, GitHub, online avatars, game profiles, and others as applicable) in addition to their physical identity and interactions.

Similarly, consider the original study that led to the formulation of the GT method—the role of the social status of dying hospital patients in the level of nursing care received and the awareness of dying (Glaser & Strauss, 2017, first published 1967). When considered in contemporary times, these can no longer be considered strictly social processes. Today, an investigation of *social status* without due consideration of the patient's online and social media profile and an *awareness of dying* without investigating the impact of readily available credible and scrupulous online medical information will be considered incomplete. Another example is that of Piaget's classic theory of cognitive development that explained the four stages of children's cognitive development as sensorimotor, pre-operational, concrete operational, and formal operational (Piaget & Inhelder, 2008). This classic theory may well need to be re-calibrated for the digital natives who are known to operate complex digital devices as early as a few months old.

STGT enables new socio-technical theories to be generated, and traditional sociological theories to be re-calibrated, by formalising and using a modern ontology that is cognisant of the extended and socio-technical realities.

5.4 Epistemology

Definition

Epistemology refers to what we consider as knowledge and how that knowledge is gained.

Researchers hold differing views about how knowledge about the reality of the research context can be captured. An *objectivist* epistemology holds that knowledge about the research world can be gained by means of measurements and/or observations that are neutral, where a replication of the study by a different observer (or measurer) reproduces the results. For example, consider the gravity experiment again. The results of the experiments are expected to be exactly the same if two different researchers follow the exact same experimental procedures (barring some margin for human error). In this case, the nature of the phenomenon being studied (e.g., gravity), instruments being used (e.g., ball, timer, slow motion video recording), and experimental conditions (e.g., set-up, airflow, angle of viewing) are relatively stable and controllable to a high degree. An objectivist epistemology works well to support such a research topic and study design.

A *subjectivist* epistemology holds that knowledge about the research world can be gained by means of interpretations of observations that are subjective to the observer (or measurer), and replacing one with another is likely to yield different findings. For example, consider a study on understanding human biases in the AI development life cycle. Say the study is designed to involve human participants such as AI practitioners and use interviews and observations as methods of data collection. In this case, the nature of the phenomenon being studied (i.e., human biases), 'instruments' being used (i.e., human participants, interviews, and observations), and research conditions (i.e., practices observed, questions, and follow-ups) cannot be considered so stable or fixed as to be able to fully replicate the study. In all practicality, a replication study will involve different participants and researchers. These humans will bring different "flavours" to the study, leading to different, equally valid, and original findings. A subjectivist epistemology works well to support such a research topic and study design.

5.4.1 STGT Expands Epistemological Choices

> "Most STGT studies are likely to align with a subjectivist epistemology, acknowledging the unique perspectives brought into the study through participants or human-related data and individual researchers. However, objectivist STGT studies of phenomena involving virtual avatars, simulations, and interactions with intelligent chatbots or robots are also possible."

The three sociological GT methods can be said to align with a specific epistemology each. For example, Glaserian GT (GGT) is often perceived to align with an objectivist view while Strauss-Corbinian GT (SCGT) and Constructivist GT (CGT) are acknowledged to align with a subjectivist epistemology (Charmaz, 2006; Stol et al., 2016).

STGT studies, on the other hand, can align with a subjectivist or an objectivist epistemology, depending on the context and research design. Most STGT studies are likely to align with a subjectivist viewpoint, acknowledging the unique perspectives brought into the study through participants or human-related data and individual researchers, who are not interchangeable beings. However, an objectivist viewpoint is also possible in an STGT study. For example, studies on phenomena occurring in artificially designed environments, such as within software games, exploring only aspects related to the virtual world, can be designed with an objectivist approach. This is because these contexts afford limited decision points, variations, and interpretations. They offer a world that is close to the idea of a stand-alone reality that is finite and deterministic. Objective measures such as game metrics can be used to manifest such an approach, e.g., by capturing accuracy, player health status, lives remaining, game levels, game points, experience points, skill level, etc. Similarly, objectivist studies of phenomena involving virtual avatars, simulations, and interactions with intelligent chatbots or robots are also possible.

5.5 Research Paradigms

Definition

Research paradigm refers to the combination of ontological and epistemological stances that informs the researcher's worldview.

Research paradigm is the formal name given to a researcher's worldview. This worldview is made up of their ontological stance, i.e., what they are willing to accept as reality in the research context, and their epistemological stance, i.e., what they are willing to accept are reliable ways of gaining knowledge about reality in the research context. Some research paradigms are positivism, postpositivism, constructivism, symbolic interactionism, and pragmatism. I explain these below, with a focus on how to conduct full STGT studies using these paradigms. For further reading on research paradigms, their impact on research, and their prevalence in SE research, the following papers can be consulted: Seaman (1999), Easterbrook et al. (2008), Wohlin and Aurum (2015), Russo and Nuseibeh (2001), and Melegati and Wang (2021).

5.5.1 Constructivism

Definition

Constructivism is the research paradigm or worldview that accepts that reality is co-created through the presence of and interactions between the researcher and the participants/data.

Constructivism acknowledges that knowledge is "*created, not discovered by mind*" (Schwandt et al., 1994). It accepts the influence of the humans involved in the study on the knowledge that is generated as a result of it. This includes the researchers conducting the study as well as the participants (or data about/from humans). The subjectivist epistemology associated with constructivism implies these people are neither neutral nor interchangeable. They bring unique perspectives and flavours to the research that cannot be replicated by involving a different set of people. Consequently, the findings from such studies apply to contexts that are the same as or similar to what was examined and are not universally generalisable. Generalisation and reproducibility are not among the desired characteristics for studies based on a constructivist approach. Instead, these studies value and can be evaluated on the basis of originality or novelty, and relevance or usefulness. Unsurprisingly, studies conducted with a constructivist approach are focused on generating new knowledge and theories over verifying existing ones.

Ethnography and case studies are research methods seen to be closely aligned to the constructivist approach (Easterbrook et al., 2008). In terms of the grounded theory suite of methods, Constructivist GT (CGT) applies an explicit and exclusive constructivist paradigm to studying social phenomena (Charmaz, 2006). STGT supports a constructivist approach to theory development in socio-technical domains, but is not limited exclusively to this research paradigm.

STGT with a Constructivist Approach

A constructivist worldview is a natural good fit for many STGT studies. Unlike in traditional sociological research where constructivism accepts a socially constructed reality, constructivism in STGT accepts a socio-technically constructed reality, as discussed in the Expanding Ontology section earlier.

When conducting an STGT study with a constructivist approach, the researcher acknowledges that they are not a neutral observer in the study, nor are they interchangeable with another researcher without any impact on the research study. This acknowledgement is often manifested in the researcher sharing their own background—who they are and what experiences, viewpoints, and assumptions they bring to the study—with the readers so they can take that background into consideration when understanding the research design choices and the interpretation, analysis, and synthesis of the findings. For example, if a researcher has professional training and experience as a software tester for charitable organisations in New Zealand, it can be assumed that they will be well placed to better study and explain the phenomenon of testing in not-for-profit business contexts in the Pacific region. This extends to how they design the research questions, what data collection procedures they select, how and from where they recruit participants or datasets, how they collect and analyse the data, and how they interpret and present the findings. In short, all aspects of the research study can be influenced by the research paradigm.

At the same time, it can also be understood that their unique background will bring its own set of limitations and opportunities. For example, it may be that they do not understand the pressures and pleasures of testing as well in for-profit business contexts in other regions such as Europe. This can be a limitation if they do not make an effort to learn as much as possible about the new context. At the same time, this can be an opportunity to study the phenomenon from an outsider's perspective and capture several nuances that those embedded in the context may have taken for granted and overlooked. Thus, sharing the background and role of the researcher can become a sort of disclaimer to understanding the research and its findings through the researcher as the lens. Similarly, it can become a disclaimer to take some things with a pinch of salt because we know how the background and role of the researcher may have influenced the findings by limiting them to what they know and understand.

For reviewers who support a positivist worldview—or are unaware of the concept of research paradigms and assume positivism by default for all research studies—reviewing a study that was conducted using constructivism can be challenging. They may end up reviewing the study rather harshly because they inadvertently end up applying the quality criteria of positivist studies to evaluate a constructivist study. They may find it lacking in many ways (e.g., this is not generalisable, this is not reproducible, this is not replicable). Alternatively, they may be aware of constructivism, but if they do not make a conscious effort to lean into it, they may not be able to perform a fair review. The same can be true for the opposite combination, i.e., a reviewer with a predominantly constructivist worldview reviewing a study conducted with a positivist paradigm as addressed later on.

5.5.2 Positivism and Postpositivism

Definition

Positivism refers to the research paradigm or worldview that accepts that reality is definite, assured, and certain and that it can be studied through direct observations by interchangeable researchers, and excludes traditional metaphysics and theology. **Postpositivism** focuses on falsification of hypotheses, increasing confidence in proposed theories with every failed attempt at falsification.

Positivism captures an approach to research that accepts reality as external and standalone. This reality exists to be discovered through observations and measurements, but is not defined or influenced by them. In other words, reality would exist and be the same irrespective of human existence or experience. The researcher's role is to study, capture, and render it *accurately*. The objectivist epistemology associated with positivism implies that changing who studies, captures, and renders this reality would not impact the findings. Reproducibility of the research process, replication and generalisability of the results, and statistical significance are desirable characteristics for studies based on a positivist approach. Consequently, studies conducted with positivism are more interested in testing and confirming existing facts, theories, and claims.

Controlled and quasi-experiments are research methods closely aligned with positivism. Typically, quantitative and closed-ended surveys and case study research also align well with positivism (Easterbrook et al., 2008). Among the traditional GT methods, Glaserian GT (GGT) is seen to be most closely aligned with a positivist approach, although it was not explicitly mentioned by the originators.

STGT with a Positivist Approach

A positivist worldview may not be the first approach that comes to mind for conducting STGT studies. However, it is possible to conduct STGT studies using a positivist approach. Since positivism accepts and expects an external and standalone reality, research contexts that offer this possibility can consider applying a positivist approach. For example, STGT studies of phenomena that take place in mostly finite and deterministic contexts such as within virtual games worlds can consider applying a positivist approach. Similarly, research involving interactions with chatbots or robots that have a finite and relatively small number of interaction possibilities offers the opportunity to apply a positivist approach. In-built analytics can be harnessed to capture objective metrics that are independent of researchers, and there is limited opportunity for subjective interpretation. In this way, the research can be conducted more or less with interchangeable researchers without any significant impact on the research study. This also makes the study replicable and the results reproducible to a large extent.

However, it could be claimed that some amount of subjectivity still remains as the background of the researcher can still influence their research design, data collection and analysis procedures, and interpretations and presentation of the findings. For example, while the in-game analytics in a massively mutliplayer online game can provide objective metrics, if the study involves some observation of game play, the findings can vary depending on whether the observing researcher has gaming experience. To be exclusively positivist, it makes sense to include only objective measures as much as possible, even if they are being collected by people.

For reviewers who support a constructivist worldview—or are unaware of the concept of research paradigms and assume constructivism by default for all research studies—reviewing a study that was conducted using positivism (or postpositivism) can be challenging. They may end up reviewing the study rather harshly because they inadvertently end up applying the quality criteria of constructivist studies to evaluate a positivist study and therefore find it lacking in many ways (e.g., this too rigid, this is too limited, this is not nuanced enough). Alternatively, they may be aware of positivism, but if they do not make a conscious effort to lean into it, they may not be able to perform a fair review.

> “A constructivist research paradigm is a natural good fit for many STGT studies. Constructivism in STGT accepts a socio-technically constructed reality. However, STGT studies can also be conducted with a positivist worldview, especially where the studied phenomenon takes place in mostly finite and deterministic contexts such as within virtual game worlds. Other paradigms such as pragmatism and symbolic interactionism and perspectives such as feminism or critical theory can also be applied in STGT studies. Selecting to consciously apply a specific research paradigm is not the same as being agnostic to research paradigms, and demands researcher awareness, maturity, and discipline.”

5.5.3 Other Approaches and Perspectives

Constructivism and Positivism are arguably the two most popular research paradigms or worldviews applied in research, especially in social sciences and theory development. Another relevant paradigm is *pragmatism*—a research worldview which accepts reality in terms of what is of practical use and seeks to understand what practical difference it will make to the observer. *Symbolic interactionism* accepts reality as what is socially understood in terms of symbols and that reality is perceived through social interactions that define and redefine symbolic meaning of concepts, and is often referred to as a theory rather than a paradigm (Schwandt et al., 1994). Strauss-Corbinian GT is said to build on both these ideas (Strauss & Corbin, 1990).

In addition to worldview, our approach to research can also be coloured by our choice of perspective. We can choose to study a topic with the lens of *feminism*, which will allow us to pay special attention to the representation of women in the studied phenomenon, which may or may not be exclusively about women. For example, a study on code review practices can take a feminist perspective to especially study how code reviews may be differently experienced by women, or what is different when the code review author and receiver are both women or not, and many other such interesting questions. We can also choose to study a topic with the lens of *critical theory*, which will allow us to pay special attention to the political purpose the study can serve and how it can be used to empower minority groups. For example, the same study on code reviews can take a critical theory perspective to especially study the experience of minority groups which may include women. It could investigate how the various combinations of minority and majority group membership may impact the process, effectiveness, and outcomes of code reviews. The ultimate aim in this case may be to conduct the study in order to raise awareness and to recommend change in practice to empower minority group members.

5.6 Summary

In this chapter, we learned about the fundamentals of research philosophy in general and how it applies to socio-technical grounded theory (STGT) studies. First, we learned abiut *why* it is important to be aware of research philosophy and its fundamental building blocks. Next, we studied simple definitions and descriptions of the fundamental philosophical concepts such as *reasoning* being inductive, deductive, and abductive, and learned how they are manifested in STGT through its different steps and procedures. After this, we learned about the concept of *ontology*, and how STGT expands ontology to socio-technical realms. Then we learned about *epistemology*, and how STGT can be performed using different epistemological options. Finally, we learned about prominent *research paradigms* such as constructivism and positivism and their application in STGT studies, as well as other approaches and combinations of perspectives such as feminism and critical theory.

References

Bruscaglioni, L. (2016). Theorizing in grounded theory and creative abduction. *Quality & Quantity, 50*(5), 2009–2024.

Charmaz, K. (2006). *Constructing grounded theory: A practical guide through qualitative analysis*. Sage.

Charmaz, K. (2014). *Constructing grounded theory*. Sage.

Douven, I. (2017). Abduction. In E. N. Zalta (Ed.), *The stanford encyclopedia of philosophy* (Summer 2017 Ed.). Metaphysics Research Lab, Stanford University.

Easterbrook, S., Singer, J., Storey, M.-A., & Damian, D. (2008). Selecting empirical methods for software engineering research. In *Guide to Advanced Empirical Software Engineering* (pp. 285–311). Springer.

Fanelli, D. (2012). Negative results are disappearing from most disciplines and countries. *Scientometrics, 90*(3), 891–904.

Glaser, B. G. (1992). *Basics of grounded theory analysis: Emergence vs forcing*. Sociology Press.

Glaser, B. G., & Strauss, A. L. (2017). *Discovery of grounded theory: Strategies for qualitative research*. Routledge (First Published 1967).

Haig, B. D. (1995). Grounded theory as scientific method. *Philosophy of Education, 28*(1), 1–11.

Hoda, R. (2022). Socio-technical grounded theory for software engineering. *IEEE Transactions on Software Engineering, 48*(10), 3808–3832.

Martin, V. B. (2019). Using popular and academic literature as data for formal grounded theory. *The sage handbook of current developments in grounded theory* (pp. 222–243). Sage Publications.

Mead, G. H. (1934). *Mind, self and society* (Vol. 111). Chicago University of Chicago Press.

Melegati, J. and Wang, X. (2021). Surfacing paradigms underneath research on human and social aspects of software engineering. In *2021 IEEE/ACM 13th International Workshop on Cooperative and Human Aspects of Software Engineering (CHASE)*.

Piaget, J., & Inhelder, B. (2008). *The psychology of the child*. Basic books.

Reichertz, J. (2007). *Abduction: The logic of discovery of grounded theory*. Sage.

Richardson, R., & Kramer, E. H. (2006). Abduction as the type of inference that characterizes the development of a grounded theory. *Qualitative Research, 6*(4), 497–513.

Russo, A., & Nuseibeh, B. (2001). On the use of logical abduction in software engineering. *Handbook of Software Engineering and Knowledge Engineering: Volume I: Fundamentals* (pp. 889–914). World Scientific.

Schwandt, T. A. et al. (1994). Constructivist, interpretivist approaches to human inquiry. *Handbook of Qualitative Research, 1*, 118–137.

Seaman, C. B. (1999). Qualitative methods in empirical studies of software engineering, *IEEE Transactions on Software Engineering, 25*(4), 557–572.

Shank, G. (1998). The extraordinary ordinary powers of abductive reasoning. *Theory & Psychology, 8*(6), 841–860.

Stol, K.-J., Ralph, P., & Fitzgerald, B. (2016). Grounded theory in software engineering research: A critical review and guidelines. In *Proceedings of the 38th International Conference on Software Engineering* (pp. 120–131).

Strauss, A., & Corbin, J. (1990). *Basics of qualitative research*. Sage Publications.

Strauss, A. L. (1987). *Qualitative analysis for social scientists*. Cambridge University Press.

Urquhart, C. (2012). *Grounded theory for qualitative research: A practical guide*. Sage.

Wohlin, C., & Aurum, A. (2015). Towards a decision-making structure for selecting a research design in empirical software engineering. *Empirical Software Engineering, 20*, 1427–1455.

Wolfe, A. (1991). Mind, self, society, and computer: Artificial intelligence and the sociology of mind. *American Journal of Sociology, 96*(5), 1073–1096.

6 Literature Reviews

Abstract In this chapter, we will learn about the different types of literature reviews possible within and alongside a socio-technical grounded theory (STGT) study. First, we will address *why* a literature review is needed in a research project, listing some of its unique advantages in an STGT study. Next, we will learn about the two literature reviews—the *lean literature review* (LLR) and the *targeted literature review* (TLR)—performed in the basic and advanced stages of an STGT study respectively, including their coverage, purpose, timing, uses, and limitations. This will be followed by an overview of the *grounded theory literature review* (GTLR) as a full-scale review method using an emergent and iterative approach native to STGT that can be performed either as a standalone review study or conducted before or after an empirical STGT study. Next, we will briefly discuss other literature review methods popular in software engineering research including informal reviews and systematic reviews such as the *systematic literature review* (SLR) and *systematic mapping studies* (SMS). The chapter will conclude with a discussion of the potential interplay between STGT studies and systematic reviews, along with presenting a *Literature Review Selection Guide* to help researchers select the most appropriate literature review methods for their general review needs.

R. Hoda, *Qualitative Research with Socio-Technical Grounded Theory*,
https://doi.org/10.1007/978-3-031-60533-8_6

6.1 Why Literature Review?

The idea that literature is to be avoided or ignored in grounded theory studies has been called out as a misconception (Suddaby, 2006). There are many practical reasons why a literature review may be desirable or even required in a research project. A literature review is often expected in order to establish the state of research and the novelty of the proposed project, for example, as part of a research study proposal, a funding or grant application, or an application for ethics approval, and in peer-reviewed research papers. In addition to such practical reasons, there are some unique advantages of performing literature reviews in socio-technical grounded theory (STGT) studies.

■ **Improving theoretical sensitivity.** Theoretical sensitivity refers to "*the propensity of the researcher to develop theoretical codes, structures, relationships, and eventually theories*" (Hoda, 2022). However, qualitative research and theory development is typically not included as part of research training in most educational programs in socio-technical disciplines such as software engineering (SE). Most of the time, novice researchers come across the need to understand theories and theory development if their specific research project involves these components, e.g., when conducting a doctorate or Masters research project that includes theory development. An effective way to develop and hone theoretical sensitivity is to read theories and learn about theory development in domains where they are more common, e.g., sociology, psychology, nursing, and education, with the aim to improve theoretical sensitivity and prepare for theory development.

■ **Improving socio-technical sensitivity.** Socio-technical sensitivity refers to "*an affinity for exploring and understanding the intricacies of human interactions and socio-technical aspects of phenomena*" (Hoda, 2022). Socio-technical sensitivity can be improved by reading literature on socio-technical topics, e.g., empirical studies on socio-technical aspects. These need not be limited to grounded theory studies, and can cover various research methods. Furthermore, they need not be focused on the same phenomenon being studied in the STGT study. How to review literature related closely to the phenomenon being studied is discussed later in this chapter.

Proceedings of conferences and workshops dedicated to human–computer interaction (HCI) and computer-supported cooperative work (CSCW) and human and social aspects such as cooperative and human aspects of software engineering (CHASE) are good resources to build socio-technical sensitivity. A variety of socio-technical studies are also published regularly in the various tracks of the ACM/IEEE International Conference of Software Engineering (ICSE), Foundations of Software

Engineering (FSE), and International Conference on Agile Software Development (XP), and journals such as *IEEE Transactions on Software Engineering* (TSE), *Empirical Software Engineering* (EMSE), *ACM Transactions on Software Engineering and Methodology* (TOSEM), *Journal of Systems and Software* (JSS), and *Information and Software Technology* (IST).

■ **Gaining domain knowledge.** Domain knowledge refers to "*an understanding of the research domain*" (Hoda, 2022). For SE researchers, developing socio-technical sensitivity and domain knowledge can go hand in hand. In addition to research literature, SE researchers can also consult practitioner literature in the specific (sub)domain. In particular, fundamental practitioner texts will help establish fundamental knowledge along with familiarity with the related terminology and popular practitioner jargon. For example, a researcher studying a phenomenon in the area of cybersecurity can consult practitioner literature on cybersecurity. Domain knowledge can be particularly useful for data collection. A researcher well versed in the basic domain knowledge can engage in much more meaningful conversations with practitioners during interviews and be able to effectively extract relevant data from public sources.

STGT studies exploring socio-technical phenomena in other domains such as medicine or nursing will require additional understanding of the relevant domain. It is advisable to have a subject matter expert on the research team to provide the necessary depth of domain knowledge to navigate the unique domain under investigation.

■ **Refining or advancing the state of theory.** Experienced researchers often become well versed over time in the relevant domain knowledge, practitioner literature, and existing theories related to the study phenomenon. Where a number of studies and proposed theoretical models of a phenomenon already exist, an STGT study can still be performed by applying a fresh approach to investigating the phenomenon. Done carefully, such STGT studies can lead to refining or advancing the state of theory. However, this requires maturity in terms of keeping an open mind that relies solely on empirical evidence as opposed to existing models and theories. As such, it is an advanced practice and is not recommended for novice STGT researchers.

An example of this approach in practice is the *theory of becoming agile* (Hoda & Noble, 2017). The topic of agile adoption had been widely studied for well over a decade. I was aware of the general stance on the topic of agile adoptions in the field, primarily through some of the adoption models I had come across. A typical first reaction may be to steer clear of such a topic, but I strongly felt something was missing. The whole premise of teams "going agile" following a set of prescribed steps using a one-off adoption approach as described in literature seemed to stand in contrast to the much more organic process I had witnessed in the industry as

Table 6.1 Literature reviews (LLR and TLR) within STGT compared to the full GTLR method

	Lean literature review (LLR)	**Targeted literature review (TLR)**	**Grounded theory literature review (GTLR)**
Definition	A lightweight and high-level review performed early to motivate and guide the STGT study design	An in-depth review targeting key concepts and (sub)categories of the STGT study, performed periodically in the advanced stages	A full-scale review of literature using an emergent and iterative approach
Coverage	Broad and landscape view	Targeted and in-depth	Full and in-depth
Purpose	Mapping the research landscape, identifying key existing works, informing research design, becoming conversant in the domain	Situating STGT findings with closely related works, aligning with standard research terminology in the field	Performing a full, typically standalone, review study
Timing	During the basic stage in an STGT study	Periodically during the advanced stage of an STGT study	Typically standalone, or done before or after an STGT research study
Uses	In research/grant/ethics proposals. As part of introduction, motivation, and early related works in papers	As part of later related works and discussion sections	As a standalone report or paper, typically generating a research framework and agenda
Limitations	Limited coverage, use limited to motivating and guiding study design	Coverage limited to target topic, use limited to comparing study findings with related works	Rigour costs time and effort, limited replicability

a researcher. But I did not know exactly how it was different or what I would end up finding. I relied on empirical evidence to guide me towards explaining what is involved in the process of software teams adopting agile methods. The resulting theory was a marked departure from the prevalent models, describing agile transformation of software teams as a complex network of transitions across multiple dimensions. The main reason I managed not to end up confirming or replicating existing models was not because I was unaware of them but rather because I strongly believed they did not fully reflect the ground reality of the phenomenon.

6.2 Literature Reviews in Socio-Technical Grounded Theory

STGT includes two types of literature reviews: *lean literature review* (LLR) and *targeted literature review* (TLR) performed in the basic and advanced stages of the STGT study respectively (see Fig. 6.1).

- **Lean Literature Review (LLR)** is a light-weight and high-level literature review performed towards the beginning of the research to identify relevant theories and theoretical models existing in the topic area and potential research gaps in order to motivate the need for the STGT study.

- **Targeted Literature Review (TLR)** is an in-depth literature review performed periodically in the advanced stages of the research, targeting the key concepts and (sub)categories emerging from the STGT study, in order to compare and place them in the wider context and latest developments in the field.

The combined application of LLR and TLR in the basic and advanced stages of an STGT study respectively enables a level and amount of literature review necessary and valuable for an STGT study. They serve specific purposes and can also be used outside of an STGT study to supplement empirical studies conducted using other research methods, such as case studies, ethnography, and survey research. However, neither of them is a full-scale review. Researchers who wish to conduct a full-scale literature review using an emergent and iterative approach native to STGT can consider the *grounded theory literature review* (GTLR) method (Wolfswinkel et al., 2013) as applied in Pant et al. (2024).

- **Grounded theory literature review (GTLR)** is a full-scale literature review, using an emergent and iterative approach native to STGT, either performed as a standalone study or conducted before or after an empirical STGT study.

Table 6.1 presents an overview of these three literature review methods, and they are detailed next, along with their coverage, purpose, timing, uses, and limitations.

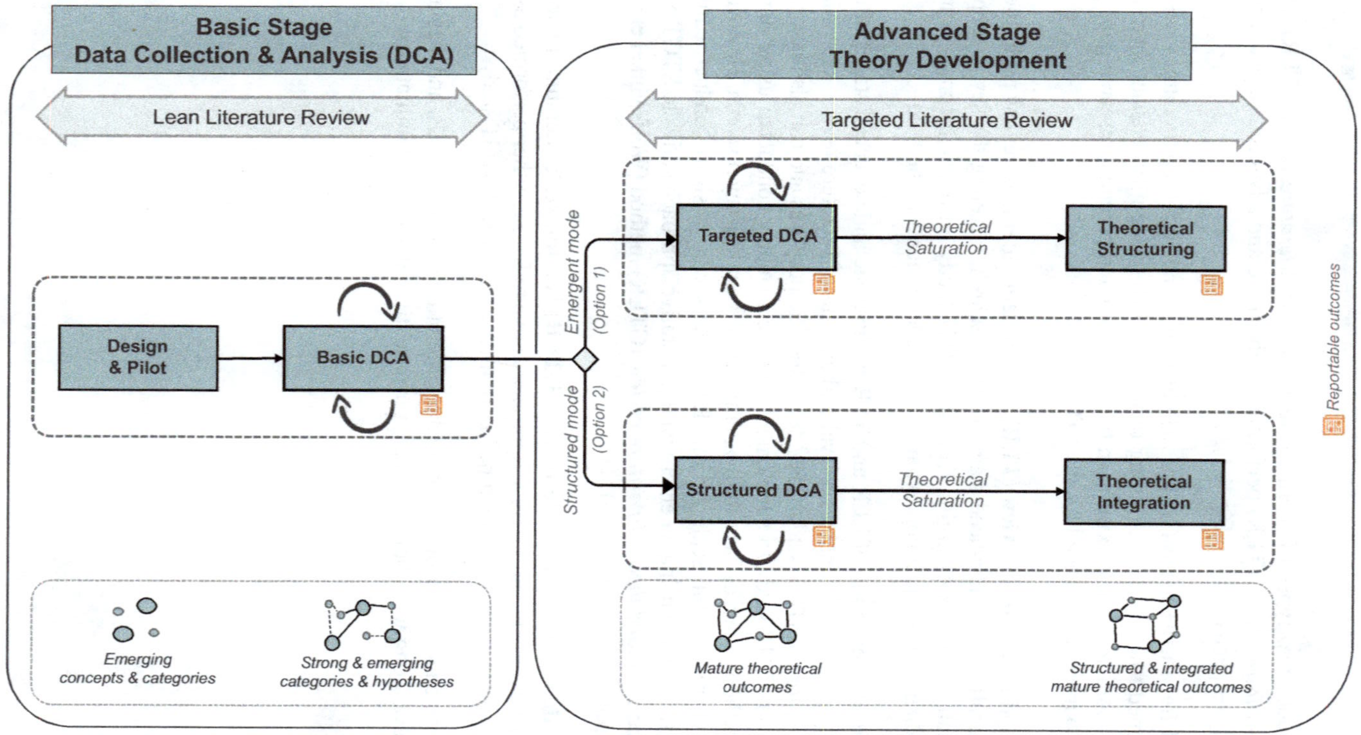

Fig. 6.1 Lean literature review (LLR) and targeted literature review (TLR) during the basic and advanced stages, respectively, of a socio-technical grounded theory study (adapted from Hoda, 2022)

6.2.1 Lean Literature Review

Definition

A lean literature review is a minimalist approach to conducting a review of the literature with the aim to scan and scope the research topic or area, depending on how much prior work exists. It is useful to provide an overview of the field and help identify the main research trends and gaps. As the term 'lean' suggests, an LLR is not meant to be extensive or exhaustive; rather, it is optimised to serve its key aims as quickly and easily as possible. It is conducted in the early, basic stage of the STGT research project, often preceding or interweaved with the formulation of research questions, instruments, tools, and approach, guiding research design. It also helps the researcher become conversant with the terminology in their research domain. Figure 6.1 visualises the LLR in the wider STGT study context.

Steps of an LLR

Conducting a lean literature review involves four steps: *scan for topic and shortlist, skim and select, read and analyse*, and *conclude and present*. The first two steps are iterated upon to finalise the list of papers to be read in-depth. The last two steps are conducted on the selected papers to achieve a high-level overview of the field. Figure 6.2 visualises these steps of an LLR.

Step 1. Scan for Topic and Shortlist

The LLR begins with conducting quick searches on online research databases and portals, such as *Google Scholar*, the *ACM digital library*, and *IEEE Xplore* for software engineering topics. Where the topic is interdisciplinary, e.g., *the use of code reviews in higher education*, other databases covering higher education research such as *ERIC* can also be consulted. Similarly, where particular journals are known to specialise in the same interdisciplinary area, e.g., *Computers & Education* and the *British Journal of Education Technology*, we can search for papers directly within those journals.

Different keywords derived from the research topic, or from research question(s) where applicable, and their combinations can be experimented with during scanning to improve the relevance of the search results. To maintain the intended lightweight nature of the review, the keywords are meant to be iteratively refined. For example, when conducting an LLR in an STGT study on the *role of the data scientists in software engineering teams*, a search string made up of keywords such as "*data scientist*", "*software engineering*", and "*team*" is a good starting point. However, it can also be broadened by adding other job titles and roles used for data scientists in

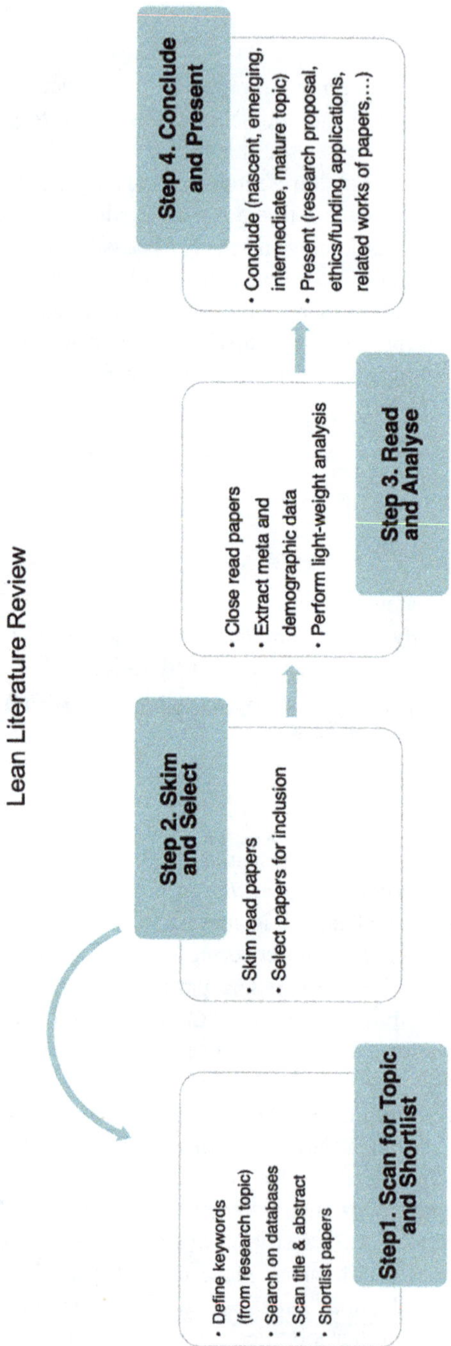

Fig. 6.2 Steps of Lean Literature Review (LLR)

some organisations such as "*data engineer*" or combinations of "*machine learning*" and "*artificial intelligence*" with "*engineer*".

The next step is to shortlist some papers from the search results to skim through. Most paper titles and abstracts provide a reasonable insight into the key focus or takeaway contributions of the paper. Some search results also list the keywords classified by the paper, which helps in judging its relevance. Inevitably we will have some criteria to judge for relevance. It is a good idea to make these explicit not only for our own reference but also for consistency of application, especially where a team of researchers is conducting the review, and process documentation for later reporting.

The criteria can be refined based on what we learn from scanning the topic landscape. For example, we may be interested only in empirical studies that report on evidence-based findings. However, it is highly recommended to search for pre-existing reviews on the topic. While finding a pre-existing review on the same topic may be a cause for disappointment when conducting a systematic review, it is a welcome discovery during an LLR! This is because an LLR is not a full, comprehensive, or in-depth review study aimed for standalone publication, rather it's main aim is to quickly ascertain the research landscape and guide the design of the STGT study. If an existing systematic review already does this reasonably well, it becomes a useful source of collective knowledge on the topic. Such a review paper can be selected for skimming and, most likely, a full read. Similarly, primary studies included in the review can also be scanned through for selection.

Another consideration for selection when scanning is the quality of the paper. This can be gauged to a large extent by looking at the publication venue and citation numbers with respect to publication date. This represents a lightweight approach to quality assessment, consistent with the lean nature of an LLR. The paper can then be selected for the next step, skim reading. Save the shortlisted papers. A link to the full paper is typically available to download as a PDF or view as an HTML page. With author preprints of papers accepted for publication and those under review becoming increasingly available on public portals such as Arxiv and ResearchGate, it is a good idea to download PDFs of these papers in case they become unavailable later for some reason.

Step 2. Skim and Select

Next, we skim read through the full content of the papers shortlisted in the previous step to better judge their relevance and quality. This involves re-reading the abstract, reading the main headings and sub-headings, the conclusion, and any other parts, e.g., key findings, figures, and tables. A second round of selection takes place at this stage as some papers are discarded after the skim reading. For example, we may realise after skim reading a paper on data scientists in software teams that it is to do with what skills are required for data scientists to function in software teams, whereas our study is mainly interested in the tools they use. So we may decide to remove this paper from our review backlog. However, in this example, it is also an indication that adding the keyword "tool" or "tools" would have been a better strategy in Step 1 if we wish to restrict our review to tools-based papers. We can return to the previous step and refine our search string in this case and continue to iterate through the process.

The papers that we keep selecting as relevant and interesting after skim reading can be saved, including a copy of the full paper and its bibliographic information. A dedicated research project drive can be used for this purpose, preferably online, to enable access for all researchers in the team. Going through the reference section of these papers and those citing them (backward and forward citations) can help select other relevant papers to potentially include in our review. However, we need to be careful not to turn the process into a comprehensive and systematic review approach! The lean nature of the review is meant to be maintained. For example, the temptation to fully read through the papers at this stage because they "*look interesting*" can be avoided as it can easily extend the review timeline.

Step 3. Read and Analyse

In this step, we read the selected papers fully and in-depth, also referred to as close reading. In line with the lean nature of the review, a lightweight analysis procedure can be applied. If we wish to report on the papers' *meta information* such as publication venue, year, author affiliation, or their *demographic information* such as the research topic, research questions, method applied, and explicitly listed limitations, recommendations, and future works, these can be extracted and collated as we read the papers. A data extraction sheet can be used for this purpose. There is no complex analysis involved for processing such information, except noting it down. Alternatively, if the LLR does not need to report on meta or demographic information, their explicit data extraction can be skipped.

The LLR focuses on analysing the key findings or takeaways of selected empirical papers and reviews as relevant to our STGT study topic. In case of empirical papers, also referred to as *primary studies*, these key takeaways can usually be found in the paper's *findings* (or *results*) and potentially the *discussion* sections. To analyse them, we can start by summarising the key takeaway points of each paper in our own words, ideally in no more than one or two short paragraphs per paper. Once this is done for all papers, the next step is to conduct analysis across the paper summaries by identifying all aspects that are common and those that are in contrast to each other. For example, we may identify that some papers (say, coded P1, P4, P9, and P11) all discuss the challenges faced by data scientists in software engineering teams, while some papers (say, coded P1, P2, P5, and P11) discuss strategies for successful integration of data scientists in software teams. Together, these are starting to tell a story about the challenges and strategies of integrating data scientists in software teams. Possible relationships between some of the challenges and the strategies may also become apparent. However, typically, we do not expect a substantial theoretical model or framework to be derived from an LLR given its lightweight nature. If a more robust GT analysis procedure such as open coding is desirable and the findings are expected to be published as a full review paper, the grounded theory literature review (GTLR) method (described later in this chapter) may be considered instead.

Similarly, the key findings of the selected review papers, also referred to as *secondary studies*, can be summarised in our own words and analysed. It is recommended to process the primary and secondary review papers separately in two groups, and not mix them. This is because primary studies report on concrete empirical evidence from a first-hand research study of practice, while secondary studies report on the review of a number of primary studies, typically presenting a high-level view across them and add a secondary level of interpretation to the primary studies.

It is also common to find papers during Steps 2 and 3 as we skim and close read them respectively that are interesting for other reasons. For example, some papers may include a exemplary research methodology section or include particularly well written recommendations for practice. We may wish to revisit such papers in our research project but they may not be directly relevant for inclusion in our LLR. Such papers can be saved in our wider collection of references for later reading during the STGT study.

In summary, a lean approach means selectively extracting the information we actually intend to use rather than aiming for comprehensive extraction of information for all possible uses. The selection of what information to extract is usually based on the nature of the report where the LLR findings are expected to be presented.

Step 4. Conclude and Present

Ideally, an LLR identifies and presents the main research trends and gaps and drafts some interesting research questions for future studies in the area, including for our planned STGT study, to address.

An LLR can result in identifying that our research topic of choice, or specific phenomenon, is very nascent in the research world and not much exists in terms of related works. This is a perfectly fine outcome of an LLR and can be reported as such. However, in the absence of research literature, the LLR can cover practitioner literature, also referred to as *grey literature*, to report on latest activities in that space. A similar process can be followed conducting an LLR with grey literature as described above for research literature. Overall, based on the LLR's finding that a topic is relatively under-researched, we can conclude that the research and practice communities will benefit from an original STGT study on the topic.

On the other hand, an LLR can result in identifying a number of relevant existing studies on the topic. Where a topic is particularly mature, a number of existing reviews may also be discovered. This does not necessarily spell doom for the research topic of our STGT study. Even where an LLR discovers that a phenomenon or topic has been extensively studied before, we can conclude that an STGT study on the same topic can still be viable and valuable if it's clear that the current state of research lacks a certain depth, breadth, or perspective that the STGT study is expected to provide. The STGT study topic can also be refined accordingly to focus on the most pertinent aspects where further depth, breadth, or perspective is required. A rare conclusion of an LLR is that there is really no room for an STGT study on the topic since everything worth saying about it has already been said. In this case, the planned STGT study can be revised to focus on a similar or completely different topic.

Whatever the conclusions, the findings of an LLR can be presented in various venues and formats, e.g., as part of a research proposal or ethics or funding application, or as part of a paper or presentation summarising preliminary findings or the overall study plans, such as a doctoral symposium paper. For most reports, such as research proposal and ethics or funding applications, meta information from the reviewed papers may not be of much use except perhaps for reporting the publication trends by highlighting the publication dates of the papers included in the review. Demographic information about the included papers, such as the research methods used, can help justify the use of a similar research method in our own study or motivate the need for a completely different approach not attempted by earlier studies.

Key information such as the main findings of the papers can help summarise what has been studied and reported so far and what is missing in terms of breadth and depth of coverage or the applied perspectives. When presenting the LLR findings in a written format, the findings can be structured to tell a story about what has been covered in the past and how our own study is expected to build on or diverge from it. Such reporting can incorporate primary studies, but also report on any relevant reviews found during the LLR.

Typically, the findings of an LLR are presented in sections that help set up the context of the research and motivate the need for the empirical study, e.g., *Introduction*, *Motivation*, *Background*, or an early *Related Works* section. An example of presenting the findings of an LLR can be seen in the *Introduction* and *Related Works* section of Dealing with Data Challenges when Delivering Data-Intensive Software Solutions (Graetsch et al., 2023). Here, the findings of the LLR are presented under two main themes, primary studies conducted in big tech organisations such as IBM and Microsoft and those conducted outside of these contexts. The section also summarises two primary studies conducted on data challenges and collaboration challenges respectively, in machine learning teams, using grounded theory. The paper uses the LLR findings to highlight its exploratory and socio-technical approach in contrast to the two studies that were heavily informed by extensive literature reviews.

Limitations of an LLR

A lean literature review is typically limited in scope and use.

- **Limited scope**. The first limitation is to do with the lean review's scope or extent of coverage. A lean literature review is not meant to be comprehensive or exhaustive. As a result, the results of the lean review do not represent the collective or complete related works in the research area. However, if conducted in the form of a systematic mapping study, the resulting findings can claim to offer better coverage.

- **Limited use**. The second limitation arises from the timing of the review. Since the research topic or question is generally rather broad to begin with, the results of an LLR done in the early stages will provide a broad overview. The studies identified and summarised in the early LLR may not be as directly relevant to the key concepts and categories that emerge later in the STGT study. For this reason, a targeted literature review (TLR) is performed in the later stages to identify, summarise, and compare related works directly relevant to the emerging categories, hypotheses, or theory.

An LLR may not be comprehensive in terms of its coverage of related works or in terms of reporting on all possible aspects of the included studies. However, it is an effective procedure within an STGT study, where the key focus is to gain a general understanding of the state of research, identify the major related works so as to delineate the planned STGT study from what has already been achieved before, and proceed with the actual empirical STGT study to generate theoretical outcomes.

6.2.2 Targeted Literature Review

Definition

A targeted literature review (TLR) is a focused approach to identifying the research studies most closely related to our STGT study findings. As the term "targeted" suggests, a TLR is focused on specific concepts, (sub)categories, and preliminary or mature theoretical outcome, depending on what is being reported. A TLR is performed periodically during the advanced stage of an STGT study, starting from when the key concepts and (sub)categories are seen to emerge to when they become strongly established and theory development is finished.

A TLR helps compare the findings of the STGT study with the findings of other closely related studies so we can demonstrate how they are distinct in some respects and potentially similar in others, and how our study contributes to the progress of the field. A TLR is a useful mechanism to firmly establish the originality and novelty of the STGT findings. While it is not meant to be exhaustive, a TLR tries to cover as many closely related works as possible. Figure 6.1 visualises the TLR in the overall STGT process.

A TLR can also help align our study and its findings with well-established terminology in the field so the research can be accessible as best and widely as possible. For example, in a study on the impact of personal characteristics of individuals on their propensity for teamwork in software projects, we may decide to use the term "*personality traits*" as a result of the TLR to replace our original term "*personal characteristics*" as the former is more well established within its originating discipline of psychology, and by association when used in interdisciplinary research contexts with software engineering. Such terminology alignment is best done after our main concepts and categories have emerged and the established terminology happens to be an accurate and suitable replacement for our own naming of those concepts and (sub)categories. It is best to be transparent about the renaming process to avoid suspicions about becoming unduly influenced by literature. To this end, we can share the original names and the revised terms post our TLR. Alignment to established terminology should not be forced as that defeats the empirical and inductive nature of STGT studies. Novice researchers can consult with their co-researchers and/or advisors to decide on the best course of action.

Steps of a TLR

Conducting a targeted literature review involves four steps: *scan for target and shortlist, skim and select, read and compare*, and *conclude and present*. The first two steps can be iterated upon to finalise the list of papers to be read in-depth. The last two steps are conducted on the selected papers to situate our own STGT findings, such as target concepts, (sub)categories, or theory, in the wider research landscape and demonstrate how they confirm, diverge from, or add to the collective knowledge. Figure 6.3 shows these steps of a TLR.

Step 1. Scan for Target and Shortlist

The TLR begins with selecting a target for the review. Depending on what is planned to be reported, the target can be a single concept or (sub)category, multiple concepts and (sub)categories, or a preliminary or mature theory. We may want to write up a key category, e.g., *skills of a data scientist*, that has become well established in the STGT study, as an independent research paper. In this case, it would make sense to perform a targeted literature review on that specific category, looking for related papers that cover the skills of a data scientist. The choice of the target in turn directs the choice of the keywords. For example, in this case, we can search for keywords such as "*skills*" and "*data scientist*", and synonyms such as "*data engineer*", "*capabilities*", "*qualities*", and so on. We can add "*software engineering*" if required to retrieve more relevant results. The choice of databases, as with the LLR, will be those most relevant to the domain. Google Scholar, the ACM digital library, and IEEE Xplore are typically useful for most research within software engineering.

Similarly, we may be looking to present an emerging or mature theory in a research paper, e.g., *the role of a data scientist in software engineering teams*. In this case, the TLR can focus on the theory as a whole. Where no other similar work exists, the TLR can focus on the theory's constituent parts, i.e., the key (sub)categories. In the example case, if no other paper has described *the role of the data scientist* as a whole, we can look for papers that may have covered key aspects such as their "*practices*", "*skills*", and "*onboarding experiences*", and the "*challenges*" they face. The choice of keywords to search for can be derived similarly, starting with an attempt to cover the whole theory and, where necessary, moving to set individual targets on its constituent parts.

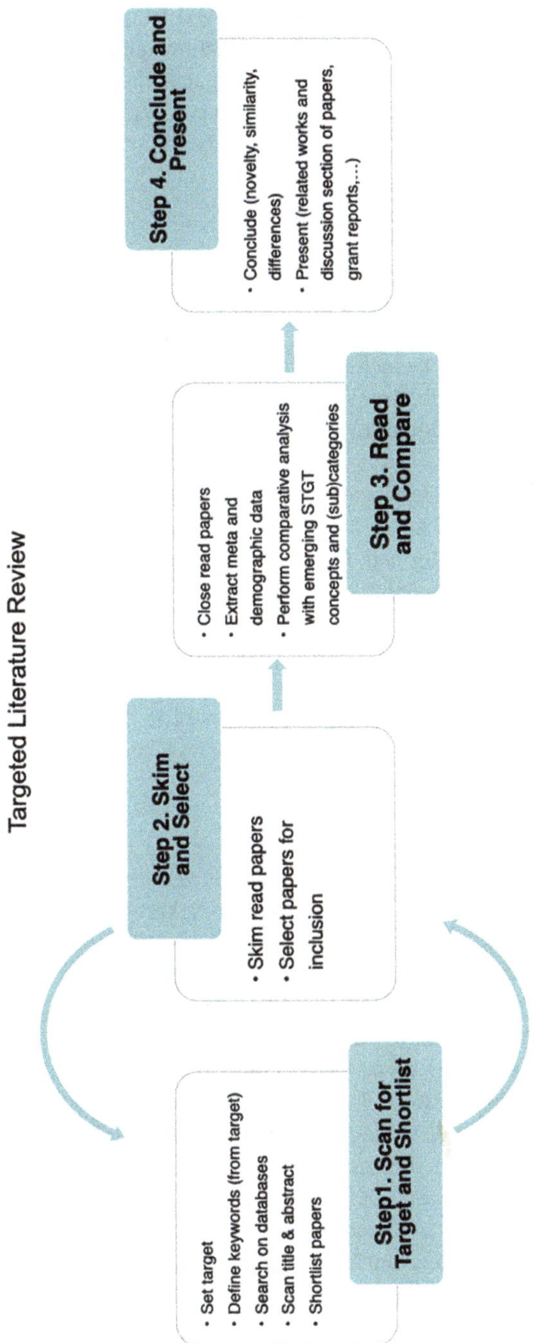

Fig. 6.3 Steps of Targeted Literature Review (TLR)

The next step is to shortlist some papers from the search results based on quick reading of their titles and abstracts. As with an LLR, these can include both empirical studies and the primary studies included in secondary reviews. Papers presenting theoretical concepts that have neither been derived from empirical evidence nor verified in practice generally do not provide the same value as those reporting empirical studies. However, in the absence of empirical studies for nascent topics, such papers can provide a useful point of reference and comparison. For example, we can show how empirical evidence from our STGT study compares to initial expectations proposed by theoretical papers.

Step 2. Skim and Select

The next step is to skim read the shortlisted papers and make final selections. For primary research papers, we can follow the same guidelines for selecting studies to include in our TLR as we did for the LLR. It is also fine to select existing literature reviews on our target topic to include in the TLR. Practically, this involves skim reading and selecting from the primary studies included in the review. It is ethical practice to reference the original review as the source of identifying the primary studies.

The *skim and select* step is arguably more straightforward in a TLR as the keywords are more clearly and finely defined at this stage as opposed to in the early phases when an LLR is performed. Copies of the selected papers can be saved for full reading and easy referencing in the next step.

Step 3. Read and Compare

This step involves reading the selected papers carefully and in-depth. The analysis approach in a TLR differs from that applied in an LLR. In a TLR, we analyse the selected papers with the aim to compare and contrast their findings to our STGT findings.

Step 4. Conclude and Present

A TLR helps draw conclusions about the state of research on the target topic and explains how the STGT findings compare to existing knowledge.

The results of a TLR can be presented in the *Discussion* or *Related Works* sections, towards the end of the paper. The main aim is to show how our study findings may be validating or contradicting existing knowledge, and, more importantly, how our study advances the state of research on that topic. The findings of a TLR can be presented in many interesting ways. For example, it can be presented in the form of a matrix or table, listing individual characteristics of the included studies and our own STGT study findings. Venn diagrams and other creative forms of visualisations can also be used, accompanied by appropriate text narrative. Where constrained by space, we can present a succinct bullet point list of the key differences and distinguishing points of our study. An example of this can be found in the "Discussion of Findings in the Context of Relevant Literature" section presented towards the end of the paper Dealing with Data Challenges when Delivering Data-Intensive Software Solutions (Graetsch et al., 2023).

Limitations of a TLR

A targeted literature review is typically limited in scope and use.

- **Limited scope**. While a TLR attempts to cover as many relevant papers related to the target topic as possible with a light approach, it is not expected to be as comprehensive as a systematic review.

- **Limited use**. Depending on the breadth of coverage and depth of analysis, a TLR can be reported as a standalone paper. However, this may not be required or desirable. The main function of a TLR is to help situate our STGT study findings in the wider research field. As such, summarising the TLR findings within a paper that presents the findings of the associated STGT study is ideal.

6.2.3 Grounded Theory Literature Review

DEFINITION

Grounded theory literature review (GTLR) is a rigorous review to present multi-dimensional findings and develop theoretical foundations for niche and emerging topics (Pant et al., 2024). With its inductive, iterative, and responsive approach, GTLR stands in contrast to the top-down, sequential, and specification-driven approach of systematic literature reviews and mapping studies. First introduced as a framework in Wolfswinkel et al. (2013), the GTLR method has been described in-depth and applied with a socio-technical approach in Pant et al. (2024).

Researchers aiming to perform a full-scale literature review using an iterative and emergent approach and publishing the findings as a standalone paper can consider performing a GTLR. A distinguishing feature of the GTLR is its emergent, iterative, and responsive approach native to traditional GT and STGT studies. A distinguishing feature of the GTLR approach is that it enables "*theory-based or concept-centric yet accurate review*" (Wolfswinkel et al., 2013). A GTLR study can not only present empirical findings but also emerging theoretical models, frameworks, insights, and research agendas, derived from applying STGT's advanced theory development procedures. An example of conducting a GTLR using STGT's data analysis can be found in Pant et al. (2024).

A GTLR is particularly suited to exploring nascent and cutting-edge topics because of its emergent approach, e.g., *the role of ethics in artificial intelligence*. Usually, it is nearly impossible to conduct a systematic review on such topics as there are not enough related works to include in the review. However, a GTLR can be employed in such cases, where its iterative approach provides flexibility in identifying related works from within the same domain and progressively refining the review protocols to accommodate related works from other domains or other credible sources of information. These can include experience reports, practitioner books and articles, industry white papers, thought pieces, and heterogeneous data from audio and video formats that are steering the new and emerging topic.

A GTLR is also suited to interdisciplinary topics because of its iterative and flexible nature. When working across multiple disciplines, especially those outside our comfort zones, we benefit from using an iterative process that is flexible and open to refinement.

Due to its methodological and philosophical alignment, a GTLR is well suited to accompany an STGT study. For example, a GTLR study can be conducted as a precursor to an empirical STGT study where the findings from the GTLR can be used to motivate the need for and narrow down on a topic for the STGT study. Similarly, a GTLR study can be conducted post an STGT study to describe how the findings of the empirical STGT study are situated in relation to related works.

Steps of a GTLR

Wolfswinkel et al. (2013) describe a framework of the GTLR with five steps: *define*, *search*, *select*, *analyse*, and *present*. The process is meant to be iterative. An overview is provided below. Further details can be found in Pant et al. (2024).

- **Define**. This step involves formulating the initial review protocol: determining the review scope, defining inclusion and exclusion criteria, and finalising the search items, databases, and search strings. A common inclusion criterion is that the studies be empirically based on primary sources of data, e.g., interviews or survey papers, so data analysis on the empirical evidence can be performed. Finalising the search string is a process that involves evolution and refinement until relevant results can be obtained. Because GTLRs are often performed in niche or nascent topics, it is common for the review protocol to be broadened by including more databases and search items (e.g., including papers on ArXiv), expanding the inclusion criteria, and relying on snowballing in the later iterations. The guidelines strongly recommend the use of a chronological logbook to record the process, especially given the possibilities of refinement, to maintain a chain of evidence around the process followed.

- **Search**. Having defined the basics, the second step involves conducting the search on the identified sources and databases. The previous *Define* step may need to be revisited here in light of the search results. As with the other steps, document the search terms, sources, and results.

- **Select**. As with most reviews, the selection step involves removing duplicates and filtering based on the titles and abstracts first, and then on full texts. This is followed by checking forward and backward references. The whole process is meant to be repeated until no new relevant papers are found. This ensures a comprehensive coverage. Oftentimes, starting with a set of *seed* papers known to the research team and following up with snowballing can be also efficient and effective. This is akin to starting an STGT empirical study with convenience sampling and moving into theoretical sampling to gather more data.

- **Analyse**. This step involves applying the data analysis procedures of open coding, constant comparison, and memoing in the basic stage and one of the two modes of theory development in the advanced stage.

- **Present**. In this last step, the findings of the review and associated insights are presented. For example, Pant et al. (2024) present a taxonomy of ethics in AI from practitioners' viewpoints that captures the key concerns of AI practitioners when considering ethics in AI, namely practitioner awareness, perception, need, challenge, and approach.

On the surface, these steps closely resemble the steps of other reviews such as a systematic literature review (Kitchenham, 2004). However, the key difference is the iterative, emergent, and responsive nature of the GTLR approach. For example, instead of finalising the full list of papers to review upfront, a GTLR runs through iterative rounds of *define*, *search*, and *select* steps to progressively identify and include related works in the review. Another key difference is the opportunity to develop theoretical models or theories, which is limited in the case of other forms of reviews. Through deeper analysis of the underlying empirical evidence, a GTLR study is also well positioned to produce recommendations and guidelines for the industry and research communities. These aspects can be seen implemented in Pant et al. (2024).

Limitations of a GTLR

There are two key limitations of the GTLR review method.

- **Rigour costs.** A well-performed GTLR is likely to be time-consuming and tedious. Having said that, other forms of full review methods such as systematic literature reviews (SLR) and mapping studies (SMS) have been acknowledged to be similarly time-intensive and tedious. There seems to be a trend these days to conduct an extensive literature review as a standalone research project or as a first step of an empirical study. This may be driven in part by the large number of citations some of these review papers tend to gather over time. However, given how elaborate it is to undertake a full review, irrespective of the method employed, carefully consider the need for a full review before diving into one. For example, a lean literature review (LLR) can be a lighter alternative, especially as a precursor to an empirical study. Consult the *Literature Review Method Selection Guide* (Fig. 6.4) to assist in this consideration.

- **Replication vs theory development**. The GTLR method recommends using a logbook to record the process of the review, including key decisions, considerations, reconsiderations, and refinements. This enables the review process to be potentially replicated if needed. In an SLR or SMS, the upfront design is meant to be more detailed and strictly specified and therefore these studies are likely easier to replicate, both in terms of the process and the results. While the logbook provides a good source of revisiting the GTLR steps, the inherent flexibility and emergent nature of those steps means it is likely not as straightforward to replicate the study and especially its results. However, similar to an STGT study, the argument for replicating an existing GTLR study is contentious given the focus on theory development instead of testing or validation through replication. What is more practical and desirable for future work is to *extend* the GTLR study from where it finished, both empirically and theoretically.

6.3 Other Literature Reviews

We now consider other forms of literature reviews and their potential role in or interplay with an STGT study.

6.3.1 Informal Review

Definition

An informal review refers to an approach to searching for literature on popular search engines or databases that does not follow a defined process or protocol.

If you wish to conduct a review for personal or other non-academic reasons such as writing a blog or an online article, performing an informal review may not only suffice but also be an effective return on the time invested. Other formal types of reviews, on the other hand, carry varying levels of process overhead which may outweigh the associated benefits depending on the intended use. An informal review can vary in scope, from being minimalist to comprehensive, based on how much literature is covered. It can cover research, practitioner, or both types of literature.

There is little motivation to conduct an informal review in an STGT study. The two review methods—lean literature review (LLR) and targeted literature review (TLR)—provide the necessary mechanisms to cover related works at different stages of an STGT study. Compared to an informal review, the LLR and TLR are well defined, more systematic, and can be documented for explanation and replication of process.

6.3.2 Systematic Reviews

Definition

Systematic reviews, such as the *systematic literature review* (SLR), *systematic mapping study* (SMS), and *tertiary review* (an SLR of SLRs) (Kitchenham, 2004), are some of the most structured and comprehensive approaches to conducting formal literature reviews.

Systematic reviews are popular in software engineering, e.g., Beecham et al. (2008), Salleh et al. (2010), Hoda et al. (2018), and Hidellaarachchi et al. (2021). However, the possibility of performing an SLR with or alongside an STGT study needs to be considered carefully. Systematic reviews are research studies in their own right and typically span a reasonably substantial time period. For example, it is not uncommon for a novice researcher to spend the better part of a year performing and reporting on a systematic review. Similarly, the smallest of STGT studies can take around six months for a single researcher to complete. If the aim is to conduct both a systematic review and an STGT study within a larger project, carefully consider the scope and size of the overall study as it will demand time and typically multiple team members to successfully complete within a reasonable time frame.

A second, and arguably more important, concern is to do with the likely conflict between the fundamental premises, principles, and approaches of these two methods. Systematic reviews are primarily based on a positivist research approach whereby they aim to achieve completeness, replicability of process, and reproducibility of the results. STGT studies, on the other hand, can be conducted using different paradigms such as constructivism or pragmatism (refer to Chap. 5 Research Philosophy). If the overall study design aims to include both a systematic review and an STGT study, it is the researcher's responsibility to be aware of and actively manage the interplay, and possible conflict, between the inherent positivist approach of their systematic review and the research paradigm applied to their STGT study. Similarly, researchers may struggle to reconcile the sequential, top-down, specification-heavy approach native to systematic reviews with the emergent, iterative, and responsive approach native to an STGT study.

Finally, researchers will need to explain the interplay between the findings from the systematic review and those from the STGT study. For example, STGT researchers applying a positivist stance, will need to explain how they avoided being biased by the findings of the systematic review. Where applying a constructivist stance, researchers will need to explain how the findings of the systematic review informed or influenced the construction of the theoretical outcomes.

Another approach would be to conduct a full literature review post an STGT study in order to compare the original empirical findings from the STGT study to the state of research established from the review. However, this objective is already met with the targeted literature review (TLR) in STGT's advanced stage.

For these reasons, novice researchers are not recommended to attempt systematic reviews with an STGT study. However, a team of researchers, with one or more experts, experimenting with such combined approaches is not ruled out. In general, those interested in performing a full-scale literature review in combination with an STGT study can consider a GTLR due to the inherent synergies between these two methods.

6.4 Literature Review Selection Guide

As seen above, there are a variety of literature review methods that can be considered for general review needs. Figure 6.4 presents a guide on selecting from six different approaches to literature reviews: *informal review*, *systematic literature review* (SLR), *systematic mapping study* (SMS), *lean literature review* (LLR), *targeted literature review* (TLR), and *grounded theory literature review* (GTLR). These literature reviews vary in their coverage, level of formality, and objectives. Depending on the purpose, different review methods can be employed.

SLR and SMS are popular in SE research for conducting comprehensive and reproducible standalone reviews (Kitchenham, 2004) on established and easily searchable topics. As a full-scale and rigorous review method, GTLR provides opportunities to present multidimensional findings and develop theoretical foundations in niche and emerging topics (Pant et al., 2024).

While LLR and TLR are directly associated with STGT studies, they can also be employed outside of an STGT study in other empirical studies such as case studies, ethnography, and survey research. If the purpose is internal use within the research study to identify and report the research gaps, help design the research instruments, or to include in a preliminary paper or research/ethics/grant proposal, the lightweight LLR approach can be used. Typically, an LLR analysis is presented in context-setting sections such as in the *Introduction*, *Motivation*, *Background*, or an early *Related Works* section in a research paper reporting on all or part of the study findings. If the purpose is to compare the findings of our own empirical study with those of others in the field, a TLR can be used. Typically, a TLR analysis is presented in a *Discussion* or later *Related Works* section in a research paper reporting the findings of the empirical study.

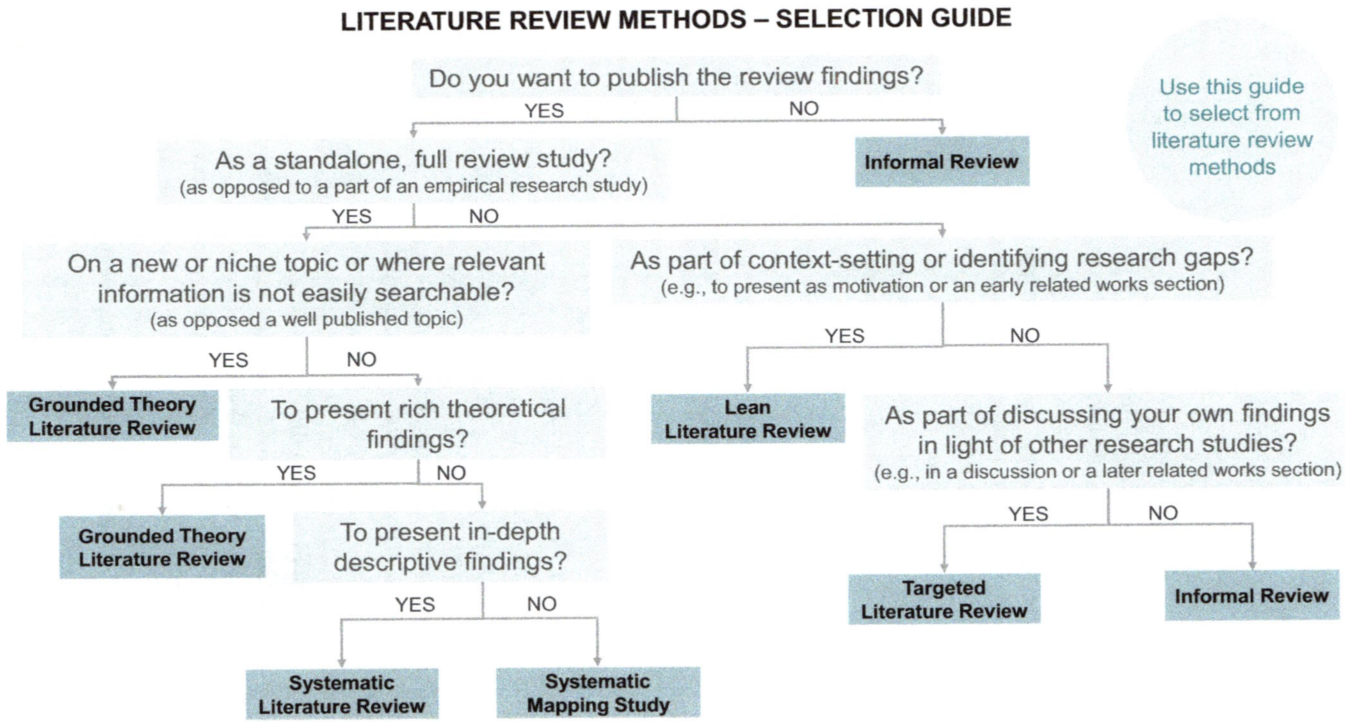

Fig. 6.4 Literature Review Method Selection Guide. Publish refers to presenting the review process and findings as part of a publicly available resource such as a technical report or peer-reviewed publication, e.g., thesis, journal, conference, or workshop paper.

6.5 Summary

In this chapter, we learned about the *benefits* of performing literature reviews within an STGT study. Next, we learned about the two types of literature reviews, *lean literature review* (LLR) and *targeted literature review* (TLR), performed in the basic and advanced stages, respectively, of an STGT study. We also learned about the *grounded theory literature review* (GTLR), a full-scale literature review method applied using an emergent, iterative, and responsive approach, for those wishing to conduct a full-scale review using STGT procedures or in combination with an STGT empirical study. Then, we learned about the possible interplay between an STGT study and other types of literature reviews popular in software engineering, such as *systematic literature review* (SLR) and *systematic mapping studies* (SMS). Finally, we learned how to select from the available options of review methods in general, using the *Literature Review Selection Guide*.

References

Beecham, S., Baddoo, N., Hall, T., Robinson, H., & Sharp, H. (2008). Motivation in software engineering: A systematic literature review. *Information and Software Technology, 50*(9–10), 860–878.

Graetsch, U. M., Khalajzadeh, H., Shahin, M., Hoda, R., & Grundy, J. (2023). Dealing with data challenges when delivering data-intensive software solutions. *IEEE Transactions on Software Engineering, 49*, 4349–4370 . https://doi.org/10.1109/TSE.2023.3291003

Hidellaarachchi, D., Grundy, J., Hoda, R., & Madampe, K. (2021). The effects of human aspects on the requirements engineering process: A systematic literature review. *IEEE Transactions on Software Engineering, 48*(6), 2105–2127.

Hoda, R. (2022). Socio-technical grounded theory for software engineering. *IEEE Transactions on Software Engineering, 48*(10), 3808–3832.

Hoda, R., & Noble, J. (2017). Becoming agile: a grounded theory of agile transitions in practice. In *2017 IEEE/ACM 39th International Conference on Software Engineering (ICSE)* (pp. 141–151). IEEE.

Hoda, R., Salleh, N., & Grundy, J. (2018). The rise and evolution of agile software development. *IEEE Software, 35*(5), 58–63.

Kitchenham, B. (2004). Procedures for performing systematic reviews. *Keele, UK, Keele University, 33*(2004), 1–26.

Pant, A., Hoda, R., Tantithamthavorn, C., & Turhan, B. (2024). Ethics in AI through the developer's view: A grounded theory literature review and guidelines. *Empirical Software Engineering, 29*, 67.

Salleh, N., Mendes, E., & Grundy, J. (2010). Empirical studies of pair programming for CS/SE teaching in higher education: A systematic literature review. *IEEE Transactions on Software Engineering, 37*(4), 509–525.

Suddaby, R. (2006). From the editors: What grounded theory is not. *Academy of Management Journal, 49*(4), 633–642.

Wolfswinkel, J. F., Furtmueller, E., & Wilderom, C. P. (2013). Using grounded theory as a method for rigorously reviewing literature. *European Journal of Information Systems, 22*(1), 45–55.

PART III

Qualitative Data Collection and Analysis

7 Basics of Qualitative Data Collection

Abstract Qualitative data is the main currency of the trade in a socio-technical grounded theory (STGT) study and in qualitative research in general. The quality of a STGT study depends first and foremost on the quality of the data collected. In this chapter, we will learn about popular *sampling techniques* such as convenience, snowball, random, representative, and theoretical sampling. Then we will learn some *tips for data collection*, including tips for effective sampling, recruitment, and engagement. Finally, we will learn about several aspects of *dealing with data* such as data ethics, data sharing, data quality using *data quality evaluation guidelines*, data usage, and data quantity including theoretical saturation. Researchers will benefit from reading this chapter in conjunction with the *Techniques of Qualitative Data Collection*, *Qualitative Data Preparation and Filtering*, and *Socio-technical Grounded Theory for Qualitative Data Analysis* chapters. Collectively, they cover socio-technical grounded theory's basic stage.

R. Hoda, *Qualitative Research with Socio-Technical Grounded Theory*,
https://doi.org/10.1007/978-3-031-60533-8_7

Fig. 7.1 Iterative steps of data sampling, collection, preparation, filtering, and analysis

7.1 Iterative Data Collection and Analysis

A distinguishing feature of socio-technical grounded theory (STGT), similar to traditional GT methods, is that it follows iterative steps of data collection and analysis instead of following a sequential approach where all data is first collected and then analysed. An iterative approach implies that small amounts of data are collected and analysed, and the emerging findings are closely inspected to assess for richness and potential gaps. This knowledge is then used to guide the next iteration, deciding what data to collect next and from which sources, also known as *theoretical sampling* explained later in this chapter. The iteration consists of five steps, data sampling, data collection, data preparation, data filtering, and data analysis, collectively referred to as data collection and analysis. Figure 7.1 shows these steps. The circular flow depicts their iterative nature. This chapter covers the steps of data sampling and data collection, focusing on the basics concepts while the techniques of data collection are covered in Chap. 8. The steps of data preparation and filtering are covered in Chap. 9 Qualitative Data Preparation and Filtering, and data analysis is covered in Chap. 10 Socio-Technical Grounded Theory for Qualitative Data Analysis.

7.1.1 Working in Batches

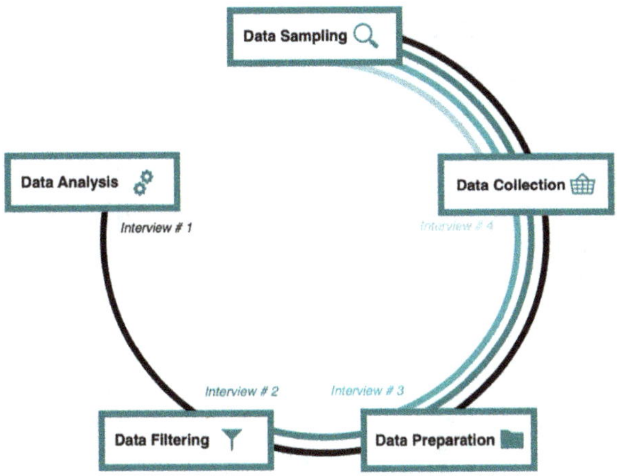

Fig. 7.2 Staggered approach to data sampling, collection, preparation, filtering, and analysis for data units within the same batch

A practical way in which the iterative nature of data collection and analysis can play out in an STGT study is to collect and analyse data in batches. For example, after the initial two or three pilot interviews are done, we can process a batch of five or six interviews before we proceed with the next batch. Novice researchers are recommended to start with smaller batch sizes, such as three or four data units at a time. With experience, as many as ten data units can be included in a batch.

A batch-based approach does not mean that each step needs to be executed completely for all data units in the same batch before the next can commence. For example, we do not have to complete data preparation for all the interviews in a batch before proceeding to filter all of them, followed by analysing all of them. Instead, we can use a *staggered approach* within the same batch. While one step is being executed for a data unit, another can commence for a different data unit. For example, while we are conducting interview #4, the first interview (interview #1) may have been fully prepared, filtered, and analysed, while the second interview (interview #2) may be in the process of being filtered, and the third (interview #3) may have been prepared for analysis. This staggered approach is represented diagrammatically in Fig. 7.2.

A key condition is that processing new iteration with a new batch of data may not commence until all data units from the previous batch have been fully collected, prepared, filtered, and analysed. This is important for theoretical sampling to work effectively. Figure 7.3 shows batch-based iterative rounds of data processing, where a new iteration begins with a new batch once the previous batch of data has been processed.

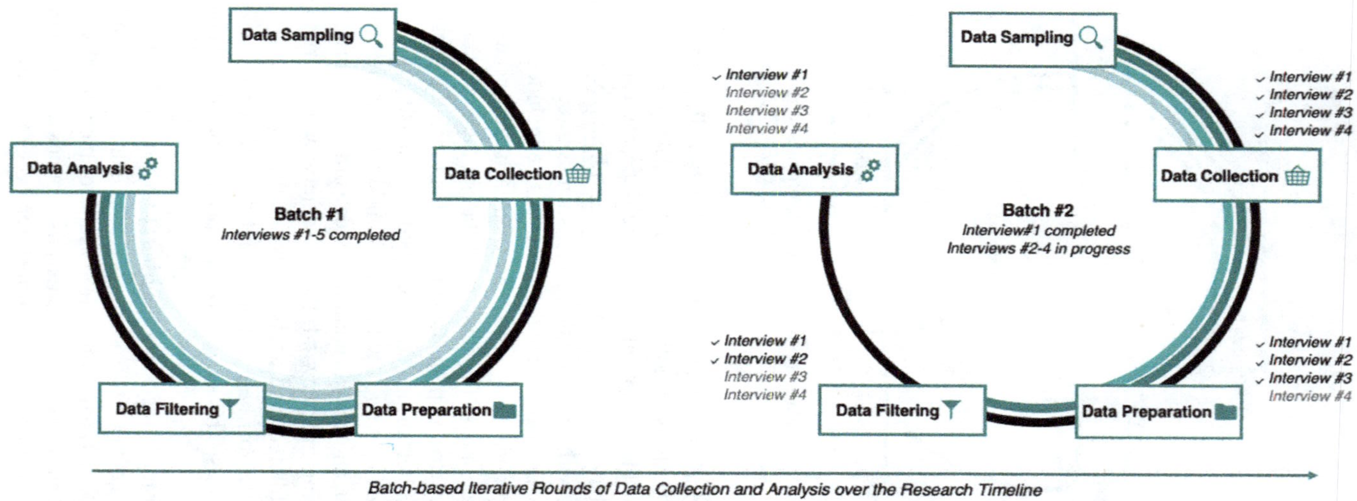

Fig. 7.3 Batch-based iterative rounds of data collection and analysis over the research timeline. A new batch starts once all steps are complete for the previous batch

7.1.2 Estimating Batch Sizes

How can we estimate batch sizes for different data sources? We can use the estimates for interview-based data as a benchmark. Consider that a single interview lasting around 30 to 40 minutes on an average is likely to produce 8 to 10 A4-sized pages in Calibri font size 11. We can use this as a benchmark for estimating batch sizes for other types of data. For example, let us consider Twitter (now called X) posts as the main data source, with the previous limit of 280 characters per post as a data unit. One A4 page will fit around six tweets with enough gaps for ease of reading. To reach a similar amount of data as contained in a single interview, we need 6 to 7 such pages, which is around 40 tweets. To reach a similar amount of data as contained in batch of 5 interviews, we need 5 such sets, which is around 200 tweets (40 tweets X 5 sets). So, 200 tweets can be considered a reasonable batch size for Twitter posts. Similar calculations can be applied to estimate batch sizes for data originating from other sources such as observation notes, focus groups, audio and video recordings, and documentation. These are no hard and fast numbers, rather estimates based on practical application.

7.2 Sampling Techniques

Definition

Sampling is the process of identifying and selecting the most appropriate data types, data sources, and collection techniques in a research project.

The research team aims to capture a *sample* from the wider selection of data sources that is relevant to the research topic and domain. To start data collection in an STGT research project, we can select from a range of sampling techniques, e.g. *convenience*, *snowball*, *random*, or *representative* sampling, based on the project context and data needs. Later on, once some concepts, (sub)categories, and relationships start to emerge, it is driven by *theoretical sampling* (Charmaz, 2006; Morse, 2010). Sampling techniques most relevant to STGT studies are described below, especially in terms of how they apply in an STGT study, followed by some tips for effective sampling.

7.2.1 Convenience Sampling

Definition

Convenience sampling involves identifying new data sources relevant to the project based on their ease of identification, recruitment, access, engagement, and data collection.

Convenience sampling involves selecting relevant data sources that are easily available to the research team. Ease of access can include considerations of leveraging existing professional relationships, networks, memberships, and subscriptions to relevant member forums, platforms, and tools, approaching local practitioners, collecting existing data, and conducting virtual data collection as opposed to travelling or commuting for face-to-face data collection.

The first part of a STGT study includes conducting a pilot study. The pilot study serves to evaluate the appropriateness and effectiveness of research design and protocols. Convenience sampling can be good approach to conducting the pilot study. It can ensure a fast and smooth start to the project. The data collected in the pilot can be included in the overall project. For more details, see Chap. 4 Research Design Canvas.

7.2.2 Snowball Sampling

Definition

Snowball Sampling is the process of identifying new data sources relevant to the research project through the recommendations from existing data sources.

Snowball sampling is another popular sampling technique that suits STGT studies. Applying snowball sampling can be as simple as asking the current participants about their recommendations for who, among their colleagues or professional acquaintances, may be a good fit to recruit for research participation. Snowball sampling can be a surprisingly effective tool for recruitment and data selection. In some cases, references from one participant can lead to recruitment of a whole team of software developers. In terms of data from publicly available sources, such as blog articles or talks recorded as YouTube videos, snowball sampling can take the form of selecting future data sources based on the references used or recommendations of related content.

7.2.3 Random Sampling

Definition

Random Sampling is the process of identifying new data sources relevant to the research project in a way that ensures random selection from a wider pool of possible sources.

Random sampling aims to capture the idea of selecting data sources at random, with the same probability of selecting one source as the other, within the pool. Random sampling is commonly applied in quantitative research, typically with a positivist approach, to achieve randomness as a means to avoid selection biases and demonstrate wider generalisability. In this sense, random sampling can be seen to contrast with purposeful sampling where sources are carefully curated and selected based on *convenience* and/or recommendations (*snowball* sampling). Most data custom collected from people are likely to be purposeful. These make up a majority of data sources in contemporary qualitative studies. However, there is room for random sampling in STGT studies. Where using publicly available data from a relatively large pool of relevant datasets, random sampling can be applied to select individual datasets to include in the study. This can be done to avoid specific biases. For example, a research team, instead of collecting data from their own repositories exclusively, may wish to select a handful of open-source software repositories for data collection and analysis at random. These can be selected from within a large pool of repositories identified as relevant to the research aims in order to demonstrate their unbiased approach to data selection and generalisability of their results beyond their native contexts.

7.2.4 Representative Sampling

Definition

Representative Sampling is the process of identifying new data sources relevant to the research project in a way that ensures they demonstrate characteristics that are typical of the wider pool.

Representative sampling goes a step beyond ensuring the data sources' relevance to the research project. It aims to capture a small-scale model or miniature version of the wider relevant domain and actors within the study. A key aim of representative sampling is to demonstrate generalisability of the findings from the sample to the wider pool. There are tools[1] available to calculate sample sizes that can be considered representative. However, these can only recommend the amount of data required. The type or characteristics of the data required for a source to be considered representative still need to be ascertained. To achieve representative sampling in a qualitative STGT study, it is important to define the characteristics of the domain and actors being studied at as fine-grained level as possible. To do this, the research team may consider questions such as: *What is it that makes the research domain and actors unique? What are the characteristics that define them?* Once this is clearly understood and defined, it can be used as a basis for selection of data sources that can be considered typical of the wider domain and actors based on the characteristics they share. For example, a study on the phenomenon of "*senior software developers maintaining relevance in the fast evolving technology sector*" may consider key characteristics such as age and length of work experience as selection criteria in addition to employment as a software developer to build a representative sample.

7.2.5 Theoretical Sampling

DEFINITION

Theoretical sampling is the ongoing process of assessing the emerging codes, concepts, (sub)categories, and hypotheses and identifying new sources for data collection in the upcoming iterations that are likely to help identify, develop, and saturate the emerging findings while filling any theoretical gaps (Hoda, 2022).

Theoretical sampling focuses on identifying new data sources based on an ongoing assessment of the emerging findings and theoretical outcomes. By definition, theoretical sampling requires some findings to emerge in the study before it can be applied. As described above, a range of sampling techniques can be applied to begin data collection in an STGT research project.

Once more key concepts and (sub)categories start to emerge, the research team can switch to applying theoretical sampling. For example, when studying self-organising roles on agile teams, we identified six roles played in agile software teams that help with self-organisation (Hoda et al., 2010). Applying theoretical sampling in this case meant we assessed the emerging findings for weaknesses and theoretical gaps. The assessment led to the realisation that key concepts and categories captured these roles as they manifested when the team was relatively new to adopting and practicing agile methods and led to the following question: *What happens to these self-organising roles as the team matures in agile practice?* Based on this, the research team decided

[1] https://www.qualtrics.com/blog/calculating-sample-size/

to collect more data from mature agile teams and managed to capture richer and more saturated definition of these roles (Hoda et al., 2012).

Theoretical sampling includes regular grooming and refinement of the research protocols such as refining the interview questions or keywords for data mining to narrow down and focus on the emerging findings. Thereby, it is also instrumental in achieving theoretical saturation, described later in this chapter.

7.3 Tips for Data Collection

7.3.1 Tips for Effective Sampling

TIPS

Tips for Effective Sampling:

- Keep it purposeful
- Keep it ongoing
- Use multiple and combined sampling techniques
- Aim for rounded perspectives
- Manage potential biases

Keep It Purposeful

The research team aims to collect data that is fit for the purpose of the research. On a high level, this involves assessing the relevance of the data to the research topic, domain, and the specific phenomenon being investigated and the ability of the data to address the research questions. On a granular level, this involves selecting data, sources, and collection techniques based on specific characteristics, also known as *purposive sampling*. Most, if not all, sampling in qualitative research is considered purposive sampling (Patton, 1990; Sandelowski, 1995). This extends to considering theoretical sampling as complex and purposeful (Coyne, 1997), where specific data, source, and technique are selected for the specific purpose of identifying, developing, and saturating emerging theoretical structures and filling any theoretical gaps.

Keep It Ongoing

A key feature of sampling in an STGT project is that it is meant to be *ongoing*, figuring out what data (type) to collect next, from where (source), and how (collection techniques). Data types, sources, and techniques are not meant to be pre-determined all at once, at the beginning of the research project. Instead, sampling in STGT follows an *inspect and adapt* approach, assessing the current state of research findings and identifying new data types and sources to help develop the findings further in each iteration.

Use Multiple and Combined Sampling Techniques

The boundaries between different sampling techniques often blur in practice (Morse, 2010), and they can be combined where applicable. For example, applying theoretical sampling, we may ask what new data do we need to add density and dimension to the emerging findings and where can we find it? If the data is easily accessible, it can be considered *convenience-based* theoretical sampling. If the data is selected based on the recommendations of existing participants, it can be considered *snowball-based* theoretical sampling. In the latter case, the criteria for theoretical sampling can be shared when requesting recommendations. For example, if the research team has identified a weakness or gap in their emerging findings about how third-party suppliers contribute to the project, they can ask about third-party suppliers in particular and request an introduction. Finding third-party suppliers directly may be challenging without combining a snowballing approach to theoretical sampling.

Aim for Rounded Perspectives

Sampling in STGT goes beyond achieving *representation* from the wider population to the sample, an approach commonly applied in quantitative research. For example, an STGT study on *understanding the journey of women students in software engineering degree programs* may aim to collect the perceptions and experiences of women software engineering students enrolled in undergraduate and graduate courses and training programs, through collection techniques such as interviews, surveys, and focus groups.

Following a quantitative approach to representative sampling, achieving a representative sample will mean estimating the size of the total population, a margin of error, and a confidence level in order to estimate the size of the sample so it can be considered representative. Imagine there are 100,000 women software engineering students worldwide, a confidence level of 95% and a 5% margin of error. Applying a popular representative sample calculator[2] suggests we need to survey at least 383 women students from the population for the sample to be considered representative. While such an approach may satisfy the quantitative needs, it does not guarantee the qualitative needs of the sample. Even if we include 383 women software engineering students in the study, such an approach still provides a limited, one-sided view of the phenomenon. We need to aim to achieve a *rounded perspective*. In this case, it would

[2] https://www.qualtrics.com/blog/calculating-sample-size/

be a good idea to also collect the perceptions and experiences of men students and the educators and instructors teaching these courses to gain a rounded perspective of the phenomenon.

Manage Potential Biases

It can be argued that some sampling techniques are more prone to potential biases than others, but none are immune. The research team needs to be aware of the biases that may arise from sampling approaches and manage them effectively. For example, approaching a software organisation through an existing professional contact may enable convenient access. However, depending on how the research team is introduced and how participants are selected, it can open doors to biasing responses received from the employees. If the research team is introduced to the potential participants in a way that establishes a sense of being audited for good practices, it can place the participants under stress "to perform" and can lead to eliciting the "right responses" as opposed to authentic responses. Similarly, if the participants were not given the opportunity to voluntarily participate and were instead assigned to participate in the research study, it can negatively impact their motivation to engage. Irrespective of the type of sampling, such aspects need to be carefully discussed and handled. The research team can discuss these aspects with their professional contact to ensure a neutral and voluntary approach for the participants.

7.3.2 Tips for Effective Recruitment

Tips

Tips for Effective Recruitment:

- Keep it open but relevant
- Be professional
- Customise and personalise
- Keep it short and practitioner-friendly
- Highlight call to action
- Networking

The digital world opens avenues for reaching out to and recruiting participants like never before. Social media platforms such as Twitter and professional networking sites such as LinkedIn enable access to international and local individual experts and interest groups. Online repositories such as GitHub provide unprecedented access to software codebases, documentation, and project data. It almost seems too easy. But in practicality, researchers compete for attention on these platforms and can risk drowning practitioners in a flood of participation requests, not to mention the associated ethical concerns (Gonzalez-Barahona, 2020; Gold & Krinke, 2022).

Recruitment and engagement approaches require careful consideration, planning, and execution to be effective. One of the key guiding principles here is being aware of the reputation we are building for ourselves in the wider practitioner and research communities. Keeping a long-term view helps steer our approach in the right direction so that we grow into becoming, and are consequently viewed as, professional and credible researchers. Here are some tips for effective recruitment and engagement practices. An example call for participation (CfP) can be seen in Fig. 7.4.

Keep It Open but Relevant

Of those whom our calls for participation reach, a small percentage will typically end up participating. This realisation can give rise to the temptation of reaching out to each and every one on our contact lists and use all possible platforms. Maintaining a long-term view helps here. Focus on the most relevant cohorts (see theoretical sampling earlier). For example, for an international and large study on a software engineering topic, a call for participation post can be requested to be shared by an international forum such as the IEEE Computer Society. For a study on agile practice in a specific country, posting a call to the national- or state-level Agile meetup groups makes more sense.

Be Professional

A sure fire way to have our *call for participation* ignored is by being unprofessional. Make an effort to carefully craft the content, format, style, and language of the call and the subject line and content of the associated emails and posts to be professional, so it's not filtered out as spam either automatically or manually. Include details of researchers and their affiliations and contact details to add transparency and credibility. Where applicable, include references to the ethics approval governing the study. Assure readers that participation is voluntary and confidential and, where applicable, anonymous. Strategically time reminders. Don't beg, don't pester!

Customise and Personalise

In a world of overflowing spam folders, customising posts and personalising emails go a long way. Emails sent to mailing list owners requesting them to share the call with their group members will benefit from personalisation, e.g. being addressed to specific individuals. Similarly, calls posted to local groups will benefit from customisation in the form of using references that make sense to that group.

Fig. 7.4 An example of a research call for participation (CfP) poster shared on Twitter and LinkedIn

Keep It Short and Practitioner-Friendly

Keep the call as short as possible, mentioning key details in a practitioner-friendly language. This means avoiding research jargon, although using common industry jargon is usually fine. Acronyms can be expanded. Mentioning how participants can benefit from the research is likely to achieve good response rates. For example, where collecting data from a number of participants or teams at the same company, I typically offer to present a research talk at the end and host question and answer sessions for knowledge exchange.

Highlight Call to Action

Highlighting a clear *call to action* that clarifies what the reader can do if they want to participate is useful. This can be in the form of a URL link leading them to fill a survey, a preliminary form expressing their interest in participating in the study, or an email address to reach the researchers. Make the call to action easy to find, e.g. in bold font, and to follow through, e.g. with a single click action, as much as possible.

Networking

Online presence and reach have their advantages but do not underestimate the value of networking with people at industry meetups, conferences, and events. These avenues are not only useful for understanding the pulse of the research domain and the local flavours of your research topic but are an effective medium to create new contacts, potentially gain individual participants and sometimes access to entire teams and organisations, and inform practitioners about our research (e.g. through presentations to the group.)

7.3.3 Tips for Effective Engagement

Tips

Tips for Effective Engagement:

- Gain the skills
- Respect participant time
- Give back

Once prospective participants respond to our recruitment efforts, the engagement phase follows. Articles have captured the examples of effective industry-academia collaboration (Carver & Prikladnicki, 2018; Salleh et al., 2018). Here are tips for effective engagement to ensure that the research participation is a valuable and pleasant experience for all involved.

Gain the Skills

As technical experts in various socio-technical fields, such as software engineering, qualitative data collection is an unlikely skill to exist in our repertoire. As described in Chap. 4, Research Design Canvas, an effective STGT research team includes people with the necessary qualitative research skills such as designing qualitative research protocols, conducting ethics assessment, and collecting and analysing qualitative data. If these skills are not pre-existing, efforts can be made to gain necessary training, for example, reading up on interviewing skills (Kvale & Brinkmann, 2009) and watching or listening to interview recordings available to researchers. Popular interview-based shows, e.g. 60 Minutes, include several aspects worth emulating.

However, their typical auditing approach is not appropriate for research interviewing, which is meant to be a lot more neutral. Shadowing experienced qualitative researchers, by helping them in their research design and "sitting in" on data collection, is also a great way to acquire these skills. Consider shadowing an expert, a senior research colleague, or your advisors. Practice to improve.

Respect Participant Time

Practitioners take time out of their busy schedule to participate in our research. Estimate and inform them of the length and frequency of the upcoming engagements with them and follow through. Consider collecting some basic information like demographic data prior to the face-to-face meeting to help save time and customise the interview. More about this in the Pre-Interview Questionnaire section covered in Chap. 8, Techniques of Qualitative Data Collection. In case of interviews, be flexible around their schedule and location, offering to meet at a time and place convenient to them and acceptable to you. For example, meeting during lunch breaks at their workplace tends to work well. In case of surveys, ensure it is designed to be time-efficient. For example, avoid unnecessarily complex or branched surveys. Design surveys in a way that can be completed in a single sitting and a reasonable amount of time, e.g. anywhere between 3 and 20 minutes. Share the estimated completion time so they are well-informed going into the survey.

Give Back

A critical part of engagement is giving back to the practitioner community. This can be in the form of a gift such as flowers and souvenirs where applicable and acceptable (e.g. through ethics approval) or sharing results via industry-friendly reports, posters, or presentations. Ideally, offer these after full data collection is complete at a given site so as not to bias the data collection in progress.

It is not uncommon for research teams to offer incentives for participation in the form of gift vouchers for all participants, parking or commute vouchers to reach specific destinations, or a chance for a few randomly selected participants to win a prize. These aspects need to be handled very careful so as to avoid any possible influence on the responses. Other forms of *koha*—Māori word for a gift—or tokens of acknowledgement and appreciation, such as flowers and chocolates for a group of teachers and students who participated in the study, may be shared once all data completion with them is complete. Increasingly, direct remuneration for research participation is becoming common, especially for large-scale data collection.

You can also follow up intermittently to update your participant base about your recent research. Practitioners appreciate us being their portal to academia, just as they are our portal to industry, providing access to relevant knowledge and advice.

7.4 Dealing with Data

7.4.1 Data Ethics

Whether we are working with pre-existing or custom-collected data, an ethical assessment needs to be conducted to gauge potential ethical concerns and to come up with a plan to address them. For example, Gold and Krinke (2020) identified a need for the Mining Software Repository community to have open discussions on the ethical issues related to data mining across sources such as version control data, developer Q&A forums, issue trackers, IDE events, and mailing lists. El-Emam (2001) raised similar concerns in the Open Source community.

In many research institutes and universities, ethics assessment takes the shape of applying for ethics approval through an official committee or panel. A number of resources can be consulted, such as (Singer & Vinson, 2002) and articles in the ethics special issue (Singer & Vinson, 2001), dealing with ethical issues such as "*informed consent*", "*confidentiality*", "*beneficence to individual and organisation*", and "*maximising benefits and minimising harm to society and participants*". Others include ethical guidelines about the use of public data in the areas of social media (Townsend & Wallace, 2016), Internet research (Markham et al., 2012), and the Menlo report on information and communication technology research (Dittrich et al., 2012), which lists principles such as *respect for persons*, *beneficence*, *justice*, *respect for law*, and *public interest*.

Some common ethical issues related to STGT studies and their mitigation plans are discussed below. For custom-collected data, such as those through interviews, observations, and surveys, the informed consent of participants is critical. Often participants share details and examples under the confidence of privacy and confidentiality. Papers presenting research findings can obscure identifiable details about individuals and their employers to maintain their privacy and confidentiality. Using participant pseudo-codes is one way to achieve this. For example, P1, P2, P3, and so on can be used to refer to participants instead of their real names or even pseudonyms since the latter can lead to assuming specific gender or ethnicity, unless that was important for the study. Similarly, any mentions of individuals and companies by the participants can be removed so the raw data is not traceable. The same applies to photographs and artefacts. These can be digitally blurred to hide any identifiable details, e.g. people's faces and visible information that can be used to identify, e.g. company name on background wall or wallpaper of Trello board and so on.

For pre-existing data, especially those in the public domain such as open-source repositories, social media posts, and YouTube videos, the research team can attempt to seek explicit consent from the owners, administrations, event organisers, or speakers to include them in the study. Where there is a risk to reputation, the identifiable information can be obscured. An example of such a scenario is a study using public data on social media as examples of "bad" programming practices with identifiable information about individuals and their employers. Finally, where possible, consult with ethics committees on the proper use of incentives, tokens of appreciations, and remuneration.

7.4.2 Data Sharing

As a part of the open science movement applied to software engineering,[3] there is a growing demand for making research instruments, protocol, and full and sample data available publicly and share them with the reviewers. For example, the IEEE International Conference on Software Engineering (ICSE), the flagship SE conference, expects and encourages data transparency[4] with the motivation to enable replication and reproducibility. However, the same motivations do not necessarily apply to empirical research, especially qualitative studies, and such expectations may alienate, if not turn away, empirical and qualitative researchers from submitting their papers. Consider an STGT study with interview data as an example. These conversations are rich in contextual information, often containing concrete examples with sensitive and identifying information. Participants who agree to share such information often do so under the guarantee of strict confidentiality and privacy, such that the data is not shared beyond the research team and all research reports maintain the anonymity of individuals and their companies, unless there is explicit permission to share them, which is a rare case. It is not possible to make raw data available publicly or even to reviewers who often sit outside the researcher's organisation, city, or even country.

However, this does not mean data collected in STGT studies and the research procedures followed cannot be verified. Samples of raw data, research protocols, procedures, tools, and instruments and working examples of data analysis can help reviewers evaluate the quality of the study and enable other researchers to extend the study in different contexts. Similarly, selected sanitised excerpts of the underlying raw data can be shared as part of the findings to provide a peak into the practitioners' world and to serve as a reliable chain of evidence. We will learn more about evaluating STGT studies in Chap. 13, Evaluation Guidelines.

Returning to the issue of open science at ICSE, I had approached the program committee chairs with my concerns and the aim to assist with drafting other ways of establishing credibility and enabling robust reviewing of qualitative research. The chairs had been working on something to that end, and a Q&A page linked to the submission instructions was added to include specific guidelines for "*empirical studies and sharing of data*[5]", which provides useful guidelines to help present empirical studies in a way enables evaluation.

---

[3] https://ineed.coffee/open-science-policies

[4] https://conf.researchr.org/track/icse-2022/icse-2022-open-science-policies

[5] https://conf.researchr.org/track/icse-2022/icse-2022-submitting-to-icse2022--q-a

7.4.3 Data Quality

The quality of research study is first and foremost based on the quality of the data collected and analysed. Given the variety of data sources and collection techniques that can be employed in an STGT study, it can be a challenge to discern their quality. Quality data sources can provide rich historical perspectives, current trends, and balanced narratives on issues relevant to our research topic. On the other hand, unverified and unscrupulous data sources can be avoided.

Data Quality Evaluation Guidelines

To help evaluate the quality of data for inclusion in an STGT study, and in qualitative research studies in general, I present the *Data Quality Evaluation Guidelines*. It covers six key quality criteria to evaluate the extent to which the data, and in many cases the source, are *relevant*, *authentic*, *accessible*, *ethical*, *credible*, and *valuable*, captured in Fig. 7.5 and described below.

- **Is it relevant?** Relevance refers to the data and its source being appropriate for inclusion in the research study. It is assumed that the reason we are assessing a data source for quality is that it has relevance to the research topic, the phenomenon under investigation, and the research questions. In this sense, relevance

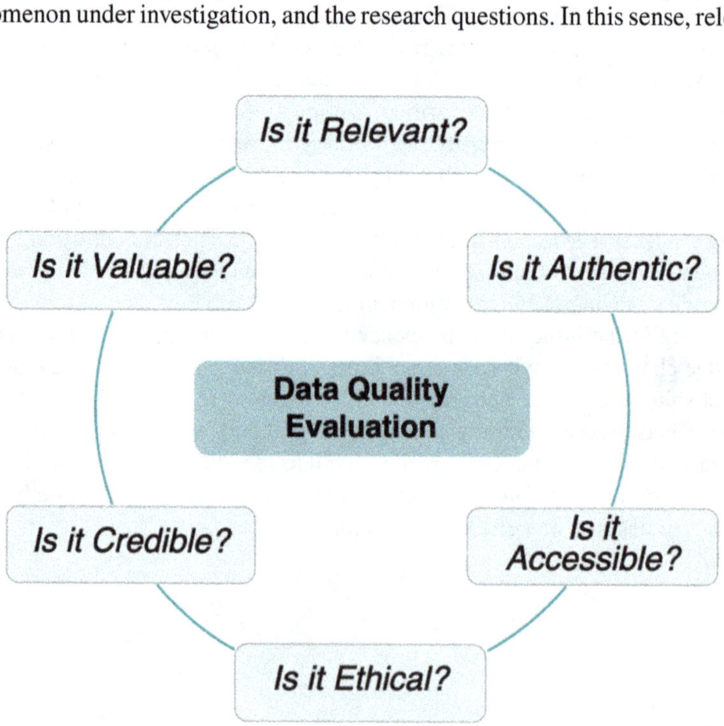

Fig. 7.5 Quality evaluation criteria for qualitative data

is almost a pre-requisite to data collection. But it will pay to explicitly consider relevance. For example, does a potential participant have the needed professional experience to provide insights on the research topic? Or is a particular GitHub project well positioned to answer research questions based on the characteristics of the contributors or details in the commit messages?
In the early days of data collection, it can be difficult to establish relevance as the scope of the study is typically rather broad and it is sufficient to establish the relevance of the data source to the research topic. For example, in a study on the role of the project manager in agile software teams, interviewing some members of an agile team or a few managers is relevant. As the research progresses and some key concepts and categories begin to emerge, theoretical sampling guides the data collection. Then on, we can better identify the data sources most relevant to our emerging findings and theoretical structures and gaps. In addition to establishing the relevance of the data source, it is also important to maintain relevance in the data collected. For example, when data mining, relevant keywords can be used, while for custom-collecting data through surveys or focus groups, consider designing questions carefully to elicit relevant information, as covered earlier in this chapter under the tips on effective data collection using some common data collection techniques.

- **Is it accessible?** The research team's ability to access the data is an important consideration. Highly relevant data that is inaccessible to the research team is of little practical value. Evaluating accessibility includes assessing the research team's ability to recruit relevant participants for custom-data collection, for example, identifying relevant meet-up groups and online LinkedIn groups where calls for participation can be posted and then evaluating how to access them responsibly, e.g. by emailing the administrations for permission to post. It also includes assessing the team's ability to access pre-existing data, which can be in the public or private domain. Publicly available data such as YouTube videos, public podcasts, and open-source software repositories offer easy access. Access to privately available data, such as project documentation, Slack chats, and individual experiences, can usually be organised through seeking permission from relevant owners and authorities.

- **Is it ethical?** Irrespective of whether it is easy or difficult to access the data, it is important to ensure ethical access and use. As discussed earlier in the section *Data Ethics*, a number of ethical considerations need to be made, including informed consent, privacy, confidentiality, anonymity, "*maximising benefits and minimising harm to society and participants*" (Singer & Vinson, 2001), and forms of incentives and remuneration.

- **Is it authentic?** Authenticity refers to the data and its source being *genuine* and not fake. For example, is the participant who they say they are? To evaluate the authenticity of the data, ask questions such as can the source of the data be identified and verified? Authenticating participants in the physical world tends to be relatively straightforward. For example, we can learn about the participants' name, job, employer, and professional background to ascertain authenticity during interviews and to some extent in voluntary surveys. Including mandatory open-ended questions that ask for specific insights is an effective way to filter out bogus or fake responses in large-scale data collection, e.g. in paid surveys on Amazon Mechanical Turk. A physical visit to the company for interviews, focus groups, and observations, in addition to its online presence, serves to establish authenticity.

When gathering pre-existing data from the public realm, such as data mining from social media channels, assessing for authenticity can be challenging. For example, a post by a well-known and respected software engineering thought leader can be easily evaluated by inspecting the posting account, e.g. number of followers, links to identifying professional websites, nature of replies to post, and other indicators. Posts by regular practitioners may need some extra effort to verify, such as visiting their professional accounts, blog, personal Web site, reading through their other posts and replies, and so on. Verifying posts by anonymous accounts, on the other hand, can be akin to mystery solving! Attempt to avoid data sources that cannot be authenticated.

- **Is it credible?** Credibility refers to the data and its source being trustworthy and evidence based. For example, is the information provided by the participant, text, or recording evidence based? Is the pre-existing dataset based on real empirical data? Is the project aimed to include simulated data? To evaluate the credibility of the data, aim to collect evidence in the form of concrete examples, contextual details, and practical intricacies. For example, when collecting custom data in physical or digital mediums, such as through interviews, credibility can be improved by asking for concrete examples and supplementing them with other data sources and collection techniques, such as through observations, to achieve data triangulation. Online public data sources can have contexts embedded in the form of links to related articles, news, research, and so forth. These can be followed up to gain a better understanding of the context and strengthen credibility.

- **Is it valuable?** Valuable refers to the data and its sources being of use and benefit to the research. Having established relevance, authenticity, and credibility, the chances of deriving value from data collection are already good. However, it still takes careful planning and execution to maximise the value derived from data collection. In case of custom-data collection, consider spending time on designing the data collection protocols well and piloting them to improve their effectiveness will go a long way. This is especially true for designing effective surveys for mixed data collection. A well-designed survey is intuitive to fill and easy to navigate. When used to collect qualitative data, it uses several open-ended questions that are easy to understand and frequently asks for rationales and examples. Tips for effective data collection through interviews, observations, and surveys have been shared earlier in this chapter. In case of pre-existing data, maximising value is driven by spending effort to filter the sources and the use of the relevant keywords to extract data. Automated techniques can be supported by some manual effort to derive value, e.g. assessing the meta-data and README files in software repositories, data labelling for novel categories, and filtering the data for noise.

Traditional GT accepts a variety of data sources and applies Glaser's dictum, "*all is data*" (Glaser & Strauss, 2017, first published 1967). STGT studies can include a variety of traditional and modern data sources and collection techniques (see Fig. 8.1 in Chap. 8, Techniques of Qualitative Data Collection). Because of the open nature of many modern and some traditional data sources, the guidance for data collection in STGT studies is *all is data, with care*. Care needs to be taken to ensure the quality of data for inclusion in our studies using the above *Data Quality Evaluation Guidelines*.

7.4.4 Data Usage

Definition

Primary data forms the core of the data for analysis in an STGT project. They are the first port of call for analysing data and developing theories. **Supplementary** data serves to support the primary data, helping clarify, extend, fill gaps, resolve conflicts, increase the range of applicable contexts, enable data triangulation, and generally improve the value derived from the primary data.

When including multiple data sources, the research team may want to specify one or more as primary data, while others may be used in a supplementary capacity. Primary data refers to the data that is first and main source of data to be analysed, from which key findings will be derived and theoretical outcomes developed. Supplementary data serves to support the primary data by helping clarify, extend, fill gaps, resolve conflicts, and generally improve the value derived from the primary data.

Supplementary data is not a must. Quality STGT studies can be conducted with primary data. However, supplementary data can serve some important functions. For example, an STGT study may use semi-structured interviews as the primary data source and supplement it with field observations. Here, the observations can validate the information shared during interviews, augment findings, and provide nuanced details. They can also help fill in any information gaps in the interview data. When we observe a meeting practice firsthand, it can provide a more complete picture than a recalled description during interviews. Similarly, they can help resolve some conflicting information provided in the interviews. For example, if two members of the same team share seemingly conflicting information about a practice, a firsthand observation of the practice can help resolve such a conflict.

Supplementary sources can also be used to increase the range of applicable contexts included in the study and in turn increase the range of contexts where the findings apply. For example, the primary data collected from interviews and observations at a handful of organisations may show software teams as severely impaired in their documentation practices. These findings can be augmented by supplementary data collected through wide-scale surveys or through data mining from popular developer forums. Such supplementary data can help improve the breadth of the findings by including a larger set of contexts.

When reporting the findings, instead of claiming generalisability, the researchers can attempt to explain the broad range of contexts studied in depth and present findings that cover those contexts. To this end, attempts can be made to capture as much of the contexts of the primary and supplementary data as possible. However, the context of the software teams represented in the online discussion forums (e.g. application domain, development tools and technologies used, organisational priorities, customer demands) may not be easily available.

Supplementary data collection can be done in parallel, as interleaved with, or in sequence after primary data is collected, depending on the research design protocols, schedule, and other constraints. Collecting supplementary data in an interleaved manner with the primary data is likely to be most effective. It will allow the research team to inspect the findings arising from the primary data and sample more primary and supplementary data to fill in the information and theoretical gaps. When collected in an interleaved manner or in sequence after collecting the primary data, supplementary data can help confirm and support the findings arising from the primary data, enabling data triangulation.

7.4.5 Data Quantity and Theoretical Saturation

How much data is enough? This is a common question asked about qualitative research studies. As with any complex question, the answer is a very thoughtful *it depends*. But let us first consider why this question arises. There are two main reasons. The first is a practical project management-based reason around attempting to estimate the scope of a project and, consequently, the effort, people, and resources required.

The other is to do with our understanding about data quantity associated with quantitative studies. Quantitative studies typically use representative or random sampling, which dictates the minimum number of data items required to ensure representation is achieved, and the results can be claimed to be generalisable to the wider population, although no matter how large the sample size, it is nearly impossible for most research studies to claim full generalisability or universality. This is especially true for those studying human and social aspects because of the vast diversity of human beings and the unpredictability of their behaviours.

Qualitative studies, on the other hand, typically value context and nuance over generalisability. STGT research projects are typically focused on investigating a specific phenomenon, using qualitative data, and their findings are generalisable to the contexts studied and those closely related. Most STGT studies do not aim for or claim wide-scale generalisability. As such, there is no specific amount of minimum data requirements for an STGT research to make valuable contributions.

However, I do not want to skirt around the issue of discussing data quantity in STGT research projects. So, I will first address some numbers that are usually mentioned in the empirical software engineering research circles, followed by explaining what is at the heart of determining quantity in STGT studies, i.e. theoretical saturation. Grounded theory studies published in software engineering seem to work with a range of around 20–50 participants. Studies with over 50 participants are rare. Studies with under 20 participants are usually early investigations that report preliminary findings or one or two key categories but not mature theoretical outcomes. They can also be studies into a phenomenon about a niche or emerging research area where there is not a lot of data available to access and analyse.

At the same time, it is rather implausible to generate novel, useful, parsimonious, and modifiable mature theories from very little data. What is *very little* data in an STGT context? I have discussed this with colleagues and, when really pressed for a number, have arrived at 20 as a bare minimum number of software engineering practitioners required in an interview-based STGT study on a common software engineering phenomenon, such as understanding specific practices and roles in a software team. Furthermore, the assumption here is that the data was derived from quality interviews of reasonable length (e.g. between 30 and 60 minutes) and were thoroughly analysed, including writing valuable memos. Twenty in this context is no magic number. It is based on the experience of conducting STGT studies in software engineering and attempting to draw meaningful mature theoretical outcomes.

By way of comparison, based on a review of a hundred articles using grounded theory across various disciplines in the years 2002–2008, and using various data collection techniques, the average data quantity was found to be 25, while the range was between 5 and 114 (Thomson, 2010). Twelve studies used sample sizes of less than 10, about a third of them (n = 32) used between 10 and 19, another third of them (n = 33) used sample sizes between 20 and 30, 22 of the studies used over 31, and only 1 study had more than a 100 for sample size.

Sample sizes vary because of a number of reasons. For example, when speaking to experts, the study may require fewer participants or if conducting multiple rounds of data collection with the same participants (Thomson, 2010). Similarly, when working on a niche topic, with other types of data, or combining collection techniques, the numbers may vary. Larger projects, such as a PhD research study, will likely have a broader scope to begin with and narrow down iteratively over time. As a result, they are likely to need a relatively larger number of participants to reach saturation. Shorter studies, such as a narrowly focused 1-year project of which the data collection period is about 3–4 months long will likely research saturation sooner if the topic and research questions were focused.

Ultimately, the sample size in an STGT study comes down to reaching a point in the study where the research team feels confident they have a strong and in-depth grasp over the phenomenon, achieving theoretical saturation.

Definition

Theoretical saturation is a point of diminishing returns in data collection when further data collection serves to confirm and validate existing conceptual findings but does not lead to significantly new information or insights. It is an indication to stop data collection.

Theoretical saturation has been labelled *mystical* and *mysterious* (Breckenridge & Jones, 2009; Aldiabat & Le Navenec, 2018) because of its rather abstract and elusive definitions. In practice, theoretical saturation is experienced once further data collection seems to serve the purpose of confirming existing findings instead of providing new insights that can significantly change the existing concepts, (sub)categories, and theoretical structure. Saturation is not aimed at the descriptive level—"*not merely descriptive redundancy*"—rather at the conceptual level (Breckenridge & Jones, 2009). This is not to be confused with the lack of any new information. New data collection is likely to provide *some* new information that can lead to descriptive changes. However, if that information does not significantly add to or change the emergent concepts and theoretical structures, and this continues to be the case for the next few data items, e.g. last few interviews, surveys, recordings, texts, or social media post threads, theoretical saturation is said to be reached.

Quality and quantity of data go hand in hand in STGT studies. Theoretical saturation, and in turn data quantity, is inherently tied to the quality of the data collected and analysed. STGT studies can be based on rich, in-depth data collected from as few as around 20 participants to as many as hundreds, e.g. collected through open-ended surveys. Theoretical sampling drives a funneling approach to data collection and analysis whereby the scope of the study becomes increasingly focused over iterations of interleaved data collection and analysis and ends with theoretical saturation. It ensures that we reach a point of saturation where data collected about emerging categories offers no significantly new information or insights. Typically, this manifests as the last few, e.g. three or four interviews serve to validate existing findings.

As described early on, STGT's data analysis procedures can be used in a limited capacity in combinations with other research methods and techniques, also known as STGT *for data analysis*. In studies using STGT *for data analysis*, as opposed to using STGT for theory development, theoretical saturation may not be reached or even be attempted. This is because guidelines around data quantity will follow those of the overarching research method being employed, e.g. case studies.

7.5 Summary

In this chapter, we learned about popular *sampling techniques* such as convenience, snowball, random, representative, and theoretical sampling. Next, we learned some *tips for data collection* including tips for effective sampling, recruitment, and engagement. Finally, we learned about a number of aspects related to *dealing with data*, such as data ethics, data sharing, data quality using the *data quality evaluation guidelines*, data usage, and data quantity including theoretical saturation. Data collection and analysis are meant to be interleaved in an STGT study and go hand in hand. Researchers will benefit from reading this chapter in conjunction with the *Techniques of Qualitative Data Collection*, *Qualitative Data Preparation and Filtering*, and *Socio-technical Grounded Theory for Qualitative Data Analysis* chapters. Collectively, they cover socio-technical grounded theory's basic stage.

References

Aldiabat, K. M., & Le Navenec, C.-L. (2018). Data saturation: The mysterious step in grounded theory methodology. *The Qualitative Report, 23*(1), 245–261.

Breckenridge, J., & Jones, D. (2009). Demystifying theoretical sampling in grounded theory research. *Grounded Theory Review, 8*(2), 113–126.

Carver, J. C., & Prikladnicki, R. (2018). Industry–academia collaboration in software engineering. *IEEE Software, 35*(5), 120–124.

Charmaz, K. (2006). *Constructing grounded theory: A practical guide through qualitative analysis*. Sage.

Coyne, I. T. (1997). Sampling in qualitative research. Purposeful and theoretical sampling; merging or clear boundaries?. *Journal of Advanced Nursing, 26*(3), 623–630.

Dittrich, D., Kenneally, E. et al. (2012). The menlo report: Ethical principles guiding information and communication technology research. *Technical Report*, US Department of Homeland Security.

El-Emam, K. (2001). Ethics and open source. *Empirical Software Engineering, 6*(4), 291.

Glaser, B. G., & Strauss, A. L. (2017). *Discovery of grounded theory: Strategies for qualitative research*. Routledge (First Published 1967).

Gold, N. E., & Krinke, J. (2020). Ethical mining: A case study on MSR mining challenges. In *Proceedings of the 17th International Conference on Mining Software Repositories* (pp. 265–276).

Gold, N. E., & Krinke, J. (2022). Ethics in the mining of software repositories. *Empirical Software Engineering, 27*(1), 17.

Gonzalez-Barahona, J. (2020). *Mining software repositories while respecting privacy*. Mining Software Repositories Tutorial. https://2020.msrconf.org/details/msr-2020-Education/1/Mining-Software-Repositories-While-Respecting-Privacy

Hoda, R. (2022). Socio-technical grounded theory for software engineering. *IEEE Transactions on Software Engineering, 48*(10), 3808–3832.

Hoda, R., Noble, J., & Marshall, S. (2010). Organizing self-organizing teams. In *Proceedings of the 32nd ACM/IEEE International Conference on Software Engineering-Volume 1* (pp. 285–294).

Hoda, R., Noble, J., & Marshall, S. (2012). Self-organizing roles on agile software development teams. *IEEE Transactions on Software Engineering, 39*(3), 422–444.

Kvale, S., & Brinkmann, S. (2009). *Interviews: Learning the craft of qualitative research interviewing*. Sage.

Markham, A., Buchanan, E., with Feedback from the AOIR Ethics Working Committee et al. (2012). *Ethical decision-making and internet research: Recommendations from the AOIR ethics working committee (version 2.0)*. http://aoir.org/reports/ethics2.pdf

Morse, J. M. (2010). Sampling in grounded theory. In *The SAGE handbook of grounded theory* (pp. 229–244).

Patton, M. Q. (1990). *Qualitative evaluation and research methods*. SAGE Publications.

Salleh, N., Hoda, R., Su, M. T., Kanij, T., & Grundy, J. (2018). Recruitment, engagement and feedback in empirical software engineering studies in industrial contexts. *Information and Software Technology, 98*, 161–172.

Sandelowski, M. (1995). Sample size in qualitative research. *Research in Nursing & Health, 18*(2), 179–183.

Singer, J., & Vinson, N. G. (2001). Why and how research ethics matters to you, yes you! *Empirical Software Engineering, 6*(4), 287–290.

Singer, J., & Vinson, N. G. (2002). Ethical issues in empirical studies of software engineering. *IEEE Transactions on Software Engineering, 28*(12), 1171–1180.

Thomson, S. B. (2010). Sample size and grounded theory. *Thomson, SB (2010). Grounded Theory-Sample Size. Journal of Administration and Governance, 5*(1), 45–52.

Townsend, L., & Wallace, C. (2016). Social media research: A guide to ethics. *University of Aberdeen, 1*(16), 1–16. https://www.gla.ac.uk/media/Media_487729_smxx.pdf

8 Techniques of Qualitative Data Collection

Abstract In this chapter, we will learn about two groups of data collection techniques: custom-data and existing-data collection. Then we will delve into the details of popular collection techniques such as pre-interview questionnaires, semi-structured interviews, and observations. We will look into other sources and collection techniques such as focus groups, surveys, recordings, texts, social media, artefacts, data mining, and immersive experiences in extended realities. Researchers will benefit from reading this chapter in conjunction with the *Basics of Qualitative Data Collection*, *Qualitative Data Preparation and Filtering*, and *Socio-technical Grounded Theory for Qualitative Data Analysis* chapters. Collectively, they cover socio-technical grounded theory's Basic Stage.

8.1 Data Collection Techniques

Socio-technical grounded theory (STGT) data analysis works best on qualitative data collected using a variety of techniques. This is because its rich data analysis procedures such as open coding and constant comparison work on qualitative data.

R. Hoda, *Qualitative Research with Socio-Technical Grounded Theory*,
https://doi.org/10.1007/978-3-031-60533-8_8

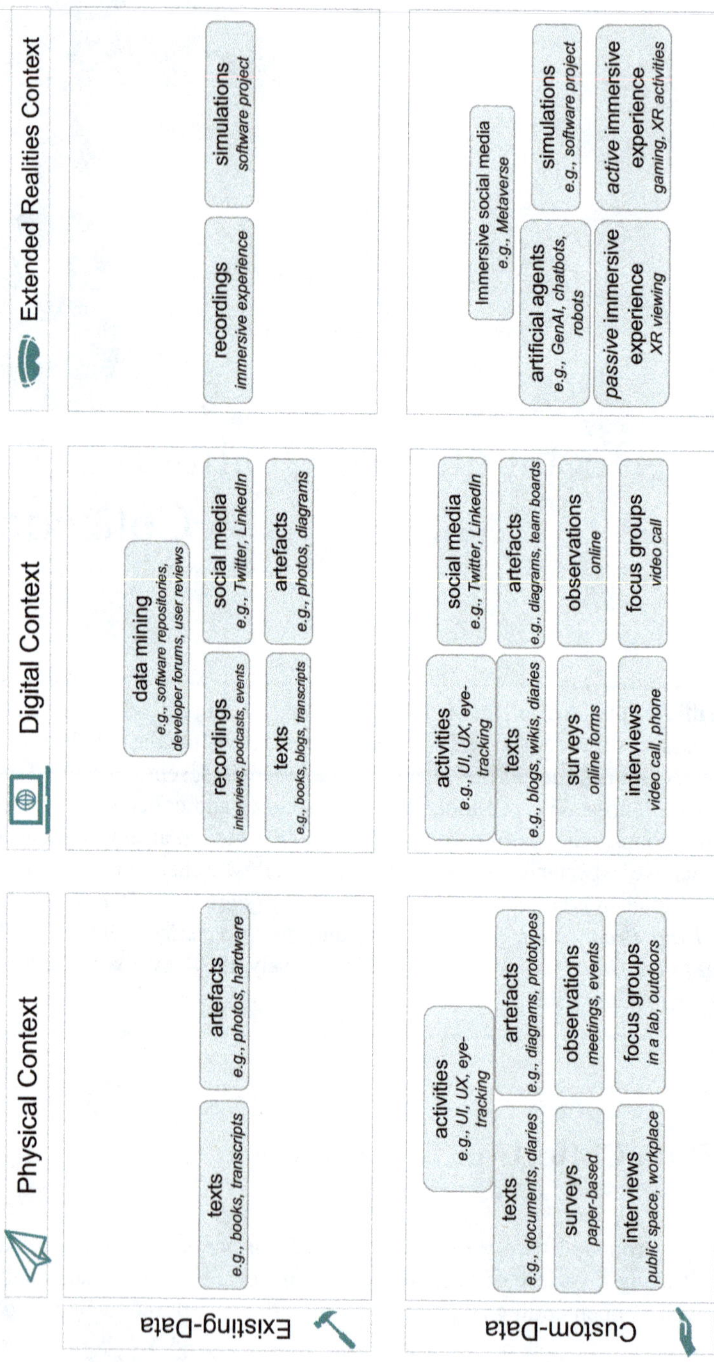

Fig. 8.1 Qualitative data sources in physical, digital, and extended reality contexts. XR = extended realities including augmented, virtual, and mixed realities; UI = user interface; UX = user experience

Quantitative data can be used to supplement the qualitative data in a mixed methods STGT study. We focus on qualitative data as it remains the main "currency of the trade" as far as STGT is concerned.

A variety of data collection techniques can be used in an STGT research project (see Fig. 8.1 for an overview). Some of these can be used in *physical*, some in *digital* contexts, and some in contexts that involve *extended realities*. Additionally, some involve *custom-data collection*, where data is specifically elicited for the research project by asking specific questions relevant to the topic and asking for concrete examples. Others involve *existing-data collection* where data already exists in some form and is gathered based on its relevance to the research project.

The two data groups can be compared. For example, in a study focused on understanding how Scrum varies in practice from how it is meant to work by the book, we used a combination of custom data and existing data (Masood et al., 2020b). By comparing custom data in terms of empirical evidence from real-world agile software teams with the existing data in terms of the Scrum Guide and the Scrum Primer, we were able to explain where, how, and why Scrum variations occur in practice.

8.1.1 Custom-Data Collection

Definition

Custom-data collection refers to techniques and sources where data is specifically elicited, and in the process created anew (not pre-existing), for the research project

Data collection techniques and sources that support custom-data collection in the physical contexts include *interviews*, *focus groups*, *observations*, and paper-based *surveys* that are typically conducted face to face, in a public space or workplace. Many of these are documented using an audio or video recorder or handwritten notes. Other custom-data sources include *texts* (e.g. custom created documents, custom written blogs, and diaries), and *artefacts* (e.g. zines, low-fi prototypes, diagrams) that are custom created as part of data collection. These custom-data collection techniques and sources applicable in the physical context are captured in the bottom-left block in Fig. 8.1.

Most of the custom-data collection techniques that work in physical contexts have their digital counterparts, including *interviews*, *focus groups*, *observations*, and *surveys* conducted in the digital mode such as over audio/video calls. Similarly, custom-data sources such as *texts* (e.g. digital blogs, wikis, diaries) and *artefacts* (e.g. diagrams, prototypes) can be utilised in digital contexts. In addition to these digital avatars of physical data sources, the digital context offers a unique source for custom collecting research data through researcher posts on *social media* (e.g. Twitter, LinkedIn, Facebook). These custom-data collection techniques and sources applicable in the digital context are captured in the bottom-middle block in Fig. 8.1.

Finally, there are existing and emerging technologies and platforms that enable extended realities, beyond the physical and digital contexts, where research data can be collected. These include *passive immersive experiences* where the researcher plays a passive role in collecting data while being immersed in the new reality created by the use of augmented, virtual, and mixed reality devices and platforms, as well as *active immersive experiences* where the researcher can play a more active role (e.g. being part of an online game.) Other sources of custom-data collection in extended realities include researcher interactions with *artificial agents* (e.g. Generative AI chatbots such as ChatGPT and Microsoft co-pilot and AI based robots) and *simulations* (e.g. a software project life cycle being played out using variables seeded by researchers). The introduction of immersive social media (Meta[1]) opens doors for data collection through passive and active *immersive social media* experiences in multiple reality contexts. However, the human and social impact of such innovations remain to be investigated. These custom-data collection techniques and sources applicable in emerging multiple reality contexts are captured in the bottom-right block in Fig. 8.1.

8.1.2 Existing-Data Collection

Definition

Existing-data collection refers to techniques and sources where data already exists in some form and is gathered based on its relevance to the research project.

Physical data sources that can be utilised to collect existing data include existing physical *texts* (e.g. books, documents, existing diaries) and *artefacts* (e.g. existing photos, hardware, prototypes). Paper-based transcripts of existing interviews, observations, surveys, and focus groups can also be used where allowed. These existing-data collection techniques and sources are depicted in the top-left block in Fig. 8.1.

[1] https://about.facebook.com/meta/.

Digital data sources and techniques can also be utilised to collect existing data such as *texts*, e.g. digital books, blogs, wikis, blogs, and digital transcripts of interviews, observations, surveys, and focus groups, as well as *artefacts* such as pre-existing photos, diagrams, and digital software artefacts, e.g. team task boards, project management tools, audio/video *recordings* (e.g. interviews, surveys, talks, events), and pre-existing *social media* posts and threads.

Some uniquely digital data sources particularly relevant for software engineering research include software repositories, developer forums, chats, and online user app reviews, which can be collected using *data mining* techniques. These existing-data collection techniques and sources are depicted in the top-middle block in Fig. 8.1.

Finally, modern data collection platforms can also be potentially used to collect existing data, e.g. *recordings* and *simulations* of previous immersive experiences. These potential existing-data collection techniques and sources are depicted in the top-right block in Fig. 8.1.

The rest of this chapter provides details of designing and applying some of the most commonly used qualitative data collection techniques relevant for STGT studies, including pre-interview questionnaires, interviews, and observations. A discussion of other techniques such as surveys and data mining is also included.

8.2 Pre-interview Questionnaires

Definition

PIQuing participant interest: a pre-interview questionnaire is a pre-cursor to the interview, not a survey in disguise! Keep the PIQ lightweight, just enough in terms of length and complexity of questions to "PIQue" the participant's interest, and get them into the right mental space for the upcoming interview.

In the early days of research, I used to ask all questions I needed from a participant during the face-to-face interview, including demographic questions such as their professional experience, current role, domain, software practices used in current project, and so on. This took up considerable time, reducing the time needed for the more focused research questions about the topic and follow-up questions during the semi-structured interviews. Over time, my students and I evolved our practice to introduce *pre-interview questionnaires* that covered all such easy to select, close-ended, demographic questions in an online format prior to the face-to-face interview.

8.2.1 Advantages of Pre-interview Questionnaires

Though the Pre-interview Questionnaire (PIQ) instrument was devised initially as a time-saver, we discovered some surprising fringe benefits over time.

- **Improved data quality**. Unlike a survey, a PIQ is not meant to be anonymous. This provides a unique opportunity for participants to clarify any questions directly with the researcher and for the researcher to clarify answers to the PIQ during their face-to-face interview with the participant. Being open to clarification opportunities means we can ensure a more robust and higher quality of data collection.

- **Focused interviews**. Having access to the demographic information beforehand meant we could tailor our interview questions accordingly to focus on certain aspects while avoiding questions that may be completely irrelevant for a participant. For an example, in a study on self-assignment, if the participant had identified themselves as regularly practicing self-assignment for over 10 years in the PIQ, we could try to elicit different examples of self-assignment working well, being challenged, and potentially failing, during the interview, whereas if the participant had reported being new to self-assignment in the PIQ, we could use the interview time to discuss a few examples in-depth rather than expect multiple examples of a variety of experiences. Such customisation is often done on the fly during the interview in the absence of the PIQ, placing additional cognitive load on the interviewer, who is already tasked with thinking up useful follow-up questions on the go. While the latter is necessarily tackled in-action during the interview, the prior can easily be managed through the use of a PIQ.

- **Documenting use and patterns**. Recounting all the possible development practices used in a project during an interview can be challenging for the interviewees. They are likely to mention the ones that come to their mind at the time and miss others. Including a question that asks them to select, or better, rank the frequency of use of the software development practices they use in a PIQ simplifies the process for the participants and ensures completeness. An example of such a question is shown in Fig. 8.2. Similar questions can be used to capture usage data and patterns for practices relevant to the research topic.

- **Supplementary quantitative data**. Much of the data collected using the PIQ forms the basis of quantitative data that can be statistically analysed and used to present quantitative results to supplement the qualitative findings. An example of this is the data resulting from the "frequency of agile practices" question can be presented in an aggregate format or through graphical visualisations. This is particularly handy to present as evidence in support of the participants identified as practicing agile methods rather than simply stating *we investigated agile teams*.

- **Data triangulation**. Information reported in the PIQ can be used for in-depth questioning in the face-to-face interviews by asking participants to share details and specific examples of reported practices. This can be further triangulated through field observations. For example, in the PIQ, the participant may have reported regular use of the retrospective practice. In the interview, we can ask for details of their typical retrospectives. During our field observations, where possible, we can observe a live retrospective session to compare and validate the information provided in the PIQ and the interview, thereby achieving data triangulation.

8.2.2 Sample Pre-interview Questionnaire

The PIQ can be designed to include two main sections: a *participant demographics* section and a *project and team information* section. The former focuses on the participant's professional background information relevant to the study such as their total work experience and work experience in a specific area (e.g. DevOps, test-driven development, mob programming). The latter covers basic information about a selected project, team, or example they will be talking about in the interview such as the domain of the project, the participant's job title and role on the project, software development method used on the project, team size, and others as relevant for the study. Ask for the participant's name so the PIQ responses can be linked to the interview data.

Using closed-ended questions with predefined list of answer options where possible and an additional open text for '*others*' option helps keep things short. Ideally, PIQs take no longer than 10 minutes to fill out. The use of pre-interview questionnaires can be found in Shastri et al. (2017); Madampe et al. (2020); Masood et al. (2020a). Some common questions used in the pre-interview questionnaire are shown in Fig. 8.2.

8.2.3 Tips for Designing Pre-interview Questionnaires

Tips

Tips for Designing Pre-interview Questionnaires:

- Keep it simple
- Keep it closed
- Don't be data greedy
- Don't get personal (unless there is a strong research requirement)

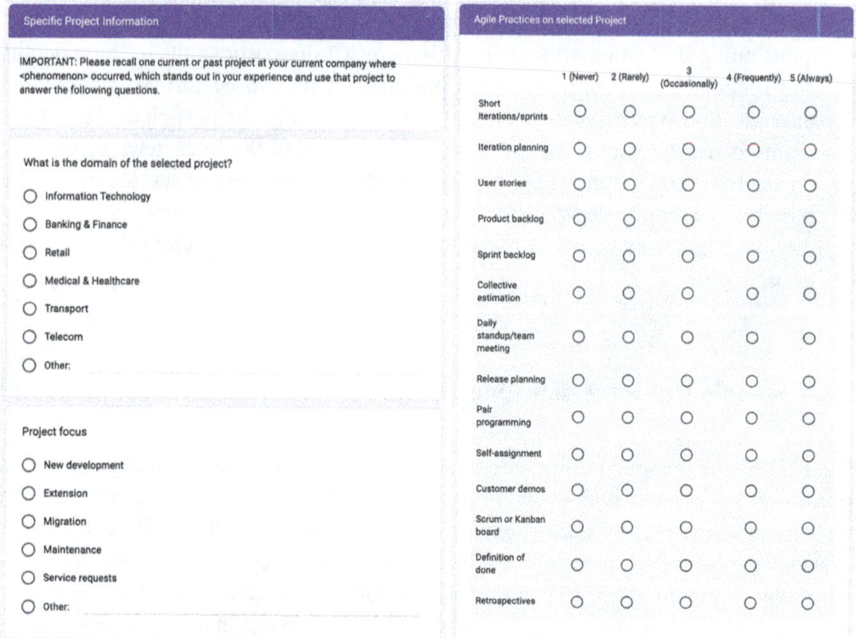

Specific Project Information

IMPORTANT: Please recall one current or past project at your current company where <phenomenon> occurred, which stands out in your experience and use that project to answer the following questions.

What is the domain of the selected project?

- Information Technology
- Banking & Finance
- Retail
- Medical & Healthcare
- Transport
- Telecom
- Other:

Project focus

- New development
- Extension
- Migration
- Maintenance
- Service requests
- Other:

Agile Practices on selected Project

	1 (Never)	2 (Rarely)	3 (Occasionally)	4 (Frequently)	5 (Always)
Short iterations/sprints	○	○	○	○	○
Iteration planning	○	○	○	○	○
User stories	○	○	○	○	○
Product backlog	○	○	○	○	○
Sprint backlog	○	○	○	○	○
Collective estimation	○	○	○	○	○
Daily standup/team meeting	○	○	○	○	○
Release planning	○	○	○	○	○
Pair programming	○	○	○	○	○
Self-assignment	○	○	○	○	○
Customer demos	○	○	○	○	○
Scrum or Kanban board	○	○	○	○	○
Definition of done	○	○	○	○	○
Retrospectives	○	○	○	○	○

Fig. 8.2 Sample questions in a pre-interview questionnaire (PIQ)

- **Keep it simple**. The format of the PIQ is meant to be lightweight and easy to use, so it's best to use simple, jargon-free, direct, and consistent language in constructing the questions and allow for flexibility in the response options.

> **Example**
>
> **Example of an indirect question with and limited options**:
> *Whose responsibility it is to maintain the project documentation?*
> *Answer options: project manager/developers/testers/business analysts*

Example

Example of a simple, direct question with flexible options:
Who is responsible for maintaining the project documentation?
(select all that apply)
Answer options: project manager/developers/testers/business analysts/others (please specify)

Here the response is set up to accept multiple-options selection. Alternatively, the word "primarily" or "mainly" can be used to act as a qualifier to assist in prioritising if the question needs a definitive answer. Where it is not possible to include all possible answer options, a final *Others (please specify)* helps. Another example where this works well is a question about the participant's current job title.

- **Keep it closed**. Open-ended questions require the participant to type their responses in free form of variable length, which takes time. Closed-ended questions with limited options are typically easier to respond to. We do not want to include open-ended questions in the PIQ. Any question requiring a detailed answer or examples can be saved for the face-to-face interview.

Example

Example of an open-ended question:
Why did your team decide to practice mob programming?
Answer in free-form text field

Example

Example of a closed-ended question:
What was the duration of the iterations on this project?
Answer options: Less than a week/1 week/2 weeks/3 weeks/4 weeks/more than 4 weeks

- **Don't be data greedy.** Becoming greedy for data is one of the biggest and constant trials of data collection. It is tempting to keep adding questions to the pre-interview questionnaire. Avoid this temptation. Making it too long or complex will not only tire the participant from filling it out but also weary of the actual interview to follow. Worst-case scenario, they may decide the whole process is too onerous and opt out before the interview.

- **Don't get personal, unless there's a research requirement**. The collection of personal information such as age and gender can be tricky as some participants may be put off by being asked these questions. It is a good idea to include a short footnote about why personal information is being collected and how it may be used. For example, reporting the demographic information of the participant may be one reason. Exploring co-relations between gender or age and other aspects may be another reason. For example, a correlation identified may be that women product owners were found to collaborate more with software teams than men product owners. Reporting aggregated information usually suffices for highlighting demographic distribution. For example, we can report that 30 % of product owners identified as women, which was representative of the wider gender distribution in the company being studied.

8.2.4 Usage and Tools for Administering the Pre-interview Questionnaire

Once a participant has agreed to participate in the research and confirmed a meeting time, send them an email outlining the arrangements for the interview and include a link to the PIQ requesting them to fill it out before the interview. For this to work, the link must be shared a few working days in advance. This provides the participant enough time to fill the questionnaire out and not rush through it 5 minutes before the interview. Since it's online, we can track whether it has been filled out appropriately and, if needed, send a gentle reminder closer to the interview time if the participant has forgotten to fill it out.

Similar to surveys, a variety of online survey tools can be used to create and administer the pre-interview questionnaire. For example, some research and educational institutes have a subscription to *Qualtrics*. *SurveyMonkey*, *LimeSurvey*, and *Google Forms* are popular free alternatives, although the latter may not be accessible everywhere in the world. Most tools are convenient and easy to use. We may have favourites depending on certain unique features they offer. Some survey tools, such as Qualtrics, can provide an estimate of the time required based on the questions included. Piloting the PIQ for comprehension, clarity, length, and appropriateness is highly recommended (see more about conducting a pilot study in Chap. 4 Research Design Canvas.)

8.2.5 Threats and Limitations of Pre-interview Questionnaires

- **Continuity loss**. A PIQ is meant to be a precursor to the semi-structured interview or other in-depth data collection techniques such as observations. It is not meant to be a stand-alone survey. If it collects information about software project or team details, it is important to design it such that continuity is maintained between the PIQ and the interview. For example, the PIQ can ask the participant to select a specific project for the purpose of answering the PIQ questions and recall the same project to answer the questions in the interview. If this link is not established, the context of application will be lost. However, the researcher is not limited to asking only about one project during the interview. Given time and willingness of the participant, the interviewer may venture to ask about other projects, in addition to the one used to answer the PIQ.

- **Context of use**. Using a PIQ may not always be the best course of action. While it simplifies the process for the research team, some participants may view it as additional time commitment required to participate in the study. It may be best to explain its purpose to the participants, e.g. highlighting how it can help contextualise the interview for a more personalised experience and save more time to spend on the conversations during the interview but leave it as an *option* to fill the PIQ beforehand. If it is met with resistance, the same questions can be included during the interview instead.

8.3 Semi-structured Interviews

Definition

Semi-structured Interviews: Face-to-face interviews can be considered a *gold standard* in qualitative data because of the richness of the information it offers. Interviews conducted online lose some of the comfort and nuances of physical interactions but offer opportunities to scale, requiring reduced time and travel.

Semi-structured interviews (henceforth referred to as interviews) are one of the most popular data collection techniques used in qualitative research studies. Interviews provide a uniquely up-close and personal access to the participants and their world. The *SAGE Handbook of Interview Research: The Complexity of the Craft* includes a number of chapters on interviews, including one on *qualitative interviewing* in the context of grounded theory by Kathy Charmaz (2012).

8.3.1 Advantages of Interviews

- **Rich data source**. Face-to-face interviews provide access not only to the information shared by the participants but also to their voice, tone, facial expressions, and body language, all adding dimensions to improve comprehension and meaning derivation. For example, we can note that at timestamp 32:10 in the interview recording, the interviewee wore a sarcastic look or walked up to the board and drew the organisational structure chart to explain their point. The ability to ask follow-up questions and delve deeper into specific areas enables richer data collection, as opposed to static forms of data collection such as surveys.

- **Examples as evidence**. Interviews provide the opportunity to ask the participants to share specific, real-world examples of the phenomenon being discussed. These in turn act as evidence to support their statements and claims.

- **Quote bank**. The evidence and examples collected in interviews become part of the data analysis, which in turn leads to the findings. This is true of other forms of data, such as project documentation. However, an added advantage of interviews is that the participants' quotes can be included as part of the narrative of the findings reported in papers and reports. These verbatim quotes open a window for the readers to glimpse into the participants' world and learn about things from the proverbial *horses' mouth* making for interesting reads. These raw forms of data also add credibility to the findings.

- **Recruitment snowballing**. Face-to-face interviews are a great mechanism to seek out more participants via snowballing. It is not uncommon at the end of an interview to ask the participant to recommend other members of their team, managers, stakeholders, customers, and so forth to participate. Such an approach may pose a bias threat if all recommended people are included in the study by default. But approaching the recommended practitioners is ultimately up to us and may be done after careful consideration of their fit for the research project based on theoretical sampling.

- **Observation gateway**. Interviews with key individuals in the team or organisation can become a convenient gateway into the rest of the organisation to collect data via other sources such as ethnographic observations of their workplace and routine or targeted observations of specific practices.

8.3.2 Sample Interview

There are many ways to go about interviewing. Below is a sample interview for illustration purposes. The actual parts of the interview are in italics and quotation marks. Actual interview questions used in previous studies can be found in Hoda et al. (2012); Shastri et al. (2017); Masood et al. (2020a). A record of how interview questions evolve can be found in Graetsch et al. (2023). More questions can be found in the *Tips for Designing and Conducting Interviews section*, presented next.

Example

Introductions and Ethics

Thank you for agreeing to participate in this research. This research is approved by the [insert name] ethics committee. Please read this information sheet and sign this consent form.

The last sentence may not be required if the consent form has been signed online in advance or as part of the pre-interview questionnaire. If not, hand over ethics document printouts for them to read. Give them few minutes to read up, fill, and sign the consent form. Then collect consent form and leave information sheet with them.

This chat is confidential, none of this will be shared with anyone in your company or outside of the research team. The research papers we write do not identify any individuals or organisations.

Setting the tone

Use this opportunity to share the planned approach and emphasise your focus on their individual practitioner experience.

I have got some questions here today, but we will keep it semi-structured, so we can discuss things that matter to you as a practitioner [or insert role, e.g. software project manager]. There are no right or wrong answers [alternative: we all know practice can differ from theory]. I am interested in your personal perspectives and real experiences [optional addition: not what the books say]. Please include concrete details and examples as much as possible. Sounds good? Let's begin.

Start recording

Explain that using an audio recorder helps you revisit the conversation later for analysis and allows you to focus on the conversation fully rather than rushing to take notes. If they agree to be recorded, start recording, else take handwritten notes.

Part A—Warm up

Can you tell me briefly about your professional background and current role.

The above is a gentle and safe warm up question. If the interviewee had filled up a pre-interview questionnaire data, you can ask more personalised warm-up questions, such as:

You mentioned your current role as [insert role, e.g. Product Owner] in the pre-interview questionnaire you filled out, please can you tell me more about how this plays out on an everyday basis?

You mentioned in the pre-interview questionnaire that your team is [e.g. highly self-organising], please can you elaborate on how this plays out in practice?

Part B—Type 1 core questions

Asking for definitions is a great way to establish a working definition of the topic and context as applicable to the participant. Then follow up with exploring various aspects of the topic with other questions. [Practice] below can be any specific concept or practice that you're focusing on, e.g. *retrospectives, sprint planning, scrum-of-scrums, self-organisation, change management*, or a sub-topic, e.g. *avoiding boredom in retrospectives, conflict resolution during sprint planning, etc.*

- *As you know, I am researching about [Practice]. Please can you explain what [Practice] means for you?*
- *What does a typical [Practice] look like?*
- *What are the main challenges of practicing [Practice]?*
- *How do you work around [specific challenges mentioned by the participant]?*
- *Based on your experience, what are the pros and cons of [Practice]?*

Part B—Type 2 follow-up questions

Ask for details and examples

- *Can you please share an example of when this happened?*
- *How often does the [Practice] take place?*
- *What do [you/team/others] do during the [Practice]?*

Ask about variations/challenges/solutions

- *What if [opposite context], how does the [Practice] work in that case?*
- *What challenges do [you/team] face with the [Practice]?*
- *How do [you/team] workaround these challenges?*

Ask for clarification—use these only if needed

- *You just mentioned [some company specific acronym]. What does it stand for?*
- *So, you mean [insert name], is that right?*

Part C—wrap-up and next steps

Anything else—open-ended invitation

- *That's all the questions I had. Is there anything else you would like to mention related to this topic that I may not covered today?*
- *Thanks again for your time and valuable perspectives today.*

Next steps
The next steps are for me to collect more data in [your/other] company. Then I will analyse the data and share the [preliminary results/papers] with you through [email/website].
Stop recording and end interview
Ask for more opportunities

- *Is it possible to have a look around the office, to get an idea of [how/where the teams are located/how the [Practice] is conducted?*
- *Is it possible to silently observe one/some of the meetings either today or another day this week/month]? Thanks.*

8.3.3 Tips for Designing and Conducting Interviews

Tips

Tips for Designing and Conducting Interviews:

- Stay curious, stay critical
- Stay conversational, stay professional
- Think theoretical, talk practical
- Stay open, narrow down over time

Here are some tips for designing effective interview questions and some important balancing acts we must perform when conducting them, including more examples of interview questions.

Stay Curious, Stay Critical

There is nothing better than genuine curiosity driving our interviews. The *bright-eyed, bunny-eared* approach and demeanour, as my PhD supervisor, Prof. James Noble, used to say, never fails. These are some ways to manifest genuine curiosity in our interviews.

- **Keep it open**. Unlike the PIQ, the interview questions are meant to be open-ended to allow the participants to share their unique ideas and experiences.

Example

Example of a closed-ended question
Do you coordinate with other teams?

Example

Examples of open-ended questions
How do you coordinate with other teams?
What does coordination with other teams look like?

Closed-ended questions provide little room for sharing details and can also create ambiance of being interrogated or audited. However, it is not as though closed-ended question cannot be posed at all. In fact, they may help participants take definitive stands on issues with *yes* or *no* responses. Use them strategically, typically accompanied by open-ended questions.

- **Listen humbly**. Acknowledging that practice can differ from theory enables us to stay humble. We may know a lot about how something is meant to work by the books (e.g. retrospectives), but the practical variations, challenges, and work-arounds can be unique to the participants' context. They are the expert in the practice field; genuinely listen to their stories.

- **It's not an audit**. Keeping our inquiry style neutral and not overly critical or demanding will help put the interviewee at ease and not feel like they are sitting an exam or are being audited for compliance.

However, when it comes to research, the dictum *stay hungry, stay foolish* (Steve Jobs) does not really apply. We must not confuse eagerness and curiosity with naïvety. It is equally important to stay critical in our data collection as it is to stay curious. It is common for researchers to be impressed by the level of experience and confidence displayed by the participants on the topic. Some participants may have a lifetime's worth of knowledge and practical experience on the topic, while you may have just started learning about the area. However, as researchers, it is our job to remain critical. There are several ways we can do this.

- **Dig deeper**. Follow-up questions are a great way to seek clarifications and details.

Example

Examples of follow-up questions:
Asking for rationale: *Why is that?*
Asking for clarification: *What is [Practice]?*
Asking for details: *What does that look like in practice?*
Asking for strategies: *How do you ensure [Practice] works?*
Asking for alternatives: *What happens when [Practice] does not work?*

- **Ask for examples**. Questions starting with *Can you think of a time when...* work well to elicit real-world examples of application. Examples can also be sought directly with *Can you share an example?* It is through concrete examples that we can learn about the participants' real experiences, with all their intricacies and nuances. Examples also serve as critical evidence bases to support the participant's perceptions and statements. In some cases, examples can reveal more than the initial statements.

- **Encourage conversation**. Sometimes asking for details does not yield much, and requesting for examples is not enough. One such scenario is when the participant genuinely does not have much to share on the topic. Sometimes, participants ease into the interview after the first few questions. Unfortunately, despite our best efforts, some never recover. Another scenario is when the participant is trying to maintain a popular narrative, the "all is well" ambience and perception, and is hesitant to share information they possess because of the sensitivity of the topic or a fear of potential consequences. One way to deal with this situation is to reiterate the confidential nature of the research and point to previous research papers by the team that do not contain any identifiable details of the participants.

Stay Conversational, Stay Professional

The idea of a semi-structured interview is to go in with a planned structure of the key areas or questions to cover but leave room for related areas and insights to emerge and flow naturally through the conversations. Herein lies another balancing act. It is important to maintain a professional approach and not become casual about the conversation. Attempt to create a level of comfort where the participants are psychologically safe sharing their stories.

A practical outcome of this approach is that no two interviews may be the same, both in terms of the full set of questions asked and the overall experience for the interviewee and the interviewer. Furthermore, interview questions, like other research protocols, are meant to evolve over the study duration, heading toward theoretical saturation, guided by theoretical sampling. The idea of not asking the exact same set of questions, phrased in the exact same way, to all research participants may appear to be a massive threat to validity for researchers used to quantitative research and inclined to the positivist research paradigm. However, for an STGT researcher, as with other qualitative research methods, the ability to personalise data collection to participants and elicit unique insights from individual experiences presents a highly valuable proposition. This is because the aim of STGT studies is to generate new findings and theoretical outcomes, not to validate hypotheses or existing theories. In STGT studies, there is a lot more emphasis on criteria such as *novelty* and *density* or depth, than there may be on criteria such as repeatability, reproducibility, and generalisability—criteria typically associated with quantitative research using the positivist research paradigm.

A related balancing act is to encourage conversation while aiming for an effective interview where most of the questions are answered within the allocated time. An introduction or ice-breaker question is a classic opportunity where the balance can easily be lost. Consider an example below.

Example

Interviewer: *Please tell me about yourself, your professional background, and your current role.*

Participant 1: *Sure. I have a bachelor's degree in chemistry; yeah, that really doesn't connect to my current role as business analyst (laughs), but I was really into chemistry at the time (laughs). In my final year, I started working on a side project with a friend of mine. We had got interested in software programming. Actually, it came out of our mutual love for video games. I am sure you've come across this before...*

(continues to recall early education and experiences with technology in general for 15 minutes out of a 40 minutes interview, several interview questions had to be dropped.)

In this example, the 15-minute introduction provided a great opportunity to set up rapport with the interviewee and bring them into ease for the rest of the interview, but it cost the interviewer several questions that they could not accommodate as they ran out of time. With practice, our interviewing skills improve. Questions can be rephrased to hint at the amount of time expected to be spent on them, by using keywords such as *briefly* or *in short*. Similarly, interjection points can be carefully created to steer the conversation back into focus. Let us revisit the previous example with enhanced interviewing techniques to achieve better outcomes.

Example

Interviewer: *Please tell me* ***briefly*** *about yourself, your professional background, and your current role.*

Participant 1: *Sure. I have a bachelor's degree in chemistry; yeah, that really doesn't connect to my current role (smiles). In my final year, I started working on a side project with a friend of mine. We had got interested in software programming. Actually, it came out of our mutual love for video games. I am sure you've come across this before...*

(gentle interjection point to steer focus)

Interviewer: *Yes, I have. What about your current role? How long have you been with Fishverse?*

Participant 1: *Currently, I am a business analyst at Fishverse. Been here for about 10 years.*

(interview continues...)

Think Theoretical, Talk Practical

This mantra is perhaps the most challenging of the balancing acts of data collection that particularly applies to interviewing. We collect data from practitioners, people who are *living* the topics that we are researching. Most of these practitioners may not understand or even be interested in what concepts or categories their experiences are being theoretically classified under. That is our job as the researcher. In designing the interview questions, or any questions for data collection, phrase the questions in way that caters to the practice space rather than the research/theoretical space.

For example, in a study on *reflective practice in agile teams*, there may be some heavy theoretical concepts to deal with, e.g. *reflection-in-action* and *reflection-on-action*. We want to discuss these with our participants and gather relevant examples and experiences. Below are examples of how *not* to phrase the interview questions, followed by examples of how to phrase them better, in the same context.

Example

Example of a theoretically heavy question
What reflection-in-action do you perform in a daily stand-up meeting?

The problem with the above question is that the participant may not be aware of the term *reflection-in-action*. By asking them about it directly, we are expecting them to translate their practical experiences into theoretical concepts for us. They will likely respond with *Sorry, I'm not sure what you mean?* or *Can you repeat the question?* or *What do you mean by reflection-in-action?* Repeating the question will not help here. Mutually establishing a working definition of *reflection-in-action* as it applies to the participant's context may help. Another approach is to rephrase the question so it indirectly refers to the theoretical concept of reflection-in-action through a practical application scenario, as below.

Example

Example of a practitioner-friendly question
What do you find yourself reflecting on during the daily stand-up meeting when it is your turn to update the team or while others are updating the team?

This question is aimed at the theoretical concept of reflection-in-action but is stated at the practical level, using practitioner-friendly terms. This allows the participant to recall how they may have applied reflection-in-action in practice without confusing them with theoretical jargon. Another related issue to note here is that using common technical jargon from the field, such as daily stand-up, is fine. The participants will be immersed in that world and language. Using complex theoretical jargon, on the other hand, is not fine. It can not only cause confusion but may also alienate and semi-intimidate the participants, who can feel inadequately informed or inexperienced to answer your questions. Worst case, they may assume a meaning and present an answer that is not relevant to the topic.

The onus of translating and presenting theoretical concepts in practical and application friendly ways lies with the researcher, not the participant. Framing questions in practitioner-friendly ways requires us to think like a practitioner. Will they be able to answer it, how? What cues might they need to recall practical scenarios from which to draw their answers and examples? It is always a good idea to discuss the interview questions with the wider research team and pilot them with real practitioners.

Stay Open, Narrow Down over Time

Designing a pre-interview questionnaire is arguably easier than designing the semi-structured questions for the face-to-face interview. Reason being, the PIQ asks for demographic type information, most of which has standard response options. The contents of the PIQ, post initial piloting and refinements, become practically standard for the duration of the research project and can be used for all participants, apart from some needed modifications to fill theoretical gaps. The interview questions, on the other hand, need to be broad enough initially to align to the overarching research question. Over time, they need to be refined to become narrow, focusing on emerging concepts and categories.

Example

Example of a broad interview question in the early data collection cycles. *What are some types of changes you typically experience on your projects? How do you manage them?*

Example

Examples of focused questions used later in the study:

- *What are some types of requirement changes you typically received from the customers on your projects?*
- *How are they conveyed to you?*
- *How do you/team respond to them?*
- *What is challenging about them?*
- *How do you overcome these challenges?*

8.3.4 Usage and Tools for Interviewing

Interviews can be conducted in physical settings, e.g. in a public space or the interviewee's workplace, or digitally, e.g. over a video or audio call. When conducting a face-to-face interview in a physical context, using a voice or audio recorder allows us to focus on the conversation at hand and not become engrossed with frantic scribbling to record things by hand. A number of powerful and easy to use recorders are available, along with accompanying or free sound organiser software for storing and re-playing the interview recordings. These days, smartphones are equally capable, but I recommend a recorder where possible as the latter typically has excellent noise cancellation and audio focusing abilities while potentially also lending more credibility and seriousness to the research endeavour.

However, using a recorder may make some participants uncomfortable. One way to ease their apprehensions is to explain to them the advantages of using a recorder (e.g. more focused conversations, better recall) and reassure them of their privacy and confidentiality (e.g. through secure storage and access). On rare occasions, despite all attempts, some participants may refuse to be recorded. We must respect their decision and continue without recording and take handwritten notes instead.

Irrespective of the audio recording, I like to keep a notepad and pen handy and tend to take some notes along the way. This can help jot down potential follow-up questions while the participant is speaking so we don't have to interrupt them. They can also assist in drawing quick diagrams to capture relationships and structures they may be explaining and show it to them for feedback on the go. Alternatively, we can pass over the pen and paper to them to draw diagrams to aid their descriptions. For interviews further along in a research project, when we have a good sense of some of the key emerging concepts and categories, we can also find ourselves noting theoretical musings during the interview, like writing a brief memo on the go or tagging a potential concept or category name that fits the description being shared.

Other tools to bring along include a pair of extra batteries for the recorder, ethics documents for participant's signing (if signing in person), and a camera or smartphone in case an opportunity to conduct a walk-through of their workplace or observation of a meeting presents itself. If conducting the interview digitally, remember to press record on the video call platform, e.g. Zoom, with the participant's permission.

8.3.5 Threats and Limitations of Interviews

- **Time and cost.** Interviews are one of the most rich sources of data but also one of the most time-consuming and costly data collective techniques, e.g. physical interviews that involve travel and commute. Interviews conducted in the digital context save on travel and commute time but are likely to take more effort than some other techniques such as surveys and data mining. A reasonable consideration would be to assess the return on investment. For example, if the nature of the topic is such that the questions are relatively straightforward with limited response options, other forms of data collection may suffice, e.g. surveys. However, to gain real-world examples and in-depth insights, interviews are well worth the investment!

- **Scaling limitations.** Because of the manual effort involved, it is difficult to scale interviews to be conducted for a large number of participants, unless there is a team of researchers dividing up the task. Even then, it may require a team workshop to design a common approach and a set of questions and follow-up questions bank to select from. It may also pay to pair up and swap around interviewer pairs for better cross-fertilisation across the team and improved consistency of approach.

8.4 Observations

Definition

Observations are a live window into the practice field. They can be used to gain in-depth understanding of the workplace and contexts, practices and activities, and interactions and dynamics, as well as to capture cues of the team and organisational cultures.

8.4.1 Advantages of Observations

- **Analysing the "mundane"**. Observations allow the researcher to take note of aspects that may appear routine and mundane to the practitioners. They may not have bothered mentioning them at all during the interviews. However, from an observer's perspective, we can note these seemingly routine aspects down, compare them to practices observed elsewhere, and also seek clarifications about our observations with the participants to gain further insights. For example, after attending a daily stand-up with a software team, the researcher can ask some of the team members about why they chose a particular order of speaking, whether the task board is always updated during the stand-up meeting or at other times, why was [insert name or description] so quiet, and how does the team follow up on the hurdles mentioned during the stand-up. Such probes can lead to other interesting insights.

- **Nuanced perspective**. When reporting things verbally, as in during an interview, the information may be presented in a manner that makes practices or actions seem highly organised and systematic. However, it is often during observations that we find nuances of the same actions playing out. For example, a participant may have informed us of consistently following a specific approach or protocol for conducting their retrospective meetings. However, during an observation session, we may find that the approach was a lot more fluid and modified in practice. We can then probe the modifications, their motivations, and consequences via more observations or through further interviews.

- **Internal verification**. Observations can also help verify information shared during interviews. During observations, we may find some of what was reported in interviews is either not accurate, partly accurate, or completely matches the actions we see in practice. When it comes to comparing interviews and observational data, actions speak louder than words. When in conflict, observational data takes precedence over verbally shared information, unless the discrepancy can be explained in some other way, e.g. as a one-off action.

8.4.2 Sample Observations

Observation notes can be made to capture as much of the context seen to be relevant as possible. If conducting the observation in person, some common things to note during observations include the location, placement, and setup of the office, project team, team desk spaces, shared boards, screens, meeting rooms, equipment, tools, platforms, and so on. A hand drawing of the team's physical setup can be found in Hoda et al. (2012). Below are a couple of observations recounted in a way one would typically record them during or after conducting them.

- **A daily stand-up**. I was being shown around the office and then, without much warning, was invited to join a daily stand-up that was about to begin. I "hurdled into the circle" the team had created, all standing around their physical scrum board. It closely followed the ideal stand-up description, team members taking turns to update others on their plans and progress and highlight any obstacles. Frequently, people would point to specific items on the board or move them to indicate progress. The conversations were brief and focused, and the meeting wrapped up in about 10 minutes. It was fun to take part in an actual daily stand-up.

- **A distributed daily stand-up**. In another instance, I was invited to observe another daily stand-up meeting that included an offshore team in Europe joining the local India team via videoconferencing. The local team created a semi-circle, facing the large screen in one of the meeting rooms. I was part of the semi-circle and was briefly introduced before the stand-up began. I greeted the remote team with a hand wave and confirmed that I'll be silently observing. On the screen, the remote team members appeared one or two at a time. The session was more informal than the other local daily stand-up. Mainly, it was used to clarify outstanding issues with the remote manager who was responsible for providing the sprint requirements, like a proxy product owner. It seemed to be more of a co-ordination meeting focused on bringing the two geographically separated teams on the same page. It lasted around 15–20 minutes, after which team members dispersed and went back to their tasks. It was useful to gather a sense of the dynamics between the local and remote team. Some of the themes mentioned in the interviews such as a slight sense of compliance to the remote manager's guidance were observable in action.

8.4.3 Tips for Conducting Observations

Tips

Tips for Conducting Observations:

- Be known
- Silence is useful
- Be a sponge
- Record
- Follow up

Observations are fun. At the same time, they can be somewhat intimidating for us and those we are observing. Here are some tips to make the most of our observation sessions.

- **Be Known**. Silent walking around and observing from a distance can appear as strange and disturbing as standing over people's shoulders and asking too many questions. It is a good idea to have your visit announced beforehand so people know what to expect. Most companies will do this automatically, but it does not hurt to remind your main contact to inform everyone. Coffee and lunch breaks are great opportunities to meet a wider group of people and answer any questions they may naturally have about us and our research.

- **Silence is useful**. "Fly on the wall" is often used as a metaphor for describing the ideal research approach to conducting observations. In other words, stay as silent and unobtrusive as possible, allowing the practitioners to go about their everyday business without being interrupted or bothered by our presence.

- **Be a sponge**. Actively soak in all the information around. How long did the meeting last? Were all members of the team actively participating in the daily stand-up? Was there a hint of tension in the team-customer interactions during the planning meeting? What was the management approach exhibited by the scrum master during the estimation session? Were testers invited and present?

- **Record**. It is easy to get carried away observing people going about their work and become unaware of our role as a researcher to record our observations. Take notes, draw or take pictures if permitted, and do what makes sense to record your thoughts and insights from the observations. The devil is in the details, and so the sooner we record, the better, ideally during the observations or immediately afterwards, so we don't forget.

- **Follow up**. Interviews and observations are meant to complement each other. Follow up on information shared during interviews by looking out for corresponding details and evidence during observations. Similarly, follow up on observations by asking relevant questions to clarify doubts or gather more details. These questions can be asked during informal talks, over a coffee or lunch, in corridors as you may be introduced to people in the organisation.

8.4.4 Usage and Tools for Observations

A notebook and pen can be used to capture the observations. We can record actions, regular and unexpected. We can also draw out things like the floorplan and seating arrangement of a team we are studying. The same can be achieved using digital writing and drawing devices such as iPads.

With appropriate ethics and participant approval, observations can also be recorded, e.g. recording an online team meeting on Zoom or video recording the daily activities of software developers. Similarly, we can also capture photographs of workspaces, artefacts, and practices. These can be shared, e.g. after obfuscating identifying details, e.g. by blurring parts of photos and videos, in our paper and media reports, so our readers can gain a glimpse of the real contexts. Similarly, snippets of observational video recordings can also be shared, e.g. in presentations, talks, and research videos.

8.4.5 Threats and Limitations

- **Time, cost, and scaling.** Similar to interviews, observations are time-consuming and have associated travel and commute costs in the physical contexts. Because of these costs, it is not easy to conduct a large number of observations, unless there is a team working on it or if the researchers are deeply embedded in context, e.g. through ethnographic observations. Observations of meetings conducted online can be effective, removing the need to travel and offering the additional benefit of recording the proceedings with participant consent. However, picking up on nuances while walking through workspaces is difficult to replicate online. Overall, like interviews, observations are a relatively "costly" data collection technique but are well worth in most cases due to the firsthand access and insights they provide into the phenomenon.

- **Observer's effect.** Participants have been reported to experience the *Hawthorne* or *observer's effect* or *researcher's effect*, behaving differently under the awareness of being observed (LeCompte & Goetz, 1982; McCarney et al., 2007). Applying a positivist stance, this can be considered a limitation of the observation technique (and, in some cases, interviews), and several steps can be taken to minimise the effect, such as those shared in the *tips for conducting observations* above. However, considered from a constructivist stance, the presence of the observer and any interactions between the observer and the observed can be considered part of the process of constructing the reality of the phenomenon being observed, not posing any threats to validity. Monahan and Fisher (2010) argue that *while outsiders may see the data as "biased", ethnographers should be prepared to argue that informants' performances—however staged for or influenced by the observer—often reveal profound truths about social and/or cultural phenomena.* Given these opposing schools of thought, it is important that researchers carefully consider their research paradigm (see Chap. 5, Research Philosophy); select to apply them consistently, including during observations; and declare them in their writings so they can be read and assessed accordingly.

8.5 Other Data Sources and Collection Techniques

Semi-structured interviews and observations, conducted in person and online, continue to be popular and rich sources of qualitative data in STGT studies. Other data sources, platforms, and collection techniques are also harnessed effectively and in combination with each other. Figure 8.1 shows an overview of a variety of data collection techniques that can be used in STGT studies in particular and in qualitative studies in general.

8.5.1 Focus Groups

Definition

A focus group is a data collection technique that involves eliciting information from a group of people together in one session. Focus groups can be thought of as group interviews; however, it can include elements of interactions between participants themselves as they discuss issues, in addition to those between the interviewer (or facilitator) and the participants. In this sense, a focus group is an interactive exercise, with the potential to discuss, debate, and develop ideas together as a group.

Typically, focus groups are designed to include people who share similar demographic or contextual backgrounds. For example, a focus group can be conducted with the members of the same software team or all the scrum masters in the organisation or product stream. For a manageable process and best outcomes, a focus group of between three and ten people is recommended, with one or two facilitators.

Research teams may gain more from conducting a focus group as opposed to individual interviews where it is imperative to collect multiple perspectives, surface potential conflicts of opinions, and establish a shared understanding or common grounds about a topic. It can also be effectively employed in cases where the topic is particularly challenging to handle in a one-on-one context and where individuals may feel psychologically safer sharing their ideas in a group setting. Similarly, it can be useful in recollecting and reconstructing specific events or experiences through the collective memory of the group.

The role of the researcher in effectively facilitating focus group sessions is critical. New researchers may wish to practice, e.g. with teammates or test participants, before stepping out to facilitate focus groups in real-world settings. They can accompany experienced researchers to a few focus groups before leading the facilitation of their own sessions. An example of the use of focus groups with grounded theory analysis can be found in O'Connor (2012).

8.5.2 Surveys

Definition

Surveys and questionnaires are structured techniques of collecting practitioner demographics, perspectives, and experiences. They can include closed-ended, open-ended, or mixed questions that elicit demographic information about the participant, their company, domain, projects, teams, and their perspectives on a variety of issues, based on their professional lifelong experiences or those on specific projects. These types of information help establish the context and enable a type of "cross-tabular" analysis across different concepts, e.g. how management approach tends to vary with years of professional experience.

Personal data such as gender and age range may also be useful to collect in some contexts, for example, in studies that are focused on gender or age as a key aspect or where some cross-tabular analysis is expected between gender or age and another concept. Collecting personal information without a clear rationale is discouraged.

When used in STGT studies, surveys are best kept short (e.g. under 20 minutes to complete) with some closed-ended and mostly open-ended questions to allow for qualitative data analysis to be applied to the results. While possible to conduct on paper, surveys are usually conducted online, using from one of many available tools such as *Qualtrics*, *SurveyMonkey*, *LimeSurvey*, and so on. Designing an effective survey form is non-trivial and typically requires a few rounds of reviews and revisions within the research team followed by testing with some people outside of the research team to assess its comprehensibility, time taken, and effectiveness to elicit the information needed. The data collected from a survey can then be analysed using STGT coding procedures.

8.5.3 Recordings

DEFINITION

Audio and video recordings can be used as data in STGT studies following quality check and ethical research practice.

A variety of rich qualitative data is available in the form of audio and video recordings that can be included in STGT studies. These include pre-existing recordings of research interviews, observations, and focus groups as well as recordings of practitioner interviews, talks, podcasts, and events such as conferences on YouTube, Spotify, and other platforms. Ethical considerations are applicable to pre-existing and freely available data as they are to custom-collected data. Carefully consider the copyright of the recordings and attempt to seek permission to include them in research. For example, if a series of relevant TED and TEDx talks are included as data sources for a research study, it is best to seek permission from the organisers or speakers to include the talks in the study, explaining its aims, expected outcomes, dissemination plans, and potential impact. While not impossible, it would be rare to perform an STGT study purely on recordings. More likely, recordings can serve as a good source of supplementary data, to support other forms of data sources and collection techniques.

8.5.4 Texts

DEFINITION

Texts refer to the category of data sources that originally appear in a text format. These include blogs, wikis, diaries, project documentation, and other written documents, that can be custom collected both in the physical and digital medium.

Software practitioners can be requested to maintain a diary for the duration of the study that captures their experiences with the phenomenon being studied. Texts can also be pre-existing, e.g. books, blogs, wikis, and meeting transcripts. For example, the data collected through the various data collection techniques, such as interviews, is typically transcribed into text formats for qualitative data analysis. Texts are one of the most convenient data sources as collecting them is typically simpler than through other means, e.g. interviews and surveys, and they are already in a form that can be analysed. However, a challenge with pre-existing texts such as books and transcripts is that they do not allow the team to pose specific questions and they have to work with what is available, including filtering content for quality and relevance.

8.5.5 Social Media

Definition

Social media platforms such as Twitter, LinkedIn, and Facebook provide people with the opportunity to express themselves and network online. Social media platforms are frequently used by researchers to advertise and recruit participants for their study. They also end up providing researchers with access to a variety of professionally curated as well as uninhibited and personal data in the form of thoughts, opinions, and experiences.

In a position paper, Storey et al. (2010) discuss the potential of social media use in improving software engineering practices. They encourage explorations into its benefits, limits, and risks for data collection in software engineering research, its effectiveness for testing software designs, and potential for supporting end-user development. While offering access to large quantities of data, the use of social media data for research is not without its challenges. For example, protecting the reputations and privacy of users has been identified as two major challenges associated with the use of social media for software engineering research (Begel et al., 2010). Responsible use of data, as with other data sources and data collection techniques, is the key to making the most of social media data in STGT studies and in empirical studies in general.

8.5.6 Artefacts

Definition

Artefacts refer to physical and digital items such as task boards, diagrams, graphs, devices, gadgets, and other items relevant to the studied phenomenon.

While conducting observations, it is common to come across artefacts used by software teams such as task boards, velocity charts, team charters, company values, and vision statements, usually posted on the walls around the office floors. Walking around the office space provides an opportunity to pause, observe, and potentially "collect" these artefacts, e.g. by taking photographs or videos, with due permission. Similarly, digital artefacts such as diagrams, team boards, photos, and diagrams can be custom collected or gathered from pre-existing sources. Artefacts may contain text and usually appear in a format that can be inspected and interpreted, e.g. user stories and tasks on a team's scrum board can inform the research team about the health of the project, how working pairs or sub-teams are formed, and even team culture through the use of cartoons and avatars to denote task ownership. Examples of the use of artefacts can be found in Masood et al. (2020a); Berntzen et al. (2022, 2023).

8.5.7 Data Mining

Definition

Data mining is the process of automating the extraction of data from various sources, usually harnessing machine learning algorithms and tools.

Some types of texts, artefacts, and data from social media channels are uniquely placed for data mining. These include texts and artefacts found in software repositories such as GitHub and BitBucket, developer community Q&A forums such as Stack Overflow and Code Project, practitioner portals such as InfoQ, developer chat portals such as on Slack and Discord, software project management platforms such as JIRA and Trello, and user reviews of the apps available on stores such as Google Play and Apple's App Store.

All of these sources are inherently digital in nature, and their data typically tend to be pre-existing. Stack Overflow is particularly popular for mining data for software engineering research, e.g. to understand the information needs of software developers (Treude et al., 2011; Liu et al., 2021). It may be possible to custom collect data from some of these sources, e.g. by asking a question on Stack Overflow.

Access to data on these forums and platforms differs. Some may be free to access such as open-source repositories on GitHub and user app reviews on app stores. However, access does not equate to permission. Research communities relying heavily on data mining such as Mining Software Repositories (MSR) are beginning to discuss their ethical challenges (Gonzalez-Barahona, 2020; Gold & Krinke, 2022). Some other channels may need special access, e.g. the researcher being given access to the software team's private Slack channel or Trello board.

Some data collection tools to support data mining from a range of sources include Perceval[2] and PyDriller[3] for mining software repositories. As with other pre-existing data sources, it is the research team's responsibility to filter for relevance and quality and prepare the mined data for analysis.

[2] https://github.com/chaoss/grimoirelab-perceval.

[3] https://github.com/ishepard/pydriller.

8.5.8 Immersive Experiences in Extended Realities

Definition

Emerging technologies such as augmented reality (AR), virtual reality (VR), and mixed realities (MR) have introduced new realities, extending beyond the material and physical reality.

Emerging technologies have fundamentally redefined human societies and communication. They have challenged the traditional sociological concepts of the human *mind*, *self*, and *society* (Mead, 1934; Wolfe, 1991). Human communication is no longer simply mediated by technology but is being redefined by it. New modes and protocols of communication have emerged in these new realities, expanding lexicon, symbols, and meaning. For example, new immersive socio-technical worlds created on modern social media platforms (e.g. Metaverse), virtual social worlds (e.g. Second Life), and virtual and new reality game worlds (e.g. Minecraft, Pokémon Go, Harry Potter: Wizards Unite) not only serve to simulate the physical world but enable the construction of new social norms and communication protocols (Kaplan & Haenlein, 2010). These brave new worlds also offer new ways to observe and study them through *immersive and experiential* approaches, e.g. as *passive* or *active* participants on immersive social media or within massively multiplayer online games.

Social science research methods originally designed to study social interactions in the physical reality need to be reassessed and refreshed to work in new realities. For example, virtual ethnography has been introduced for *novel social spaces* created by online interactions (Hine, 2008). Similarly, STGT acknowledges these new realities and encourages the exploration of responsible data collection in such modern contexts. It motivates the need to consider multiple ontology, epistemology, and research paradigms (see Chap. 5 Research Philosophy). For example, games are generally rule-based and can be designed to offer limited decision-making. Possibilities in a virtual game world can be designed to be finite and deterministic, manifesting closely the idea of an external stand-alone reality best captured by a positivist research paradigm or mindset, whereas social interactions between real people on online social media platforms is a different type of reality, informed by the intermixing operational contexts, symbols, languages, and guidelines of both real and virtual worlds, offering the same, if not more, complexity than the real world. Here, an *interpretive* or *constructivist* mindset may be more suitable. Chapter 14. Future Directions in Qualitative Research covers some of the opportunities and concerns of using Generative AI tools such as ChatGPT for qualitative research.

8.6 Summary

In this chapter, we learned about the two groups of *data collection techniques* in STGT studies: custom-data collection and existing-data collection. We learned about some popular data collection techniques in more detail: pre-interview questionnaires, semi-structured interviews, observations, and other sources and collection techniques such as focus groups, surveys, recordings, texts, social media, artefacts, data mining, and immersive experiences in extended realities. Data collection and analysis are meant to be interleaved in an STGT study and go hand in hand. Researchers will benefit from reading this chapter in conjunction with the *Basics of Qualitative Data Collection*, *Qualitative Data Preparation and Filtering*, and *Socio-technical Grounded Theory for Qualitative Data Analysis* chapters. Collectively, they cover socio-technical grounded theory's basic stage.

References

Begel, A., DeLine, R., & Zimmermann, T. (2010). Social media for software engineering. In *Proceedings of the FSE/SDP workshop on Future of software engineering research* (pp. 33–38).

Berntzen, M., Hoda, R., Moe, N. B., & Stray, V. (2022). A taxonomy of inter-team coordination mechanisms in large-scale agile. *IEEE Transactions on Software Engineering, 49*(2), 699–718.

Berntzen, M., Stray, V., Moe, N. B., & Hoda, R. (2023). Responding to change over time: A longitudinal case study on changes in coordination mechanisms in large-scale agile. *Empirical Software Engineering, 28*(5), 114.

Charmaz, K., Belgrave, L., et al. (2012). Qualitative interviewing and grounded theory analysis. *The SAGE Handbook of Interview Research: The Complexity of the Craft, 2*, 347–365.

Gold, N. E., & Krinke, J. (2022). Ethics in the mining of software repositories. *Empirical Software Engineering, 27*(1), 17.

Gonzalez-Barahona, J. (2020). Mining software repositories while respecting privacy. In *Mining Software Repositories Tutorial*. https://2020. msrconf. org/details/msr-2020-Education/1/Mining-Software-Repositories-While-Respect ing-Privacy

Graetsch, U. M., Khalajzadeh, H., Shahin, M., Hoda, R., & Grundy, J. (2023). Dealing with data challenges when delivering data-intensive software solutions. *IEEE Transactions on Software Engineering*. https://doi.org/10.1109/TSE.2023. 3291003

Hine, C. (2008). Virtual ethnography: Modes, varieties, affordances. In *The SAGE Handbook of Online Research Methods* (pp. 257–270).

Hoda, R., Noble, J., & Marshall, S. (2012). Self-organizing roles on agile software development teams. *IEEE Transactions on Software Engineering, 39*(3), 422–444.

Kaplan, A. M., & Haenlein, M. (2010). Users of the world, unite! the challenges and opportunities of social media. *Business horizons, 53*(1), 59–68.

LeCompte, M. D., & Goetz, J. P. (1982). Problems of reliability and validity in ethnographic research, *Review of Educational Research, 52*(1), 31–60.

Liu, M., Peng, X., Marcus, A., Xing, S., Treude, C., & Zhao, C. (2021). API-related developer information needs in stack overflow. *IEEE Transactions on Software Engineering, 48*(11), 4485–4500.

Madampe, K., Hoda, R., & Singh, P. (2020). Towards understanding emotional response to requirements changes in agile teams. In *Proceedings of the ACM/IEEE 42nd International Conference on Software Engineering: New Ideas and Emerging Results* (pp. 37–40).

Masood, Z., Hoda, R., & Blincoe, K. (2020a). How agile teams make self-assignment work: A grounded theory study, *Empirical Software Engineering, 25*, 4962–5005. https://doi.org/10.1007/s10664-020-09876-x

Masood, Z., Hoda, R., Blincoe, K. (2020b). Real world Scrum: A grounded theory of variations in practice. *IEEE Transactions on Software Engineering, 48*(5), 1579–1591.

McCarney, R., Warner, J., Iliffe, S., Van Haselen, R., Griffin, M., & Fisher, P. (2007). The hawthorne effect: a randomised, controlled trial. *BMC Medical Research Methodology, 7*(1), 30.

Mead, G. H. (1934). *Mind, self and society* (Vol. 111). Chicago University of Chicago Press.

Monahan, T., & Fisher, J. A. (2010). Benefits of 'observer effects': Lessons from the field. *Qualitative Research, 10*(3), 357–376.

O'Connor, R. (2012). Using grounded theory coding mechanisms to analyze case study and focus group data in the context of software process research. In *Research methodologies, innovations and philosophies in software systems engineering and information systems* (pp. 256–270). IGI Global.

Shastri, Y., Hoda, R., & Amor, R. (2017). Understanding the roles of the manager in agile project management. In *Proceedings of the 10th Innovations in Software Engineering Conference* (pp. 45–55).

Storey, M.-A., Treude, C., van Deursen, A., & Cheng, L.-T. (2010). The impact of social media on software engineering practices and tools. In *Proceedings of the FSE/SDP workshop on Future of software engineering research* (pp. 359–364).

Treude, C., Barzilay, O., & Storey, M.-A. (2011). How do programmers ask and answer questions on the web? (NIER track). In *Proceedings of the 33rd International Conference on Software Engineering* (pp. 804–807).

Wolfe, A. (1991). Mind, self, society, and computer: Artificial intelligence and the sociology of mind. *American Journal of Sociology, 96*(5), 1073–1096.

9 Qualitative Data Preparation and Filtering

Abstract Qualitative data collection and analysis also involves data preparation and filtering. In this chapter, we will learn about *data preparation* including preparing interview, observation, recording, survey, and text-based data and their storage and organisation. Then we will learn about *data filtering*, including the filtering key information, contextual information, and noise. Finally, we will learn about some *tips for data filtering*. Researchers will benefit from reading this chapter in conjunction with the *Basics of Qualitative Data Collection*, *Techniques of Qualitative Data Collection*, and *Socio-technical Grounded Theory for Qualitative Data Analysis* chapters. Collectively, they cover socio-technical grounded theory's basic stage.

R. Hoda, *Qualitative Research with Socio-Technical Grounded Theory*,
https://doi.org/10.1007/978-3-031-60533-8_9

9.1 Data Preparation

Definition

Data preparation *is the process of converting the raw data into formats (typically text-based) where qualitative analysis can be performed effectively, efficiently, and with ease and confidence.*

Before coding can commence, the raw data collected needs to be prepared for analysis. Data preparation involves converting the data from its raw form into formats in which analysis can be performed effectively and efficiently. Text-based formats are ideal for qualitative analysis, e.g. Google Docs, Microsoft Word, or paper printouts provide a full overview of individual units of data such as a single interview. They also enable convenient comparison of information within the same and with other units of data, e.g. across several social media posts (Fig 9.1).

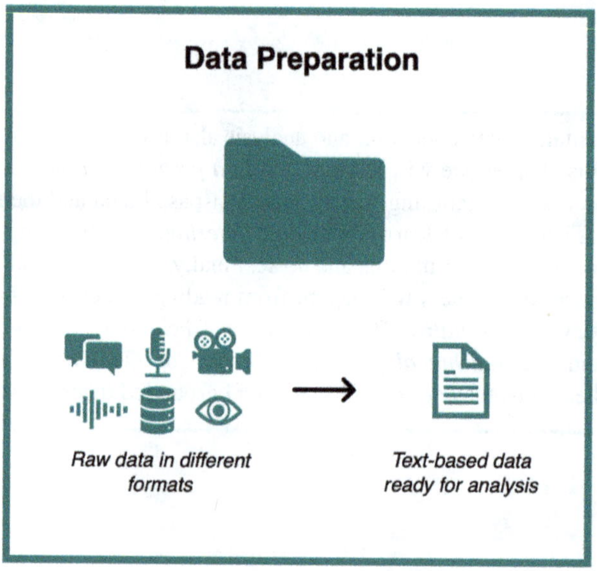

Fig. 9.1 Data preparation: converting raw data into a format convenient for analysis, typically text-based

While data analysis can be conducted on the non-text formats directly, such as using audio or video files, it can be somewhat ineffective and inefficient. Analysing data naturally requires constantly going back and forth. If done on audio or video recordings, it can introduce unnecessary cognitive overload and fatigue as the researcher constantly stops, rewinds, and replays recordings over and over again. They risk missing useful information and are more likely to introduce human errors. Another benefit of data preparation is that it provides easy access to the verbatim raw data for reporting. For example, duly sanitised and pertinent quotes and excerpts can be easily extracted from the transcripts and included in manuscripts, presentations, posters, and videos as needed.

Data preparation is almost always done ahead of data filtering and analysis. It can also be considered a pre-step to data analysis since it can be partially executed by non-analysts, e.g. by outsourcing audio recordings to professional transcribers for transcription, with due ethics approval. Emerging transcription tools are making this task simpler. However, analysts inevitably have to become involved in data preparation, e.g. to confirm the accuracy of transcriptions, whether manual or automated. Data filtering can be performed alongside coding or ahead of coding where the data is expected to contain considerable noise.

9.1.1 Preparing Interview Data

Data collected through semi-structured interviews is typically saved in the form of audio or video recordings. In preparation for analysis, the recordings are transcribed into text format. Transcription is a time-intensive activity. Novice researchers may find transcribing their interview recordings useful as a means to revisit the conversations and relive their data collection experiences. Manually transcribing interviews can help them reflect on their interviewing skills, notice moments where they asked a good follow-up question and where they missed an opportunity. As the research project progresses and the novice researcher gains experience, the benefits of manually transcribing may diminish in comparison to the benefits of time gained from semi-automating the process or employing professional transcribers. For example, automated transcription tools such as *Jarvis.ai* and *Otter.ai*, voice typing features embedded in *Google Docs*, *Google Live Transcribe*—an Android-based transcription app—and voice command assistants can help.[1] It is also common for researchers to outsource this step to professional transcribers, following appropriate ethics guidelines. Irrespective of the approach, someone from the research team, preferably the researcher who originally collected the data, can go over and confirm the accuracy of the transcription, correct any errors, and fill in any gaps.

9.1.2 Preparing Observational Data

Observational field notes and sketches are usually taken using a pen and paper or digital tools and devices. To prepare them for data analysis, a number of aspects need to be addressed. Notes taken during observations may have been taken in shorthand

[1] Discretion is recommended in using AI and cloud-based tools when working with particularly sensitive data.

or may be missing details. Expand and finalise them while the observation experience is still fresh. If they exist in a paper format, saving digital copies is a good idea for safekeeping. If observations were conducted by multiple researchers, notes can be compared, any conflicting information discussed and resolved, and complementary information combined to produce a detailed set of notes. If the data analysis is going to be performed by multiple researchers, it is important to prepare the observational notes in a way that makes them easily accessible, legible, and shareable for all.

Observations can also result in photographs and video recordings. Preparing them involves storing them securely in the research folders, named appropriately for ease of access and participant confidentiality. Video recordings can be further transcribed verbatim, or observational notes can be taken based on viewings of the recordings. These notes can then be prepared for analysis as detailed earlier.

9.1.3 Preparing Recordings Data

Rich qualitative data can be found in the form of audio and video recordings, e.g. recordings of pre-existing research interviews, observations, and focus groups, practitioner talks, podcasts, documentaries, short films, and so on. If including these in an STGT study, the researchers can make use of the text narratives that often accompany such recordings or transcribe them as discussed earlier.

9.1.4 Preparing Survey Data

For paper-based surveys, the responses can be typed up into spreadsheets in preparation for analysis. Responses to online surveys and questionnaires can be conveniently exported into spreadsheets. While the respondents are typically anonymous, each response can be numbered for ease of reference, e.g. R1, R2, corresponding to each row of the spreadsheet. Where mixed data was collected, the qualitative responses can be further extracted out into separate spreadsheets for qualitative analysis while maintaining the respondent mapping to the main spreadsheet using the reference numbers. This helps avoid excessive horizontal scrolling during analysis. Many online surveying tools such as *Qualtrics*, *SurveyMonkey*, *LimeSurvey*, and *Google Forms*[2] offer the ability to produce basic statistical analysis and graphs of quantitative data on the click of a button. However, we may wish to apply different visualisations or analyse the data in advanced ways, e.g. exploring various possible co-relations and co-variances. In this case, consider exporting the raw responses into spreadsheets and performing desired analysis and visualisations.

---

[2] Google Forms may not be accessible everywhere in the world, causing researchers to miss certain geographic locations in their survey.

9.1.5 Preparing Text-Based Data

Some data sources originally appear in text formats, e.g. blogs, wikis, diaries, project documentation, text-based artefacts, and other written documents. Similarly, social media posts, software repositories, developer question-and-answers, community forums, and developer chat platforms are examples of data sources where the data originally appears in a text format. These are near ready for analysis and require relatively little preparation. However, the researchers will need to consider three key aspects when dealing with such data. First, consider making local copies of these datasets to avoid losing access to them if the original sources are modified or retracted. Second, if the amount of data is inundating, as can happen with online public data, they will need to define the scope of the workable data and perform data mining or extraction accordingly, prior to data analysis. Finally, given many of these data sources have low regulation and work on complaint-based censorship, they may need to be further filtered for relevant and useful content, as explained in *data filtering* later in this chapter.

The same applies to data in the form of academic and practitioner literature and articles that appear in text formats. In such cases, it is recommended to design a data extraction sheet so that the data can be extracted using a consistent approach. For example, the *Research Methodology* details can be extracted in a separate column or sub-sheet to the *Findings*. This will also help multiple researchers distribute the analysis workload. Details of the grounded theory literature review method, where STGT data analysis can be employed to analyse literature, are provided in Chap. 6, Literature Reviews.

9.1.6 Data Storage and Organisation

Once the data is in a text form, adding page and line numbers makes for easy referencing during data analysis. For example, to maintain participant confidentiality and privacy, interview transcripts can be named using a consistent alphanumeric protocol instead of using the real participant and/or company names. For example, "P21-July2021" can be used to name a transcript where "P21" is the participant number and "July2021" captures when the data was collected. The mapping of real participant details and transcript numbers can be stored separately. Additionally, the researchers may wish to further sanitise the transcripts by replacing all possible identifying details such as company name, names of peers, managers, and other references, with pseudo-names to provide further security. Removing these details entirely is not recommended as it can cause some key and contextual information to be lost during analysis. However, examples of data that is included within manuscripts and shared with reviewers need to be sanitised to maintain participant confidentiality.

Prepared data can be stored on secure, password-protected local or offline storage such as on official laptops or desktops. Saving backups on multiple devices ensures avoidance of nightmarish scenarios of losing precious data as a result of hardware failure or software corruption. Increasingly, researchers use secure online and cloud-based storage, such as Dropbox combined with Boxcryptor for security, Google Drive with strict access control, and other online platforms or shared drives provided by their institutions.

Over time, we can end up with staggering amounts of data. Organising this data logically, in well-labelled folders, will greatly assist in not only data management but also with data analysis, reducing look-up time and unnecessary cognitive overload. Data analysis tools such as NVivo, ATLAS.ti, and MAXQDA offer data storage and management features.

9.2 Data Filtering

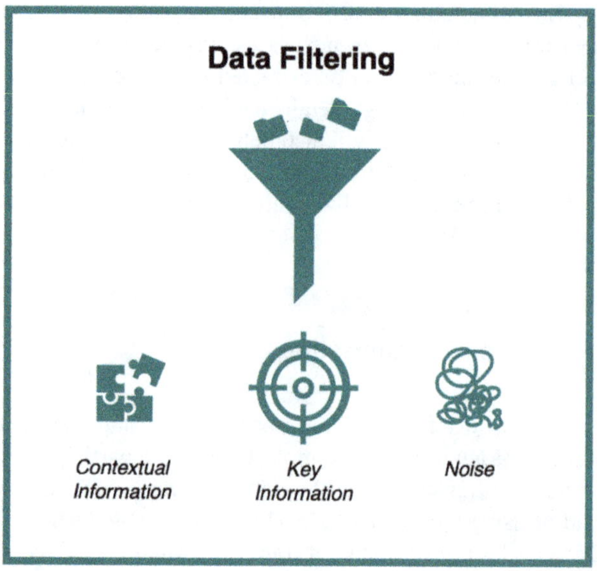

Fig. 9.2 Data filtering: separating key information, contextual information, and noise

Definition

Data filtering *is the process of identifying the key information, contextual information, and noise in the raw data.* Data filtering can be performed alongside coding or ahead of coding in cases where the data is expected to contain considerable noise.

Once data has been prepared in a format that is easily accessible, the next step is to filter the data for useful information. Data filtering involves roughly grouping the data into chunks of *key information*, *contextual information*, and *noise*, visually represented in Fig. 9.2. Key information and contextual information are relevant and useful information, while noise represents the bits that are irrelevant or of little value, from a coding perspective.

Researchers tend to improve over time in their data collection skills to reduce the collection of noise, but some noise in data is inevitable. For most types of prepared data, such as interview transcripts, data filtering can be done while performing coding. Other types of data, especially pre-existing data such as those collected from software repositories, developer forums, and social media, can contain more noise. This is because they pre-exist independently for other purposes and happen to be harvested for research (see Chap. 8, Techniques of Qualitative Data Collection, for ethical considerations of data mining). In these cases, we need to filter the data to discard or disregard the noise and analyse the useful bits. Depending on the amount of expected noise in such cases, data filtering can be done as a separate step, prior to coding.

- **Key information** is information that is related directly to the topic of our research, including concrete details and examples. Key information is analysed using STGT's coding procedures of open coding, constant comparison, and memoing.
- **Contextual information** is background and demographic information that supports and enhances the understanding of the key information. Contextual information can be extracted from the data and processed using descriptive analysis and typically does not need STGT's coding procedures.
- **Noise** is data that has little or nothing to do with the research topic or phenomenon under investigation and provides little or no research value to the project. Noise is not analysed using STGT's coding procedures or any other qualitative analysis techniques.

Not all data needs to be analysed using rigorous coding procedures such as open coding and constant comparison. Some data may not need to be analysed at all. Effectively identifying and treating these different types of information can greatly improve the efficiency of our data analysis. For example, consider the data collected from a semi-structured interview. As humans, we tend to speak in flow, reflecting on perceptions and lived experiences while also recalling related stories and details on the go. The human ability to move across space and time during conversations is unparalleled! Sometimes, interviewees will go on a tangent that may add useful additional insights, and at other times, these tangents can fully digress from the topic and provide little valuable information. Similarly, when mining data from developer forums or app reviews, despite our best efforts and using the most relevant keywords, a fair bit of noise can creep into the datasets. For each of these types of information, we will consider how to identify them and, broadly speaking, what to do with them.

9.2.1 Key Information

Definition

Key information *is the information directly related and most relevant to our research topic and helps address our research questions. Key information across the various data sources requires deep analysis to make sense of and typically sparks the need for reflections to be captured through memoing.*

Key information can be thought of as the *main course*, the *star performance*, and the *raison d'etre* for collecting data in the first place. It is likely to be found throughout the raw data, whether custom collected or pre-existing. During an interview, key information is most likely to present itself in response to questions directly related to the research topic and in examples that the participants share in an effort to explain or expand on their response. For example, here's an excerpt from an interview for a research project focused on understanding how software teams become self-organising agile teams.

Example

Question: *What were some of the main challenges in the process of transitioning into becoming self-organizing?*
Answer: *I think the culture is the main thing.*

Question: *You mean the work culture or the national culture?*
Answer: *Work culture. I don't think that the national culture is so important...[later]...If the company believes it and the team believes it, they can create a good culture in the team, irrespective of the national culture. That is the overriding fact and many times they use that as a proxy to blame their dysfunction on the national culture.*

The above excerpt contains information that can be classified as key information as it is directly addressing the research topic, highlighting *culture* as an important aspect of transitioning into becoming agile. All these data fragments can be considered key information. This key information will need to be analysed using open coding, constant comparison, and memoing. Similarly, key information within observational notes, documentation, software repository data, social media posts, and other types of data can be identified and analysed.

Applying data filtering refers to identifying data fragments as key information, contextual information, and noise. It does not include analysis, rather identifies data and data fragments that need to be analysed.

Key information, once analysed, typically makes up the details of the *Findings* section of the study report. Along with memos, it fuels insights and discussions in the *Discussion* section. Snippets and condensed summaries of the analysed key information are frequently presented in the *Abstract*, *Introduction*, and *Conclusion* sections to summarise the main findings of the study.

9.2.2 Contextual Information

Definition

Contextual information *provides valuable information about the context in which the phenomenon occurs. It serves to support, supplement, complement, complete, nuance, enhance, and enliven the key information.* Contextual information can be **demographic**, **organisational**, and **practice-based** information.

Contextual information provides valuable information about the context in which the phenomenon occurs. It helps makes better sense of the key information. Contextual information can be *demographic*, *organisational*, and *practice-based*, as described next. It commonly ends up comprising the *Background, Context*, and *Case Description* sections of the study report. It can also be added within the *Findings* and *Discussion* sections to support and better explain the key findings.

Demographic Contextual Information

Definition

Demographic information *is information about research participants such as their age, gender, professional role, years of work experience, years of experience in a particular practice, and so on that are relevant to the research project.*

Demographic information helps us understand the participant, their background, and their worldview, all of which has bearing on the key information they share. For example, in a study on *onboarding experiences in software teams*, we may be able to compare the experience of novice software developers being onboarded into their first job, with those of more experienced developers being onboarded to a new company, role, team, or project. This will be possible if we collect the relevant demographic information about the respective participants.

Capturing demographic information can be built into the research protocols for custom-collected data. For example, most semi-structured interviews start by asking for a general introduction of the participant as an ice-breaker question. This introduction section of the interview is a prime candidate for collecting demographic information about the participant such as their professional background. Additionally, demographic information can be captured in a more structured manner using a pre-interview questionnaire. Similarly, surveys can include a section to explicitly collect demographic information. Capturing demographic information in pre-existing data such as about the director and writers of documentaries and authors of online articles and blogs can be relatively straightforward. However, tracing the demographic information in some other data sources can be challenging. For example, if an open-source software project does not already include the demographic information about its contributors, it can be rather cumbersome, and sometimes near impossible, to trace such details.

Demographic information can be identified during data filtering. Processing demographic contextual information does not require deep coding procedures of open coding and constant comparison. It needs extraction of relevant information from reading and processing the raw data. In this example, we extract demographic information from the participant response by first highlighting it in bold font in the raw data and then extracting, e.g. into a spreadsheet.

Example

Interviewer1: *Please tell me briefly about your professional background and your current role.*
Participant3: *My name is Rabia Sol. I am a* ***senior developer*** *at* ***Letfix****, for umm...* ***nearly five years*** *now. (thinks) Yeah. I was* ***previously working at MyDish as a Web developer for two and a half years.***

Example

participant	**P21**
current role	**senior developer**
current company	**Letfix**
experience at current company (in years)	**5**
previous role	**web developer**
previous company	**MyDish**
experience at previous company (in years)	**2.5**

Demographic information is usually compiled across participants and presented in the form of a *Participant Demographics Table* or are visualised as graphs (e.g. bar graphs and pie charts) and figures (e.g. a marked up world map to show geographic spread of participants). Depending on the ethics conditions, typically all the real names of individual participants, people they refer to, and companies they work at are kept confidential and are reported using pseudonyms or alpha-numeric codes, such as **P1-P(n)** for participants, **T1-T(n)** for teams, and **O1-O(n)** for organisations.

Extracting the real names of the companies enables us to follow up on those companies and gather further information such as the company's domain, size, location, vision, and recent news related to it, which can form the *organisational contextual information*, discussed next.

Organisational Contextual Information

Definition

Organisational information *is the background information about the world where the phenomenon occurs, including the domain, company, or group, and their vision, goals, structure, size, composition, values, norms, culture, and related aspects that help understand that world better.*

Organisational information has to do with aspects that make up the world where the phenomenon occurs. The world can be the domain (e.g. medical practice, primary education), the company (e.g. a particular hospital, school), a certain service division (e.g. human resources, customer service), a group (e.g. meetups, special interest groups, communities of practice), or project ecosystems (e.g. GitHub projects), all the way up to the smallest organisation unit such as a single software development team. The aspects of interest include their vision, goals, structure, size, composition, values, norms, culture, and so on. The more organisational information we can gather relevant to the phenomenon, the better we can understand and explain it.

Organisational information is not limited to the early parts of interviews but can be found later, intertwined with key information. Sometimes, it may be available neatly presented in README files within their software repositories, but more often, it needs to be extracted from related sources. For example, organisational information of a participant's company may be extracted from their public Web site or LinkedIn account. Observations and artefacts are effective ways to capture organisational information. A walk down the participant's workplace can help capture the company's vision statements, ideologies, and cultural cues.

Once extracted and shaped into desired texts, tables and figures, organisational information is typically presented in the *Research Method* and *Case Overview* sections of the study report. It can also be used to provide context in the *Findings* section. Summaries of organisational information can be presented in the *Abstract, Introduction*, and *Conclusion* sections to provide a sense of the study's scope, size, and context.

A study can report organisational information on single or multiple levels, as relevant to the research topic. For example, in a study of *inter-team coordination in large-scale software development*, we can report the composition of the individual software teams participating in our research in terms of their size, distribution of professional roles, and distribution of years of work experience across the team. We can also report on the organisation of the larger inter-team ecosystem including the size and composition of the product owner community of practice. These bits of information can help explain some of our main findings derived from analysing key information. For example, a key finding of our study on *inter-team coordination challenges* (Bick et al., 2017) was that effective inter-team coordination is incumbent on the awareness of dependencies across individual teams, which in turn is achieved through alignment of planning activities such as estimation and prioritisation across the team and inter-team levels. In this case, the organisational information such as number of teams, team sizes, and details of the product owner community of practice helped us explain why dependencies exist across individual teams and how a lack of dependency awareness causes coordination challenges.

Practice-Based Contextual Information

Definition

Practice information *is the information about the research topic or phenomenon under investigation that serves to validate the relevance, authenticity, and credibility of the data but does not require deep data analysis or coding to process.*

An important concern when collecting data is to ensure it is relevant, authentic, and credible (see *Data Quality Evaluation Guidelines* in Chap. 7, Basics of Qualitative Data Collection). In particular, it is important to establish that the candidate data source is well suited to provide valuable information about the research topic or phenomenon. For example, when studying a topic in agile software development, attempt to establish that the teams are indeed practicing agile software development. Observations and documentation help in this regard. However, we can be more structured and consistent about how we establish this across different data sources and units.

For example, a common question my research teams include in our pre-interview questionnaire for studies in the agile domain is shown in Fig. 9.3. Collecting this information provides valuable insight into the extent and maturity of the participant's agile practice. It also provides a reference point for explaining some of the practice details shared in the interviews and as seen to be played out during observations. Unless these practices are the key focus of our research, they can be considered practice-based contextual information or, simply, practice information.

Agile Practices on selected Project

	1 (Never)	2 (Rarely)	3 (Occasionally)	4 (Frequently)	5 (Always)
Short iterations/sprints	○	○	○	○	○
Iteration planning	○	○	○	○	○
User stories	○	○	○	○	○
Product backlog	○	○	○	○	○
Sprint backlog	○	○	○	○	○
Collective estimation	○	○	○	○	○
Daily standup/team meeting	○	○	○	○	○
Release planning	○	○	○	○	○
Pair programming	○	○	○	○	○
Self-assignment	○	○	○	○	○
Customer demos	○	○	○	○	○
Scrum or Kanban board	○	○	○	○	○
Definition of done	○	○	○	○	○
Retrospectives	○	○	○	○	○

Fig. 9.3 Question to capture practice-based contextual information in the pre-interview questionnaire

Practice information, such as an overview of the frequency of common agile practices performed by the participating teams, is typically presented in text, tabular, or figure formats in the *Cases Overview* and *Findings* sections of the study report.

9.2.3 Noise

Definition

Noise *is data that provides little or no research value to the project or has little or nothing to do with our research topic and can be left alone from a rigorous coding perspective.*

Traditional grounded theory follows Glaser's dictum and accepts *all is data* (Glaser & Strauss, 2017, first published 1967). In light of the vast variety of traditional and modern data sources available to STGT studies and the open and often unregulated nature of modern data sources such as social media, STGT accepts *all is data, with care*. Care needs to be taken in not only collecting data from quality sources but also ensuring the quality of the data that has been collected. If we do not learn to minimise the collection of low-quality data and noise in the collected data and to deal with them, we can end up spending copious amounts of time and effort analysing parts of data that have little or no value to add to our research topic. This is not only cumbersome and costly but can also demotivate us as we start to feel overwhelmed trying to find relevance and meaning where little exists. This is true for most qualitative data analysis procedures such as thematic analysis. However, it is critical for STGT data analysis procedures such as open coding and constant comparison because they are especially rigorous. We need to identify and deal with noise in data and apply rigorous STGT data analysis procedures to quality data so it can yield a good return on the time and effort invested.

Whether we classify noise manually or using machine learning algorithms, a key concern is to define noise. Noise is data that has low relevance for the research topic or phenomenon under investigation or adds little or no research value and can be left alone from a deep data analysis or coding perspective. The *Data Quality Evaluation Guidelines*, presented in Chap. 7, Basics of Qualitative Data Collection, lists six criteria to evaluate data and source quality for selection and inclusion in the study. When applied during data sampling, prior to collection, they can ensure the collection of quality data from sources that are *relevant*, *authentic*, *accessible*, *ethical*, *credible*, and *valuable*.

Selecting relevant, authentic, and credible data sources improves the chances of collecting relevant and valuable data. However, once collected, it needs to be re-examined during data filtering since not all parts of the collected data may be relevant or valuable, albeit they may be generally interesting ideas. *Relevance* refers to the data being related to the research topic and phenomenon. *Valuable* refers to the data benefiting the research project. These are both rather subjective and elusive terms. They are particularly difficult to grasp during the early stages of the research project when the topic is still being solidified and by novice researchers who may not have experience in discerning what makes for valuable data or even valuable research. The researcher's understanding of noise improves over the research project duration as they gain experience and as the key findings begin to emerge and solidify.

For these reasons, it is recommended to be gentle in classifying noise during the early stages of the study. Later on, it becomes easier to do and can be applied more widely and confidently, as needed. Below we explore some examples to understand what noise in data looks like along with tips on how to deal with it.

Noise in Pre-interview Questionnaires and Surveys

Custom-collected data in the form of valid responses to well-designed pre-interview questionnaires and surveys that are distributed through credible channels are likely to contain the least amount of noise, compared to some other data collection techniques. Survey data collected through paid services such as Amazon Mechanical Turk[3] may need to be carefully assessed for noise. Voluntary survey responses can also contain noise. Survey responses may be authentic in terms of being filled by the genuine software practitioners with relevant experience of the research phenomenon; however, some responses may have been filled without much thought and add little to no value to the research project. For example, the respondent may have answered the early, often demographic, questions well but may have lost interest in the later, typically open-ended questions requiring typing, leading to one-word and short answers or answers that are generic, repeating the questions verbatim, not addressing the question, or providing little to no insights into the research topic. Consider an example of a survey response.

Example

Question 6a: *Select all the human values you consider important when developing software in your domain.*
Answer: *<selects options from given list>*
Question 6b: *Why do you consider the selected human values important?*
Answer: *Human values are important when developing software in your domain.*

When asked to select from a list of human values (*Question 6a*), the respondent makes their selection. When asked to share *why* they consider the selected human values important (*Question 6b*), the response is seen to be copied from the previous question verbatim. This goes to show that the respondent probably did not deliberate on the question but rather chose to provide *some* answer. In this case, verbatim copying from the question. This response to *Question 6b* can be considered noise. If there is a pattern of such noisy responses throughout the survey entry, that particular entry can be considered bogus and can be safely discarded.

Consider another entry for the same survey questions, where *Question 6a* is answered well but the answer to *Question 6b* is different to the earlier response.

[3] https://www.mturk.com/.

Example

Question 6b: *Why do you consider the selected human values important?*
Answer: *Human values are important when developing software.*

Here the respondent has confirmed that they consider human values important when developing software, which can be considered a generic statement, a confirmation, or part repetition of the previous question. If this is a one-off such response throughout the survey entry, the whole survey entry from this respondent does not need to be classified as noise. While it does not answer the question asked, it is still *relevant* to the topic and *valuable* in the sense that it serves to confirm the importance of human values when developing software, which can be reported separately.

Noise in Interview Data

Tips to maximise the effectiveness of interviews can be found in Chap. 8, Techniques of Qualitative Data Collection. Despite our best attempts, some interviews can generate noise in the form of data that is of little use to the research project and certainly does not require STGT's rigorous data analysis procedures such as open coding and constant comparison. Consider an example of an ice-breaker-type question and answer from a semi-structured interview.

Example

Interviewer: *Please tell me about yourself, your professional background, and your current role.*
Participant 1: *Sure. I have a bachelor's degree in chemistry; yeah, that really doesn't connect to my current role as business analyst (laughs), but I was really into chemistry at the time (laughs). In my final year, I started working on a side project with a friend of mine. We had got interested in software programming. Actually, it came out of our mutual love for video games. I am sure you've come across this before... (continues to recall early education and experiences with technology in general for 15 minutes out of a 40 minutes interview.)*

When we consider this interview excerpt, it becomes apparent that some useful *demographic information* is shared. Applying data filtering, we revisit this interview excerpt below to note the demographic information (in **bold** font), and everything else can be considered noise (in light gray font), i.e. information that may be interesting but has little to no value to add to our research topic. We can disregard the noise for STGT data analysis purposes.

Example

Applying data filtering: *Sure. I have a* ***bachelor's degree in chemistry****; yeah, that really doesn't connect to my current role as* ***business analyst*** *(laughs), but I was really into chemistry at the time (laughs). In my final year, I started working on a side project with a friend of mine. We had got* ***interested in software programming****. Actually, it came out of our mutual* ***love for video games****. I am sure you've come across this before... (continues)*

The information *bachelor's degree in chemistry* and *current role of business analyst* can be noted as demographic information. The reported *interest in software programming* and *love for video games* can also be noted in case links to some *key information* arise later in the same interview when we analyse it or in relation to data from some other interview or data source when we compare them later. Unlike noise in survey responses that is best discarded, noise in interview transcripts can be left in and low-lighted using lighter font colours as shown in the example above, using digital transcripts. An easier option is to underline the parts of the text that need to be analysed, leaving the rest as it is and considering it noise. Where using physical copies, words and phrases considered noise can be left unmarked or without highlighting, while other useful information is highlighted using coloured markers or by drawing circles or boxes around them with appropriate coding annotations and notes. Another option is to strike out bits classified as noise using a light hand. These formatting techniques ensure the interview transcript still reads well, without any abrupt gaps on account of deleted text, and can be revisited later as needed.

Noise in Observational Data

Observations are an important source of data collection. When we walk around a participant's workspace or sit in during software practices of interest to observe how they are performed, there are numerous things that can be observed. Often we find ourselves in meetings that include sensitive project and team information. While allowed to observe and take notes with confidentiality in mind, most teams are not comfortable having such sessions audio or video recorded. This leaves us with the challenging task of making keen observations while also trying to take useful notes. A number of actions, reactions, and happenings can be vying for our attention. If only we had inbuilt *noise cancelling* technology! Noise in observations can be handled *in action* in such cases. In other words, we can be somewhat selective about what we choose to observe and note down. This can be achieved by reminding ourselves of our research topic and focusing on aspects that appear relevant. When new to observations, it is recommended to observe and note down more rather than less. In time, our skills improve as we become more used to conducting observations.

Where permitted, we can record observations. In this case, the identification and elimination of noise will need to happen *afterwards* when revisiting the recordings or observational notes. It then becomes similar to the process of identifying and disregarding noise in interview data.

9.3 Tips on Data Filtering

Tips

Tips on Data Filtering:

- Discard invalid data
- Go gentle on noise cancellation
- Treat sensitive demographic information carefully
- Distinguish between key and contextual information
- Distinguish between process of abstraction and noise
- Leverage fringe benefits of "interesting noise"

9.3.1 Discard Invalid Data

Every so often, we can end up with data that is invalid for inclusion in the study. For example, we may have carefully designed a survey and distributed it to reliable cohorts using credible channels such as meet up groups or LinkedIn groups. Still, once the responses come through, we can receive some responses that are invalid. They can include unfinished entries where some of the questions were responded to, while others were not, entries with gibberish words and "test" responses where random text was filled out. These are usually the case when someone wants to run through the survey questions without actually answering them. They can also include responses that are clearly irrelevant to the questions asked or filled out in jest, e.g. consistently sarcastic responses or jokes. Invalid data can be considered the most blatant form of noise and can be safely discarded.

9.3.2 Go Gentle on Noise Cancellation

Classifying parts of data as noise is the decision to not analyse those parts of data. This is not a trivial decision. Be gentle in classifying noise as it risks discarding potentially valuable data because of a lack of experience or assumptions. Both novice and experienced researchers are recommended to go gentle on noise classification in the early days of open coding data. This is because open coding requires the researcher to remain *open* to ideas emerging from the data. Aggressively classifying data as noise can risk losing what could have been important codes leading to valuable concepts and categories through analysis.

Avoid extensive noise classification unless dealing with a dataset that is particularly noisy. This is likely to be the case in large pre-existing datasets that contain both information that is valuable to the research project and also a significant amount of data that is irrelevant to the project. For example, applying data filtering on Stack Overflow query logs can require a fair amount of noise classification or data cleaning, e.g. in the form of removing duplication (Cao et al., 2021).

If custom-collected data such as through interviews and observations continue to contain a lot of noise and very little relevant and valuable information, the data collection protocols such as interview questions can be revisited and revised to improve the quality of data collection and, thereby, the efficiency of data analysis.

9.3.3 Treat Sensitive Demographic Information Carefully

Collecting information about the gender, age, and geographic location of participants can help keep the participant base as balanced as possible. If we report on these aspects, with due permissions, it can serve to inform the wider researcher and practice communities about the diversity of our participant base. Reporting on these aspects can also help address equity, diversity, and inclusion issues in the software and technology industries through raising awareness (Albusays et al., 2021). However, reporting sensitive demographic information can make some participants particularly vulnerable to identification in their company. For example, if P21 was the only female senior developer in the team we interviewed, all quotations attributed to P21 can be traced back to her. To protect their identity and preserve the confidentiality of the information participants agreed to share, we can report gender, age, and ethnicity type demographic information as an aggregated distribution across the complete participant base rather than listing it for individual participants.

9.3.4 Distinguish Between Key and Contextual Information

Sometimes, it can be difficult to distinguish between key and contextual information. For example, a project manager describing their interactions with their team may provide information about how the team is set up internally (*team composition*), who interacts with whom (*team interactions and dynamics*), how the team interacts with other teams (*inter-team coordination*) and management layers (*hierarchical setup*), and more. If these aspects, such as team composition and coordination, are the key focus of our research, they are considered key information. Otherwise, if they serve to add value or relate to the key information in some way, these are organisational contextual information.

Another way to distinguish between key and contextual information is to consider the estimated effort required to process each of them. For example, demographic and organisational contextual information is typically readily available from the context studied. Similarly, processing practice-based contextual information such as those gathered from pre-interview questionnaires or surveys is relatively straightforward. The survey tool usually enables basic descriptive analysis on the click of a button and also visualises the results as bar graphs or pie charts. On the other hand, key information requires rigorous data analysis to make sense of and spark the need for further data collection and for memos to be written.

9.3.5 Distinguish Between Process of Abstraction and Noise

Data is progressively transformed and condensed in the analysis process. The procedures of open coding and constant comparison are meant to naturally raise the data in levels of abstraction, accompanied by a narrowing down of the research focus. For example, through coding, phrases and paragraphs in the raw data are condensed into short codes. As similar codes are grouped to form concepts, there will naturally be fewer concepts than codes. At the same time, not all codes may be significant or common enough to form concepts. Some will remain practically unused in the research project. Finally, as similar concepts are grouped to form sub-categories or categories, there will be naturally fewer (sub)categories than concepts. At the same time, not all concepts make it to form categories. This process of abstraction and surfacing of the most significant patterns leads to a natural reduction in the quantity of text being handled over the course of the project. The bits of data that eventually do not make it into concepts and categories are not the same as noise. Unlike noise, it cannot be identified and removed in advance and has to go through the analysis process to see if it "floats" to the top through increasing levels of abstraction.

9.3.6 Leverage Fringe Benefits of "Interesting Noise"

When filtering data, we find most data will fall into key information, contextual information, and noise. However, every now and then, we will come across bits of data that seem very interesting but are not really about our research topic. Such data, if analysed, can potentially lead to what is known as incidental findings, unrelated to the main purpose of the research. Experienced researchers are likely to spot such data with more ease, based on their experience of the wider research field, beyond the topic of the current research project. Technically speaking, from the perspective of the project, this is still noise. However, it may be too interesting to simply disregard! What we do with this *interesting noise* depends on our personal preference and the project's resource and time constraints. For example, it may lead the research team to completely revise their research focus. This is typically easier to do in the early stages and is more costly to do later on.

In a large stand-alone STGT study, such as a PhD project typically spanning three or more years, the researchers may decide to keep this data, explicitly revising the research focus to include the new dimension it covers and refining the research protocols to gather more of it. The decision to broaden the project scope in this way will inevitably increase research time and costs. The additional findings may not make it into emerging theoretical outcomes but can make for solid, stand-alone concepts and categories, interesting enough to report on their own. For example, during my doctoral study, I used a broad approach to data collection and analysis, especially in the early stages, which resulted in some interesting "fringe" findings. These did not make it into my doctoral thesis (Hoda, 2011). However, they were written up and published, e.g. *agility in context* (Hoda et al., 2010) and *negotiating agile contracts* (Hoda et al., 2009). Arguably, my PhD could have been finished sooner had I been more focused in my approach, but at the same time, I learned a lot about the wider agile discipline in the process, which benefited me in years to come. These are some aspects for the research team to consider when faced with interesting noise.

In a small stand-alone STGT study of around 6 to 12 months' duration, on the other hand, the time constraints mean the researchers may need to take a tough call and disregard the bits of interesting noise and proceed with the analysis of only the key and contextual information directly related to the topic. They can save that data for future projects and research topics, since their relevance and interest have been empirically established.

9.4 Summary

In this chapter, we learned about *data preparation* including preparing interview, observation, recording, survey, and text-based data and their storage and organisation. Then we learned about *data filtering* including filtering key information, contextual information, and noise. Finally, we learned some *tips for data filtering*. Researchers will benefit from reading this chapter in conjunction with the *Basics of Qualitative Data Collection*, *Techniques of Qualitative Data Collection*, and *Socio-technical Grounded Theory for Qualitative Data Analysis* chapters. Collectively, they cover socio-technical grounded theory's basic stage.

References

Albusays, K., Bjorn, P., Dabbish, L., Ford, D., Murphy-Hill, E., Serebrenik, A., & Storey, M.-A. (2021). The diversity crisis in software development. *IEEE Software, 38*(2), 19–25.

Bick, S., Spohrer, K., Hoda, R., Scheerer, A., & Heinzl, A. (2017). Coordination challenges in large-scale software development: A case study of planning misalignment in hybrid settings. *IEEE Transactions on Software Engineering, 44*(10), 932–950.

Cao, K., Chen, C., Baltes, S., Treude, C., & Chen, X. (2021). Automated query reformulation for efficient search based on query logs from stack overflow. In *2021 IEEE/ACM 43rd International Conference on Software Engineering (ICSE)* (pp. 1273–1285). IEEE.

Glaser, B. G., & Strauss, A. L. (2017). *Discovery of grounded theory: Strategies for qualitative research.* Routledge (First Published 1967).

Hoda, R. (2011). *Self-organizing agile teams: A grounded theory*, PhD thesis, Open Access Te Herenga Waka-Victoria University of Wellington.

Hoda, R., Kruchten, P., Noble, J., & Marshall, S. (2010). Agility in context. In *Proceedings of the ACM international conference on Object oriented programming systems languages and applications* (pp. 74–88).

Hoda, R., Noble, J., & Marshall, S. (2009). Negotiating contracts for agile projects: A practical perspective. In *International Conference on Agile Processes and Extreme Programming in Software Engineering* (pp. 186–191). Springer.

10 Socio-technical Grounded Theory for Qualitative Data Analysis

Abstract Qualitative data analysis forms the heart of socio-technical grounded theory (STGT). In this chapter, we will start by learning about the *basics of qualitative data analysis* and *preparing for qualitative data analysis* as it applies in STGT, including the mindset, approach, and worldview applied to analysis. This is followed by a visual notes-taking analogy to help explain the general idea of qualitative data analysis using STGT procedures. Then we will learn about the STGT procedure of *open coding* using hashtags, the zoom out–zoom in technique, and how to draw out analytical and socio-technical codes as well as considering options and revising codes. Next, we will learn about the procedure of *constant comparison* through which data is condensed and raised in levels of abstraction and the procedure of *memoing* to draw insights and relationships. This is followed by *tips for data analysis*, including tips for creating codes, coding for richness, context filling, role of research paradigm, and improving theoretical sensitivity. Next, we will consider *team-based coding*, including guidelines for achieving alignment in a coding team. Finally, the chapter ends with explaining the *expected outcomes* of applying STGT for data analysis.

R. Hoda, *Qualitative Research with Socio-Technical Grounded Theory*,
https://doi.org/10.1007/978-3-031-60533-8_10

10.1 Basics of Qualitative Data Analysis

Qualitative data analysis forms the heart of socio-technical grounded theory (STGT). STGT offers two possible applications:[1] *STGT for data analysis*, a limited application for qualitative data analysis, and *full STGT study*, the full application of both the basic and theory development stages for theory development.

STGT for data analysis can be used to generate rich, nuanced, and layered descriptive findings, taxonomies, theoretical models, frameworks, and in some cases emerging hypotheses and preliminary theories. Examples of the application of STGT for data analysis can be found in Hidellaarachchi et al. (2023); Madampe et al. (2023); Pant et al. (2023); Li et al. (2023); Wang et al. (2023); Chan and Hauser (2023). The full STGT method, on the other hand, can be used to generate novel, useful, parsimonious, and modifiable theories and other mature theoretical outcomes. Examples of the application of the full STGT method can be found in Graetsch et al. (2023); Chan and Hauser (2023).

In STGT, the term *basic data analysis* refers to the procedures of open coding, constant comparison, and memoing. Basic data analysis is core to both *STGT for data analysis* and to the basic stage of a *full STGT study*. Table 10.1 presents a glossary of terms associated with STGT data analysis for ready reference.

Definition

Basic data analysis in socio-technical grounded theory (STGT) comprises the procedures of *open coding*, *constant comparison*, and *memoing*.[2]

- **Open coding** is the process of coding data inductively and comprehensively, with an open mindset, to enable emergence of information and insights, without looking to find anything specific in the data.
- **Constant comparison** is the process of comparing newly arising codes with all existing codes, both from within the same data unit and with those across different data units, to identify similarities or common patterns among them.
- **Memoing** is the ongoing process of documenting the researcher's thoughts, ideas, questions, and reflections on emerging codes, concepts, and categories and evidence-based conjectures on possible links between them.

[1] Traditional GT methods—Glaserian GT (Glaser & Strauss, 2017, first published 1967), Strauss–Corbinian GT (Strauss & Corbin, 1990), and constructivist GT (Charmaz, 2006)—are dedicated to theory development and do not support limited applications of only their data analysis procedures.

[2] Open coding and constant comparison are core procedures common to all versions of GT - traditional and modern. STGT presents a socio-technical approach to conducting these procedures.

Collectively, they transform raw data into valuable information and insights. *STGT for data analysis* can be used to generate rich, nuanced, and layered descriptive findings, taxonomies, theoretical models, frameworks, and in some cases emerging hypotheses and preliminary theories.

10.2 Preparing for Qualitative Data Analysis

Before we explore the steps of open coding and constant comparison, it is important to understand the necessary mindset, approach, and the choice of worldview with which to conduct data analysis.

10.2.1 The Mindset

The term *open* in open coding refers to two specific aspects. First, it refers to the scope of application. In open coding, the analysts code openly or comprehensively, for all data at hand. The exceptions are the bits of data that have been identified as *noise* as part of data filtering. Data filtering can be applied simultaneously with coding or as a pre-step to coding, as explained earlier in Chap. 9 Qualitative Data Filtering and Preparation. Other than any apparent noise, open coding is applied to all data, not selectively to some parts of it.

Second, the term open refers to the analyst's mindset remaining open. Researchers are urged to understand the difference between "*an open mind and an empty head*" (Dey, 1999). While researchers are likely to possess some prior knowledge of their research topic that can help understand the data better, "*prior conception should not become preconceptions*" (Dey, 1999). Instead, the analyst is driven by curiosity and the motivation to learn from real-world evidence and allow it to inform and, in some cases, transform their understanding.

> An example of openness can be found in the reflections of Dr Brene Brown, the renowned author and speaker. Dr Brown applied GT to her research study on *professional helping* (Brown, 2002). She notes the following in her thesis, which is also quoted by Barney Glaser in his article, *The Novice GT Researcher* (Glaser, 2009):
>
> "*Through the use of grounded theory, I was forced to challenge my own interests, investments and preconceived ideas in order to understand the concerns, interests and ideas of the research participants. The process evolved from 'I think this is important – are you doing it?' to 'what do you think is important to helping and why?' This evolution transformed my narrow quest for verification into the development of a complex theory about a basic socialpsychological process of professional helping.*"

Table 10.1 STGT data analysis terminology—glossary of terms

Terms	Description
Raw data	The data in its raw form. It can be in the form of interview data available as audio-recordings, observational data saved as hand-written notes, or pre-existing data in the form of developer comments on GitHub repositories. Typically, the raw data requires some preparation before it can be analysed.
Code	The term or phrase that summarises the key points from the data being analysed. These are typically two to four words, representing the key point in a summarising manner and shorthand format.
Concept	A common umbrella term or phrase that summarises and represents a set of similar codes. The next level of data abstraction above codes.
Category	A common umbrella term or phrase that summarises and represents a set of similar concepts. The highest level of data abstraction, above concepts. Sometimes, *subcategories* and *super-categories* may also arise below and above the category level, respectively, depending on how layered the findings are.
Key categories	Categories that are the strongest and most meaningful of the emerged categories and that best relates to other key categories and through which most of the research findings can be explained.
Theory	Theory refers to the key categories and hypotheses (relationships between categories) that taken together explain the phenomenon or topic under investigation.
Coding	Coding is the process of closely inspecting, deeply making sense of, and inferring meaning from data and giving those meanings some labels or names, also called codes.
Open coding	Open coding is the process of coding data inductively and comprehensively, with an open mindset, to enable emergence of information and insights, without looking to find anything specific in the data.
Constant comparison	Constant comparison is the process of comparing newly arising codes with all existing codes, both from within the same data unit and with those across different data units, to identify similarities or common patterns among them.

10.2.2 The Approach

Open coding applies an *inductive* reasoning approach (refer to Chap. 5 Research Philosophy). An inductive approach implies "*drawing general conclusions from patterns evidenced across specific instances*" (Hoda, 2022). The direction of inductive reasoning goes from the specific to the general, or bottom-up. In contrast, a deductive reasoning approach involves "*drawing conclusions about specific instances from general facts or existing theories*" (Hoda, 2022). The direction of deductive reasoning goes from the general to the specific, or top-down.

The STGT researcher (or analyst) does not approach the analysis with a view to look for certain predefined patterns. Their task is to enable patterns to emerge from the data through following a systematic and rigorous application of the open coding and constant comparison procedures. *Systematic* refers to following specific procedures and steps, in the recommended manner and sequence. Once committed to STGT, the research team needs to exercise discipline in maintaining a systematic approach. *Rigorous* refers to being diligent and thorough in approach, aiming to uncover deep insights from the data, rather than surface-level findings. In the upcoming sections, we will see how to achieve this in practice through examples of inductive open coding.

The inductive approach to coding, along with constant comparison, leads to increasing levels of data abstraction. Analysing raw data gives rise to *codes*. Newly arising codes are constantly compared to existing codes to identify similarities. Similar codes are then grouped together under an umbrella term. This next level of abstraction is called *concepts*. The same procedure is applied to group similar concepts together under to form *categories*, a higher level of abstraction. In some cases, there may be an additional level of *subcategories* between concepts and a category or a *super-category* formed from combining several categories, also known as an *epic*. This procedure of constant comparison is illustrated later in the chapter.

10.2.3 The Assumptions List

Maintaining an open mindset involves acknowledging our assumptions. To create an open mindset, I recommend creating an *assumptions list*—a list of ten (or more) statements the researcher believes to be true about their research topic *before* they earnestly begin data collection and analysis. This exercise allows the researcher to become aware of their assumptions about the topic, whether it comes from their first hand professional experience, observations, having heard ideas from others, or having read on the topic. For example, based on the first hand experience of working as a software developer, the researcher may have certain views about how a software team operates. They may have experienced a hierarchical form of management and may therefore assume that is the status quo for most software teams. These assumptions can influence what they see during data collection and how they choose to interpret it. The same is true for when they are analysing data.

Assumptions are not inherently problematic. Some of our experiences can help us understand the context better. However, some assumptions may be biases. For example, based on their previous professional experience as a developer, if the researcher believes that the developer role is more important than the tester role, this is a bias. A more open and mature perspective would be to acknowledge the importance of different roles in the software team for their unique contributions to the project and how they complement each other.

Many times our assumptions help us formulate hunches about what we see in the data. These hunches can be explored through subsequent data collection, forming the cornerstone of abduction. Abduction or abductive reasoning is key to theorising (see Chap. 5 Research Philosophy for more on its role in theory development.) We can leverage our experiences and assumptions to make sense of the data and derive candidate hypotheses. This can be followed through with further evidence collection to learn more about the proposed hypotheses, where they may be strengthened, discarded, or modified as a result of our data collection and analysis.

The role of the assumptions list is to remind us of what we believe to be true *prior* to the research investigation and to continue evidence generation that may support, negate, or help change our assumptions. Having an explicit assumptions list also helps others—advisors and peers—help the researcher check themselves if they find that they are leaning heavily on their assumptions without enough evidence from the research study.

TIPS

Tips on Maintaining an Open Mindset:

- Make an *assumptions list* about the topic before data collection and analysis begin and keep it handy.
- Focus the data collection and analysis on the participants' main concerns, as opposed to what may interest you personally.
- Focus on what can be seen in the data and allow it emerge, instead of trying to find something specific in the data.
- Be ready to have prior beliefs, knowledge, and experiences challenged by the evidence at hand.

10.2.4 The Worldview

How we approach and deal with pre-existing notions also depends on our choice of research paradigm or worldview (refer to Chap. 5 Research Philosophy).

If the research team has decided to apply a *positivist* worldview to their STGT study, they can try to actively acknowledge and handle their preconceptions about the research topic. One way to do this is for the research team, especially the analysts, to independently create their individual assumptions list, along with brief rationales of how and why they arise. The research team can then compare notes and discuss them together, arriving at a collective list of statements capturing their pre-existing knowledge and beliefs. They can help each other list the known biases and reveal unconscious biases by asking each other critical questions. This list can be readily referred to when conducting data collection and analysis to actively avoid potential biases from creeping in. Ultimately, it will enable the team to stay as objective and neutral as possible, a desirable feature in positivist research.

If the research team has decided to apply an *interpretivist* or *constructivist* worldview to their STGT study, they can still conduct the same exercise of compiling a collective assumptions list. However, instead of using it to *avoid biases* (a positivist perspective), it can be used to explain how and why the analysts made sense of the data and constructed meaning *because of* their background and prior knowledge and beliefs (a constructivist perspective). Such explanations can be captured in reflective memos, e.g. on the role of the researcher, and shared as supplementary materials alongside the findings.

> "We make our research but our research also makes us. Indeed, as we create new knowledge from our research, we can impact the research field. At the same time, the research process itself serves to support, challenge, and help us grow as professionals as we continue to learn from the empirical evidence and our research experiences along the way."

10.2.5 A Visual Notes-Taking Analogy

To help explain the general idea of open coding and constant comparison at an abstract level, I will use the example of visual notes-taking. Visual notes-taking is a popular way to capture and share key takeaways from talks and presentations. It involves listening to a recorded or live talk and capturing its main takeaway points and sub-points in condensed formats. These are usually captured on a sheet of physical or digital paper, in creative fonts, and accompanied by relevant drawings and icons that best represent those points. While the visualisation aspects may not apply to STGT research, the process that goes into creating the content of the visual notes is similar to the general idea of open coding. If you are comfortable with or enjoy sketching, you can use the creative visualisation process to accompany the open coding exercises.

Let us consider the similarities between visual notes-taking and open coding. In both cases, the visual notes-taker and analyst do not go in with any prior expectations other than that the content will be about the stated topic. They are curious to learn from the talk or the data source respectively. They aim to capture all the key ideas shared, comprehensively, as they come up. Both good visual summaries and open coding aim to go beyond transcribing or recording the highlights, such as is done when taking the minutes of a meeting. Instead, both pay careful attention to the nature and flow of arguments made. They aim to capture the key ideas, using verbatim words and phrases where appropriate, or by giving them their own labels.

Figure 10.1 shows an example of a sketch note I created live while listening to Rachael Slattery's talk at Agile Australia 2023 conference in Sydney. The process of noting the key points from the talk was similar to how I would approach open coding. Listening to Rachel speak, I tried to summarise the key points she was making in her talk. First, she talked about the concept of *getting older*, which is a natural phenomenon. At the same time, she highlighted how we are *lucky to grow old.* Immediately, this set the tone for the talk as being different to our usual perspective on getting older. Next, Rachel asked the audience what we appreciate about older role models and summarised three key points—*optimism*, *vitality*, and *sense of purpose*. Because this was a structured talk, the concepts were handed out on a plate. When open coding empirical data, on the other hand, we can hardly expect our data sources, e.g. interviewees, to summarise their key points into neatly named concepts for us. That's something we have to do, and we will see how in the upcoming sections. She then went on to suggest we *reframe aging* as something to look forward to and plan for. She highlighted the role of *play*, *health*, *relationships*, and *joy* as *rituals* to be

Fig. 10.1 Example of visual notes of Rachel Slattery's Agile Australia 2023 talk

built into our lives as we grow older. Similarly, there were other wonderful nuggets shared in this beautiful talk.[3] Each of these key ideas can be seen captured in the sketch note (Fig. 10.1.)

Another commonality between visual notes-taking and the general idea of open coding is that the outcomes in both cases are likely to vary, at the conceptual (and not only the visual) level, based on who undertakes it. This is because both require some level of creativity, individual interpretation, and judgement calls about what makes for key ideas in a talk or interview. For example, if you search the Internet

[3] Video of this particular talk is not available, but you can read more about Rachel's Silver Futures initiative here: https://www.innovationaus.com/rachel-slattery-on-ageing-and-the-next-tech-wave/.

for visual notes of Sir Ken Robinson's iconic TED talk *Do schools kill creativity?*, one of my favourite TED talks, you will find a variety of visual notes representations that have summarised that talk. Most of them will share common points, typically the key takeaways from the talk, but they will also differ in terms of their judgement of the relative importance of the key points and how they link to each other. Some notes may highlight a really subtle and nuanced idea that others may have missed. Others may have missed what most would consider as an essential takeaway. The former is an example of deep work, while the latter is likely a case of rushed work. The same is true for open coding. For this reason, where multiple coders are working on the same data, it will be beneficial to conduct joint coding sessions and to agree on coding norms, in order to achieve shared understanding, and then compare notes frequently to maintain alignment. Guidelines for team-based coding are shared later in the chapter.

The analogy can be extended beyond open coding to constant comparison and the general approach to theory development. For example, the notes-taker can follow the same process to create visual notes of several talks on the topic of *schools and creativity*. They can then compare one visual note to the other, to find the most significant patterns of ideas across all the notes of the various talks. Next, they can combine similar ideas from different talks to form overarching patterns and identify new relationships between them. This process is similar to the general idea of constant comparison. The outcome is expected to be an overarching set of ideas and links between them that capture what several TED speakers have to say about schools and creativity.

In addition to serving an as analogy, STGT analysts can learn and leverage new aspects from visual notes-taking that can enhance their efficiency and effectiveness. For example, visual notes-takers leverage the visual format to highlight the relative importance of ideas using different font sizes (e.g. using bigger fonts for more important concepts), positioning on the paper (e.g. placing key ideas in central locations), and linking them using labelled lines and arrows to depict relationships. Open coding does not need to include such high levels of creative visualisation. In its most basic form, coding can be purely text based. However, visualising emerging codes and the relationships between them, using simple visualisations (e.g. text boxes and arrows) is a powerful way to organise key ideas. Easy-to-use tools such as pen and paper, Microsoft PowerPoint, and mind-mapping tools (e.g. miro.com, draw.io, Canva) can help. Similarly, visualisation can be used to explore how key ideas "*hang together*" to form preliminary hypotheses. Going back and forth between visualisations and textual formats can be a synergistic exercise in making sense of the large amounts of data that ends up being gathered and analysed. Finally, most research outputs are expected to include a visualisation of the emerging theoretical model or mature theory, typically using boxes and arrows, and "visual coding" can help generate a useful visualisation. You can use such TED talks and other credible videos online to practice open coding—either exclusively through words or including sketching, as you find useful.

As with most analogies, this one has its limitations. First, for most visual summaries, the input content is a mostly structured professional talk or some mostly organised text. When it comes to research data, we are more likely to come across unstructured or semi-structured data. Key information usually appears alongside contextual information and is often hidden within noise. It is also likely to be spread across the text, rather than being neatly organised into points and sub-points with logical flow, as in a professional talk. The job of an STGT analyst in open coding semi-structured data demands a lot more effort than analysing well-structured and organised professional talks. Additionally, open coding is also meant to be more comprehensive than visual notes-taking. Open coding aims to capture as much as possible, extracting and constructing meaning beyond what is easily seen on the surface level.

Second, while it includes some room for revisions, visual notes-taking is typically an intense, one-time, time-boxed activity. Visual notes are often completed by notes-takers and sketch artists in real time as they listen to live presentations, which requires a combination of cognitive, linguistic, analytical, and artistic abilities. I am constantly in awe of good visual notes-takers! Such intense time frames mean the notes-takers make some critical decisions on the go. Open coding, on the other hand, does not face such extreme time pressures. The analyst is at relatively more leisure to create new codes and refine them in light of new knowledge, repeatedly, until satisfied with the results. At the same time, do not keep the pace of open coding too leisurely as it may trap the analyst into continuously doubting their analysis and refining their codes. There is a balance to be achieved, which comes with practice and the very real timeline pressures of the research project.

Finally, what is seen in the sketch note (Fig. 10.1) is my summary of what I took away from the talk. Because of the time-boxed and live nature of sketch noting, and the very personal approach to it, the process lacks in rigour. I may have missed some important key points (sometimes literally running out of time or space on the page) or somehow misinterpreted others. If this was a scientific research endeavour such as open coding, a lot more rigour will need to be built into the process through comprehensive coding, refining codes, and seeking feedback from others, e.g. the data source (also known as member checking) or other researchers such as our advisors and peers.

10.3 Open Coding

Definition

Coding is the process of closely inspecting, deeply making sense of, and inferring meaning from data and giving those meanings some labels or names, called codes.

Open coding is the process of coding data inductively and comprehensively, with an open mindset, to enable emergence of information and insights, without looking to find anything specific in the data.

10.3.1 Open Coding with Hashtags

Definition

Coding with hashtags is the process of creating hashtags—a word or short phrase prefixed with a hash symbol (#)—to conceptualise and represent a key idea in a parsimonious (concise and elegant) way.

To help understand the general approach to creating codes, I will use the example of hashtags.[4] Hashtags are a word or short combination of words prefixed with the hash (#) symbol, popular on social media platforms such as Twitter.[5] Hashtags are created and used to conceptualise and represent key ideas. In social media platforms, such as Twitter, hashtags are a powerful tool used to "tag" a post to link it with all other posts on the same topic. Using hashtags, all related content from multiple sources can be easily searched, accessed, and read. Hashtags that become popular are featured as *Trending Topics* on Twitter.

In its condensed format, hashtags allow users to conveniently and effectively refer to and cross-reference the entire gamut of ideas, experiences, sentiments, and comments related to the topic. Some hashtags capture names of things and places, e.g. *#Kiwi* or *#TajMahal*. These can be considered *descriptive* tags and are mainly used to convey contextual information. Other tags capture significant events, moments, and phenomena, using words taken literally from the phenomenon, e.g. *#MelbourneLockdowns*. Some are created anew to associate with a phenomenon, e.g. *#MeToo*. These can be considered *conceptual* tags that give a name or label to a complex underlying concept. For example, the *#MeToo* hashtag initiated a massive movement[6] acknowledging and exposing sexual harassment, across industries and countries. It served to capture the movement, the motivation behind it, individual cases and stories shared on various platforms, and the drive for justice against sexual harassment. In other words, it helped conceptualise a complete phenomenon using a combination of two words. When we come across a *#MeToo* tag, it reminds us of the movement and all its related aspects.

I find coding, or the process of creating new codes, similar to the process of creating new hashtags. A code is a short phrase, typically one to four words, that

[4] https://en.wikipedia.org/wiki/Hashtag.

[5] https://help.twitter.com/en/resources/glossary.

[6] https://en.wikipedia.org/wiki/MeToo_movement.

helps conceptualise the key ideas in a given text. The analyst considers a piece of text and then has to come up with a code. Figure 10.2 shows the use of hashtags for open coding. A key advantage of using hashtags is that it can be easier to think of them as codes than regular English phrases. For example, *#portfolioApproach2Career* can be considerably easier to remember as a code and use as a catch phrase than a regular phrase such as *taking a portfolio approach to one's career*.

Using hashtags also allows for more creative code names. For example, we can use numbers to present words in shorthand, such as are commonly used in modern online discourse, e.g. using the number 2 for "two" or "to", 4 for "for", e.g. *#call2Action*. Other kinds of common shorthands such as "yrs" for "years" are also acceptable in this format. The first letter of each next word, mainly nouns and verbs, are capitalised for better readability, e.g. *#growingConcernsOverEthics*. Similarly, underscore (_) can be used to separate words for better readability, e.g. *#growing_concerns_over_ethics*. These naming conventions are similar to how variables are named in software coding or programming.

Using hashtags for coding also helps us avoid the temptation to create really long codes that sound more like sentences than codes. Over time, the researcher may drop the use of the hash sign # as they become accustomed to open coding. This is not a problem if you are still applying the key principles of creating hashtags, i.e. capturing the main points, keeping it short, and using shorthand where possible.

10.3.2 Open Coding: An Example

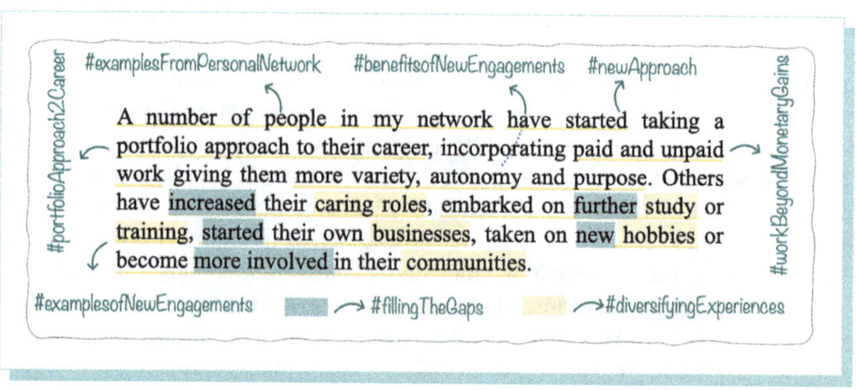

Fig. 10.2 An example of open coding with hashtags

To illustrate an example of open coding with hashtags, I will use an excerpt from Rachel Slattery's thoughts on aging captured on the Silver Futures platform,[7] shown

[7] https://silverfutures.com.au/investing-in-future-you/.

in Fig. 10.2. The verbatim text can be seen in the centre in black font. Parts of the text that are used to generate codes are highlighted using yellow underlines. The codes generated from analysing the text appear in a teal-coloured font. This approach mimics the manual, coding *by hand on the margins* approach, as is usually done with a pencil and highlighters on paper.[8]

The coding has been done on a line-by-line and sentence-by-sentence basis. Two codes were generated from the first line. I coded the text "*A number of people in my personal network*" as *#ExamplesFromPersonalNetwork* and the next part "*have started taking*" as *#newApproach*. The second code is far from the verbatim text and serves to show how analytical codes can be drawn from text, as compared to summarising the words. Next, we come across "*portfolio approach to their career*" which I coded nearly verbatim as *#portfolioApproach2Career*. We can keep this code until we learn more about what it means, and decide later if it needs to be refined. Next, the text "*incorporating paid and unpaid work*" is coded as *#workBeyondMonetaryGains*, which lends a new dimension and is worth capturing. Next, the text "*more variety, autonomy, and purpose*" is coded as *#benefitsofNewEngagements*.

All these five codes are gathered from a single sentence. This is an example of how exhaustive open coding needs to be. Sentences in other data can give rise to more or less codes. The key is to keep coding openly for all possible codes. This lends rigour to the process and ultimately richness to the findings.

The second sentence goes on to list other engagements. I code this as *#examplesofNewEngagements*. Each of them can be further coded as *#increasedCaringRoles*, *#furtherStudy*, and so on. I do not include these in the figure to avoid visual clutter as it may take away from the illustrative example. In practice, it is recommended to generate as many codes as possible as part of comprehensive open coding.

Next, we continue coding by asking questions such as: What else is being said here? Are there more codes to be captured? The answer is, yes. I draw your attention to something else that can be inferred from these examples. Some words of these examples are highlighted in teal colour. These are words that taken together seem to capture an emerging concept (grouping of similar codes). For example, the words *increased*, *further*, *started*, *new*, and *more involved* are words that indicate something more or something new. Taken together, they can be seen to be leading to an emerging concept of completing the missing or lacking parts of our life experiences. I code this as *#fillingTheGaps*. Similarly, the words highlighted in light yellow such as *caring roles*, *study* (or training), *businesses*, *hobbies*, and *communities* together seem to capture the common idea of *#diversifyingExperiences* in work and life.

This is a good time to write a memo about what we see in the data. We learn about memo writing later in the chapter. For now, consider it as taking notes about the key insights we have gathered from the analysis. For example, we can say that much of this quote is about people taking on a new work–life approach that involves

[8] There are a number of modern tools available for coding, such as NVivo, ATLAS.ti, MAXQDA, spreadsheets, Google docs, and so on. My recommendation to those new to qualitative data analysis is to practice with pencil and highlighters on paper as it is less structured and more forgiving. Of course, it is not environmentally sustainable to keep printing datasets for coding. Once comfortable with the basic procedures, feel free to experiment with and select digital tools of your choice.

#fillingTheGaps that are seen to exist in their work–life portfolios and in the process they are *#diversifyingExperiences*. These reflections may also nudge us to revisit our earlier codes. For example, the first half of the quote is about work and career, including *#workBeyondMonetaryGains*, while the second half of the quote is more about finding richer life experiences. This is as far as we can go based on the given text. The next steps would be to continue coding and adding to our codes and memos. We will find that some codes and emerging concepts will become stronger, while others may dwindle away for lack of further evidence from within the same and across other data sources.

Open coding can give rise to scores, and even hundreds, of codes per data unit. This can be overwhelming, and so appropriate systems and tools need to be put in place to manage the growing set of codes (see Chap. 8 Techniques for Qualitative Data Collection for more on tools). At the same time, we were able to condense two full sentences with rich ideas into eight codes (additional five if we consider each of the engagement examples). This condensing, combined with constant comparison (covered in the next section), raises the data to new levels of abstraction, progressively reducing it in size until it is condensed down into a few sentences that explain the key categories and hypotheses, and a few diagrams representing the findings, theoretical models, and theories. That is the power of STGT's qualitative data analysis procedures.

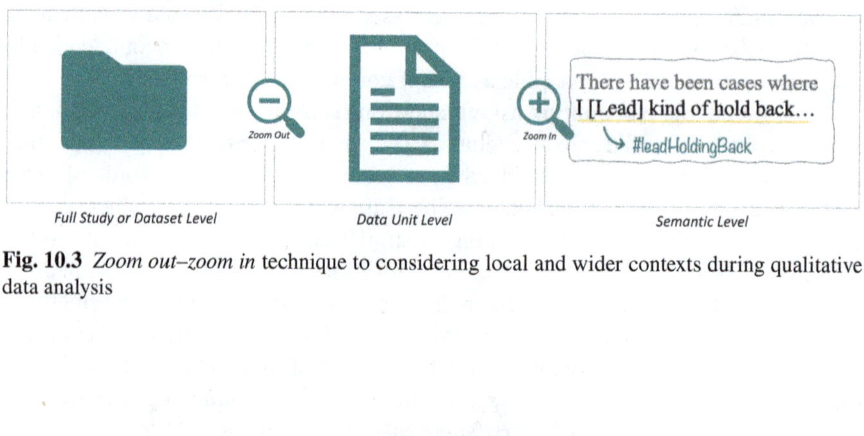

Fig. 10.3 *Zoom out–zoom in* technique to considering local and wider contexts during qualitative data analysis

10.3.3 The Zoom Out–Zoom In Technique

In the previous example, I coded the text "*A number of people in my network*" as *#examplesFromPersonalNetwork*. I derived this information from combining the present text with information shared earlier in the article. In the article, Rachel first drew on research to support her arguments about what keeps us working as we age. That could have been coded as *#evidenceFromResearch*. Then she quoted Theodore Roosevelt on "*work worth doing*". This could have been coded as *#wisdomofWorldLeaders*. Knowing about the earlier context helps us code the present text as *#examplesFromPersonalNetwork*, rather than *#myPersonalNetwork*, for instance, because we know this is following a line of argument to support the key ideas from multiple sources, be it research or world leaders or personal networks.

This is an example of how coding at the micro level still needs to consider the wider context of the full data unit. I call this the *zoom out–zoom in* technique, where we zoom out to consider the wider/macro context and then zoom back in to continue coding at the micro level, complimenting current data with prior information. It enables us to separate the woods from the trees as we become increasingly inundated with codes.

Let us consider another example: the code *#benefitsofNewEngagements*. Here, I could have used the word *work* instead of *engagement* as the line talked about "*paid and unpaid work*". However, I decided to go with *engagement* keeping the rest of excerpt in mind which talks about aspects beyond work, such as "*caring roles*" and "*hobbies*". I could have used *activities* instead of *work*, but again, careful re-reading of the excerpt in light of the rest of the article—applying the *zoom out–zoom in* technique—suggested *engagement* was a better alternative that captured the idea of providing fulfilment and purpose to life as we grow older.

Figure 10.3 shows an illustration of the *zoom out–zoom in* approach of considering the context at the widest full study or entire dataset level, the individual data unit level (e.g. within a single interview), and at the closest, data chunk level (e.g. one sentence or paragraph). The zooming in and out also serves as a great opportunity to write memos about what we see in the data from the two vantage points, connecting local discoveries within individual data units to the wider context of the study dataset.

10.3.4 Drawing Out Analytical Codes

Considering the above example, creating codes may seem like a simple exercise. While it is not necessarily complex, there is certainly a sense of quality and depth that differentiates good coding from satisfactory and poor coding. Poor coding practices fail to extract the meaning, attribute the wrong meaning, or miss identifying key points in the data. Coding practices that lead to merely summarising underlying data into condensed formats are mostly limited to being descriptive and can be considered satisfactory at best. Good coding, on the other hand, aims to reach beyond merely describing the underlying data and represents the analysis that goes into finding its deeper meanings.

It is not uncommon for analysts, especially those new to qualitative analysis, to start off with poor codes. This is similar to our experience of producing our first "horrible" draft when we are writing a report. We can easily see there is much room for improvement. The key is to press on and try again. The next attempt(s) will lead to a better set of codes that can be considered satisfactory. If we are committed to our analysis, we will be ready to refine our codes some more. With patience and practice, we will can get closer to good codes. Over time, we can get to good codes faster.

Now, let us consider an example of how we can move from our first poor (unsatisfactory) codes to more descriptive (satisfactory) codes and finally, to the analytical (good) codes, working on the same underlying data. The data excerpt has been taken from a semi-structured interview with a senior software technical lead, as part of a study on understanding what drives and sustains self-assignment in agile teams (Masood et al., 2021). I have deliberately coded it in different ways to demonstrate progress from poor to descriptive to analytical coding.

Open Coding: Attempt #1

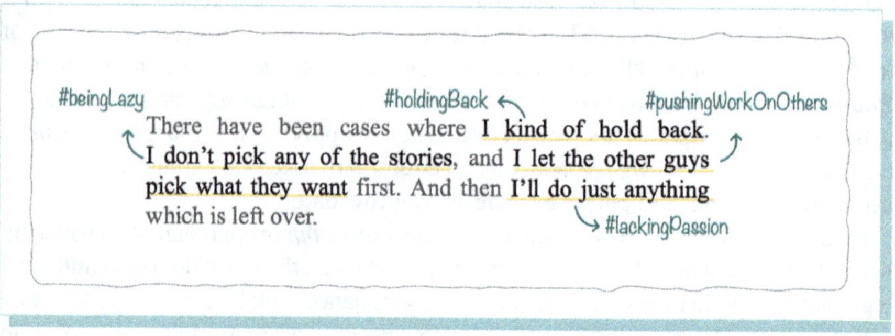

Fig. 10.4 Open coding attempt #1: An example of *poor* coding from a first attempt that misses key points, infers wrong meaning, and makes inappropriate attributions

Figure 10.4 shows a first attempt at coding where most of the codes derived can be considered inappropriate and even wrong as they fail to capture the meaning of the data and seem to make inferences on the face value of the text, without due consideration for the complete context and source. For example, "*I don't pick any of the stories*" is interpreted here as the speaker being lazy to pick tasks and is coded as *#beingLazy*. Similarly, "*I let the other guys pick what they want*" is coded as *#pushingWorkOnOthers*. Here the analyst misses an important word "*first*" which completes the sentence and gives it a different meaning as we will see in the second coding attempt. Next, "*I'll do just anything*" is coded as *#lackingPassion* which is inappropriate because, like in the previous code, it fails to take the whole sentence and the wider context into account when deriving the meaning. The very first code *#holdingBack* is not necessarily wrong but is still missing some important information that impacts not only this code but how the rest of the codes in this example are derived, as we will see in a better coding attempt presented next. Overall, this first, likely quick attempt at coding is closer to judging than analysing. Unless we are assuming an explicit critical stance, our job as analysts is not to judge the participants or the situation but to analyse it as fairly as possible.

Open Coding: Attempt #2

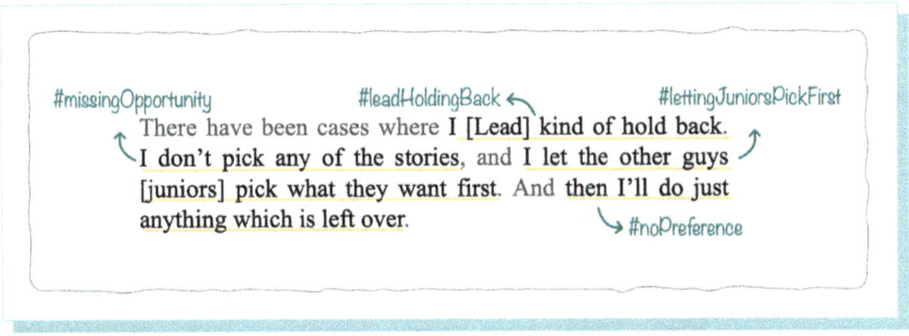

Fig. 10.5 Open coding attempt #2: An example of *descriptive* coding from a second attempt which is satisfactory but has more room for improvement

Figure 10.5 shows the second attempt at coding. We see better codes being generated based on more careful analysis, such as by analysing the complete sentence and the wider context and also taking the source into account. Here the *source* of the quotation is a senior technical lead. This information has now been inserted into the raw data in square brackets to complete the context, because it makes a difference to how their statements can be interpreted. Applying our zoom out–zoom in approach, the word "*juniors*" is also inserted in square brackets because we know from elsewhere in the same interview that the tech lead is referring to their juniors when they say "*other guys*" (sexist use of the term "*guys*" notwithstanding.) Now, the first code reads *#leadHoldingBack* which lends more context to the code as it identifies the source, which is relevant in this case. Then, this first code is used as a guide to draw better inference from the statement "*I don't pick any of the stories*". Considering this is being said by the tech lead, they probably have every opportunity to pick the tasks they want to self-assign from the task list and can even have early access to the task list in some cases. We will typically know this from our knowledge of the domain, e.g. arising from first hand experiences or observations of others. However, we know of the code *#leadHoldingBack* and therefore them not picking any tasks is related more to missing the opportunity they had, coded as *#missingOpportunity*, rather than *#beingLazy* as poorly coded in the first attempt. They then go on to explain their stance by stating "*I let the other guys [juniors] pick what they want first*" which clearly shows that they are *#lettingJuniorsPickFirst*. Finally, they say "*then I'll do just anything which is left over*" which is coded as them displaying *#noPreference*.

We can see that these new set of codes are an improvement over the previous set. Most of these codes serve to describe *what* is happening, as best as possible. However, we can do better than this. We can analyse more deeply to extract the best quality codes possible, as we will see in the final attempt.

Open Coding: Attempt #3

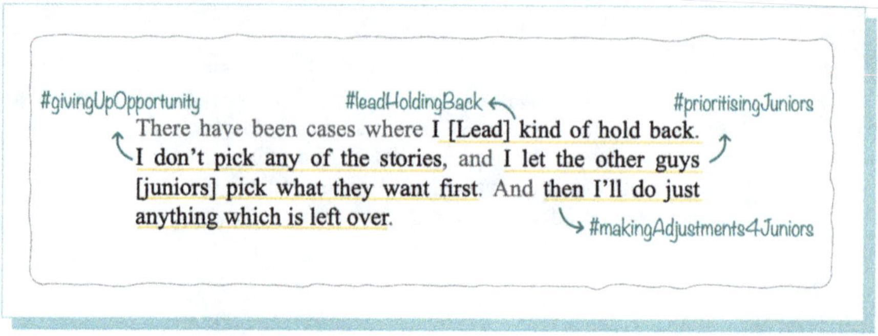

Fig. 10.6 Open coding attempt #3: An example of *analytical* coding from the final attempt which represents quality and depth

Figure 10.6 shows the final attempt of coding. We see what rich analytical codes look like once the researcher has engaged deeply with the data, inspecting it from multiple angles and at multiple levels. The first code is still *#leadHoldingBack*. The second code is now refined to *#givingUpOpportunity* which better captures the essence of the statement than *#missingOpportunity*, since the tech lead willingly gives up on their opportunity to self-assign tasks first. Next, the code *#lettingJuniorsPickFirst* is reconsidered. We can see that it serves to describe what is happening, i.e. the tech lead is letting junior members pick tasks first. This is a descriptive approach to coding. We want to move to a deeper, more analytical approach. Analytical here refers to carefully considering not only what is happening but also, as much as possible, *why* and *how* it is happening. When we ask these questions of the data at hand (e.g. *why would they do that?*) and placing things into the wider context (e.g. what else are they doing? taken together, what are they trying to achieve?), we can see that this action is about giving priority to the juniors, coded as *#prioritisingJuniors*.

Finally, the last code *#noPreference* is refined following the same analytical approach to understanding the *why* and the *how* behind the *what* we can see on the surface. And so we move from a descriptive code to a more analytical code *#makigAdjustments4Juniors* which serves to capture and explain both *why* the tech lead chooses to "*do just anything which is left over*" and *how* they end up *#prioritisingJuniors*. Taken together, these codes start to tell a story about how senior developers and tech leads will sometimes display deference to juniors when it comes to practicing self-assignment in agile teams.

The above examples of multiple attempts at coding the same raw data serve to highlight the journey of the analyst as they learn how to perform open coding and get progressively better at it. Another couple of aspects to note here are the role of memoing—explained later in the chapter—in improving coding quality and that of peer or expert review and feedback. As we gain experience with open coding different types of data, the time it takes to go from the first poor attempt to the good coding outcomes becomes shorter and our confidence in our analysis capabilities grows.

Tips

Tips for Open Coding:

- Apply an open mindset and approach.
- Apply the *zoom out–zoom in* technique to consider the local and wider contexts.
- Analyse and don't judge.
- Dig deeper to discover the *why* and the *how*, not just the *what* that is happening.
- Apply domain knowledge.
- Write memos to capture insights.
- Seek peer or expert review and feedback.
- Repeat and refine to improve code quality.

10.3.5 Drawing Out Socio-technical Codes

In addition to coding analytically, researchers working with data representing socio-technical contexts need to code in a way that extracts the complete socio-technical meaning of the data and thereby derive socio-technical codes. Socio-technical context here refers to contexts where "*the social and technical aspects are interwoven in a way that studying one without due consideration of the other makes for an incomplete investigation and understanding*" (Hoda, 2022).

Open Coding with a Social Science Approach

Arising from sociology, it is not surprising that traditional GT methods apply a sociological lens to analysis, draw out social codes and concepts, and develop social theories. On the other hand, STGT applies socio-technical analysis and aims to draw socio-technical codes and concepts and develop socio-technical theories. To illustrate the difference between coding using traditional GT approaches (such as Glaserian GT (Glaser & Strauss, 2017, first published 1967), Strauss–Corbinian GT (Strauss & Corbin, 1990), and constructivist GT (Charmaz, 2006)), and STGT's socio-technical approach, let us consider two examples of coding the same underlying raw data with the sociological and socio-technical approaches, respectively.

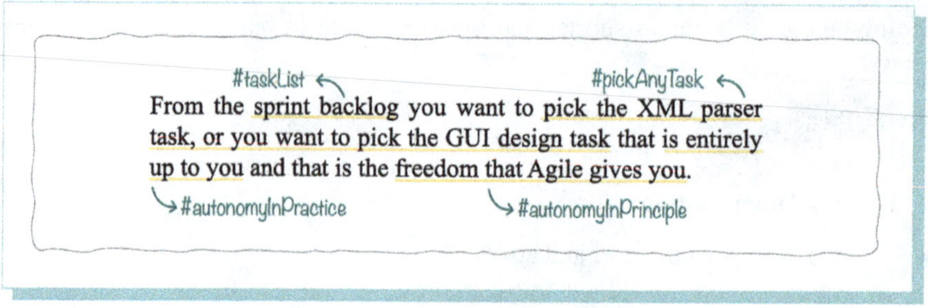

Fig. 10.7 Example of open coding with traditional GT methods' sociological approach

Figure 10.7 depicts a traditional sociological approach to open coding. We find that the text "*...you want to pick the XML parser task or you want to pick the GUI design task that is entirely up to you*" is understood to represent the developers' ability to pick different tasks, coded as *#pickAnyTask*. It also captures the use of the jargon "*sprint backlog*" to effectively mean a *#taskList*. The last part of the sentence "*...that is the freedom that Agile gives you*" is inferred to represent the freedom or autonomy that Agile methods promise in principle, coded as *#autonomyInPrinciple*. Having captured this, we can also create a code *#autonomyInPractice* to capture and emphasise how the autonomy promised by Agile methods in principle is being applied in practice in this case. While there is nothing wrong with this analysis per se, we can achieve more depth of information and insight by applying a socio-technical lens to open coding the same raw data, as demonstrated next.

Open Coding with a Socio-technical Approach

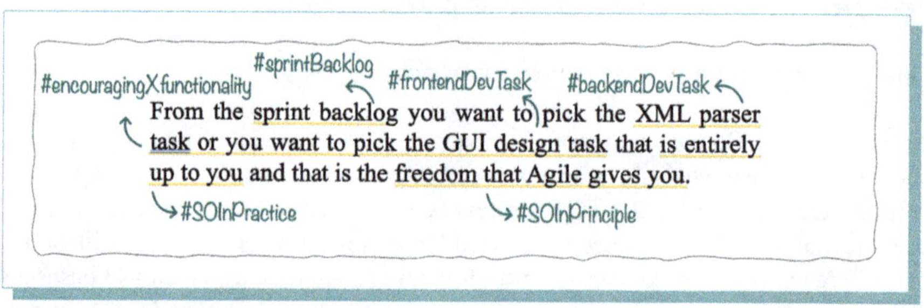

Fig. 10.8 Example of open coding with STGT's socio-technical approach

Figure 10.8 depicts STGT's socio-technical approach to open coding. We find the code *#taskList* is replaced with *#sprintBacklog*, the code *#autonomyinPractice* is replaced with *#SOinPractice* where SO is short for self-organisation, and the code *#autonomyinPrinciple* is replaced with *#SOinPrinciple*. These new codes reflect the application of domain knowledge and the use of the appropriate technical terms which makes a difference to the open coding and eventual findings. For example, by coding *#sprintBacklog*, we have captured the idea of a specific list that is relevant to the current software development cycle or sprint. This is different to a *product backlog*, which captures the overarching list of all desired functionality, not all of which may make it into the software product. These technical nuances can make a significant difference to what else we code in the future and the possible relationships that might emerge through memoing.

Similarly, using the technical term self-organising (abbreviated as SO) as opposed to autonomy can have a similar effect as self-organising agile teams are known to possess not only autonomy but several other characteristics, such as cross-functionality and continuous learning. Such depth and richness would have been lost if we were not open coding using a socio-technical approach.

Next, the code *#pickAnyTask* derived using a social lens is now replaced with two new codes derived using a socio-technical approach. The social approach to open coding treats the raw data terms of "*XML parser task*" and "*GUI design task*" as technical placeholders or black boxes,[9] taken as a whole to represent different types of technical tasks, and therefore representing the developers' ability to pick any tasks. Applying a socio-technical approach to the same would yield more nuanced insights as to the level of flexibility on offer for the developers. With relevant domain knowledge of software engineering, we can examine the text "*...you want to pick the XML parser task or you want to pick the GUI design task that is entirely up to you*" more closely and deeply. Now, the term "*XML parser task*" is understood to be used as an example of back end development tasks, coded as *#backendDevTask*, and "*GUI design task*" as front end development tasks, coded as *#frontendDevTask*.

Having broken down these technical aspects using our domain knowledge, we can now relate them back to the social aspects to derive comprehensive socio-technical codes. Typically, back end and front end developers tend to specialise in their respective functional areas. Allowing self-assignment to cross these traditional boundaries is a noteworthy insight. Thus, breaking down the technical details here allows us to appreciate the wide *range* of functional tasks that are available for self-assignment, where the same may be restricted in other teams. These insights lead to the creation of a new code, *#encouragingXFunctionality* (where *X* stands for cross), that captures how the freedom to self-assign across a wide range of functional tasks in this case effectively promotes the development of cross-functional skills among the developers. In this context, *#encouragingXFunctionality* carries both social and technical meaning and can be considered a socio-technical concept.

It is through applying a socio-technical approach to open coding that we are able to harness more comprehensive, deeper, and nuanced meanings and insights from the data in socio-technical domains. Let us also note that this is a great opportunity to write a memo on the proposed relationship between self-assignment and cross-functionality. With the strength of evidence gathered from the analysis of further data, the proposed relationship may become solidified.

---

[9] Refer to the socio-technical research framework in Chap. 3.

Role of Domain Knowledge and Socio-technical Sensitivity

Definition

Domain knowledge is *the knowledge of the domain being studied*, e.g. knowledge of the domain of software engineering, computer science, information systems, human-computer interaction, artificial intelligence, and so on. The research team needs to have the relevant domain knowledge in order to perform effective literature reviews, design the research protocols, collect relevant data, analyse data, derive findings, and present them.

Socio-technical sensitivity is the *ability to explore, identify, and understand the intricacies of human interactions and socio-technical aspects of phenomena* (Hoda, 2022).

Let us break down this socio-technical approach further to understand the forces at play. The socio-technical nature of STGT manifests itself primarily in two ways. First, through the *domain knowledge* that is required to conduct the study. Second, through the *socio-technical sensitivity* of the researchers. Both these aspects predispose software engineering researchers to perform STGT better than those who may be new to either. However, both domain knowledge and socio-technical sensitivity skills can be learned by individuals and also distributed within the research team to achieve the best results, as discussed in Chap. 4 Research Design Canvas.

When considering the STGT data analysis procedures, researchers with the necessary domain knowledge are likely to better comprehend the data, derive meaning from it, and create rich codes. For example, software engineering researchers conducting STGT studies in SE and related domains are more likely to be able to extract the complete socio-technical meanings as compared to someone with no knowledge of these domains. The need to understand the terminology specific to the study domain is particularly important in socio-technical domains such as software engineering. The data in these domains, be it interviews or stack overflow threads, is likely to contain large amounts of domain-specific details, acronyms, and jargon. We cannot treat these details like black boxes or placeholders, only acknowledging their presence but not really understanding their meaning and function. Domain-specific terms carry specific meanings that augment what can be inferred from the data. Most of the time, they represent socio-technical concepts.

To further illustrate the importance of domain knowledge in drawing socio-technical codes, consider the raw data examples in Fig. 10.9, taken from a semi-structured interview about how software teams engage with their product owners or customer representatives (Hoda et al., 2011). Let us focus on the domain-specific terminologies used. These have been coded in blue, and others have been coded in grey for illustration purposes. The interviewee refers to the software engineering role of a "*developer*", coded as *#SERole*, and an agile-specific role of a "*product owner*" which stands for a customer representative, coded as *#agileRole*. Researchers with the requisite domain knowledge may not need to code these explicitly as they are part of their standard vocabulary. Nonetheless, these domain-specific terms have been highlighted here to show how they may appear foreign to researchers without the necessary domain knowledge and may need to be explicitly coded. Another scenario where it may be useful to code them explicitly is where the study involves understanding the role of technical language in communication, e.g. between developers and end-users.

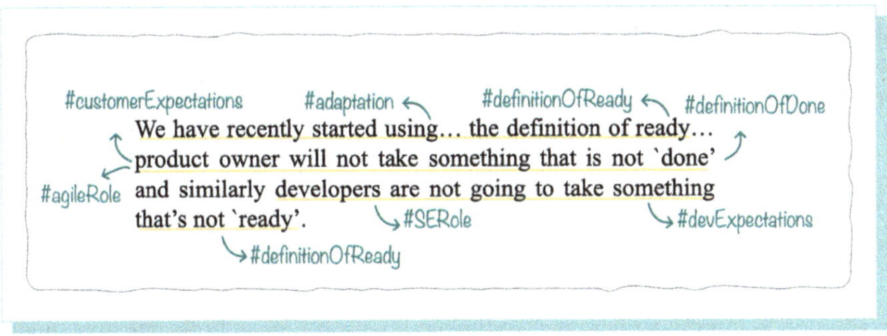

Fig. 10.9 Example of socio-technical coding for domain-specific terms and jargon

Next, by referring to "*something that is not 'done'...*", the participant makes an indirect reference to the scrum concept of *definition of done* from fundamental agile literature,[10] coded as *#definitionOfDone*. This is an example of the domain knowledge that the analyst needs to possess in order to make complete sense of what is being said. At the same time, it represents an inherently socio-technical concept because it includes both the technical details of the acceptance criteria requisite to considering a task done and the social implications for the team to negotiate them with the customer and have them signed off. In the same excerpt, the interviewee talks about the idea of "*definition of ready*", coded as *#definitionOfReady*.

In addition to domain knowledge, the research team needs to possess socio-technical sensitivity. A researcher with mature socio-technical sensitivity will reach beyond identifying the domain-specific terminologies used directly and indirectly in the raw data, such as *#definitionOfDone* and *#definitionOfReady*. Applying a socio-technical lens to their analytical reasoning, they can also identify the socio-technical reasons *why* these definitions are being used. They can see that using the *#definitionOfDone* is like an informal socio-technical contract to capture and satisfy *#customerExpectations* (new code generated), such that the product owner will not accept a task as done until it meets the criteria they have laid out and agreed upon with the team. Similarly, the *#definitionOfReady* can be considered an informal socio-technical contract that addresses developers' expectations such that developers will not agree to start working on a task until its technical requirements are well explained by the product owner, coded as *#devExpectations*. Both definitions and set

[10] https://www.agilealliance.org/glossary/definition-of-done/.

of expectations have technical and social implications. Taken together, the participant is explaining how the agile team has adapted a new practice of *#definitionOfReady* to balance the established agile practice of *#definitionOfDone*. Another piece of analysis that is relevant here is that the new practice of *#definitionOfReady* is a home-grown *#adaption* (another new code generated) to the regular agile practices, introduced by the team.

These inferences can be arrived at by applying the relevant domain knowledge and socio-technical sensitivity to analytical reasoning, and by carefully considering the full social and technical implications. Zooming out to the wider context of the conversation and with enough supporting evidence from the study at large, the researcher can conclude that such an adapted strategy is evidence of how agile teams practice self-organisation. In this context, self-organisation is not a social concept. It carries both social and technical meaning and is a socio-technical concept.

10.3.6 Considering Options and Revising Codes

In addition to improving our open coding abilities through multiple attempts, finalising the name of a code may require a few iterations. Creating codes can sometimes involve coming up with options for code names and selecting one that seems to best capture the inferred meaning. Figure 10.10 shows one such example. Here, the initial question by the interviewer is coded as *#RCDefinition* because it is asking for the participant's own definition of what they consider as a requirements change. Here requirements change is abbreviated as RC for ease of use. The participant response starts with "*Well, two parts*" and then goes on to identify *#customerDemand* and *#forcedExternalCircumstances*. In this sense, the participant does not really provide a definition as expected, but they identify "*two parts*" that can be coded as *#RCParts?*, or *#RCTypes?*, or *#RCComponents?*. In other words, we are considering options of possible code names represented by the use of question marks.

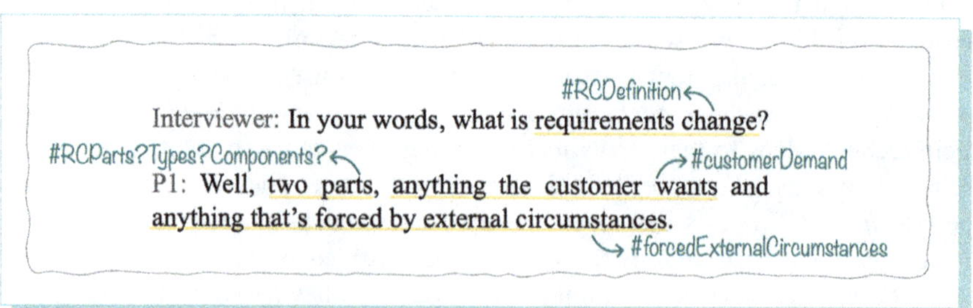

Fig. 10.10 Example of considering options and making revisions when creating code names

Next, we consider each option of possible code names carefully. What does "*two parts*" stand for? Considered in the context of the question, it stands for *two parts of requirements change* which can be coded in the first instance as *#RCParts*. Now, let us consider the word *parts* at a semantic level. The dictionary defines *part* as "*an amount or section which, when combined with others, makes up the whole of something*". While the examples given by the participants may be part of a wider set of examples, it would not make sense to say *#customderDemand* is a *part* of requirements change. The same goes for the options *#RCComponent* and *#RCType*. We could say these are *#RCExamples*, but again, while the participant is sharing examples, they are not examples of RCs; rather, they seem to be examples of the *reason* why an RC might arise. To see if this fits, we put it into a sentence: *#customderDemand* and *#forcedExternalCircumstances* are two *reasons* why RCs arise. That makes sense. Thus, the final code derived here is *#Reasons4RCs*, which was not even one of the options to begin with but goes to show how initial options and reasoning about them leads to better codes. Code names with options (using question marks) also make for excellent candidates for detailed discussions with the wider research team. The team can consider the pros and cons of selecting one name over the other and help finalise one.

Note, the code *#forcedExternalCircumstances* is taken almost verbatim from how the participant mentioned it. Avoid the temptation to use verbatim code names too often as they can lead to descriptive coding. However, sometimes the words used in the raw data are the best suited to capture what is implied. Another aspect to note is that the code *#RCDefinition* does not progress further because while it was expected, no direct information was provided about it. If it comes up again in the same interview (*zoom out* to data unit level) or from other data sources (*zoom out* to dataset level), we can include it in our list of potential codes (*zoom in*). It is also worth noting that the text "*Well, two parts*", while seemingly casual, ended up giving rise to an important code that could have been easily missed if not considered carefully, at the semantic level, with the related context in mind.

It is also common for analysts to revisit codes in light of new evidence and revise them to better fit the emerging meanings. Sometimes this can take the shape of revising the code name or breaking up codes into two or three different ones. Code name revision is a natural part of the coding process. It is expected to occur more in the early stage of coding and less in the later stages where the codes have firmed up and started giving rise to concepts. With experience in open coding, coming up with appropriate code names becomes an easier and faster process. However, every now and then, experienced analysts will still come across data that requires considering multiple code name options. It can also serve as an opportunity to write memos, comparing and combining similar codes together and exploring relationships between them, which is a great segue into the next section.

10.4 Constant Comparison

Definition

Constant comparison is the process of comparing codes derived from within the same data unit and across all data units to find common patterns among them. Using constant comparison, similar *codes* are grouped to form a *concept*, and similar concepts are combined to form a *category*. Sometimes, an additional level of *subcategory* may arise between concept and category levels and *super-categories* above the category level.

Open coding can result in large numbers of codes, leaving the researcher feeling inundated. It is difficult to imagine how the mountains of data we have collected and the large numbers of codes arising from the analysis can lead to a coherent theoretical outcome. What makes this possible is the increasing levels of abstraction achieved through the *constant comparison* procedure.

10.4.1 Increasing Levels of Abstraction

Figure 10.11 depicts the increasing levels of abstraction resulting from inductive open coding and constant comparison. Researchers can use Fig. 10.11 as a template to visualise their emerging codes, concepts, and (sub-)categories (either in portrait or landscape modes as best suits). Such visualisations give the researchers the opportunity to step away from their mountains of raw data and help them make sense of the big picture with regard to their emerging findings. Visualisations can be an effective mechanism to share the emerging findings with others, seek feedback, and have discussions. For example, by drawing a preliminary model of how the codes, concepts, and (sub-)categories relate to each other, the research team can carefully consider the suggested groupings, asking questions such as *Is this dense enough to be a category on its own or is it really a concept within another category? Is this category encompassing too many disparate concepts and is it better off being two separate categories?* Moving between text-based coding and visualisations can be a synergistic exercise.

Visualisations are best done with pen on paper initially so it is easy to change and move things around. Once near final, they can be transferred into digital forms using tools such as Canva, Microsoft PowerPoint, or various annotation tools. Through iterations of review and revision, the theoretical model or taxonomy diagram—or a theory diagram if proceeding to theory development—can be finalised and presented in articles and reports, often in the form of a graphical abstract, as seen in Madampe et al. (2021); Graetsch et al. (2023); Berntzen et al. (2023); Pant et al. (2023).

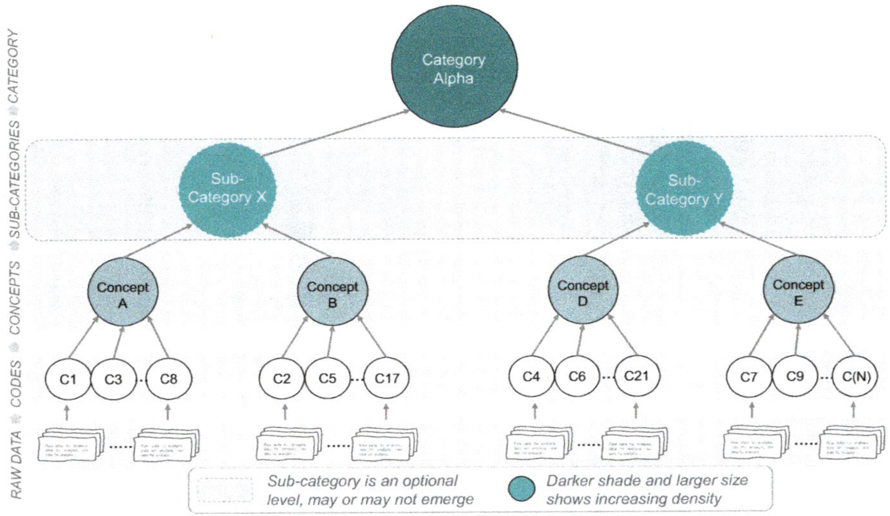

Fig. 10.11 An inductive (bottom-up) approach of open coding and constant comparison with increasing levels of abstraction, from raw data to codes to concepts to subcategories (if applicable) to categories to possibly, super-categories (not depicted here)

10.4.2 Constant Comparison: An Example

To see how constant comparison is applied in practice, let us follow an example in Fig. 10.12. It is taken from an ongoing study on applying STGT for data analysis to user app reviews (Haggag et al., 2024). The open coding done on the margins shows that this is an example of a poor review from a user. The one-star rating also confirms the same. The company name is kept anonymous for privacy reasons.[11]

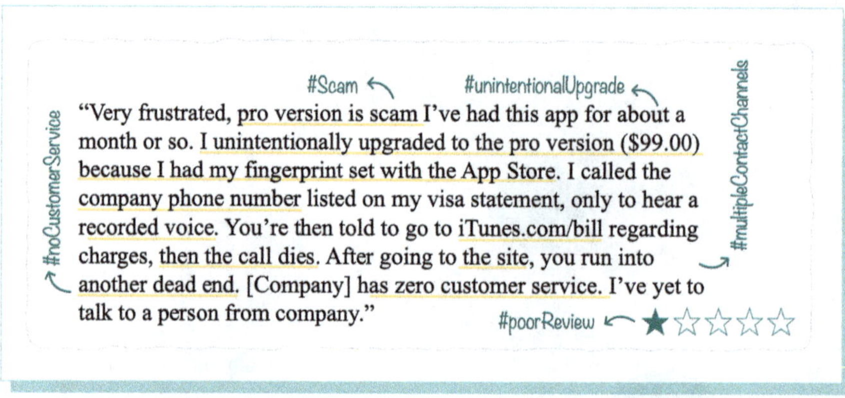

Fig. 10.12 STGT's open coding performed on an app review, including star rating confirming the poor review in the text

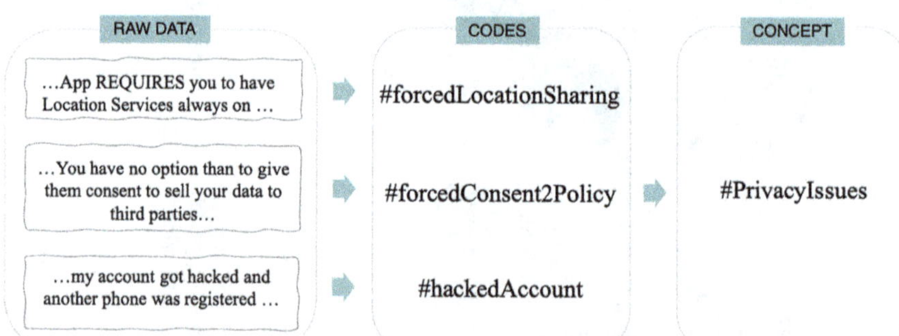

Fig. 10.13 Constant comparison applied to identify and group similar codes into a common concept

Figure 10.13 shows excerpts of three other reviews under *raw data* in the first column. Applying open coding to each of these, three codes were generated as

[11] It may be possible to trace the user's identity which raises wider data privacy concerns regarding the use of public data for research purposes, something that is increasingly being considered an ethical concern in many parts of the world.

#forcedLocationSharing, *#forcedConsent2Policy*, and *#hackedAccount*, shown in the middle column. These three and other similar codes are grouped together to give rise to one common concept, *#PrivacyIssues*. This is a simplified view of what is in reality a much more messy process of comparing codes to identify which are similar enough to group under a common concept and to generate the name for that concept.

Typically, a concept is created from combining codes from different data units, and preferably multiple sources, which lends strength of evidence to the analysis. To achieve higher strength of evidence, it will make sense to support this dataset with data from other sources, e.g. through interviews with some end-users or by analysing social media posts regarding the same app.

Applying the constant comparison procedure at the concept level, concepts are grouped to form (sub-)categories and so on. As new data comes in through the iterative rounds of data collection and analysis, it is open coded. The codes arising from the new round are compared with the existing ones and can serve to strengthen existing concepts and lead to new ones. It is worth noting here that the same code may contribute to giving rise to multiple concepts. However, this is rare and not to be expected generally from open coding. It may also be a sign that the generated code may be representing too many ideas within it and may benefit from being broken down into two or more codes. The same concept leading to multiple categories is arguably even rarer and the same advice applies as for codes above.

Both open coding and constant comparison are rigorous procedures. Imagine the number of comparisons required to ensure each code has been considered in light of all the other codes to find similarities, across the entire dataset! It demands a lot from the analysts in terms of time, effort, care, and reflection. The outcome is robust, rich, and multilayered findings and reflections that add to the rigour of the research study. At the same time, sharing examples of the *chain of evidence* from the raw data all the way up to the category levels ensures credibility. This is why a well-done STGT analysis can be claimed to be both credible and rigorous. More about this in Chap. 13 Evaluation Guidelines.

However, not all codes make it to the concept level and some naturally drop out while others "bubble to the top". Figure 10.14 presents a metaphorical representation to show how codes rise up and group to form concepts and categories, while some codes and concepts are left behind (at the bottom) in the process. Whether a code "survives" the rigorous analysis process and makes it to the concept level depends on the strength of evidence, typically from multiple instances within the same data unit and from across multiple data units. In rare cases, a code makes it to the concept level because of its novelty even if arising from a single instance. In the latter case, it is especially important to explain why the code was promoted to the concept level despite being supported by a single instance. For example, the code may be the "missing piece" that completes the concept, or it may present a novel artefact or practice that is worth documenting.

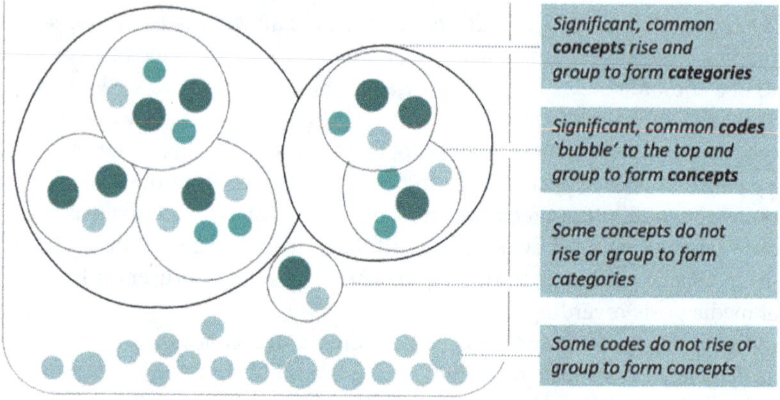

Fig. 10.14 A representation of how codes "bubble up" to concepts and categories and how some codes and concepts are left at the bottom in the process

The end of the *basic data analysis stage* in STGT is marked by the emergence of some significant concepts and categories, strongly supported by the underlying codes. Through data analysis and the writing of memos (also known as *memoing*, covered next), some relationships between concepts and some between categories are also likely to emerge. At this stage, the research team may decide to end their STGT project and report the findings in the form of the strongest categories identified and the preliminary theoretical outcome seen to emerge, e.g. a model, framework, taxonomy, or beginnings of a theory. Alternatively, they can decide to progress to the *advanced theory development stage* to build one or more mature theoretical outcomes. Theory development is covered in Chap. 12 Theory Development. There we will learn about the advanced memo writing as it applies to theory development. For now, let us consider the process of basic memoing, which plays an important role in the basic data analysis stage.

10.5 Memoing

Definition

Memoing is the ongoing process of documenting the researcher's thoughts, ideas, questions, and reflections on emerging codes, concepts, and categories and evidence-based conjectures on possible links between them (Hoda, 2022). Memos can be in the form of written notes, sketches, maps, diagrams, photos, annotations, and audio and video recordings. Memoing is an imperative procedure that distinguishes socio-technical grounded theory from other qualitative research methods, generates insights, and drives theory development.

Memoing allows the researcher to take a step back from the mountains of raw data to consider wider aspects such as identifying patterns in the data, write about interesting insights gained during analysis, and discuss the gaps in the emerging theoretical model or theory.

While memos can contain field observations, both brief and detailed, it is critical that they don't stop there. Researcher insights, thoughts, questions, and ideas can be included in memos. Indicate whether the statements captured in memos are researcher assumptions, ideas arising from some other external sources such as a book or talk, or direct evidences from the research dataset. Embedding references to original data sources helps establish a chain of evidence.

Example

For example, once an insight is captured in a memo, the researcher can write about it and record questions such as

- *Why is this so?*
- *Why isn't it some other way?*
- *How does concept A relate to concept B?*
- *What kind of relationship is this?*
- *What are the barriers here?*
- *What are the enablers here?*
- *What is missing?*
- *What data can be collected next and from where/whom?*

Such questioning helps the researcher to engage more deeply with the data. Another key function of memoing is that it activates theoretical sampling by encouraging the researcher to think about what they need to collect next and from where/whom.

10.5.1 Types and Forms of Memos

Memoing is an imperative procedure in STGT that differentiates it from other qualitative methods (Hoda, 2022). Memos can serve different purposes and are generally of three types:

- ***Basic memos*** that are written to identify and discuss key insights about the data, question the data, and consider the patterns and gaps in the emerging theoretical concepts and categories. Basic memos can also include preliminary suggestions of relationships evidenced across concepts and categories. They are generously written in STGT's basic stage and serve to explore and formulate key codes, concepts, categories, links between them, and preliminary theoretical outcomes.

- ***Advanced memos*** that are written to explore the relationships across concepts and categories, delving into the details of the relationship such as its nature and facets. They are written in STGT's advanced stage of theory development and can occasionally also uncover new concepts and categories. Advanced memoing is indispensable to theory development.
- ***Reflective memos*** that capture reflections about the research process and researcher experience, e.g. capturing research design decisions, limitations, threats, implications for future work, and recommendations for future research. They can be written at any time during an STGT project.

All three types of memos are meant to be regularly revisited, revised, and expanded on, as the project progresses and the researchers gain experience. Memos can be created in many forms. Text-based memos are rather standard, written on physical or digital mediums. Some researchers may find textual memos too formal and restrictive and may benefit from the impromptu nature of recording their thoughts and ideas as audio notes or video recordings.

Memos can include sketches and photos, e.g. of office layouts as seen in Hoda et al. (2012) or placement of particular physical items of interest. More examples of memos can be found in Graetsch et al. (2023); Madampe et al. (2022); Hidellaarachchi et al. (2023). As with raw data and emerging analysis, store memos carefully and confidentially and back them up regularly (e.g. through local version control or on the cloud).

> “Memoing is the secret ingredient that adds richness to qualitative data analysis in STGT studies through supporting researcher reflexivity. Memos are where abductive reasoning is most evident and where concepts, categories, hypotheses, and theoretical outcomes take shape. Memoing is a glue that binds data collection to data analysis iteratively and progressively, helping drive theoretical sampling and theorising.”

10.5.2 Quality and Quantity of Memos

There is no fixed number of memos expected in relation to the data size. One data unit (e.g. an interview) can lead to multiple memos and others may not lead to any. As with most elements of STGT, what is more important is the quality of the memos in terms of how deeply we have thought about things and how well we document them for future use. Even basic memos need to reach beyond descriptions and consider the layers, facets, nuances, insights, and possible patterns and links in the data.

10.5.3 Using Memos

Besides driving data analysis and theoretical sampling, memos serve a number of other functions. Memos themselves are not data to be open coded. Rather, basic and advanced memos form the basis of rich discussion sections in papers and contribute to recommendations for research and practice. Reflective memos can be leveraged to include a reflections section in the paper and to contribute to describing any method adaptations with rationales and acknowledging threats to validity and limitations, as these are part of reflecting on the study design and method application. Reflective memos can also help with the writing of rebuttals or response letters during the review process, drawing on the captured research design rationales to answer reviewer questions. Examples of memos can be shared in manuscripts to establish the chain and strength of evidence and to lend credibility to the method application as seen in Graetsch et al. (2023); Hidellaarachchi et al. (2023); Pant et al. (2023).

10.6 Tips for Data Analysis

Tips

Tips for data analysis:

- Create clear and strong codes.
- Code for richness.
- Fill in the context.
- Apply a research paradigm.
- Improve theoretical sensitivity.

10.6.1 Create Clear and Strong Codes

A study on how software developers come up with variable names (Feitelson et al., 2020) with 334 developers identified a three-step process of naming variables that involved *selecting the concepts to include in the name*, *selecting the words to represent each concept*, and *constructing a name using these words*. These steps were not found to be necessarily in sequence or applied with awareness. A subsequent experiment established that the conscious application of the three-step process resulted in significantly better variable names. A similar approach can be adopted when creating codes during STGT data analysis with some additional considerations.

- **Selecting what to code**. All key and contextual information is worth coding, as described in Chap. 9 Qualitative Data Preparation and Filtering. Open coding can be done on a line-by-line and sentence-by-sentence basis. A sentence may be considered worth coding as a whole by creating a single code name. Alternatively, the analyst may find multiple words or phrases within a sentence worth coding, i.e. one phrase of raw data can lead to multiple codes.
- **Deciding what is conceptually represented**. As explained with the example of creating hashtags in Sect. 10.3, the analyst needs to identify what the selected part of the data being coded represents conceptually. Does it represent a practice, a time period, a role, an individual, a limitation, a range, a challenge, a strategy, a reflection, or a grievance? What is key idea captured in the raw data chunk under consideration?
- **Giving it a name.** A name given to the idea captured in the raw data is called a code. Typically, a code name is between one and four words long. It can be of our own making or include words taken verbatim from the raw data. The last two steps, identifying the idea and naming it, may happen in sequence or together in a way that it is difficult to distinguish.

10.6.2 Code for Richness

There are a few of things to keep in mind about coding. First, avoid poor coding, which mostly results from not spending enough time with the data, rushed analyses, and not thinking carefully and deeply about the data when analysing it, and not writing memos. Second, the inherent iterative nature of GT also applies to its coding practices. In particular, the path to deriving analytical codes often goes through first deriving descriptive codes (Charmaz, 2014). This means researchers need not be afraid to start with a first attempt at coding and follow up with revising those codes until they are richer. As we attempt to capture and summarise *what* is happening in the data, we produce descriptive codes. This is a good first step. Next, aim to analyse more carefully and deeply by asking analytical questions such as *why*, and where applicable, *how*, as they relate to what is happening. For example, Charmaz suggests asking questions such as "*what do the data suggest? pronounce? leave unsaid? from whose point of view?*" (Charmaz, 2014, pg. 116). While the data may not always provide answers to all these questions, they make for excellent triggers to write memos and, where applicable, drive theoretical sampling to collect relevant data.

Drawing out analytical codes requires thinking deeply about the raw data at the micro and macro levels, what I call the *zoom-in/zoom-out approach*. At the micro level, we "zoom in" and read sentences and chunks of data to try to infer meaning and make logical and semantic sense. But this is not enough. The researcher needs to also "zoom out" and infer meaning based on the wider context of the data. For example, Glaser suggests asking "*what is this data a study of?*" (Glaser, 1978, pg. 57) as a way to understand the overall essence of the data unit so we can derive better meaning of the smaller chunk in relation to the overall context. To take an analogy, this is like painting where the painter zooms in and works close to the canvas, focusing on the lines, colours, and shapes up close. Every now and then, they have to step back and widen their field of vision, focusing on how the close-up area they are currently working on sits with respect to the rest of the painting.

At the same time, in coding analytically, it is important not to overreach for explanations. Remember, anything we code has to be grounded in the data. At the code level, stay as close to the data as possible (Charmaz, 2014, pg. 116).

Finally, it may not always be possible to derive analytical codes for all underlying data, and some portion of the codes may remain descriptive. We can live with this, so long as most of the codes are analytical.

For those new to qualitative coding, it may be difficult to gauge the difference between descriptive coding and analytical coding, and sometimes even poor coding. A good way to avoid poor coding is to double-check the inferences drawn with the participant directly, also known as *member checking*. However, this may not always be possible to do, especially in case of pre-existing data from publicly available sources. Another approach to learning to work towards analytical coding is to seek early and frequent feedback from others in the research team, including those with coding experience. Investing time and effort in learning how to code well in the early stages of the STGT journey will provide great returns throughout the current project and in future projects.

10.6.3 Fill in the Context

Data analysis relies heavily on understanding the context of the raw data at hand. Context filling, which is embedding contextual knowledge (e.g. in square brackets) to make the raw data more complete and standalone for analysis, is an important step in consciously considering the context in order to perform quality coding. Conversely, if we do not consciously consider and fill the contextual details, our brains tend to do this unconsciously. Consider how the human brain is able to make sense of sentences with words that have missing and scrambled letters. For example, try reading this:

Example

Yuo cna porbalby raed tihs esaliy desptie teh speillgn msitaeks.

Apparently such sentences can be read by most people so long as the first and last letters are in order and are not scrambled to the extent that they are anagrams, e.g. tried vs tired.[12] We can do this because of our ability to anticipate what comes next based on our knowledge of how the language works.[13]

Similarly, when analysing data, if the context is not provided, our brains can promptly fill up those gaps based on assumptions, often drawing on our knowledge base, e.g. reading of literature and prior experiences. An advantage is that it allows us to draw on our knowledge and experiences to better understand the data we are analysing. For example, where the raw data contains a lot of domain-specific technical jargon and the analyst has the relevant domain knowledge, it can work to their advantage to make better sense of the data. However, a disadvantage is that there is a possibility that the analyst may start assuming things because they know them to work a certain way in their prior experience instead of attempting to understand what is going on based on the data and its associated context.

Unconscious context filling can lead to poor coding, where we can become judgemental as opposed to analytical, and end up drawing incorrect inferences, for example, in the cases where we have not bothered to grasp the contextual evidence, which may in fact contradict our assumptions and prior experience. The analyst needs to be careful in not assuming things when analysing data and instead consciously perform context filling based on evidence. Where there is not enough contextual information, the analyst can make a note of this (e.g. in a memo) and attempt to fill this gap by collecting more relevant data. A more proactive approach is to spot such gaps during data collection where possible, e.g. during an interview, and ask for clarifications and more contextual information. Having said that, there is a balancing act between trying to gather as much contextual information as possible and moving ahead with the research.

Having avoided incorrect assumptions, the researcher's knowledge and experience can still have an influence on data analysis. Whether and how we acknowledge this depends on our choice of research paradigm.

10.6.4 Apply a Research Paradigm

Where following a positivist research paradigm, the data and its analysis are separated from any insights based on the researcher's personal or professional experiences and not combined with the research evidence. However, noting them down is a good way to both get it off our chests and to become consciously aware of our own preconceptions, considered biases in a positivist view. These can be written up as reflective memos and shared with practitioners and researchers in the form of blog posts, videos, or other formats that are not claimed to be research findings but are nonetheless insightful for the community.

---

[12] http://www.mrc-cbu.cam.ac.uk/people/matt.davis/cmabridge/.

[13] As a fun little exercise, I tried this with ChatGPT, and it could read it correctly too.

Where following a constructivist approach, personal insights can still be recorded, e.g. as reflective memos, along with documenting how they inform the formulation of the emerging findings. For example, an STGT researcher can reflect on how their own experience of being a software developer has shaped their understanding of their study on the role of AI developers in implementing ethical AI.

10.6.5 Improve Theoretical Sensitivity

Definition

Theoretical sensitivity *is the propensity of the researcher to identify codes, concepts, and categories in the data and to explore and establish relationships between them.* Theoretical sensitivity improves with coding experience until it becomes second nature.

Theoretical sensitivity improves with exposure to and experience in open coding. The more codes we create, the better we get at identifying parts of the raw data that contain information worth coding and naming the codes. Gradually, the analyst's constant comparison skills improve as they are able to see how certain codes group together to form concepts and concepts group to form categories. Similarly, writing memos helps them explore and establish relationships between various concepts and categories. At an advanced stage, the analyst is able to draw hypotheses that spell out the relationships. The more the analyst immerses in analysis and seeks and applies feedback, the more their theoretical sensitivity improves.

As an analogy, this is similar to how software programmers improve their object-oriented design skills such that designing new classes and applying the principles of encapsulation, inheritance, and composition—with may have been difficult or confusing at first—start to become manageable and eventually, second nature, with experience.

While increased theoretical sensitivity improves analysis abilities, it can also pose a threat to our ability to remain open. Much like experienced software programmers, experienced STGT analysts can develop favourites when it comes to identifying concepts and categories. For example, analysts comfortable with identifying "*types of*" things in the data can become limited to producing taxonomies.

Ideally, the expertise gained from previous project experiences will help improve our effectiveness, accuracy, depth, and speed of analysis, but not unduly influence how we analyse new data. With heightened awareness and conscious effort, experienced analysts can remain open in their analysis. When working in a team, the experienced analyst should avoid the temptation of making quick calls and instead leverage the freshness of approach that the other, less experienced team members can bring. It takes humility and trust in the team. I often use an innocent child learning about a new world as an analogy to remind myself and others to hit the reset button before and after each project.

10.7 Team-Based Coding

STGT coding can be performed by a single analyst or a team of analysts. In the former case, it is a good idea to have the codes regularly reviewed by others such as advisors, colleagues, and qualitative research experts and to refine the approach as needed based on their feedback. The latter case of multiple coders is more complex. How can we ensure consistency and shared understanding (sometimes referred to as reliability) of the coding approach across multiple coders?

The process of coming up with codes is a creative exercise. Each researcher looking at the same piece of raw data may find different ideas worth coding. Each is also likely to come up with a different name to capture the same idea. This creative subjectivity is widely acknowledged in qualitative research and is not unique to open coding. By way of comparison, let us consider (software) coding in the software engineering context. An empirical study of how software developers choose variable names showed a 6.9% median probability of two developers selecting the same name (Feitelson et al., 2020). However, once a name was chosen, it was seen to be understood by the majority of developers. This finding reflects my experience of running coding workshops where people tend to come up with different code names for the same raw data but also seem to understand each other's codes most of the time, sometimes after some discussion of rationales.

When it comes to qualitative coding in a team, some teams seem to act as a *single mind*. They find it relatively straightforward to be able to discuss and arrive at mutually acceptable codes. Any minor differences are discussed and resolved with the team deciding on a final name or interpretation. Other teams may exhibit strong differences and trying to achieve consistency in coding can seem next to impossible. Before trying to "fix this problem", e.g. by applying quantitative-based approaches such as inter-rater reliability measures, let us first try to better understand the problem.

10.7.1 Why Inconsistencies Arise Across Multiple Coders

- **Multiple coders don't make a team.** One of the key underlying causes of major differences, and hence inconsistency, across multiple coders is that they do not function as a team. Lack of teamwork can hinder the quality of the outcomes.
- **Silos don't help.** A second underlying cause is the segregation of research roles in ways that are seemingly efficient but in reality impede cross-learning and consistency in qualitative studies. For example, medium to large research teams

tend to separate researchers into those that collect data, those that analyse it, and those that report and present the findings. Useful tacit knowledge can be lost in handovers between these silos.

- **Ignorance is not bliss.** A third underlying cause is not acknowledging and addressing the members' fundamental differences in human values and research philosophies. These fundamental differences can manifest themselves in concrete terms, e.g. what an analyst classifies as key and contextual information versus noise, which parts of the useful information they decide to code, how they draw inferences, how they create codes, and what key patterns and relationships they see in the data. Lack of shared values and research philosophy can hinder the team's ability to achieve its best research work.
- **Not having a plan hurts.** Finally, even where the above-mentioned issues are addressed, a team that does not have concrete strategies to enable the members to align themselves to each other's analysis "*wavelength*" will likely struggle.

The above-mentioned issues are not dissimilar to those that arise in software engineering. For example, a team of software developers is likely to produce better products and services than a group of individual developers working in parallel with little communication, coordination, and collaboration. Similarly, a cross-functional software team where the various functional roles are involved in almost all parts of the software development life cycle (e.g. developers involved in requirements gathering) is likely to produce better outcomes for the customer than a team where these functional roles are working in silos (e.g. developers only perform software coding.) Finally, in software teams made up of diverse team members, it is important to address the diversity of coding approaches and to active working toward defining team norms and coding standards that help the team perform better together. For example, collective code ownership and coding standards have been shown to improve technical quality of the software project (Maruping et al., 2009).

10.7.2 A Word About Inter-coder Reliability

Inter-coder reliability (ICR) is "*a numerical measure of the agreement between different coders regarding how the same data should be coded*" (O'Connor & Joffe, 2020). Inter-rater reliability (IRR) is a related concept with subtle differences in the context of application. These measures are rather controversial and have received objections from various quarters (Hollway & Jefferson, 2012; Vidich & Lyman, 2000; Clarke & Braun, 2013). ICR and IRR are deeply seated in a positivist tradition, aiming to discover the one objective reality of the research topic. They are seen by many to contradict the philosophical underpinnings of most qualitative research as most qualitative research tends not to be positivist and welcomes multiple perspectives and shared understanding of the context (Guba & Lincoln, 1994; O'Connor & Joffe, 2020).

Another related concept is that of *intra-coder reliability* that aims to establish whether the same individual will code the same data in the same way at different points of time. This is equally problematic in qualitative research. While the data being analysed remains the same, the wider context surrounding the research topic may have changed in a way that demands a new perspective to the analysis. Indeed, the individual performing the analysis may also have changed as a person and a professional over time as they learn and grow. We can relate to this by looking back at some of our previous research from decades ago and identifying areas of improvement. Trying to *freeze* the outcomes of qualitative data analysis in time through such measures is not only philosophically problematic but is also limiting.

> “Conducting qualitative research is like stepping into a river. Adapting from the beautiful quote by Heraclitus, no one ever steps into the same river twice. For it's not the same river, and they are not the same person.”

Returning to our software coding analogy, imagine mandating numeric scores from code reviews as a way to claim reliability without addressing any of the underlying issues. Will that solve the root problems? Most likely not. Similarly, team alignment in qualitative analysis is more complex as we have discussed above and naturally requires a more nuanced and inherently qualitative approach.

10.7.3 Guidelines for Achieving Alignment in a Coding Team

TIPS

Guidelines for achieving alignment in a coding team:

- Become a team.
- Be more than analysts.
- Acknowledge the differences.
- Decide on most suitable values and research philosophy for the project.
- Conduct coding workshops.
- Develop coding principles.
- Maintain a coding repository.
- Seek expert review.
- Leverage participant feedback.

Approach data analysis with the aim of conducting rigorous analysis and producing rich codes together as a coding team. With an organised approach to team-based coding, the team can harness their multiple perspectives and combined strengths to achieve high-quality analysis outcomes. Below I share some guidelines to achieving alignment, and by extension shared understanding and consistency, in a team of analysts. These steps address the underlying issues more deeply and in ways better suited to most common qualitative research philosophies and encourage *reflexiv-*

ity and dialogue, often cited as the key benefits of measures such as inter-coder reliability (O'Connor & Joffe, 2020).

- **Become a Team.** Becoming an effective team is critical to effective team research, and that includes analysis. It is vitally important that the group of analysts working on the data analysis in the same project become a team and not remain individual coders working in parallel. This includes social aspects such as making conscious efforts to get to know each other and establish protocols for effective communication, coordination, and collaboration. They are also recommended to conduct a *Research Team Values Assessment and Alignment Exercise* as a team workshop to arrive at a general shared list of human values, as described in Chap. 4 Research Design Canvas.

- **Be More than Analysts.** In qualitative research, the more the same researchers are involved across the various research steps such as data collection and analysis, the better the outcomes can be expected to be in terms of quality, rigour, and consistency.

- **Acknowledge the Differences.** A first step to resolving differences is to acknowledge them. Team members can get together to share their individual research *mindsets* (e.g. how they are applying openness to their coding; see Sect. 10.2.1), *approach* (e.g. how they perform inductive reasoning; see Sect. 10.2.2), and *worldview* (e.g. what research paradigm they subscribe to, including ontological and epistemological stances they hold; see Sect. 10.2.4). Senior members of the team can encourage a psychologically safe environment in the team to express such differences through open dialogue.

- **Decide on Most Suitable Values and Research Philosophy for the Project.** Once the fundamental differences are apparent, the team can discuss these in relation to the specific context of the research project. For example, instead of selecting the most common worldview held by most members of the team or that recommended by the most senior researcher outright, the team can conduct a *Research Project Values Assessment and Alignment Exercise* and a *Research Philosophy Alignment Exercise* as team workshops, as described in Chap. 4 Research Design Canvas to arrive at the shared values and shared research philosophy best suited to their specific project.

- **Conduct Coding Workshops.** Coding workshops involve multiple analysts considering the same piece of raw data, together, and coming up with their own codes, followed by sharing their codes with each other, questioning each other's codes, offering rationales, and discussing similarities and differences. They help the team come up with a shared understanding of the data and with a shared approach to the analysis. Regular workshops can be held at the start of data analysis and then less frequently to ensure continued alignment.

- **Develop Coding Principles.** Qualitative data analysts can develop a set of coding principles that they agree to abide by. These can include guidelines on what to do in specific cases and include anonymous examples from prior experience of conflict resolution. For example, a coding principle can be that for data with lacking details and relevant contextual information, the team will aim to collect more data to supplement it. Where that is not possible, the team will mark the concepts arising from that data as weak and emerging. These will likely not make it to the final set of findings or theory, but can be reported as possible areas of future work.

- **Maintain a Coding Repository.** The coding team can set up a shared workspace where they have all raw data securely saved along with the coding principles for ready references, a project timeline, and planned workload distribution and task ownership. It can also include the results of the various values alignment, philosophy alignment, and coding workshops. This is where everyone on the team can save their analysis and add their memos. Like a software repository, the STGT coding repository can include a README file that describes the project, the aims and objectives, the team setup, and shared access and version control protocols.

- **Seek Expert Review.** Another way to achieve consistency is to seek expert review of the team's collective coding practices. They can be an independent, third-party reviewer or a member of the team with robust expertise and experience who can provide insights into the strengths and weaknesses of the team's approach, highlight areas of inconsistencies, and help resolve conflicting views. Expert review and advice can be elicited at key points in the project: e.g. after the first round of analysis, when it feels like the basic stage is complete, when the team conducts a first round of their selected mode of advanced theory development (if they decide to proceed), and when the team thinks they have reached saturation. The expert can help review the analysis at these critical milestones.

- **Leverage Participant Feedback.** Finally, the team can check their coding outcomes with the participants of the research, where possible. For example, they can share drafts of research manuscripts to gain participant feedback. Sharing the analysis of individual lines of raw data or individual data units (e.g. an interview transcript) may not be productive because of the aforementioned fundamental differences in how people approach coding, and this applies to practitioners who additionally may not have the requisite qualitative research background to assess the coding on a fine-grained level. However, most practitioners are good at judging the relevance and resonance of the key concepts, categories, and emerging hypothesis against their lived experiences and provide feedback that way.

10.8 Expected Outcomes

Qualitative data analysis using STGT's basic procedures of open coding, constant comparison, and memoing allows researchers to make sense of large amounts of raw data, condense it, and raise it through increasing levels of abstraction. The application of STGT's basic stage of data collection and analysis is expected to result in the identification of some significant patterns in the data in the form of key concepts and categories. With ongoing memoing, some relationships between these concepts and categories as well as insights are also expected to emerge. The research team can decide to stop here. This would be considered a limited application of STGT, known as *STGT for data analysis*. The key categories and emerging relationships identified at the end of the basic stage can be reported in publications in various forms such as conference papers, journal articles, workshop papers, doctoral symposium papers, short papers, posters, and videos. Examples of the kinds of outcomes achievable from the application of STGT for data analysis can be found in Hidellaarachchi et al. (2023); Madampe et al. (2023); Pant et al. (2023); Li et al. (2023); Wang et al. (2023); Chan and Hauser (2023).

The research team may decide to continue to the advanced stage of theory development, covered in Chap. 11 What Is Theory? and Chap. 12 Theory Development.

10.9 Summary

In this chapter, we learned about the *fundamentals of basic data analysis*, including the mindset, approach, and worldview applied to analysis, followed by a visual notes-taking analogy to help explain the inductive approach to qualitative data analysis in socio-technical grounded theory. Then we learned about the procedure of *open coding* with hashtags, the zoom out–zoom in technique, drawing out analytical and socio-technical codes as well as considering options and revising codes. Next, we learned about *constant comparison* through which data is condensed and raised in levels of abstraction and the procedure of *memoing* to draw insights and relationships. This was followed by *tips for data analysis*, including creating codes, coding for richness, context filling, role of research paradigm, and improving theoretical sensitivity. Next, we considered the idea of *team-based coding*, including guidelines and strategies for achieving alignment in a coding team. Finally, we learned about the *expected outcomes* of STGT's basic stage. Researchers interested in the advanced stage of theory development can proceed to Chap. 11 What Is Theory? and Chap. 12 Theory Development.

References

Berntzen, M., Stray, V., Moe, N. B. & Hoda, R. (2023). Responding to change over time: A longitudinal case study on changes in coordination mechanisms in large-scale agile. *Empirical Software Engineering, 28*(5), 114.

Brown, C. B. (2002). *Acompañar: A grounded theory of developing, maintaining and assessing relevance in professional helping*. University of Houston.

Chan, Y.-C. & Hauser, E. (2023). Understanding reactions in human-robot encounters with autonomous quadruped robots, *Proceedings of the Association for Information Science and Technology, 60*(1) 86–97.

Charmaz, K. (2006). *Constructing grounded theory: A practical guide through qualitative analysis*. Sage.

Charmaz, K. (2014). *Constructing grounded theory*. Sage.

Clarke, V. and Braun, V. (2013). Successful qualitative research: A practical guide for beginners. In *Successful qualitative research* (pp. 1–400).

Dey, I. (1999). Grounding grounded theory: guidelines for grounded theory inquiry.

Feitelson, D., Mizrahi, A., Noy, N., Shabat, A. B., Eliyahu, O., & Sheffer, R. (2020). How developers choose names, *IEEE Transactions on Software Engineering, 48*(1), 37–52.

Glaser, B. (1978). *Theoretical sensitivity: Advances in the methodology of grounded theory*. Sociology Press.

Glaser, B. G. (2009). The novice GT researcher. *The Grounded Theory Review, 8*(2), 1–21.

Glaser, B. G. and Strauss, A. L. (2017). *Discovery of grounded theory: Strategies for qualitative research*. Routledge (First Published 1967).

Graetsch, U. M., Khalajzadeh, H., Shahin, M., Hoda, R. & Grundy, J. (2023). Dealing with data challenges when delivering data-intensive software solutions. *IEEE Transactions on Software Engineering*. https://doi.org/10.1109/TSE.2023.3291003

Guba, E. G. & Lincoln, Y. S. (1994). Competing paradigms in qualitative research, *Handbook of Qualitative Research, 2*(163–194), 105.

Haggag, O., Hoda, R., & Grundy, J. (2024). Towards enhancing mobile app reviews: A structured approach to user review entry, analysis and verification. In *In the proceedings of Evaluation of Novel Approaches to Software Engineering (ENASE)*.

Hidellaarachchi, D., Grundy, J., Hoda, R., & Mueller, I. (2023). The influence of human aspects on requirements engineering-related activities: Software practitioners' perspective, *ACM Transactions on Software Engineering and Methodology, 32*(5), 1–37.

Hoda, R. (2022). Socio-technical grounded theory for software engineering. *IEEE Transactions on Software Engineering, 48*(10), 3808–3832.

Hoda, R., Noble, J., & Marshall, S. (2011). The impact of inadequate customer collaboration on self-organizing agile teams. *Information and Software Technology, 53*(5), 521–534.

Hoda, R., Noble, J., & Marshall, S. (2012). Self-organizing roles on agile software development teams. *IEEE Transactions on Software Engineering, 39*(3), 422–444.

Hollway, W., & Jefferson, T. (2012). *Doing qualitative research differently: A psychosocial approach.* Sage.

Li, Z. Z., Wang, H., Gasevic, D., Yu, J., & Liu, J. K. (2023). Enhancing blockchain adoption through tailored software engineering: An industrial-grounded study in education credentialing, *Distributed Ledger Technologies: Research and Practice, 2*(4), 1–24.

Madampe, K., Hoda, R., & Grundy, J. (2021). A faceted taxonomy of requirements changes in agile contexts. *IEEE Transactions on Software Engineering, 48*(10), 3737–3752.

Madampe, K., Hoda, R., & Grundy, J. (2022). The emotional roller coaster of responding to requirements changes in software engineering. *IEEE Transactions on Software Engineering, 49*(3), 1171–1187.

Madampe, K., Hoda, R., & Grundy, J. (2023). A framework for emotion-oriented requirements change handling in agile software engineering. *IEEE Transactions on Software Engineering*. https://doi.org/10.1109/TSE.2023.3253145

Maruping, L. M., Zhang, X., & Venkatesh, V. (2009). Role of collective ownership and coding standards in coordinating expertise in software project teams. *European Journal of Information Systems, 18*(4), 355–371.

Masood, Z., Hoda, R., & Blincoe, K. (2021). What drives and sustains self-assignment in agile teams. *IEEE Transactions on Software Engineering, 48*(9), 3626–3639.

O'Connor, C., & Joffe, H. (2020). Intercoder reliability in qualitative research: Debates and practical guidelines. *International Journal of Qualitative Methods, 19*. https://doi.org/10.1177/1609406919899220

Pant, A., Hoda, R., Spiegler, S. V., Tantithamthavorn, C., & Turhan, B. (2023). Ethics in the age of AI: An analysis of AI practitioners' awareness and challenges. *ACM Transactions on Software Engineering and Methodology*. https://doi.org/10.1145/3635715

Strauss, A., & Corbin, J. (1990). *Basics of qualitative research.* Sage Publications.

Vidich, A. J., & Lyman, S. M. (2000). Qualitative methods: Their history in sociology and anthropology. *Handbook of Qualitative Research, 2*, 37–84.

Wang, W., Khalajzadeh, H., Grundy, J., & Madugalla, A. (2023). Adaptive user interfaces for software supporting chronic diseases. *2023 IEEE Symposium on Visual Languages and Human-Centric Computing (VL/HCC)* (pp. 215–218). IEEE.

PART IV

Theory Development

11 What Is Theory?

Abstract In this chapter, we will learn about *what is theory?* ranging from random and education guesses, research-based predictions to scientific theories and laws, including what makes hard or soft theories. Then we will learn about *socio-technical grounded theories* as outcomes of a full STGT study, followed by learning about the four genres of theories as broad and high-level theories, broad and in-depth theories, focused and high-level theories, and focused and in-depth theories.

11.1 What Is Theory?

Definition

Theory is an evidence-based explanation of a phenomenon, derived systematically by considering the evidences available in the studied context.
Random guesses, **educated guesses**, and **research-based predictions**, while useful in their own contexts, are not theories. Theories range from "*soft*" and "*hard*" ***scientific theories*** to ***scientific laws***, with increasing levels of evidence

R. Hoda, *Qualitative Research with Socio-Technical Grounded Theory*,
https://doi.org/10.1007/978-3-031-60533-8_11

and certainty. Theories are often seen to make predictions about future behaviours in similar contexts, with varying degrees of certainty depending on the nature of the phenomenon studied. Useful theories are accepted by the experts and resonate with the people who experience the phenomenon in the studied or similar contexts.

The term *theory* is freely used in both formal and informal contexts. It is used to refer to ideas ranging from *random* or *educated guess* in everyday parlance, *research-based predictions* in sports, politics, and economics, to *scientific theories* defined as "*scientifically acceptable principles to explain a phenomenon*" (Merriam-Webster). This includes *"soft" scientific theories* in psychology, sociology, and socio-technical fields such as software engineering, *"hard" scientific theories* in physics and biology, and *laws* in physics and mathematics. The word theory is also used to describe an ideal set of circumstances, e.g. "it was meant to work *in theory*". With such wide-ranging use and misuse, it is important to unpack the term and clearly define what is meant by theory in a socio-technical grounded theory (STGT) study.

To demonstrate and make sense of these varying definitions, I present a visualisation in Fig. 11.1. It has two dimensions:

- **Certainty**, on the horizontal x-axis, which captures the level of stability of the inherent nature of phenomenon being studied and the certainty of predicted outcomes, e.g. random guesses have low certainty, while scientific laws have high certainty associated with them.

- **Evidence**, on the vertical y-axis, which captures both the quantity and quality of the underlying observations, data, and facts as well as the rigour and systematic nature of the research approach to derive them, e.g. random guesses are low on the quantity and quality of underlying evidence, while scientific laws are based on strong evidence and systematic research methods.

Note that this visual representation is not meant to be interpreted as a chart drawn to scale or created from accurate underlying data through systematic research. Neither is it meant to be a puritan approach to classifying the sciences. The definitions and explanations I offer are based on my own reading and understanding, which in turn are informed by my training and experience in science and engineering, basic knowledge and research on theories in psychology and sociology, and a deep seated interest in theory development irrespective of disciplines.

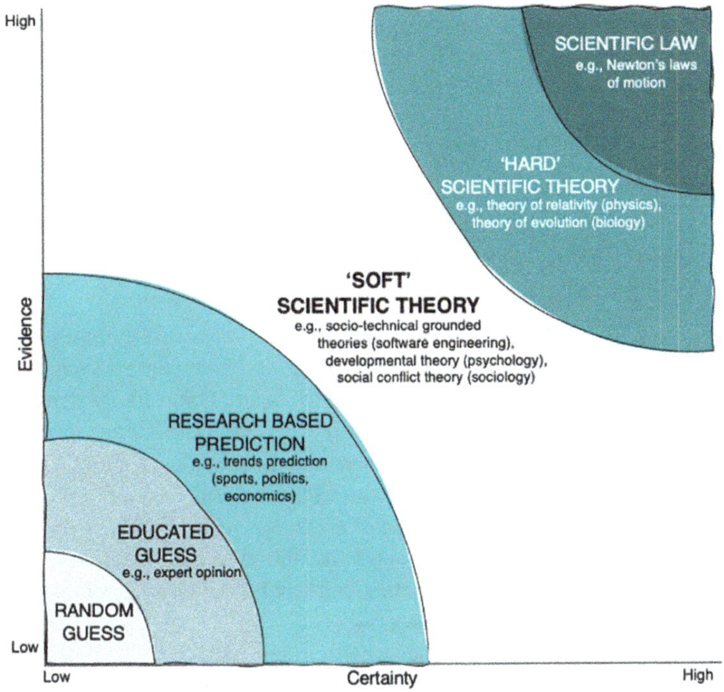

Fig. 11.1 Meanings associated with the term "theory" ranging from *random guess* as the layperson's use of the term to established *scientific laws*. The x-axis represents increasing *certainty* of the nature of the phenomenon studied and the predicted outcomes (e.g. individual behaviour, stock market behaviour, automated test suites, rainfall, and gravity), and the y-axis represents increasing quantity and quality of the supporting *evidence*

11.1.1 Random and Educated Guesses

The term *theory* in everyday parlance is often used to mean a hunch, assumption, or a *random guess* that is typically a personal opinion based on either limited or no supporting evidence (see bottom left corner of Fig. 11.1). An example is "*I have a theory about why Adam always arrives early on Wednesdays*", which suggests that (a) it has been observed that Adam arrives early on Wednesdays and (b) the speaker has some clues that can help explain why it (a) occurs. Depending on the strength of the clues or evidence, the speaker can make a random guess, or an educated guess at best, at explaining the phenomenon and predicting future behaviour. For example, a media journalist providing their expert opinion on election polls is an **educated guess**. Needless to say, the time taken to come up with such guesses is negligible as compared to the rigorous research studies required to come up with scientific theories or laws. Guesses can also be made about macro-level phenomenon, such as "*I have a theory that the universe is infinite*". However, made by a layperson with little or no evidence, it is at best a guess, and not even close to a theory in the formal sense of the word. Conversely, using the phrase "*it's just a theory*" is inaccurate for the same reasons.

11.1.2 Research-Based Predictions

Definition

Research-based predictions are based on some formal research conducted to collate and analyse relevant evidences. The certainty of the predicted outcomes in this case is higher than in the case of an educated guess.

For example, through an analysis of the past 10 years of Olympics medal tallies, current team performances, and a number of other factors such as relative team strength, research-based predictions can be made about likely winners in the Olympics games. Such predictions are usually listed with confidence levels because they cannot be guaranteed. For example, based on previous 5 years' data on the election outcomes and the latest pre-election opinion polls, a journalist might say: "*The Labour party has an 86% chance of emerging as a winner in the upcoming elections in New Zealand*". The percentage likelihood represents the level of uncertainty present due to the numerous factors that can influence an election result, or a sports team performance for that matter.

Because of the nature of the phenomenon being studied, e.g. specific events in sports, politics, economics, and the need for regularly updated predictions, the research applied to derive these predictions is often quick and lightweight. Many of them rely on predictive tools that apply basic algorithms or more sophisticated artificial intelligence models. Such research-based speculations are used not only in sports and political systems but also in financial systems such as stock markets and mutual fund investments, guiding transactions worth billions of dollars everyday.

11.1.3 Scientific Laws

Definition

Scientific laws are *highly objective and plausible explanations of a phenomenon repeatedly observed and studied using systematic and rigorous methods.* Scientific laws are strongly supported by evidence and afford the highest certainty possible of all theories.

Next, we move to the top right corner of Fig. 11.1. Fields of research that apply the scientific method and a scientific mindset are referred to as the sciences. Laws and theories developed in these fields are called *scientific laws* and *scientific theories*.

Sciences are often concerned with the study of natural phenomena. Natural phenomena, such as gravity and acceleration, are highly stable within the standard range of observable contexts and therefore display high levels of certainty. Collecting evidence through observations and experimentation to form scientific laws requires extensive time and effort. Developing a scientific law is a significant human and individual achievement, and it is often named after the scientist who develop it.

Example

Newton's second law of motion states that *objects will accelerate in the direction of the force applied. The acceleration is directly proportional to the force and inversely proportional to the mass of the object.* It is represented using the formula

$$F = ma$$

where F denotes *force*, m denotes *mass*, and a stands for *acceleration*.

This is referred to as a law, not a theory, because it is supported by mathematical proofs, and repeated observations and experiments, and is known to be highly certain in its predicted outcomes within the normal range of application, e.g. matter studied in the physical world accessible to humans.

However, even scientific laws are limited to contexts within which they are near certain and outside of which they start to wobble. For example, Newton's laws of motion work well for objects in the everyday physical world we are familiar with. But when objects reach the speed of light, the same laws are not able to explain the observed and predicted behaviours and need adjustments.

The debate on whether mathematics is a science or a conceptualisation of the natural order of things notwithstanding, mathematical laws are another example.

Example

The *commutative laws* of mathematics state that swapping the order of numbers in the mathematical operations of addition and multiplication will produce the same result. The term commutative here refers to the commuting or moving around of numbers.

$$a + b = b + a$$

$$e.g., 2 + 8 = 8 + 2$$

Similarly, there are *associative and distributive laws* that predict behaviour of numbers and display certainty under the assumed contexts.

11.1.4 Scientific Theories

Definition

Scientific theories *are proposed explanations of a phenomenon as established by the underlying calculations (e.g. mathematical proofs on paper) and/or repeated practical observations and experiments (where possible) derived using systematic and robust methods.* Scientific theories have lower supporting evidence and lower certainty of predicted outcomes than scientific laws (as shown in Fig. 11.1).

"Hard" Scientific Theories

Some sciences such as physics and chemistry are traditionally referred to as *hard sciences*. They deal with physical and chemical world, entities, their relationships, and influences. Generally, scientific theories arising out of these sciences are supported by numerous observations and experiments and have high (though not absolute) certainty when it comes to predictions. I refer to these as **"hard" scientific theories**.

Example

As part of his *special theory of relativity*, Albert Einstein challenged the notion that mass and energy are distinct entities and argued for an interchangeable relationship between them, denoted by the equation

$$E = mc^2$$

where the kinetic energy of an object (E) can be calculated by multiplying its mass (m) with the speed of light (c) squared.

Ethical arguments of possible applications notwithstanding, a significant consequence of the ideas introduced by the special theory of relativity is seen in nuclear physics, where the mass of a small amount of uranium is converted to incredible amounts of energy. However, the interchangeability of mass and energy in general has not been observed and measured in nature or experiments because of our physical limitations to move matter at the speed of light. If this was possible, the special theory of relativity and its generalised version, known as the general theory of relativity, would qualify as scientific laws.

Other examples of scientific theories include the *Big Bang theory* that explains the evolution of the universe into its current and likely future states. *Darwin's theory of evolution by natural selection* explains the biological evolution of species in terms of adaptations that occur in species where heritable traits favouring survival and reproduction become more common across populations over time.

"Soft" Scientific Theories

Fields of science that specialise in studying humans and human-related phenomena, follow the scientific method, and apply a scientific mindset are commonly referred to as *soft sciences*, e.g. psychology and sociology. They focus on the workings of the human brain, observed human behaviour, and social interactions. Theories in these fields have lower certainty of predicted outcomes than in the hard sciences (see placement in the middle range in Fig. 11.1). I refer to these as **"soft" scientific theories**.

Example

Piaget's theory of cognitive development defined children's brain as fundamentally different to the adults' brains, growing through four stages of children's cognitive development: *sensorimotor stage (0–2 years), preoperational stage (2–7 years), concrete operation stage (7–11 years), and formal operational stage (12 years and over)*. The theory had far-reaching implications on the applied approaches to children's education, being guided by these stages of development.

However, in the digital age, such classic theories need to be re-examined and recalibrated in light of modern human experiences. For example, how well does Piaget's theory account for the cognitive development of *digital natives* who differ from the children in Piaget's time? Similarly, other psychological theories such as *attachment theory* and *theories of personality* remain modifiable to account for the changing human experience.

This does not make "soft" scientific theories (or the research that goes into developing them) inferior to "hard" scientific theories. The certainty associated with a theory typically aligns with the stability of the phenomenon studied. In many ways, explaining human and social behaviour through scientific theories can be considered as challenging, if not more, than explaining and predicting naturally occurring phenomena due to the inherent uncertainty in people's behaviour and level of complexity of their interactions with each other and their world. Even the most powerful of computational devices and advanced simulation models are yet not capable of predicting human behaviour in the same way as gravity can be predicted.

What Makes Theories "Hard" or "Soft"?

Why is it that theories developed in the sciences such as psychology and sociology have lower certainty of prediction than those developed in the fields of sciences such as physics and chemistry? In other words, what makes them soft or hard? To understand this, let us consider the nature of the objects and phenomenon they study and how they are observed and measured.

Sciences such as physics are the study of the natural world and entities. Entities such as *matter* have properties such as mass, velocity, and acceleration, and fundamental physical *forces* such as gravity have relatively negligible ranges of variations. For example, the mass of a ball can be measured to a high level of accuracy across repeated measurements. Some entities such as the speed of light are known to be constant. To study the effect of a force on the mass of an object, other factors can be relatively easily controlled, e.g. experiments can be conducted in zero gravity. Furthermore, observing and measuring stable entities and forces does not alter them. Neither do the results vary to any significant extent depending on the individual researchers conducting the experiments (not considering human errors). In short, the relative *certainty* inherent in natural entities and forces and our ability to repeatedly observe and measure them (increased quantity of evidence) with consistent results and without influencing the results (increased quality of evidence) contributes to the certainty of their predicted actions, reactions, and interactions. Dealing with objects and forces of *hard* nature, i.e. those with little room for variations, leads to the name hard sciences and hard scientific theories.

At the same time, it is worth noting that even hard scientific theories are bound by their context of operation, however wide or "universal" they may be. For example, the *Heisenberg uncertainty principle* states the location and momentum of very tiny objects moving at very high speeds such as electrons cannot be predicted precisely, rather only within a range of possibilities. However, the accuracy of the predictions can be improved by increasing the number of measurements. Similarly, the "*Schrödinger cat*" thought experiment presents an interesting take on the stability of observations and predictions in hard sciences.[1] Discoveries in the quantum and relativistic realms have questioned the assumed absolute certainty of science and reconsidered it as *fallible but rationally justified* (Andersen & Hepburn, 2016).

Now consider the fields of psychology and sociology that study humans and phenomenon involving human behaviour and interactions. The inherent variance in the nature of humans such as personality, physiology, and emotions is relatively large when compared to the properties of inanimate objects. Similarly, there is much higher unpredictability in the behaviour of individuals across the human population such that the outcomes of repeated measurements with the same subject and across subjects have lower replicability than when repeating measures with inanimate objects and fundamental physical forces. There is also a very large range of factors that can influence human behaviour and social interactions, making it difficult to control for and study individual factors.

---

[1] https://www.nationalgeographic.com/news/2013/8/130812-physics-schrodinger-erwin-google-doodle-cat-paradox-science/.

A fundamental reason behind these issues is that humans, both those studying and those studied, are not interchangeable and replaceable in the way inanimate objects are. Each human participant carries their own unique set of characteristics, experiences, opinions, and free will which dictates multiple possible interaction scenarios. Similarly, each human researcher carries their own unique set of expertise, backgrounds, experiences, worldviews, and conscious or unconscious presumptions and biases leading to different possible interpretations of the same underlying evidences and therefore different overall explanation of the phenomenon, i.e. different theories. In short, the relative complexity and *uncertainty* inherent in the nature and characteristics of human subjects and our limited ability to repeatedly observe and measure them (limited quantity of evidence) with consistent findings and without influencing the results (limited quality of evidence) contributes to the uncertainty of their predicted actions, reactions, and interactions. Dealing with subjects and phenomenon of *soft* nature, i.e. those with large room for variations, leads to the name soft sciences and soft scientific theories.

Systematic and robust research methods exist in both hard and soft sciences, commensurate with the nature of what they study. Assuming careful and rigorous application of their respective research methods, the inherent differences in the nature of what they study imply that the certainty of the results will still vary. While this limits generalisability, repeatability, and reproducibility in soft scientific theories, it does not undermine their *credibility*, *rigour*, and *usefulness*. They remain the best possible scientific explanations for what is studied, supported by underlying evidences and observations derived using systematic and robust methods.

11.2 Socio-technical Grounded Theories

Definition

The theory derived from the application of the socio-technical grounded theory (STGT) method is a soft scientific theory comprised of the key identified patterns (referred to as concepts and categories) and relationships between them (expressed as hypotheses). It is grounded in quality evidence collected and analysed through *credible* and *rigorous* application of the full STGT method. It captures the essence of the socio-technical context of the phenomena studied and exhibits the characteristics of *novelty*, *usefulness*, *parsimony*, and *modifiability*.

Software engineering is a fundamentally socio-technical field. Socio-technical activities in software engineering are influenced by a wide variety of factors. They pose limitations and challenges similar to those faced in psychology and sociology, making it *complex* and *open to variations* and therefore, rather *unpredictable*. For example, how a software team interacts with its customers can be influenced by factors such as *team composition*, *team maturity*, the *length of the customer relationship*, the *level of trust* within the team and between the team and their customer, the *type of contract* governing the software project, and much more. Attempting to isolate any one factor for observation in the real world is rather impractical. Similarly, the certainty of the outcomes tends to vary as discussed earlier.

Having considered the wide range of use and misuse of the term theory, the theories derived from applying the socio-technical grounded theory (STGT) research method are typically soft scientific theories with limited certainty and supporting evidence (see middle range of Fig. 11.1). Arguably, if applied to study more stable phenomena, say in artificially created contexts with predefined deterministic behaviours and interaction outcomes, such as in some software games, it can lead to "harder" scientific theories.

A theory derived from the application of the full STGT method that is made up of the key *patterns* identified along with the strongest *relationships* between them. The theory statement identifies the key categories and defines the relationships between them.

- **Patterns.** While many patterns emerge over the course of an STGT study, only the ones most significant in terms of their ability to explain the phenomenon and supported by *strength of evidence* survive and emerge to the top most levels of data abstraction. In STGT terminology, these patterns are referred to as *concepts* and *categories*.

- **Relationships.** "*A grounded theory is more than just a set of descriptive categories: it also describes the key relationships between those categories*" Hoda and Noble (2017). Relationships explain how the key concepts/categories relate to each other and can be represented as a set of hypotheses.

At an abstract level, scientific laws and theories typically follow the same format, i.e. they describe the relationship between well-defined key concepts. For example, $F = ma$ is an abstract representation of a very specific relationship between three concepts, *force*, *mass*, and *acceleration*. Similarly, socio-technical theories identify and define the key categories and describe the relationships between them. For example, a grounded theory may capture the relationship between the *level of customer involvement* in agile projects and the *self-organising ability* of the relevant teams, where inadequate customer involvement is seen to negatively impact their self-organising ability, leading to the introduction of coping mechanisms and adaptations to agile practice (Hoda et al., 2011). Empirically derived theories can be explained in text and represented as visual model diagrams, e.g. see Hoda et al. (2011); Hoda and Noble (2017); Masood et al. (2020b,a); Shastri et al. (2021); Graetsch et al. (2023).

11.3 Expected Outcomes

The expected outcomes from the basic stage include preliminary theories, early theoretical models and frameworks, indicative relationships, hypotheses or propositions, and lightweight taxonomies. These are discussed in Chap. 10 Socio-Technical Grounded Theory for Qualitative Data Analysis. The expected outcomes from a full STGT study, applying the advanced stage, include mature theories, theoretical frameworks, models, and taxonomies. The outcome is considered mature once it comprises well-supported and dense categories and, in case of theories, mature relationships. The term "mature" does not mean the theory is expected to be universally applicable nor some kind of a "final" theory. In fact, one of the key evaluation criteria for a mature theory is *modifiability*. Both the application of the STGT research method and its outcomes—whether partial or mature—can be evaluated using the STGT evaluation guidelines, presented in Chap. 13 Evaluation Guidelines.

Theoretical outcomes can vary in the breadth of the phenomenon covered, i.e. they can be *broad* or *focused*, and in the depth or level of detail in which it is explained, i.e. they can be *high-level* or *in-depth*. Most theories derived from the application of an STGT study align to one of the four possible combinations or genres: *broad and high-level*, *broad and in-depth*, *focused and in-depth*, or *focused and high-level* (Fig. 11.2).

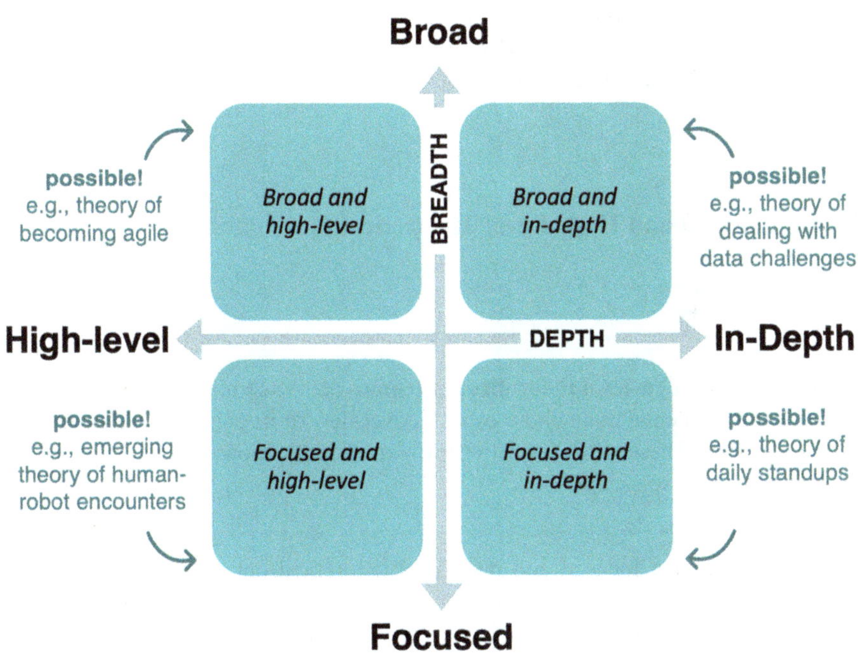

Fig. 11.2 Genre of empirically grounded theoretical outcomes

11.3.1 Broad and High-Level Theoretical Outcomes

Definition

Broad and high-level theoretical outcomes are outcomes that present a high-level explanation of a relatively broad phenomenon. They present an overarching view of a phenomenon, laying out the field, identifying the key constituents of the phenomenon, and how they interact with each other in enough detail to define them clearly, but not necessarily in-depth. These theoretical outcomes can be treated as research agendas where each of the constituent elements identified can in turn be studied individually to produce focused and in-depth theoretical outcomes.

An example of a broad and high-level theory is the *theory of becoming agile* (Hoda & Noble, 2017) which explains the phenomenon of agile transformations, a broad phenomenon. The theory describes the main constituents of this phenomenon as the five dimensions of software development practices, team practices, management approach, reflective practice, and culture. Arguably, each dimension can be investigated individually to produce focused and in-depth theories and guidelines for practice.

Some research topics that are likely to result in broad and high-level theoretical outcomes include investigating *how innovation occurs in software development*, *the effects of human factors (age, gender, personality) on software engineering process or products*, and *how artificial intelligence supports software engineering and vice versa*.

11.3.2 Focused and High-Level Theoretical Outcomes

Definition

Focused and high-level theoretical outcomes are outcomes that are focused on a narrow phenomenon and present an overview of its constituent elements or activities. These often take the form of classifications, categorisations, mappings, or taxonomies.

An example of a focused and high-level theoretical outcome is the emerging *theory of human reactions in encountering an autonomous quadruped robot* (Chan & Hauser, 2023). Another example is the study on *self-organising agile roles* (Hoda et al., 2012) which identified the different types of informal *roles* played by members of software teams in an effort to self-organise. The description of each of the roles included enough information to understand the role definition so individuals playing these roles in practice could be identified, along with identifying the stakeholders the role interacts with and how, a mapping of the informal roles to the formal Scrum roles, and an understanding of how the informal role definitions evolve from their manifestation in relative new teams as compared to that in more mature agile teams.

Some research topics that are likely to result in focused and high-level theoretical outcomes include investigating *what changes occur in software projects, ways in which software developers respond to change requests*, and *range of emotions exhibited in retrospective meetings and how they relate to team cohesion and process improvements*.

11.3.3 Focused and In-Depth Theoretical Outcomes

Definition

Focused and in-depth theoretical outcomes are outcomes that focus on a narrow phenomenon in detail. They typically achieve practical relevance and significance through detailed, in-depth accounts of how that phenomenon manifests in practice, when it does not work, when it's challenging, and the associated how's and why's.

For example, the *theory of daily standup meetings* (Stray et al., 2016) presents an example of a focused and in-depth theory on the Scrum practice of the daily standup meeting. The study presented seven constructs and six propositions in its theoretical framework and practical accounts of how standups varied in practice, factors that effected attitudes negatively and positively, and guidelines for making the most of standup meetings. Another example is the *impact of inadequate customer collaboration* (Hoda et al., 2011) which laid out the six C's, namely, the context, condition, causes, consequences, covariance, and contingencies related to the phenomenon of inadequate customer collaboration experienced by self-organising agile teams.

Some research topics that are likely to result in focused and in-depth theoretical outcomes include *value of sprint reviews* based on how developers and customers interact during a sprint review and what we can learn from those interactions. In the grand scheme of the entire Scrum software development process, the sprint review is a subpart and so the topic can be considered focused. Similarly, the perceived value of other software development practices can be explored. *How software teams support and enable well-being, how code reviews impact software quality, how self-assignment impacts cross-functionality*, and *how emotions can be embedded in generative artificial intelligence* are all topics that can be studied using STGT to produce focused and in-depth outcomes.

11.3.4 Broad and In-Depth Theoretical Outcomes

Definition

Broad and in-depth theoretical outcomes are outcomes that are simultaneously broad and in-depth. These are challenging to achieve because of the time and effort required to explore something in sufficient depth and breadth and are often done as part of larger projects.

A theoretical outcome that can be said to be broad and in-depth is the *theory of multidisciplinary software teams (MDSTs) dealing with data challenges when delivering data-intensive software solutions* (Graetsch et al., 2023), developed through the application of the *full STGT method*, including its basic and advanced stages. The theory explains the *challenges* faced by MDSTs such as gaining access to data, aligning data, understanding data, and resolving data quality issues, the *context* in and *condition* under which these challenges occur, their *causes*, the *consequences* of the challenges, the *contingencies* or strategies applied to address the challenges, and the *covariance* relationships between strategies and causes and/or challenges.

Another outcome that comes close is the *theory of Scrum variations* which explains the variations in Scrum roles, practices, and artefacts seen in practice as compared to their by-the-book definitions (Masood et al., 2020b). In this study, the topic, *how Scrum varies in practice as compared to by-the-book*, is a broad one, and the study covers all the key constituents of the Scrum method, the *roles*, *practices*, and *artefacts*. At the same time, under each of the key categories, the study provides nuances of the variations and grounded evidence from the underlying raw data. Detailed examples of *how, when, and why* real-world Scrum teams practice the Scrum roles, practices, and use the artefacts in variation to their definition in the fundamental Scrum books provide depth.

Some research topics that will benefit from broad and in-depth theoretical outcomes include *moderation of harmful content in social media*, *identifying biases in artificial intelligence*, *embedding of ethics in software engineering education*, and *the impact of a pandemic on research adaptations*.

11.4 Summary

In this chapter, we learned about *what is theory?* ranging from random and education guesses and research-based predictions to scientific theories and laws, including what makes for hard or soft theories. Then we learned about *socio-technical grounded theories* as outcomes of a full STGT study, followed by the four genres of theories as broad and high-level theories, broad and in-depth theories, focused and high-level theories, and focused and in-depth theories.

References

Andersen, H., & Hepburn, B. (2016). Scientific method. In E. N. Zalta (ed.), *The stanford encyclopedia of philosophy* (summer 2016 edn). Metaphysics Research Lab, Stanford University.

Chan, Y.-C. & Hauser, E. (2023). Understanding reactions in human-robot encounters with autonomous quadruped robots. *Proceedings of the Association for Information Science and Technology, 60*(1): 86–97.

Graetsch, U. M., Khalajzadeh, H., Shahin, M., Hoda, R. & Grundy, J. (2023). Dealing with data challenges when delivering data-intensive software solutions. *IEEE transactions on software engineering*. https://doi.org/10.1109/TSE.2023.3291003

Hoda, R., & Noble, J. (2017). Becoming agile: a grounded theory of agile transitions in practice. In *2017 IEEE/ACM 39th International Conference on Software Engineering (ICSE)* (pp. 141–151). IEEE.

Hoda, R., Noble, J., & Marshall, S. (2011). The impact of inadequate customer collaboration on self-organizing agile teams. *Information and Software Technology, 53*(5): 521–534.

Hoda, R., Noble, J., & Marshall, S. (2012). Self-organizing roles on agile software development teams. *IEEE Transactions on Software Engineering, 39*(3): 422–444.

Masood, Z., Hoda, R. and Blincoe, K., (2020a). How agile teams make self-assignment work: a grounded theory study. *Empirical Software Engineering, 25*: 4962–5005. https://doi.org/10.1007/s10664-020-09876-x

Masood, Z., Hoda, R., & Blincoe, K. (2020b). Real world Scrum: A grounded theory of variations in practice, *IEEE Transactions on Software Engineering, 48*(5): 1579–1591.

Shastri, Y., Hoda, R., & Amor, R. (2021). The role of the project manager in agile software development projects. *Journal of Systems and Software, 173*, 110871.

Stray, V., Sjøberg, D. I., & Dybå, T. (2016). The daily stand-up meeting: A grounded theory study. *Journal of Systems and Software, 114*, 101–124.

12 Theory Development

Abstract In this chapter, we will begin by addressing the *attitude* and *approach* to theory development in software engineering. Then we will learn about *theory development* using socio-technical grounded theory (STGT), including how to select between the emergent and structure modes. This is followed by the *common procedures* of theory development, including theoretical sampling, advanced memoing, targeted literature review, and theoretical saturation, that appear in both the modes of theory development. Then we will learn about the *emergent mode*, including its unique procedures such as targeted data collection, targeted data analysis, and theoretical structuring and a practical example of *applying the emergent mode*. Next, we will learn about the *structured mode*, including its unique procedures such as structured data collection, structured data analysis, and theoretical integration and a practical example of *applying the structured mode*. Next, we will go over the options for *reporting outcomes* as traditional and other outputs, followed by recommendations for *presenting outcomes* including theory statements, theory diagrams, and examples of raw data. Then we will consider the *nuances of theory development*. Finally, the chapter ends with an *Is Theory Development for Me?* Quiz, designed to help researchers self-assess their readiness for theory development and work on identified areas of improvement to become capable theorists.

R. Hoda, *Qualitative Research with Socio-Technical Grounded Theory*,
https://doi.org/10.1007/978-3-031-60533-8_12

12.1 Attitude to Theory Development

Experienced software engineering (SE) researchers have highlighted the importance of developing theories in the SE discipline from time to time (Sjøberg et al., 2008; Herbsleb, 2018). A handful of SE researchers have been attempting theory use and development through the decades, especially in agile software development (Stray et al., 2022). Despite this, the performance of our research community in this area has been underwhelming. There may be a number of contributing factors.

Many SE researchers tend to have a conflated understanding of *what* constitutes theory. Those on one extreme consider hypotheses that are proposed based on individual experiences as theory, whereas these can be considered educated guesses at best. Those on the other extreme regard theory as only those statements that have been proven to be universal facts or widely generalised findings, what I call the *grand theory syndrome*.

To understand the latter, consider SE research projects aiming to develop a tool or a technique. If the community expectation was to support only those projects that result in the creation of something as significant and grand scale as the Google search engine, how many tools and techniques would be developed and published in SE research? Not many! When it comes to tools and techniques, we value the role of incremental and cumulative progress. On the other hand, unrealistically high standards expected from the development of theories and theoretical models have stifled incremental and cumulative progress in this area.

An empirically *grounded* theory that is inductively derived from empirical evidence using a systematic research method—or what I call an empirical theory—can be placed much higher than educated guesses and much lower than universal facts. It is often referred to as a *mid-ranged* theory (Glaser & Strauss, 1966; Strauss & Corbin, 1990; Charmaz, 2006; Hoda, 2022), where its range of application is neither severely local (such as those based on an individual experience) nor significantly general (representing the entire population). Theories derived from applying the full STGT method are applicable to the contexts that were studied and, by some stretch, to similar contexts. Naturally, theories based on a wider range of contexts will have wider applicability. Furthermore, good quality theories exhibit strength and chain of evidence and remain modifiable in light of new evidence. For more details on the nature of what constitutes theory, see Chap. 11: What Is Theory?

Another possible reason behind the low uptake of theory development in SE is to do with popular beliefs about *who* can develop theory. A common misunderstanding here is that theory development is a niche activity, reserved for selected individuals. Possibly because of the element of creativity involved (often exhibited as abduction), it is also often assumed that theory development can only be done by a few gifted individuals. It also points to our unconscious biases about what age group, gender, and ethnicity these experts may represent. For example, if I asked you to name some theorists, names such as Einstein and Darwin will likely come to mind. These individuals are commonly regarded as geniuses contributing to universal theories, and we may struggle to think of everyday researchers—men and women—to contribute to more localised but useful empirical theories.

Besides the grand theories of universal applicability, there is plenty of room for more localised theories to be developed that help explain practical phenomenon in limited contexts. For example, the *theory of dealing with data challenges when delivering data-intensive systems* explains how data-intensive multidisciplinary teams deal with data challenges (Graetsch et al., 2023). While it does not claim to be universal, the theory is expected to be applicable in many contexts that are similar to those investigated in the study.

A related aspect here is that many SE researchers feel under confident or unqualified to attempt theory development and struggle to imagine themselves as theorists. The background and training of SE researchers are typically rooted in the technical aspects of software programming, processes, architecture and design, maintenance, and operations. When software engineers become researchers through higher education (e.g. Master's or PhD) or training, they do not necessarily undergo training in qualitative research and theory development. If training in theory development is offered in higher degree courses and professional training programs, all those who may be open to the idea of theory development will benefit from the opportunity. By considering theory development to be a niche area reserved for the selected few, we do a disservice to the SE research community, which could otherwise benefit from many more useful theories and theoretical outcomes to build a stronger foundation of the discipline.

> "It does not take Einstein to develop theory. As with any other research endeavour in software engineering (e.g. prototype tools development), we need a balanced attitude and approach to theory development in SE, where we neither trivialise it nor put it on a pedestal for the selected few to practice. With investment in reading up on theories within and outside of their domain, learning theory development skills and procedures, and applying them, more researchers can confidently attempt and succeed with theory development. Socio-technical grounded theory (STGT) provides a robust framework to learn about basic qualitative research skills and procedures as well as theory development."

12.2 Approach to Theory Development

In SE, we find two main approaches to theory development:[1] First is the *hypothesis testing approach* also known as the *hypothetico-deductive* approach (Glaser & Strauss, 2017, first published 1967). In this approach, researchers begin by formulating hypotheses. These can be drawn from a review of literature, existing theories in other disciplines, and/or based on expertise and experience from research or industrial practice. As a next step, they go about collecting evidence that can help conclude whether the hypotheses hold true or not. In some cases, the collected evidence may not be able to support any clear conclusions either way. Overall, this approach serves to validate or refute the initially proposed hypotheses. If the hypotheses are not backed up by non-trivial empirical evidence, they can be classified as educated guesses or research-based predictions. Such attempts cannot be classified as theories, as we know from the types of "theories" in Chap. 11 What Is Theory?

The second approach is a primarily inductive approach where there are no hypotheses to begin with, only a research topic or area of interest. Collection and analysis of empirical evidence lead to preliminary hypotheses. These are progressively strengthened (or disregarded) through iterative data collection, analysis, and memoing. The result of this approach to theory development is an evidence-based theory also known as *grounded* theory. Socio-technical grounded theory (STGT), like the traditional GT methods, offers an inductive approach to theory development.

12.3 Theory Development: Selecting a Mode

Having unpacked the definition of theory more generally across disciplines and specially as it applied in STGT (see Chap. 11: What Is Theory?), let us focus on how to go about developing theory. If you are still wondering whether to continue to the advanced stage of theory development, consider revisiting the *STGT Application Selection Guide* in Chap. 3: STGT Overview. To assess if theory development may be your cup of tea personally, consider taking the *Is Theory Development for Me? Quiz* at the end of this chapter.

As we continue from the basic stage into the advanced stage of theory development, there is a natural narrowing down of focus (see Fig. 12.1). In comparison to the

[1] The term theory is used to capture a range of possible theoretical outcomes such as mature theoretical frameworks, models, taxonomies, and mid-ranged theories.

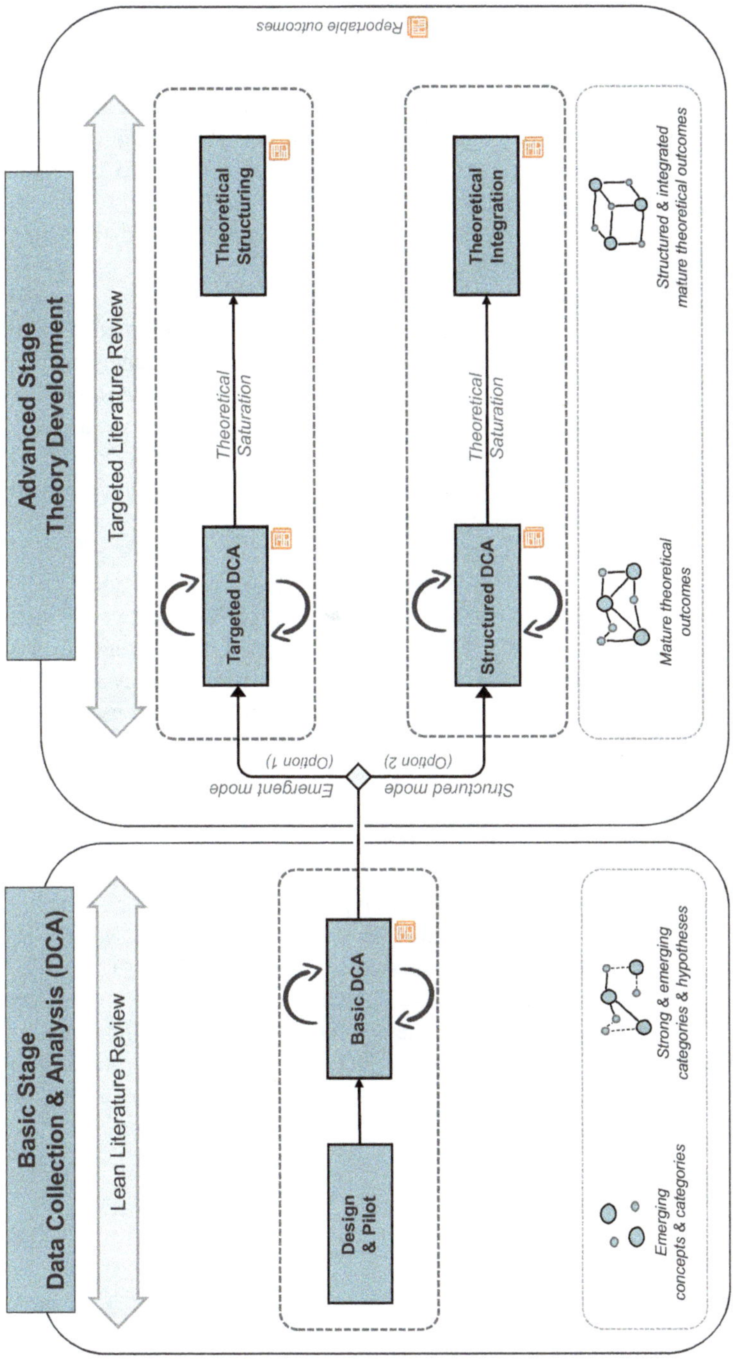

Fig. 12.1 Basic and advanced stages of the socio-technical grounded theory study (adapted from Hoda, 2022)

open approach to data collection and coding in the basic stage, the research team is meant to narrow their data collection and analysis to focus on the developing theory. The team collects data driven by the needs of the emerging theory, also known as *theoretical sampling*. For example, where a category is considered important but not yet strong or nuanced enough, the team can focus their sampling to collect data from sources that are most likely to provide more information about that category. Similarly, if a link is starting to emerge between two categories, future data collection and analysis can be focused on finding out more about that link, and so on, until the team reaches a point where additional data collection does not yield any significant new concepts, categories, or insights, also known as *theoretical saturation*.

This natural narrowing down of focus in the process of theory development can be done in one of two ways, captured in STGT as the two modes of theory development: the *emergent* mode or the *structured* mode. The emergent mode is inspired by Glaser's version of GT, also known as *classic* or *Glasserian GT*, where the theory, specifically the theoretical structure, is seen to emerge towards the end of the development process (Glaser & Strauss, 2017, first published 1967). The structured mode is inspired by *Strauss-Corbinian GT*, where a structure is identified sooner in the research project and used to guide the remaining data collection and analysis (Strauss & Corbin, 1990).

In STGT, the choice of the two modes of theory development is deliberately left to until after the research team has had experience with STGT's data collection and analysis procedures in the basic stage. This is motivated by two reasons: First, it is very challenging for those new to STGT or qualitative data analysis and theory development to decide on their preferred mode upfront, captured as the *#NoVersionControl* challenge in Chap. 2: Traditional Grounded Theory Methods. Once they have gained experience with the basic steps and procedures of STGT during the basic stage—open coding, constant comparison, and memoing—have started deriving concepts and categories, and have improved theoretical sensitivity, they are in a much better position to understand the differences between the two modes of theory development and make an informed decision. Second, it enables a respectable exit point for those who decide not to continue with theory development. Having distinct basic and advanced theory development stages allows researchers to use *STGT for data analysis* only or to conduct a *full STGT study* that includes theory development.

Table 12.1 presents an overview of the two modes, including differences in their context of use and distinct steps. It also includes a list of steps that are common to both modes. Irrespective of the mode used, the end result of the advanced stage is an integrated and structured mature theory.

Table 12.1 Two modes of theory development: emergent versus structured, their contexts of use, distinct steps, and their common steps and outcomes

	Emergent mode	Structured mode
Context of use	Studying a broad phenomenon (e.g. *agile transformations*)	Studying a narrow phenomenon (e.g. *limitations of using JIRA for issue tracking in DevOps teams*)
Distinct steps	Open coding applied widely on the broad phenomenon	Open coding applied on the narrow phenomenon
	Basic stage ended with the emergence of some strong and some not so strong categories and indicative relationships between them	Basic stage ended with the emergence of a clear set of categories that form an overarching structure
	Iterations of *targeted* data collection and analysis, targeting most significant categories and continuing to establish relationships between them	Iterations of *structured* data collection and analysis, focusing on saturating individual categories and firming up relationships between them
	Theoretical structuring	Theoretical integration
Common steps	Targeted literature review, theoretical sampling, advanced memoing, theoretical saturation	
Outcome	Structured and integrated theory or theories	

Context of Use

To select between the emergent and the structured modes, consider their contexts of use, using the following questions:

- *Is this a study of a broad phenomenon?* Broad phenomenon, e.g. agile transformation or ethics in AI, are naturally likely to take longer to narrow down over the course of the study. Therefore, they are more likely to benefit from selecting an emergent mode of theory development. On the other hand, if the phenomenon being studied is narrow, e.g. a specific software practice such as the limitations of using JIRA for issue tracking in DevOps teams, it is more likely to benefit from selecting a structure mode of theory development.

- *Was open coding applied widely across the broad phenomenon for a considerable time period?* Sometimes, the research begins by focusing on an extremely broad phenomenon/topic and may end up having to narrow down the research focus rather rapidly until it is a lot narrower than when it started. In this case, the team is more likely to benefit from selecting the structured mode. On the other hand, if open coding was applied on a broad phenomenon/topic for a considerable period of time such that many distinct aspects of the phenomenon were identified and still no clear structure connecting those aspects was visible, an emergent mode of theory development would be better suited.

- *Is a structure of the theory becoming apparent?* Oftentimes, the basic stage can result in the identification of some strong and some not so strong categories, as well as some preliminary relationships between those categories. In this case, the research team can expect the weaker categories to either continue maturing with new concepts being identified or fizzle out due to the lack of supporting evidence.[2] Similarly, the links between the categories can be expected to emerge in earnest only much later in the study, in a sort of a "*eureka*" moment or a slow dawning of "*what this is all about*". This is a classic example of an emergent mode of theory development where the structure of the theory is expected to emerge later on. On the other hand, the basic stage can lead the team to a point where the key categories are looking more or less stable, i.e. most of the data being collected and analysed seems to fit within the categories that have already emerged. It may also be that an overarching structure becomes apparent, such that we can see how the categories relate to each other and more or less "*hang together*". This structure can be a unique one or may resemble one of the popular theory templates (more about templates later in this chapter). This is a classic case where it would make sense to continue with a structured mode of theory development, building on that structure.

The two modes of theory development are both systematic and rigorous. Neither is better than the other. It is a matter of what mode makes more sense for a given research project, judging by where things are at towards the end of the basic stage. Answering the probing questions about the context of use will help with mode selection. There are some steps unique to each mode and some steps that are common. The common steps of targeted literature review, theoretical sampling, advanced memoing, and theoretical saturation are described in the following sections:

12.4 Theory Development: Common Procedures

Some procedures of theory development are common in both modes:

- *Theoretical sampling* to drive data collection
- *Advanced memoing* to capture insights
- *Targeted literature review* to align the findings with existing literature
- *Theoretical saturation* to mark the end of data collection

These are outlined in the following sections:

[2] Weaker categories can be shared as additional insights and ideas for future works which the research community can explore in the future.

12.4.1 Theoretical Sampling

Definition

Theoretical sampling is the ongoing process of assessing the emerging codes, concepts, (sub)categories, and hypotheses, and identifying new sources for data collection in the upcoming iterations that are likely to help identify, develop, and saturate the emerging findings while filling any theoretical gaps (Hoda, 2022).

Theoretical sampling focuses on progressively filling theoretical gaps. For this reason, it is typically not possible to start a study with theoretical sampling. An exception maybe when a study is part of a series of studies, building on the findings from the previous study. A majority of STGT studies can begin with sampling techniques such as convenience, snowball, random, and/or representative sampling. As soon as some concepts start to emerge, the study can switch to applying theoretical sampling to guide the data collection. By the time the team reaches the advanced stage of theory development, they will be applying theoretical sampling exclusively. Applying theoretical sampling implies carefully considering the key emerging categories and relationships to identify weaknesses and theoretical gaps and steering the data collection accordingly to strengthen the weak concepts, categories, and links and to fill the gaps in the emerging theory.

Theoretical sampling is one of the main practices that lends STGT its responsive and agile nature. As a result of theoretical sampling, the research team regularly grooms and refines their research protocols, e.g. interview questions in case of traditional data collection through interviews or data extraction keywords in case of modern data mining of online repositories, to focus on the needs of the emerging theory, thereby assisting with theoretical saturation. More information about theoretical sampling can be found in Chap. 7: Basics of Qualitative Data Collection.

12.4.2 Advanced Memoing

Definition

Advanced memoing focuses on developing the patterns and relationships in the data. It also includes carefully revisiting, reassessing, refining, and comparing memos to confirm and strengthen existing relationships, reject unsupported indicative relationships, and establish new links across concepts and categories (Hoda, 2022), progressively enabling the formulation of the theory. Memoing is indispensable to theory development.

Basic memoing, conducted in the basic stage, allows the researcher to get used to the practice of reflection and serves to explore and formulate key codes, concepts, categories, links between them, and preliminary theoretical models. More details of basic memoing are available in Chap. 10: Socio-technical Grounded Theory for Qualitative Data Analysis.

In the advanced stages of theory development, advanced memoing focuses on developing the relationships in the data, delving into the details of the relationship such as its nature and facets. Often, basic memoing on a certain insight progresses on to advanced memoing on the same, building it up. For example, in a research on *the role of the project manager in agile projects*, a basic memo may be captured about how the project manager was seen to enable certain agile practices such as the daily stand-up for some teams. Over the course of the research study, as more data was collected and analysed, it may become apparent that there may be a relationship between what happens in the team when the project manager is present during an agile practice and when they are not. The memo can be further developed to capture the emerging relationship, moving beyond *enabling agile teams* (early name during basic memoing) to *influencing agile team practices* (revised name during advanced memoing). In this way, basic memoing leading to advanced memoing can enable the formulation of the *hypothesis* that *the presence of the project manager has a positive influence on certain agile team practices and a negative influence on certain others.* The details of the specific practices and the nuances of the influence can also be captured in the advanced memos and shared as part of the study findings.

Advanced memoing also involves carefully revisiting, reassessing, refining, and comparing memos, where similar memos can be compared and consolidated. Occasionally, it can lead to the identification of completely new insights that force the team to reconsider and make major revisions to a key category or relationship. Most of the time, it serves to progressively strengthen key categories and build the links between them. Unlike basic memoing which is more open and exploratory, advanced memoing is more focused and selective. Here, the stakes are higher. Only those insights and relationships that are strongly supported by the growing evidence survive. Weak and unsupported indicative relationships are rejected. Memos can be written to document the rationales for their rejection and serve as chain of evidence in theory development. Those that are promising but need further evidence can be pursued through theoretical sampling to drive new data collection and analysis that is *targeted* or *structured*, depending on the mode of theory development. Alternatively, some promising relationships that were not strong enough to make it into the theory can be listed as additional insights, so they can be researched in depth in future studies. Ongoing advanced memoing replaces the one-time step of *theoretical sorting* found in *Glaserian* and *Strauss-Corbinian* GT (Glaser & Strauss, 2017, first published 1967; Strauss & Corbin, 1990) performed towards the end of the research project. Critically, advanced memoing acknowledges hypothesis development as iterative and incremental rather than a one-time activity.

12.4.3 Targeted Literature Review

Definition

A **targeted literature review** (TLR) is a focused approach to identifying the research studies most closely related to the STGT study findings that serve to situate the findings in the wider research landscape and highlight their role in advancing the relevant body of knowledge. A TLR is a relatively lightweight step within an STGT study for handling related works as opposed to being a standalone and comprehensive systematic review method in its own right.

STGT presents two types of literature reviews that are common to both modes of theory development: a lightweight *lean literature review* (LLR) conducted during the basic stage to identify research gaps and motivate the need for the study and an in-depth *targeted literature review* (TLR) performed periodically during the advanced stage of theory development.

A TLR is an approach to target the identification of literature that is most closely related to the emerging findings. TLR serves the purposes of (a) comparing and situating the key emerging findings (categories and relationships) in the wider research landscape and (b) highlighting the role of the original findings in filling research gaps and contributing to the relevant body of knowledge. In this way, a TLR also helps establish the originality and novelty of the STGT findings.

A TLR can be relatively lightweight and informal, focusing on identifying related works quickly and effectively. It can also be conducted using more formal and systematic procedures. However, in most cases, high levels of formality, rigour, and systematic treatment are not required. The findings of a TLR are meant to serve the specific function of comparing them to the STGT study findings and are not aimed to be published as a standalone set of findings.

As the theory develops, TLR can be performed to search for relevant literature using specific keywords aligned to the emerging concepts, categories, and relationships. A TLR is usually conducted when enough original findings and insights have emerged where they can be written up as a paper. In other words, as soon as the team is ready to report some findings, they will need to perform a TLR. For example, in an STGT study on the *challenges of applying ethical AI principles in practice*, the research team may decide to write a dedicated paper on the key category of *tool-related challenges*. In this case, a TLR can be conducted, targeting the search on keywords such as *tools*, *challenges*, *ethics*, and *AI*. The results can be filtered based on relevance and quality, selected, read, and compared to the original STGT findings. The TLR will help draw conclusions about what is already known about tool-related challenges from literature and explain how the original STGT findings compare to and extend existing knowledge.

The results of a TLR can be summarised in the *Discussion* or *Related Works* sections, after the original findings are presented. For example, see the description of the TLR in the *Methodology* section and the results of the TLR in the *Discussion of Findings in the Context of Relevant Literature* section of *dealing with data challenges* paper (Graetsch et al., 2023). The text description can be accompanied by other formats, such as comparison tables or figures. Further details of lean and targeted literature reviews can be found in Chap. 6: Literature Reviews.

12.4.4 Theoretical Saturation

Definition

Theoretical saturation is a point of diminishing returns in data collection when further collection serves to confirm and validate existing conceptual findings but does not lead to significantly new information or insights. It is an indication to stop collecting more data.

In both modes of theory development, when the advanced data collection reaches a point of diminishing returns, the study is said to have reached *theoretical saturation*. For example, the last few data collection attempts (e.g. last three to four interviews) serve to validate what we already know. Saturation can be sought and achieved through theoretical sampling for each key category individually or for the theory as a whole.

Reaching theoretical saturation is a sign to finish data collection and perform one of theoretical structuring (for the emergent mode) or theoretical integration (for the structured mode).Further details on data quantity and theoretical saturation can be found in Chap. 7: Basics of Qualitative Data Collection.

12.5 Emergent Mode

The emergent mode of theory development is designed to enable a gradual and progressive emergence of theory over the course of the advanced stage. The emergent mode does not necessarily take longer than the structured mode. It allows for the theoretical structure to emerge in an organic manner and be finalised progressively, more towards the later part of the research project. It includes distinct steps and procedures of *targeted* data collection and analysis and *theoretical structuring* as a means of providing structure to the emergent theory, typically using one of many theory templates or by creating a bespoke structure. These are described below followed by a practical example of conducting a full STGT study applying the emergent mode of theory development.

12.5.1 Targeted Data Collection

Definition

Targeted data collection refers to applying theoretical sampling to drive data collection in a way that *targets* data sources that are most likely to help fill theoretical gaps and strengthen the key categories that have emerged strong or are starting to emerge strong from the basic stage.

Targeted data collection is named so because it targets data sources that are likely to provide more insights into the emerging key categories and help fill theoretical gaps. These include categories that have emerged strong from the basic stage and those that seem to have good potential to develop into strong categories in the future. As in the basic stage, data can be collected from a variety of traditional and modern sources, such as through interviews, focus groups, observations and/or data mining of online relevant repositories, videos, digital documents, and so on. However, the choice of sources becomes more strategic and targeted to those that can help with building the emerging theory.

12.5.2 Targeted Data Analysis

Definition

Targeted data analysis involves the application of the procedures of *targeted coding*, which is the same as open coding but applied in a targeted manner, and *constant comparison. Advanced memoing* ensures the relationships between the categories are established and strengthened.

Targeted data analysis involves very similar data analysis procedures as used in the basic stage, except they are applied in a limited and *targeted* manner. These include *targeted coding* and *constant comparison* procedures. Similar to open coding, targeted coding is inductive such that the coding is done bottom up. Freshly derived codes are constantly compared with the other codes, and similar codes are grouped into concepts. These codes and concepts can be from those previously identified in the project or entirely new ones. In this sense, the inductive coding procedure is the same as in open coding. The key difference between open coding and targeted coding is that targeted coding is limited to coding only for the most significant concepts and categories that have emerged or are looking very promising to develop into key categories going ahead.

Research protocols, such as interview questions, will be revised accordingly to enable targeted data collection. The data in this way is already expected to be a lot more focused than what is typically collected during the basic stage. Therefore, the amount of noise expected and data filtering required is much lower compared to the basic stage. Even so, the targeted coding and constant comparison procedures keep things tight by focusing mainly on the key categories.

Occasionally, an entirely new category can be identified through targeted coding and becomes part of the emerging theory. For example, this can happen in cases where fresh data collection, typically in the early parts of the advanced stage, reveals interesting new insights that compel the research team to revisit the data from the basic stage. They may then start identifying hitherto undiscovered codes and concepts supporting the new findings. Such revisiting and reanalysis can be time- and effort-consuming. In many cases, time and funding constraints may mean that the research team will need to discuss the possible consequences, including potential return on investment, before proceeding with a full reanalysis of their entire dataset.

More commonly, targeted data analysis serves to find new insights, in the form of new codes and concepts, that help build the emerging categories into key categories and those supporting them, until they are saturated. Ongoing advanced memoing enables the team to identify new relationships and strengthen indicative relationships between categories, giving rise to a theoretical structure, i.e. how the key categories relate to each other. It also becomes progressively clear how the categories and relationships are integrated, i.e. what does it all mean taken together as a theoretical outcome in the form of a rich theory, framework, model, or taxonomy.

Targeted data collection and analysis continue until theoretical saturation is reached, as described in the common procedures. Once saturation is reached, the theoretical outcome is considered integrated and mature and ready for further structuring using theoretical structuring.

12.5.3 Theoretical Structuring

Definition

Theoretical structuring is an optional but highly recommended step that involves identifying the genre of theory best suited, exploring theory templates that naturally align, and where one fits, using a theory template to further arrange the key categories into a structured theory.

The emergent mode of theory development focuses on the gradual emergence of the theory, working towards identifying and saturating the key categories and identifying and strengthening the relationships between them. In the emergent mode, the structure of the theory is typically not apparent until much later in the project when "everything finally falls into place". Therefore, those applying the emergent mode will benefit from an explicit structuring step.

Theoretical structuring involves carefully assessing the mature findings from the study to identify the genre of theory we have come up with. Experienced theorists are likely to be aware of the genre of the theory as it develops. Novice theorists are recommended to consider the expected outcomes to discern if their findings represent a broad and high-level theory, a focused and high-level theory, a broad and in-depth theory, or a focused and in-depth theory (see Chap. 11: What Is Theory for more). For example, if the theory captures a narrow phenomenon and presents an overview of its constituent elements, it is most likely a taxonomy or a classification.

The next step is to carefully assess pre-defined theory templates and see if any seem to naturally fit the findings. Glaser presented a number of theory templates or common structures of theories that he referred to as theoretical coding families (Glaser, 1978). Theory templates define the hollow skeletal structure that can be used to shape our empirical theory. It is not the same as using an existing theory[3]

A popular theory template is the "process" template used to capture mature findings that present a process of some sort, e.g. process of becoming a woman software engineer. A process template is usually defined by having stages (or phases) and indicative entry and exit points into each stage. Another popular template is the six Cs template, consisting of conditions, context, causes, consequences, contingencies, and covariances associated with a key category, e.g. the theory of dealing with data challenges in multidisciplinary teams (Graetsch et al., 2023). A similar template is proposed by Strauss and Corbin, called the *Coding Paradigm*, consisting of the context, causal conditions, intervening conditions, action-interaction strategies, and consequences related to the phenomenon (Corbin & Strauss, 1990). Other templates include degrees, dimensions, identities, and so on. Table 12.2 summarises some of these theory templates.

The research team can consider the characteristics of these templates to decide whether any of them naturally align and can be used to depict the mature theory they have developed. Where none fits, they can continue to finalise the original structure that emerged from the targeted data collection and analysis. However, more often than not, a theory template is found to be well suited. Using a pre-defined template can lend a clearer structure to the theory when presenting it, than if one was not used. For this reason, while structuring is optional, it is highly recommended.

[3] To understand the idea of theory templates, consider design patterns in programming. Design patterns are not software code. They represent specific configurations that can be used to arrange or structure the software codebase.

12.5.4 Applying the Emergent Mode: A Practical Example

To understand what an emergent mode of theory development looks like and how targeted data collection and analysis and theoretical structuring can be applied in practice, consider the following example of a full STGT study starting with the basic stage and continuing to the advanced stage using the emergent mode.

Theory template	Description	Examples (real and hypothetical)
Coding paradigm	Captures the context, causal conditions, intervening conditions, action-interaction strategies, and consequences related to the phenomenon	How agile teams practice self-assignment (Masood et al., 2020a)
Degree	Captures the extent, level, amount, range, intensity, magnitude, proportion, or ratio of something	Degrees of freedom in academia
Dimension	Captures the aspects, features, facets, properties, elements, or divisions of something	The dimensions of change during agile transitions (Hoda & Noble, 2017)
Process	Captures the stages/phases of a process or a journey, typically including entry/exit (or start/end) indicators for each stage/phase	The journey of becoming a woman in STEM
Six Cs	Captures that contexts, conditions, causes, consequences, contingencies, and covariances associated with a phenomenon or key category	The six Cs of dealing with data challenges (Graetsch et al., 2023)
Strategy	Captures plan, approach, mechanism, way, scheme, techniques, tactics, or management of something	Strategies data scientists use to ensure data quality
Type	Captures the kind, variety, category, classification, grouping, genre, or family of something	Types of biases in AI software

Table 12.2 Some common theory templates that can used to structure the findings, based on (Glaser, 1978, pp 75–82) and Corbin and Strauss (1990). Examples include real (with reference) and hypothetical studies

The Basic Stage

Imagine a research team of three software engineering researchers decides to delve into understanding the phenomenon represented by one of the four core values of the agile manifesto, "*responding to change over following a plan.*" They estimate the study to be roughly 1 year long. The overarching research question is as follows: *How do agile practitioners respond to changes?* The terms "changes" and "respond" are not limited to specific definitions and are open to interpretation. As such, the research topic and the research question are both very open and broad. While the research team is experienced, none of the individuals have applied traditional GT or STGT before, and all of them are new to theory development.

A *lean literature review* conducted by the team suggests there is not much available on their chosen research topic although a variety of papers on requirements engineering were identified. An in-depth empirical investigation into the topic makes sense. They consider methods such as case study and ethnography; however, they do not expect to have the level of in-depth and on-site access into a specific case or multiple cases as these methods demand.

The team finds STGT to be a good option to utilise data from practitioners representing a variety of companies, domains, roles, and technologies. They select STGT because their research project fits the socio-technical (ST) framework very well: how agile software practitioners respond to change is an ST phenomenon or topic, software engineering is an ST domain and agile practitioners are ST actors, the research team are ST researchers, and they plan to use ST data, tools, and techniques to conduct the study. Furthermore, they knew they would be dealing primarily with large amounts of qualitative data, and they were open to learning qualitative data analysis. Based on these conditions, STGT seemed like a good choice to derive rich findings and insights.

Over the next month, the research team works on gaining ethics approval, and team engages in *study preparation* and conducts a small *pilot study* where they interview three agile practitioners about their experiences of responding to changes. *Open coding* and *constant comparison* applied to the pilot interview data quickly reveal the true breadth of the topic as participants describe various types of changes they have encountered on agile projects, including changes in specification or requirements, changes in technology, changes in the team composition, changes to the product owner role, changes brought on as a result of an agile transformation underway at their organisation, and so on. At the same time, participants describe different types of responses to these changes, which primarily seem to fall under socio-technical responses and emotional responses. Based on the insights offered about each of these and in order to align the study scope to the 1-year plan, the team decides to perform an in-depth study on requirements changes and socio-technical responses. As a result of the pilot, they were able to revise their topic to "*socio-technical responses to requirements changes*" and their research question to *how do agile practitioners respond socio-technically to requirements changes.* They revise their interview protocol accordingly, e.g. some of the questions were revised to improve clarity, a couple of follow-up questions were added, and more examples from real-world practice were explicitly sought from the interviewees.

Over the next 3 months, the team conducts iterative data collection and analysis, working their way through 20 interviews. Through *open coding* and *constant comparison*, they identify codes and concepts such as estimating the effort required to implement a proposed change, to perform product backlog refinement, to develop a prototype solution, and to integrate it into the software. They also identify a number of related concepts, such as how requirements changes originate, how they are relayed to the team, how they are documented, and so on. These findings and insights were enabled by regular *memoing* by the team. At this point, the team has some decent findings on two key categories: the requirements changes and the socio-technical responses to the requirements changes. They decide to report these in the form of two conference papers, one focusing on each key category. They write them up over the next few months. As a part of writing these papers, they perform a targeted literature review on their revised research topic and report how prior knowledge compares to their findings.

At this point, around 6 months into the study, the team considers their options. They could conclude their empirical investigation here, at the end of the basic stage. This approach would mark a limited application of *STGT for data analysis*. As a next step, they could move on to developing solutions to support some of challenges they have identified in responding to requirements changes. For example, they could focus on implementing tools and guidelines over the remaining 6 months of the study. Alternatively, they could continue to delve deeper into the empirical investigation, conducting a *full STGT study* to develop mature theoretical outcomes and leave the tools development for a follow-up study or for another research team. Both are perfectly viable and acceptable options.

Upon deliberation, the team concludes that by now they are comfortable with the procedures of STGT and their chosen research topic could do with a deeper dive. They are confidential that they can recruit more practitioners for further data collection. They also like the idea of developing and publishing a mature theory on the topic and decide to proceed to the advanced stage.

The Advanced Stage: Emergent Mode

Having decided to continue to the advanced stage, the research team consults the differences between the two modes of theory development (see Sect. 12.3 and Table 12.1). They note that they have been studying a relatively broad phenomenon. They have applied open coding broadly resulting in two strong and a few weaker categories and have identified some indicative relationships between them. However, no clear overall theoretical structure is discernible. With these conditions, they conclude that an emergent mode of theory development best suits their study.

The team proceeds to iterative and interleaved rounds of *targeted data collection* and *analysis*. They now aim for data sources that are likely to provide more insights on the key and related categories and concepts. Instead of inviting all agile practitioners as they had done earlier, they target agile practitioners with at least 2 years of experience in handling requirements changes in their upcoming participant recruitment. Since one of the key categories—requirements changes—needed more depth on how, when, and why requirements changes originate, they focus on recruiting product owners and other agile practitioners responsible for providing requirements to share their experiences. An interesting emerging co-relation identified through *advanced memoing* is that people with previous experience of working in traditional software development settings seem to have remarkably different responses to proposed requirements changes as compared to those who have little to no such experience. Therefore, the team decides to investigate this in more depth by asking participants to compare their experiences of handling requirements changes in the two software development contexts in their upcoming interviews. These are examples of theoretical sampling in action, as applied to drive targeted data collection.

Targeted data collection and analysis continue until the key categories are saturated, i.e. they are rich with detailed evidence supporting their various facets. For example, the team identifies further responses about requirements changes. These include the concepts of *technical dependencies introduced by the change* and *the impact of the proposed change on sprint delivery*. These new concepts add richness to the category.

The last few interviews have mainly served to confirm what they already know about the topic. With *theoretical saturation* reached, the team stops data collection and analysis. At this point, roughly 9 months into the study with 28 interviews, the team can present the key categories and the relationships between them as a mature theory in the form a publication. However, they are aware of the recommendation to apply *theoretical structuring* and decide to give it a go. First, the team carefully considers their findings by answering prompting questions such as the following: *Have we answered the research question(s)? What have we discovered in this study? What is this theory about?* In response, they acknowledge that their findings cover a comprehensive range of aspects related to the key categories, requirements changes, and socio-technical responses to requirements changes. For example, their findings explain types of requirements changes; how, when, and why they originate; how they are relayed to the team; and the impacts of introducing requirements changes. The findings also capture the responses to requirements changes, e.g. how they are documented, estimated, added to the product backlog through refinement, prioritised, assigned, integrated, implemented, reviewed, and maintained. All together, these represent a comprehensive understanding of what constitute a requirements change and its journey from originating to being handled by agile teams.

As part of the theoretical structuring step, the team then discusses the genre of the theory they have identified (see Chap. 11: What Is Theory). They conclude that what they have ended up with is best classified as a focused and in-depth theory. Even though the initial topic was rather broad, the team progressively narrowed it down through the pilot, basic, and advanced stages to where the final outcome is relatively focused. Since the various aspects of the theory are detailed with multiple layers of rich codes, concepts, and sub-categories supporting them, it is considered an in-depth theory.

Next, they consider the pre-defined theory templates (see Sect. 12.5.3 and Table 12.2). They identify three possible templates that can fit their findings: the taxonomy template, the process template, and the six Cs template. They consider each in turn. A taxonomy of requirements changes seems to fit at a first glance. However, closer consideration reveals it is likely to leave some parts of the findings unaccounted for as they don't fit the notion of such a classification. Applying the process template is also considered but quickly discarded as the study evidence does not support the notion of stages of requirements change or responding to them. The six Cs template seems to be the best fit as it enables the findings to be represented as a theory of responding to requirements changes in terms of six aspects: the *context* and *conditions* (when, how, and where requirements changes originate), *causes* (why requirements changes occur), *consequences* (impacts of requirements changes), *contingencies* (ways in which teams respond to and handle requirements changes), and *covariance* (how responses vary with the presence or lack of previous experience of working in traditional environments). The team decides to restructure or arrange their findings into the six Cs template as it was found to be best suited.

The research team is ready to report the theory in a journal format which allows them enough space to go through all the details. They design a theory diagram based on the six Cs template (e.g. see Fig. 12.3) and also use it to structure the Findings section of their manuscript with each of the six Cs becoming a detailed subsection. They perform a *targeted literature review* to find studies most closely related to the overall theory and to each of the categories and underlying concepts. While they don't find anything that compares to the overall theory, they do find some studies that relate to the category requirements changes and to several concepts underlying the other category, responding to requirements changes. These related works and their comparison with their own findings are presented in the Discussion section of the manuscript. A number of insights, recommendations, and guidelines for practice drawn from the effective use of basic and advanced memoing are also shared. With the completion of the manuscript, they have completed the full STGT study and reported a structured and integrated mature theory.

12.6 Structured Mode

The structured mode of theory development is designed to enable a structured development of theory, building on the structure apparent through the basic stage. It includes distinct steps and procedures of *structured* data collection and analysis and *theoretical integration* as a means of finalising the theory for presentation. Because it builds on the preliminary structure emerging from the basic stage, it does not include an explicit structuring step as is applied the emergent mode. However, theoretical integration is recommended to build the theory to its maximum potential. These are described below followed by a practical example of conducting a full STGT study applying the structured mode of theory development.

12.6.1 Structured Data Collection

Definition

Structured data collection refers to applying theoretical sampling to drive data collection in a way that is guided by the theoretical structure emerging from the basic stage, selecting data sources that are most likely to deepen and saturate the emerging concepts and categories. It can include the use of explicit theory templates early on to guide the rest of the theory building.

Structured data collection is named so because it involves data collection that is guided by the theoretical structure emerging from the basic stage. As in the basic stage, data can be collected from a variety of sources. However, a key selection criterion is to focus on those that support and build on the emergent structure.

12.6.2 Structured Data Analysis

Definition

Structured data analysis involves the application of the procedures of *structured coding*, which is the same as open coding but limited to the emerging theoretical structure, and *constant comparison. Advanced memoing* ensures the relationships between the categories are established and strengthened.

Structured data analysis involves very similar data analysis procedures as used in the basic stage, except they are applied within the boundaries of the emerging theoretical structure. These include *structured coding* and *constant comparison* procedures. Similar to open coding, structured coding follows an inductive approach. Unlike open coding, it is not open to identifying all possible codes. Instead, it is mainly limited to the categories and relationships that have emerged from the basic stage. This is helped by the fact that the data collection is also structured, meaning it is less likely for the research team to encounter noise in the data during structured coding since it was already collected to support the emerging theoretical structure.

Of the three types of coding, open coding is the most open. It aims to comprehensively identify all possible codes, concepts, and categories present in the data. This is followed by targeted coding (used in the emergent mode) which leaves room for identifying new categories. Structured coding (used in the structured mode) is the most closed of the three, working closely within the boundaries of the emerging categories and relationships. It is extremely rare for a brand new category to emerge from structured coding and become integrated in the emerging theory. Ongoing advanced memoing enables the team to strengthen the existing relationships between categories, serving to strengthen the overall theoretical structure.

Since the general structure of the theory is more or less finalised early on in the structured mode, the research team can consider the pre-defined theory templates (see Sect. 12.5.3 and Table 12.2) to identify if any of them fit their own emerging structure. They can then use it to further shape the structure of their emerging theory. For example, if the structure emerging from the basic stage seems to more or less fit the *Coding Paradigm* theory template, they can apply it straight away to structure the categories and concepts emerged thus far, revise research protocols accordingly, and use this structure to guide further data collection and analysis. This would imply they focus entirely on the *context*, *causal conditions*, *intervening conditions*, *action-interaction strategies*, and *consequences*. The research team can also identify the genre of their theory early on in the advanced stage. They can identify whether their emerging theory represents a broad and high-level theory, a focused and high-level theory, a broad and in-depth theory, or a focused and in-depth theory (see Chap. 11

What is Theory). Unlike in the emergent mode, in the structured mode, the theory structure and genre are established earlier on and serve to guide the rest of the theory building effort.[4]

Structured data collection and analysis continue until theoretical saturation is reached, as described in the common procedures. Once saturation is reached, the theory is considered structured and mature and is ready for further integration through *theoretical integration*.

12.6.3 Theoretical Integration

Definition

Theoretical integration is an optional but highly recommended step that ensures all the categories are fully integrated into the overall theoretical structure and involves finalising the "*storyline*" of the theory. Sometimes, it involves the emergence of an additional theoretical layer that serves to enhance the existing structure and make additional sense of the theory as a whole.

The structured mode of theory development relies on the structure of the theory becoming clear earlier on, e.g. towards the end of the basic stage or early in the advanced stage. As such, it does not require an explicit structuring step later on. However, despite having a clear structure to the theory, those applying the structured mode will benefit from ensuring that all the concepts and categories are fully integrated into the overall theoretical structure. Practically, this means carefully reassessing the current placements of the concepts and categories within specific parts of the theory structure or template, moving things around as necessary for better fit, and also ensuring there are no concepts and categories floating around without a clear place in the theoretical structure. For example, as part of theoretical integration, a research team using the *Coding Paradigm* theory template can reassess the placement of their concepts and categories and move things around for better fit, e.g. moving codes from under *causal conditions* to *intervening conditions* if that is a better representation of the underlying evidence. They can similarly go through all concepts and categories to ensure they are integrated well into the *Coding Paradigm* template.

Sometimes, the team may find a concept or a category that is interesting but does not fit into the overall theoretical structure. This is usually a sign that the concept or category is an incidental finding that is not directly related to the theory and should

[4] Structured coding is similar to axial coding introduced by Strauss and Corbin (1990), which adds a structure to the theory development earlier on in the process, rather than how the structure emerges gradually and much later on in the Glaserian version. Structured coding is not limited to using the Coding Paradigm template and can use from a variety of templates based on best fit.

not be forced into the theory. Guidance on reporting such findings is shared later in this chapter.

Occasionally, theoretical integration can also provide the opportunity to identify an additional theoretical layer that enhances the existing structure and helps understand the theory as a whole from a different perspective. For example, a research team may have developed a taxonomy which contains six categories or groups with detailed explanation of each group and its characteristics with plenty of examples. This in itself would be a mature theory and a robust research contribution. However, after carefully considering the categories in the taxonomy and the relationships between them, it may become apparent that each group in the taxonomy is linked in a way that builds on top of each other to form a hierarchy. The last step of deriving the hierarchy, beyond the classification or taxonomy, would be an example of theoretical integration. Consider, for example, Bloom's taxonomy[5] and Maslow's hierarchy of needs,[6] both representing hierarchical taxonomies and being visually represented using tiered pyramid diagrams. Of course, we do not know how these two hierarchical taxonomies were developed. However, we can imagine cases where theoretical integration is applied in the later stages that ends up adding more value to the theoretical structure.

We will revisit theoretical integration in the context of explaining the role of abduction in theory development through a real example of its application in Graetsch et al. (2023), explained later in this chapter.

12.6.4 Applying the Structured Mode: A Practical Example

To understand what a structured mode of theory development looks like and how structured data collection and analysis and theoretical integration can be applied in practice, consider the following example of a full STGT study starting with the basic stage and continuing to the advanced stage using the structured mode.

The Basic Stage

Imagine a research team of three experienced researchers decides to conduct a study on '*self-assignment in agile teams*' which aims to answer the following question: *How do agile software development teams perform the practice of self-assignment?* The study is expected to be 1 year long. While the team is experienced, none of the individuals have applied traditional GT or STGT before, and all of them are new to theory development.[7] The team wishes to conduct an in-depth study and expects to

[5] https://en.wikipedia.org/wiki/Bloom's_taxonomy

[6] https://en.wikipedia.org/wiki/Maslow's_hierarchy_of_needs

[7] As with the emergent mode, I select an example of a team that is new to theory development to demonstrate the structure mode too. This is done to reiterate that researchers do not need to be experienced in theory development to attempt either mode. On the other hand, a team that has prior experience in theory development may naturally find the process easier to follow, including deciding which mode best suits their needs.

unravel the inner workings of agile teams as they perform self-assignment. A *lean literature review* conducted by the team suggests there is not much research available on this topic although topics such as motivation and task allocation are well studied in traditional software development settings. They find STGT to be a suitable research method for the project as it is well aligned with STGT's underlying socio-technical research framework; it was expected to yield non-trivial amounts of qualitative data for analysis and and included the option to proceed to theory development.

Over the next month, they work towards gaining relevant ethics approval, study preparation, and conducting a small pilot study where they collect data from four software practitioners through an online survey. The survey was designed to ask about self-assignment in the context of a specific project, probing aspects such as frequency of practice, when it was practiced, what a typical self-assignment process looked like through an example, challenges in practicing self-assignment, and strategies to overcome the challenges. *Open coding* and *constant comparison* applied to the survey data quickly revealed a variety of ways in which self-assignment was being practiced, as well as related challenges and strategies. Next, necessary refinements were made to the survey protocol to improve understanding, ask for specific examples, and provide answer options for some questions to reduce the amount of typing required.

Over the next 3 months, as part of the next *basic data collection and analysis* steps, the research team has collected around 60 responses to their survey. They identify a range of challenges in practicing self-assignment, both from team and manager perspectives, and also identify many strategies and workarounds used to overcome them. To probe deeper into the identified areas, the team decides to supplement the survey findings with observations.

The team conducts observations of three agile teams across two companies that agreed to participate. They observe several sprint planning meetings and daily stand-ups as their survey findings showed these to be the most commonly mentioned occasions where self-assignment was reported to be practiced. The team also analyses JIRA boards and Slack communication, where possible, to gain a comprehensive understanding of the phenomenon. They decide to report these findings in a journal paper.

At this point, around 6 months into the study, the team considers their options. They could finish their empirical investigation here and proceed to a different part of the study, such as developing guidelines on how to practice self-assignment effectively followed by an intervention study in a case company using an action research approach. This would have constituted a limited application of *STGT for data analysis*. Alternatively, they could continue to delve deeper into the topic, focusing on the challenges and strategies as applied in different project contexts, in a *full STGT study* and develop a mature theory. Both are perfectly viable and acceptable options.

The team find themselves comfortable with the procedures of STGT. They also have enough contacts that they created during the study to gather more data. The prospect of developing a theory on the topic sounds exciting to them, and so they proceed to the advanced stage.

The Advanced Stage: Structured Mode

To decide which mode of theory development to apply, the research team consults the differences between the two modes (see Sect. 12.3 and Table 12.1). They consider the current state of their findings. So far, they have two strong categories, challenges and strategies, that they have reported in a journal paper. They also have a few other categories that are clearly and strongly related to these two but could do with more depth. These include the project contexts in which challenges occur and are overcome, the reasons leading to the challenges, and the impact of the challenges on the team. The overall structure of the theory seems to be closely aligned to the *Coding Paradigm* theory template, covering the *context*, *causal conditions*, *intervening conditions*, *action-interaction strategies*, and *consequences* related to challenges of practicing self-assignment. They are also able to assess that once saturated, their theory will fall into the focused and in-depth genre. They decide to restructure their findings using the *Coding Paradigm* template. Since the structure of the emerging theory is now relatively clear and stable, they conclude that a structured mode of theory development is best suited to their study going forward.

The team proceeds to iterative and interleaved rounds of *structured data collection* and *analysis*. They now aim for data sources that can help them achieve more depth and saturate all the categories. Guided by the theory structure, they apply theoretical sampling. The team revises their observation protocols to focus more on the causal conditions leading up to the challenges and aim to interview some managers to gain more depth in the managers' perspective. They also analyse more JIRA logs to ascertain the impacts of direct or manager-led assignment (as opposed to self-assignment) on the team and the project. *Advanced memoing* helps reveal relationships between manager's approach to team empowerment and the number and extent of self-assignment challenges faced by the team, among other relationships that fall under intervening conditions.

Structured data collection and analysis continue until each element of the *Coding Paradigm* template is rich with detailed underlying codes, concepts, and categories. Now, the team finds that further data collection is mainly serving to confirm what they already know. Having reached *theoretical saturation*, the team stops further data collection. At this point, around 9 months into the project, the team can present the structured and mature theory in a publication. However, they follow the recommendation to apply *theoretical integration*. In doing so, they test the placement of all concepts and (sub)-categories under each element of the *Coding Paradigm* template. They decide to move some concepts around from causal conditions to intervening conditions. They find some concepts under consequences are better grouped into higher-level sub-categories of team-based consequences and manager-based consequences instead of being reported as 15 individual consequences. The final placements are reviewed by all three researchers as well as a colleague who was not part of the project. The theory is now integrated, in addition to being structured and mature, and serves to explain the phenomenon of challenges of self-assignment using the *Coding Paradigm* template.

The research team is ready to report the theory in a journal format which provides enough room to explain all aspects of the theory in depth. They design a theory diagram to represent the *Coding Paradigm* template and also use it to structure the Findings section of their manuscript with each element of the Coding Paradigm model becoming a detailed subsection. They perform a *targeted literature review* to find studies most closely related to the overall theory and to each of the categories and underlying concepts. Nothing close to the overall theory is discovered, but literature about the contexts in which self-assignment and direct assignment are practiced are identified in a few papers. These related works and their comparison with their own findings are presented in the Discussion section of the manuscript. A number of insights, recommendations, and guidelines for practice drawn from the effective use of basic and advanced memoing are also shared. With the completion of the manuscript, they have completed the full STGT study and reported a structured and integrated mature theory.

12.7 Reporting Outcomes

12.7.1 As Traditional Outputs

STGT outcomes, both final and interim, can be reported as traditional research outputs, i.e. peer-reviewed publications. Mature theories, theoretical frameworks, and taxonomies resulting from the application of a full STGT study are best reported in longer formats that provide enough room to describe all the details of the theory and discuss its various components in depth. Journals, thesis manuscripts, and books are good formats for reporting mature theories. It is also possible to present a condensed version of a mature theory in a shorter format, such as a conference paper, e.g. theory of becoming agile (Hoda & Noble, 2017).

Interim or partial outcomes from a full STGT study can include emerging or saturated categories, preliminary or indicative relationships between categories, and possibly both presented as preliminary forms of theories, theoretical frameworks, models, and taxonomies. Depending on the level of depth achieved in the analysis, such interim outcomes can be reported in workshops, in conferences, and in journals. When reporting interim or partial outcomes, the research team can note that the paper reports on a specific category or set of categories or indicative relationships or preliminary theory, as the case maybe. Avoid reporting interim findings in a way that comes across as a mature theory. It will not be accurate and will likely attract more intense evaluations. At the same time, reviewers need to be open to enabling the publication of interim outcomes to support the progress of the field. Typically, STGT studies are conducted on topics that lack empirical evidence and theories. As such, it is important to not stall interim outcomes from being shared with the international community simply because they are interim. Authors and reviewers can refer to the evaluation criteria for interim outcomes to assess the quality of the findings and their readiness for publication (see Chap. 13). An example of a publication of an interim STGT outcome can be seen in Gama and Lacerda (2023).

Interim outcomes reported in conference papers can sometimes be extended into journal publications once the findings have matured. An example of this is a conference paper on self-organising agile team roles, based on 24 participants, published at the international conference on software engineering (Hoda et al., 2010). Later on, when the study was completed and the roles had matured with further data collection and analysis, based on a total of 58 participants, an extended version of the paper was reported as a longer journal paper which described the final outcomes (Hoda et al., 2012). In such cases, the extended version of the paper referenced the conference version and briefly listed the extensions.

Where a research team reports their study outcomes through multiple publications, which is usually the case, they can consider including a brief description of how the various publications are related as part of a larger STGT study in each of their publications. The team may also consider reporting an "overall" paper that summarises all the findings together, if that applies to their context. Usually, a master's or PhD thesis manuscript serves this function for master's and PhD researchers.

Outcomes from the limited application of *STGT for data analysis*, typically applied in combination with other research methods, are likely to yield a few strong or promising categories and potentially a set of preliminary relationships, hypotheses, or propositions. The application of *STGT for data analysis* can also result in high-level taxonomies. These outcomes can be presented as descriptive findings, same as when reporting qualitative research findings from applying other qualitative methods. For example, a study was conducted on developer's emotional responses to requirements changes using *STGT for data analysis* with a mixed methods approach (Madampe et al., 2022). It reported a set of descriptive findings in the form of reporting the key emergent categories: emotional responses to requirements changes, stimuli triggering emotions, stages of requirements changes handling, emotion dynamics, and time-related aspects. As part of reporting future work on theory development, the paper presented an emerging theoretical model of emotion dynamics of software team contexts, including its diagrammatic representation and suggestions for future work (Madampe et al., 2022). In another example, a study on the influence of human aspects on requirements engineering-related activities reported key findings from the application of *STGT for data analysis* on survey data, including factors that motivate individuals and important personality characteristics that influence effective performance of RE-related activities. It also reported a number of insights, reflections, and recommendations drawn from the data analysis including effective use of memoing (Hidellaarachchi et al., 2023).

Finally, sometimes, data analysis yields an interesting category that does not necessarily fit the rest of the emerging theory or answer any of the planned research questions. This is typically common during a PhD study which allows for an extended basic stage where open coding is applied widely and results in many concepts and categories, not all of which proceed to be integrated into mature theories. If they represent interesting and detailed outcomes worth reporting, such incidental findings can be reported as standalone research papers.

12.7.2 As Other Outputs

STGT researchers can also choose to supplement their publications with other forms of reporting. Increasingly, research is being reported in the form of posters, videos, demos, artefacts, patents, blog posts, presentations, talks, performances, podcasts, news articles, and posts on social media to gain wider reach beyond research audiences. I like to call these "Alt+Pubs" or alternate publications, which represent non-traditional outputs beyond publications. STGT findings, both interim and mature, can be reported in many of these creative formats to achieve research impact beyond academia.

Over the years, I have presented my research findings at many industry conferences such as Agile Australia, Agile New Zealand, Agile India, and Agile Middle East. I have also talked about research findings in news interviews and podcasts such as ABC Radio National's Ockham's Razor and Agile Caravanserai. Many of these Alt+Pubs can be found on my website. Finally, I like to share synopsis of latest research papers on social media such as on LinkedIn and Twitter with industry practitioners and the wider public in short and easily accessible formats. I encourage my students to do the same, so research findings do not remain limited to academic audiences and can have a wider impact on society.

12.8 Presenting Outcomes

In presenting an emerging or mature theory, I recommend including a few standard elements: a theory statement, a theory diagram, and plenty of examples of sanitised raw data. Not only do these elements improve the overall presentation, they also serve to establish *credibility* and *rigour*, described further in Chap. 13: Evaluation Guidelines.

12.8.1 As Theory Statement

A theory statement is a statement that presents the theory in a succinct text format. It can be thought of as an "elevator pitch" of the study findings. Typically, it makes reference to all the key categories and relationships between them. The rationale for this is to demonstrate *parsimony*, i.e. "*compactness of the theory such that it exhibits conceptual density and explains potentially complex phenomenon in simple and elegant ways*" (Hoda, 2022). Ideally, the theory statement is a single sentence. Where the sentence becomes unnecessarily long or complex, it is recommended to break it down into a few sentences or a succinct paragraph.

Theory Statement Examples

Example

Our theory about multidisciplinary teams dealing with data challenges explains (a) the challenges faced by MDSTs including gaining access to data, aligning data, understanding data, and resolving data quality issues; (b) the context in and condition under which these challenges occur; (c) the causes that lead to the challenges; (d) the related consequences of these challenges; (e) the contingencies or strategies applied to address the challenges including high-level strategic approaches, implementing new tools and techniques, and building stronger teams; and (f) the relationships between strategies and causes and/or challenges represented as covariances (Graetsch et al., 2023).

Example

The theory of becoming agile explains agile transformation as a network of ongoing transitions across five dimensions: software development practices, team practices, management approach, reflective practices, and culture. The unique position of a software team through this network, and their pace of progress along the five dimensions, explains why individual agile teams present distinct manifestations of agility and unique transition experiences (Hoda & Noble, 2017).

Example

The theory of lack of customer involvement explains the context, conditions, and causes of the lack of customer involvement in agile projects, its consequences on the self-organising ability of the team, the contingencies (strategies) that teams come up with to continue delivering solutions, and how some of these strategies vary with the causes (Hoda et al., 2011).

Example

The theory of multiple levels of project management challenges describes the project management-related challenges resulting from and experienced by self-organising teams at multiple levels of project, team, individual, and task on agile projects (Hoda & Murugesan, 2016).

Example

The theory of the role of the project manager in agile projects explains how the project manager performs five different activities—facilitating, mentoring, negotiating, protecting, and coordinating—on an everyday basis, by using three different management approaches, hard, moderate, and soft, and the possible influence of the project manager on the frequency with which agile practices are carried out by teams (Shastri et al., 2021a).

12.8.2 As Theory Diagram

As the famous proverb goes, *a picture is worth a thousand words*. Theory diagrams are a great way to visually and elegantly depict the key findings. Not only does it serve to present the theory in a compact and appealing format, it can also become a signpost for leading the reader through its various aspects in the text. Additionally, theory diagrams make for excellent graphical abstracts and can easily be included in presentations, posters, and videos to provide an overarching view of the key findings.

In drawing the theory diagram, the research team can come up with their own model of placing the key categories and depicting links between them, e.g. Hoda and Noble (2017); Hoda and Murugesan (2016), Shastri et al. (2021a,b). Where applicable, they can leverage established theory templates such as the six Cs to depict their theory, e.g. Hoda et al. (2011), Masood et al. (2020a), Graetsch et al. (2023).

Theory Diagram Examples

Figure 12.2 shows the theory diagram associated with the *theory of becoming agile* using a bespoke researcher-defined model. Figures 12.3 and 12.4 show the *theory of inadequate customer involvement* and the *theory of multidisciplinary teams dealing with data challenges*, respectively, using the six Cs template (Hoda et al., 2011; Graetsch et al., 2023). Finally, Fig. 12.5 shows an emerging theoretical model developed using *STGT for data analysis* (Madampe et al., 2022).

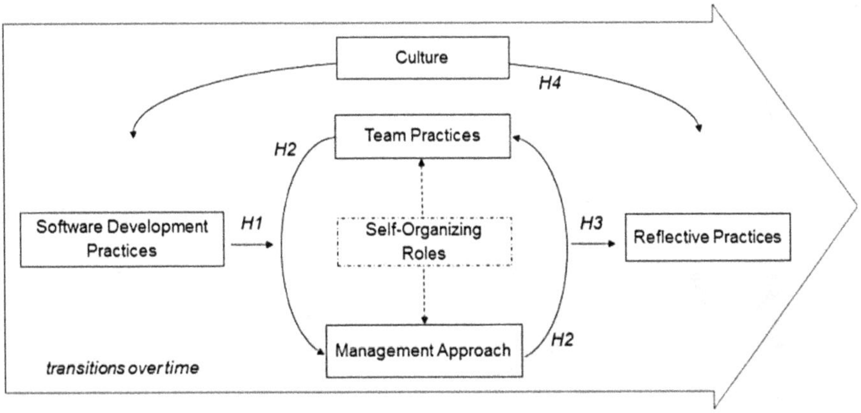

Fig. 12.2 Theory diagram depicting the *theory of becoming agile* (Hoda & Noble, 2017), where H1–H4 represent the four hypotheses that emerged in the study

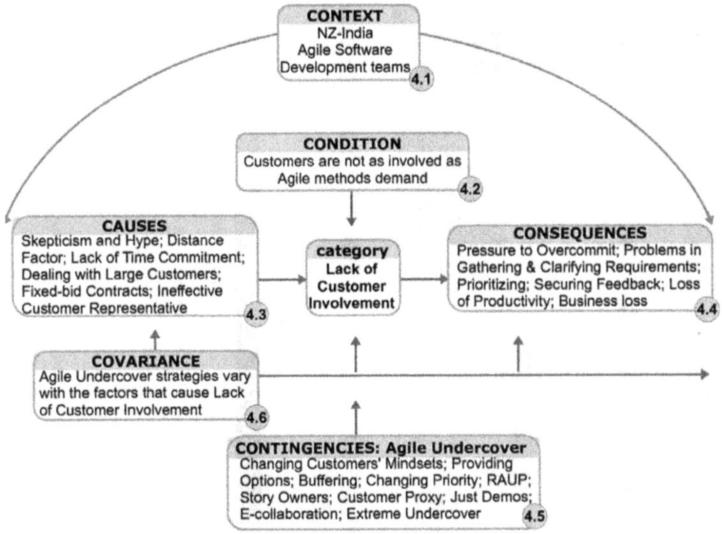

Fig. 12.3 Theory diagram depicting the *theory of lack of customer involvement* (Hoda et al., 2011) using Glaser's six Cs theory template (Glaser, 1978), where 4.1–4.6 refer to the section number where each of the six Cs is described in the paper

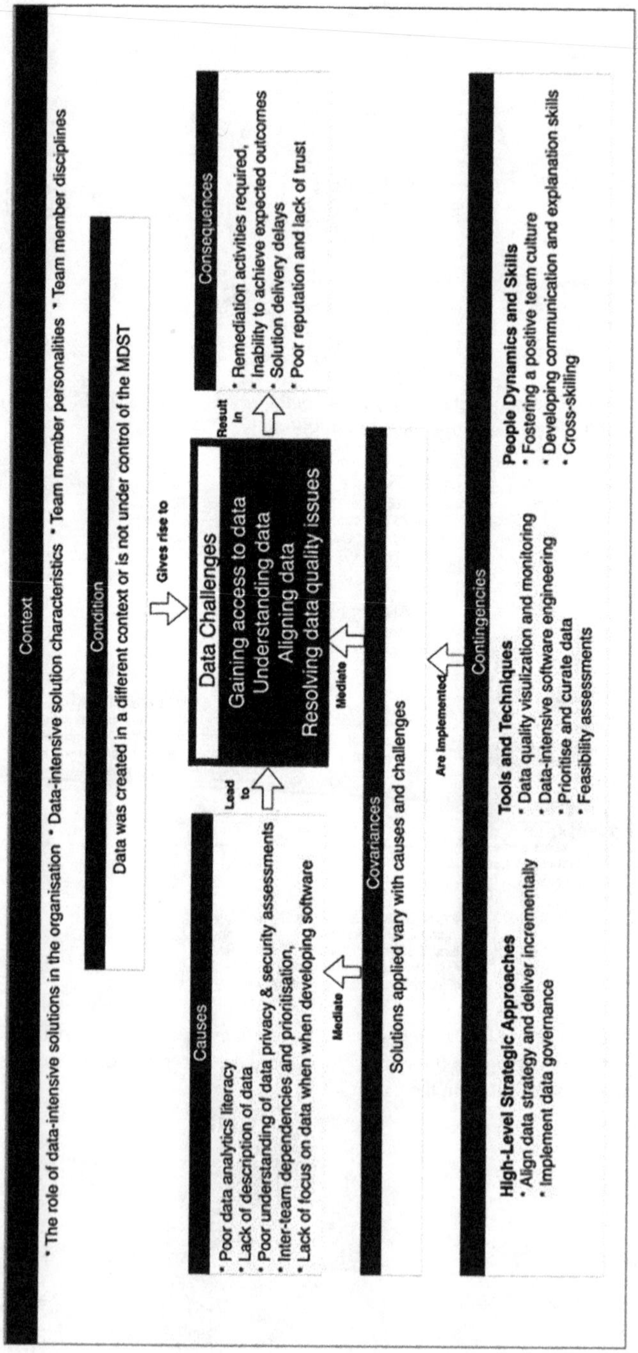

Fig. 12.4 Theory diagram depicting the *theory of multidisciplinary teams dealing with data challenges* (Graetsch et al., 2023) using Glaser's six Cs theory template (Glaser, 1978)

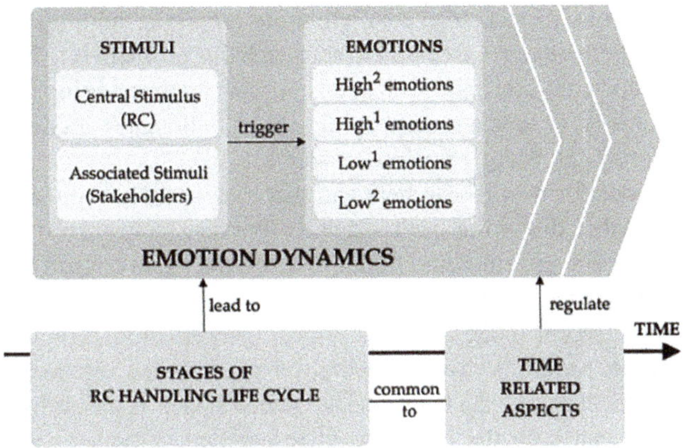

Fig. 12.5 Emerging theoretical model depicting emotion dynamics of software team contexts (Madampe et al., 2022) using STGT for data analysis

12.8.3 With Examples of Raw Data

In addition to the theory statement and diagram, STGT studies will benefit from including a variety of verbatim examples of appropriately sanitised and anonymised underlying raw data, e.g. quotes from interviews, photos of observations and artefacts, links to relevant tools and demos, and so on. Including raw data examples at pertinent places in the manuscript not only lends credibility and rigour to the study but also makes for an interesting read, as the readers get an opportunity to experience the field and the original sources directly.

12.9 Nuances of Theory Development

12.9.1 Role of Theoretical Sensitivity

Researchers who are new to qualitative research and theory development can struggle to see a structure emerged from their data analysis. This is primarily because they have not been through the process of theory development before and may not know what to expect. Reading up on theories in other research domains and on other topics can greatly benefit new researchers to improve their ability to identify and formulate theoretical concepts and structures, also known as *theoretical sensitivity*.

Experienced researchers, on the other hand, face the opposite challenge. Due to increased theoretical sensitivity on account of experience, they run the risk of prematurely identifying a theoretical structure before it has been fully established through the analysis and memoing procedures. Sometimes, they can begin to "see" one of their previously used structures while the emerging findings may be better suited to some other structure. One way to approach this problem is to be conscious of this temptation and continue to have an open approach to discovering new theoretical structures. Another is to seek a second opinion from colleagues not directly involved in the study as they can bring a fresh perspective.

It is a good idea for new researchers and theorists to discuss their progress with experts when further down the basic stage as they can help identify a theoretical structure best suited to the emerging findings. They can again consult with the expert during the advanced theory development stage to finalise their theoretical structure when using an emergent mode or to assist with theoretical integration when using a structured mode. Similarly, it is beneficial for experienced researchers to engage with new researchers during the basic and advanced stages as they afford a freshness of approach that can help the experienced researchers remain open to emerging structures.

12.9.2 Role of Deduction

Classifying grounded theory as purely inductive is naïve (Haig, 1995). While STGT is primarily driven by an inductive or bottom-up approach, it also includes some element of deductive or top-down reasoning. The role of deduction is most explicitly seen in the practice of theoretical sampling where the existing findings are assessed to decide what data may be required to collect next and from where. Theoretical sampling encapsulates a deductive approach, moving from the general (high-level findings) to the specific (new evidence to be collected).

Historically, Glaserian GT also acknowledges the role of *deduction* in guiding theoretical sampling (Glaser & Strauss, 2017, first published 1967, chapter II), while *Strauss-Corbinian GT* suggests a greater role of deduction in the later stages of theory development where the emergent theory is seen to be verified against the data (Strauss & Corbin, 1990). However, Glaserian GT is opposed this view, referring to it as "*forcing*" rather than emergence of theory (Glaser, 1992).

STGT acknowledges the deductive approach present in theoretical sampling as a means to drive data collection for theory development. However, that is not the same as a hypothetico-deductive approach where pre-formulated hypotheses are actively tested and validated against evidence. Instead, theoretical sampling allows the researchers to be guided by the emerging theory, collect new data to provide richness to the existing categories and concepts, strengthen indicative relationships, find new relationships, and, overall, help progress the theory towards maturity.

12.9.3 Role of Abduction

Theory development is a systematic and rigorous process. While being systematic and rigorous is necessary, it is not sufficient. This is because theory development is also inherently a creative process. Theorists are creators of new knowledge and new ways of capturing, conceptualising, and presenting knowledge, which typically requires some out-of-the-box thinking, connecting of ideas in new and original ways, and conducting thought experiments.

One mechanism that encapsulates creativity in theory development is abduction. Charles Sanders Peirce described abduction as "*a process of forming an explanatory hypothesis*" (Haig, 1995). The role of abduction in the process of coming up with hypotheses and developing theories has a long lineage. For example, consider Einstein's famous *Gedankenexperimente* or thought experiments, Stephen Hawking's hunches on black hole theory, and Darwin's connecting the dots from visual clues to develop the theory of evolution. Similar approaches can be seen in everyday medical practice where hypotheses are developed based on the available evidence, e.g. symptoms, history, and patient's lifestyle. Similarly, abductive reasoning is generously applied in criminal investigation in coming up with hypotheses around how events unfolded based on the available evidence at hand, e.g. clues, artefacts, and testimonies. The latter was referred to by Peirce in a personal "detective" experience (Reichertz, 2007) and famously portrayed in the engaging pursuits of the fictional character, Sherlock Holmes. As the author, Sir Arthur Conan Doyle states "*when you have eliminated all which is impossible, then whatever remains, however improbable, must be the truth.*" Abduction applies a similar approach, "*to propose the best possible explanation based on all the evidence, albeit incomplete, available* (Hoda, 2022).

In an STGT study, researchers can apply a variety of abductive reasoning modes, such as reason, hunch, clue, metaphor, analogy, symptom, pattern, and explanation (Shank, 1998), for creative thinking which is considered key to theorising and theory development (Martin, 2019). Basic memoing in the early stages of an STGT study can give rise to indicative relationships between categories and preliminary hypotheses and propositions. These are further developed during *advanced memoing*, based on the available evidence and insights. Some relationships, hypotheses, and propositions become stronger with evidence, while others dwindle away and are discarded.

Abduction is also applied in the procedures of *theoretical structuring* in the emergent mode of theory development. As part of theoretical structuring, in trying to "see" a structure in the key categories and emerging relationships, the researcher will benefit from brainstorming ideas and considering relevant metaphors that help explain the "big picture" view of the key findings.

Similarly, abduction can be applied during *theoretical integration*. For example, in a study on how real-world Scrum practice differs from how it is described in agile literature, we had identified a number of variations across Scrum practices, roles, and artefacts (Masood et al., 2020b). These variations together formed the *theory of Scrum variations in practice*. As a final step, it became apparent that different variations seemed to be motivated by different rationales, e.g. some arose due to a lack of clarity in the original guidelines, some due to contextual factors, others due to need, and yet others due to choice. Based on this realisation, I proposed a nuanced classification framework of the variations, classifying them into *standard, necessary, contextual* variations, and *clear deviation*, in addition to the ideal but rare, *by-the-book* practice. Arriving at the framework was an experience in abductive reasoning. The challenge with abduction is that it is difficult to teach someone to do it. There is no formula that can be readily applied. Deeply engaging with the data and theory development, while keeping an open mind about what we see in the patterns, helps. Staying open to insights gained from other experiences outside of research can also help. The experience of abduction can be shared and aught to be acknowledged in research reporting, as we did in our paper (Masood et al., 2020b).

While the role of sudden or slow-dawning "*sensitive insights of the observer*" is acknowledged as "*the root sources of all significant theorising*" (Glaser & Strauss, 2017, first published 1967, chapter XI), *Glaserian GT* does not explicitly acknowledge the role of abduction in theory development. *Strauss-Corbinian GT* is seen to be influenced by abduction but remains limited to a footnote in Strauss' book (Charmaz, 2014; Strauss, 1987). Constructivist GT is the most vocal about the use of abduction in theory development, describing it as a type of "*inferential leap*" made when the researcher arrives at a surprising finding and comes up with useful explanations, also known as *theoretical conjectures* or inferences, and collect more data if necessary to explain it (Richardson & Kramer, 2006; Charmaz, 2014).

12.9.4 Importance of Visualisation

Visual representations of the STGT outcomes in the form of theory diagrams are valuable for theory presentation. Visualisation serves another important function. It can be used as a simple yet powerful tool or approach to support coding and theory formulation. For example, as the codes give rise to the concepts and indicate the emergence of the first few categories, visualising them as a hierarchical diagram will help understand which codes group to form which concepts and how they together make up the category. An example can be seen in Chap. 10: STGT for Qualitative Data Analysis.

Such coding diagrams can be very useful as a clear overview of the copious number of codes growing rapidly in our spreadsheets or on our computer-aided qualitative and mixed data analysis software such as NVivo and MaxQDA. They can help the analyst make sense and keep track of the coding. The number of codes and concepts under each category will help establish and convey the breadth of each category, providing a good sense of coverage. Adding information on the source of the code in the diagrams will help establish and convey their strength of evidence, providing a good sense of depth. For example, code names can be followed by participant numbers in brackets to capture all those participants whose inputs led to that code. Coding diagrams are also very handy for demonstrating coding progress to the team, colleagues, and advisors and having discussions about the coding decisions and rationales. Such discussions can lead to refinements in terms of renaming and rearranging of codes and concepts more appropriately, leading to quality outcomes.

Similarly, visualisation of categories and the indicative relationships between them in the form of in-progress theory diagrams are valuable means to make sense of the emerging theory. Mind maps can be created to visually represent categories and underlying concepts and codes using tools such as Microsoft PowerPoint, Canva, Draw.io, and other diagram creation tools. They are especially valuable for structuring and integrating the theory. They enable the team to carefully consider the "bigger picture view" by looking at an overview of the findings and enable discussions that can lead to refinements and rearrangements. Considering the emerging theory diagram as it currently stands can help identify the theory templates that best fit the findings. Visualising all significant codes, concepts, and categories can help identify any "rouge" ones that need to be grouped, dropped, or reported separately.

Finally, theory diagrams can also help in planning out a publications strategy for the whole research project. For example, the team can consult their emerging theory diagram to plan for future publications focusing on a key category or a set of categories and relationships between them.

12.9.5 Structuring and Integration

Theoretical structuring happens early and progressively in the structured mode of theory development and does not require an explicit step dedicated to it. However, the structure mode benefits from an explicit integration step, as demonstrated through thought experiments and examples earlier.

Similarly, theoretical integration happens organically in the emergent mode and does not require dedicated step. However, the emergent mode benefits from an explicit structuring step, as demonstrated through examples earlier in this chapter.

Steps such as theoretical structuring and integration help demystify and take away the guesswork from theory development by (a) breaking down the process of theory development into well-defined steps or procedures that can be practiced by theorists and (b) providing a vocabulary to demonstrate, explain, evaluate, and debate how theories are developed.

12.9.6 Narrowing Down Versus Validation

Targeted and structured data collection are not the same as looking for data that can confirm the current findings. That would be validation. Taken to an extreme, validation can get close to manifesting confirmation bias, where the research team selectively uses materials that confirm their findings and do not leave room for new insights or counter ideas. In contrast, targeted and structured data collection procedures are focused on finding out as much as possible about the emerging key and related categories, including new codes, concepts, and sub-categories that help describe these categories better and in more depth. Some of this can be in the form of codes and concepts that are diametrically opposite to what is known about a category so far and helps to develop a comprehensive and rich understanding of the various facets of that category. Focusing the data collection on the key, potential key, and related categories is a practical way in which the research study progressively narrows down in scope until it can be completed.

12.10 Is Theory Development for Me? Quiz

There are a number of factors that can help determine if pursuing qualitative research and theory development is a good idea for a given project, for example, the nature of the phenomenon being studied, the opportunities available for qualitative data collection in that area, and the quality of the data. The collective skill set of the research team also plays a role in whether and how well they can conduct socio-technical qualitative research. As explained in the *socio-technical research framework*, the collective skill set of socio-technical researchers includes skills in social sciences, philosophy, qualitative research, theory development, and technical skills and/or experience. Not every person on the team needs to be skilled in all areas; rather collectively, they may possess reasonable skills across the set. More about this in Chap. 3: STGT—An Overview.

To go a step above and beyond basic qualitative data analysis, researchers can also consider their personal readiness for theory development. Not everyone *needs* to develop theory. Not everyone *wants* to do it either. Of those who are interested, some find it easier than others. Based on my experiences of conducting STGT studies and supervising students, I present the **Is Theory Development for Me? Quiz** that can be used to assess one's current levels of readiness for theory development. Some of the traits in the quiz are common good researcher traits, irrespective of the research method. Taken together, the complete set is especially suited to assess readiness for theory development.

I like to believe in the growth mindset (Dwek, 2007). The quiz does not aim to suggest that researchers without the listed traits will fail at theory development. Those who already possess or are predisposed to these traits are likely to have a head start, while those on the other end will need to put in more effort. These traits can be learned and enhanced. The readiness quiz can be used to self-assess traits from time to time as researchers grow into them over the course of their STGT study.

Is Theory Development for Me?

Rate yourself on 1–5 for each of the traits, where **1 is most unlike you** and **5 is most like you**. Sum up all the scores and use the scale at the end of the quiz to self-evaluate current readiness for theory development. I say *current* because these can be worked on and improved:

- *I observe and question both the mundane and the strange.*
- *I find patterns in everyday objects/events.*
- *I can think in abstract terms.*
- *I like analysing and deep thinking.*
- *I can connect the dots across seemingly disparate ideas/disciplines.*
- *I am creative.*
- *I am comfortable with uncertainty.*
- *I am systematic and disciplined.*
- *I do not give up easily.*
- *I can manage self-doubt and biases.*

Interpreting Your Scores

Between 34 and 50	You will likely enjoy theory development. Preserve and strengthen these traits.
Between 16 and 33	You can work on theory development while improving selected traits.
Between 5 and 15	You may struggle with theory development unless you improve relevant traits.

Skills for Theory Development

Keen observation captured as *I observe and question both the mundane and the strange* is the ability to notice and ask questions of the mundane as well as identify and delve into the uncommon. Observation is a highly desirable quality in theory development. Imagine if Newtown hadn't *really observed* and questioned something as mundane as an apple falling to the ground, he would not have discovered theoretical concept of gravity. Keen observation[8] applied in STGT studies enables discovery of the rationales and nuances of a phenomenon which in turn make for in-depth, rich, and interesting set of findings.

[8] Observation here refers generally to observing the data and the research process along with reflecting on our own role as a researcher. It does not refer exclusively to observations as a data collection technique.

■ **Pattern recognition** captured as *I find patterns in everyday objects/events* is the ability to identify *similarity* in objects, events, or ideas across a range of instances. What led Darwin to ultimately come up with the theory of evolution started with close attention to detail (observation) and pattern recognition as he identified patterns of beak sizes, shapes, and thickness across the range of flinches he observed on the Galápagos Islands. Similarly, pattern recognition in terms of identifying key points and concepts within and across different data sources in STGT studies is at the heart of the data analysis approach.

■ **Abstraction** captured as *I can think in abstract terms* is the process of removing the concrete details and capturing the essential characteristics or essence of an event or piece of information. Software engineers are used to the idea of abstraction. Consider the components of a programming language in the form variables, classes, objects, and interfaces. These are all abstractions of concepts we wish to represent and implement. Other examples include quadratic equations in algebra, Venn diagrams, and abstract art where seemingly foreign-looking shapes and non-traditional colours are used to capture and represent real-life objects and ideas. In STGT studies, abstraction is the key to data analysis, as concrete evidences are abstracted into key ideas (codes) and subsequently into concepts and categories.

Together, pattern recognition and abstraction are essential to making sense of large amounts of data and form the core of STGT data analysis and theory development process.

■ **Analysis** captured as *I like analysing and deep thinking* is the researcher's disposition to asking questions of the data and seeking meaning in ideas, situations, and behaviours for sense making. *What is the meaning of this statement? Why are these behaviours being observed? How did this situation arise?* Given the interwoven nature of data collection and analysis, questions in the analysis phase guide next rounds of data collection. Investing in deep analysis will lead to rich and deep theories.

■ **Synthesis** captured as *I can connect the dots across seemingly disparate ideas, events, and disciplines.* While pattern recognition looks for similarities, synthesis focuses on bringing related ideas together to form a whole. Theory development in STGT requires constant comparison and synthesis of information across multiple sources, e.g. across all interviews and observations, and large amounts of project data. Data analysis software such as NVivo can help with organising and managing the data.

■ **Creativity** captured as *I am creative* is the researcher's ability to be original, think outside the box, go with the flow, and ultimately produce an original explanation that has not been empirically derived before. Theory development is arguably one of the most complex and advanced research endeavours. Applying Bloom's taxonomy, creating original theories can be seen as a higher-order objective that requires and builds on the other research skills of observation, comprehension, analysis, evaluation, and synthesis (Anderson et al., 2001). Presenting the theory in easy-to-understand and visual ways also demands creativity.

■ **Embracing uncertainty** captured as *I am comfortable with uncertainty* is the ability of the researcher to accept all types of uncertainty inherent in research projects in general and with theory development in particular. While dealing with uncertainty is a natural part of research, STGT is marked by higher levels of uncertainty compared to other methods. The basic data analysis procedure of *open coding* requires the researcher to remain open to all key points emerging from individual data sources, not necessarily knowing *what it all means* until later when patterns start to emerge. Similarly, deriving codes, concepts, categories, relationships, hypotheses, and the overall theory development relies on emergence. Researchers who are naturally able to work with uncertainty or can learn to trust the process are likely to effectively deal with any associated anxiety and frustration and succeed with STGT.

■ **Discipline** captured as *I am systematic and disciplined* is critical to applying a systematic research method such as STGT. A disciplined approach is imperative to achieving high-quality outcomes in STGT studies. While some adaptations to the process are inevitable, skipping critical steps or performing shallow practice will defeat the purpose of conducting an STGT study. Any theory resulting from a shallow or inconsistent application of STGT will easily show the weaknesses in the evidence and analysis and the lack of depth, richness, and nuance.

■ **Persistence** captured as *I do not give up easily* is at the heart of any research endeavour. However, it is particularly true for theory development. Einstein famously said "*It's not that I'm so smart, it's just that I stay with problems longer.*" While we can all agree Einstein was uncommonly smart, it is also true that many smart people do not end up developing fundamental laws or making profound discoveries. Persistence or grit is the key.

■ **Self-awareness and regulation** captured as *I can manage self-doubt and biases* are useful traits for a socio-technical researcher. Being aware of our own worldview and potential biases and being able to deal with them appropriately will lead to theories that are truly grounded in evidence and representation of the participants' points of view. Remaining open to possibilities is essential to making new discoveries. But constant self-doubt and revisiting of decisions can severely inhibit our ability to make progress in an STGT study. The typical trajectory of an STGT study involves starting broad and narrowing down iteratively and incrementally towards key patterns and relationships. Achieving this successfully requires a careful balance between remaining openness and self-regulating doubts.

A few **additional traits** can be considered for theory development in fields such as software engineering:

- *I have a good grasp on software technology concepts and the socio-technical context surrounding software engineering.*
- *I like observing and analysing human behaviour to find meaning.*
- *I have a good grasp on qualitative research.*

Previous training and/or practical experience in software engineering, sociology, and qualitative research can certainly provide a head start. But theory development in socio-technical fields is not limited to individual or teams of software engineers and/or sociologists. Theory development can be undertaken, learned, and successfully completed by anyone committed to working towards and excelling in the above-mentioned areas.

12.11 Summary

In this chapter, we addressed the *attitude* and *approach* to theory development in software engineering. Next, we learned about *theory development*, starting with selecting between the emergent and structure modes. This was followed by the *common procedures* of theory development, including theoretical sampling, advanced memoing, targeted literature review, and theoretical saturation, that appear in both modes of theory development. Then we learned about the *emergent mode*, including its unique procedures and a practical example of *applying the emergent mode*. Next, we learned about the *structured mode*, including its unique procedures and a practical example of *applying the structured mode*. Next, we considered the options for *reporting outcomes* as traditional and other outputs, followed by recommendations for *presenting outcomes* and the *nuances of theory development*. Finally, we took the *Is Theory Development for Me?* Quiz to self-assess readiness for theory development and identify areas of improvement to become capable theorists.

References

Anderson, L. W., Bloom, B. S. et al. (2001). *A taxonomy for learning, teaching, and assessing: A revision of Bloom's taxonomy of educational objectives*. Longman.

Charmaz, K. (2006). *Constructing grounded theory: A practical guide through qualitative analysis*. Sage.

Charmaz, K. (2014). *Constructing grounded theory*. Sage.

Corbin, J. M., & Strauss, A. (1990). Grounded theory research: Procedures, canons, and evaluative criteria, *Qualitative Sociology, 13*(1), 3–21.

Dwek, C. (2007). *Mindset: The new psychology of success*. Balantine Books.

Gama, K.,& Lacerda, A. (2023). Understanding and supporting neurodiverse software developers in agile teams, *Proceedings of the XXXVII Brazilian Symposium on Software Engineering* (pp. 497–502).

Glaser, B. (1978). *Theoretical sensitivity: Advances in the methodology of grounded theory*. Sociology Press.

Glaser, B. G. (1992). *Basics of grounded theory analysis: Emergence vs forcing*. Sociology Press.

Glaser, B. G., & Strauss, A. L. (1966). *Awareness of dying*. Transaction Publishers.

Glaser, B. G., & Strauss, A. L. (2017). *Discovery of grounded theory: Strategies for qualitative research*. Routledge (First Published 1967).

Graetsch, U. M., Khalajzadeh, H., Shahin, M., Hoda, R., & Grundy, J. (2023). Dealing with data challenges when delivering data-intensive software solutions. *IEEE Transactions on Software Engineering, 49*, 4349–4370 . https://doi.org/10.1109/TSE.2023.3291003

Haig, B. D. (1995). Grounded theory as scientific method. *Philosophy of Education, 28*(1), 1–11.

Herbsleb, J. (2018). What would a science of software engineering look like?, *Keynote address delivered jointly to the Cooperative and Human Aspects of Software Engineering (CHASE) and Crowd Sourcing in Software Engineering (CSI-SE) Workshops (ICSE 2018).* https://herbsleb.org/web-pres/slides/crowd-chase-2018-final-dist.pdf

Hidellaarachchi, D., Grundy, J., Hoda, R., & Mueller, I. (2023). The influence of human aspects on requirements engineering-related activities: Software practitioners' perspective, *ACM Transactions on Software Engineering and Methodology, 32*(5), 1–37.

Hoda, R. (2022). Socio-technical grounded theory for software engineering. *IEEE Transactions on Software Engineering, 48*(10), 3808–3832.

Hoda, R., & Murugesan, L. K. (2016). Multi-level agile project management challenges: A self-organizing team perspective, *Journal of Systems and Software, 117*, 245–257.

Hoda, R., & Noble, J. (2017). Becoming agile: A grounded theory of agile transitions in practice. In *2017 IEEE/ACM 39th International Conference on Software Engineering (ICSE)* (pp. 141–151). IEEE.

Hoda, R., Noble, J., & Marshall, S. (2010). Organizing self-organizing teams. In *Proceedings of the 32nd ACM/IEEE International Conference on Software Engineering-Volume 1* (pp. 285–294).

Hoda, R., Noble, J., & Marshall, S. (2011). The impact of inadequate customer collaboration on self-organizing agile teams. *Information and Software Technology, 53*(5), 521–534.

Hoda, R., Noble, J., & Marshall, S. (2012). Self-organizing roles on agile software development teams. *IEEE Transactions on Software Engineering, 39*(3), 422–444.

Madampe, K., Hoda, R., & Grundy, J. (2022). The emotional roller coaster of responding to requirements changes in software engineering. *IEEE Transactions on Software Engineering, 49*(3), 1171–1187.

Martin, V. B. (2019). Using popular and academic literature as data for formal grounded theory. In *The sage handbook of current developments in grounded theory* (pp. 222–243). Sage Publications.

Masood, Z., Hoda, R., & Blincoe, K. (2020a). How agile teams make self-assignment work: a grounded theory study. *Empirical Software Engineering, 25*, 4962–5005. https://doi.org/10.1007/s10664-020-09876-x

Masood, Z., Hoda, R., & Blincoe, K. (2020b). Real world Scrum: A grounded theory of variations in practice. *IEEE Transactions on Software Engineering, 48*(5), 1579–1591.

Pant, A., Hoda, R., Spiegler, S. V., Tantithamthavorn, C., & Turhan, B. (2023). Ethics in the age of AI: An analysis of AI practitioners' awareness and challenges. *ACM Transactions on Software Engineering and Methodology* . https://doi.org/10.1145/3635715

Reichertz, J. (2007). *Abduction: The logic of discovery of grounded theory*. Sage London.

Richardson, R., & Kramer, E. H. (2006). Abduction as the type of inference that characterizes the development of a grounded theory. *Qualitative Research, 6*(4), 497–513.

Shank, G. (1998). The extraordinary ordinary powers of abductive reasoning. *Theory & Psychology, 8*(6), 841–860.

Shastri, Y., Hoda, R., & Amor, R. (2021a). The role of the project manager in agile software development projects. *Journal of Systems and Software, 173*, 110871.

Shastri, Y., Hoda, R., & Amor, R. (2021b). Spearheading agile: the role of the scrum master in agile projects. *Empirical Software Engineering, 26*(1), 1–31.

Sjøberg, D. I., Dybå, T., Anda, B. C., & Hannay, J. E. (2008). Building theories in software engineering. In *Guide to advanced empirical software engineering* (pp. 312–336). Springer.

Strauss, A., & Corbin, J. (1990). *Basics of qualitative research*. Sage Publications.

Strauss, A. L. (1987). *Qualitative analysis for social scientists*. Cambridge University Press.

Stray, V., Hoda, R., Paasivaara, M., Lenarduzzi, V., & Mendez, D. (2022). Theories in agile software development: Past, present, and future introduction to the XP 2020 special section. *Information and Software Technology, 152*, 107058.

PART V

Evaluation and Future Directions

13 Evaluation Guidelines

Abstract In this chapter, we will learn about the general *evaluation approach* to be applied when evaluating research applications and outcomes which involves assessing reviewer suitability, acknowledging the default review position, establishing an acceptance threshold, and cultivating a constructive review style. Then we will learn about the two sets of *evaluation criteria* for socio-technical grounded theory (STGT), one for *evaluating the application* and the other for *evaluating the outcomes*. We will learn about the two evaluation criteria for STGT application: credibility and rigour. Next, we will learn about the criteria for evaluating the outcomes of applying STGT in a limited context for data analysis: originality, relevance, and density. Then we will cover the criteria for evaluating the outcomes of a full STGT study, including both basic and advanced stages, to produce mature theoretical outcomes: novelty, usefulness, parsimony, and modifiability.

R. Hoda, *Qualitative Research with Socio-Technical Grounded Theory*,
https://doi.org/10.1007/978-3-031-60533-8_13

13.1 Evaluation Approach

Tips

Tips for Approaching Research Reviews

- Assess review suitability—Are you well equipped to evaluate the research method in addition to the research topic?
- Acknowledge default position—Do you have a *neutral*, *accepting*, or *rejecting* default position?
- Establish an acceptance threshold—What is the basic minimum level below which you will reject certain technique applications, tool usages, research design choices, conclusions, and so on?
- Cultivate a constructive feedback style—Be professional, respectful, constructive, and helpful in your feedback. Empathy is key!

As a first step to evaluating socio-technical grounded theory (STGT) applications and outcomes or any research method and its outcomes for that matter, it is important to consider some fundamental aspects that define our evaluation approach. These can be broken down into *assessing review suitability*, *acknowledging default position*, *establishing an acceptance threshold*, and *cultivating a constructive feedback style*. Being consciously aware of each of these aspects will allow program chairs, editors, and reviewers to avoid unconscious bias, to ensure consistency across reviews, and to be constructive while enabling high-quality reviews.

13.1.1 Assessing Review Suitability

If you have been invited to review a research paper, most likely a program chair or an associate editor has invited you because they found your expertise to be relevant to the paper. Despite this, we cannot simply assume it is a good match. Assess suitability. A quick glance over the abstract, or the full paper if available, will help us assess whether the research topic and area are matching our expertise and experience. However, this is not enough. It is vital to consider the research method employed in the paper and our expertise in those types of methods. A study on a highly relevant topic in our area of expertise may have been conducted using a research method we are not familiar with. For example, imagine you have received an invitation to review a paper in your core area of research. While the topic and area are a good match, you realise from reading the abstract and browsing the paper that you are not at all familiar with the research method applied. It may be a quantitative experimental study while you work almost exclusively with qualitative research methods, or vice-versa. In such cases, consider declining the invitation and recommending a colleague who may be better placed to review that paper. The research method is almost as important a factor to assess suitability for review purposes as the research topic or area.

13.1.2 Acknowledging Default Position

Once you find the review invitation suitable, you can proceed to consider your position as a reviewer. There are three possible default or starting positions, which are either clearly or somewhat inclined towards being *neutral*, *accepting*, or *rejecting*. Arguably, these positions stem from what we fundamentally believe the aim of peer review and the job of a reviewer to be, i.e. to accept research in good faith unless challenged or disappointed (accepting), to reject research unless convinced otherwise or pleasantly surprised (rejecting), or to be a neutral reader until evidence convinces us one way or the other (neutral). It is important to be aware of our default position and to acknowledge any changes detected during the review. For example, we may have started off with a positive position, and somewhere down the line, we seem to be moving towards a negative position. We need to ask ourselves: What changed? Has the paper lost our trust because the calculations don't add up? Are we tired on account of poor readability of the paper while the results may be interesting? Are the claimed contributions too grandiose and unsupported, and is that a deal breaker? Or are we annoyed they did not cite a relevant paper, which sometimes happens to be our own? Awareness is the first step to battle and defeat unconscious bias! Acknowledging our default and changing positions allows us to self-correct and provide evidence to support our overall evaluation of the paper.

13.1.3 Establishing an Acceptance Threshold

Related to the default position is the idea of an acceptance threshold, a basic minimum level below which we reject certain technique applications, tool usages, research design choices, conclusions, and so on. We all inherently have personal tolerance thresholds when it comes to reviews—hence why some reviewers have a reputation for being strict (high threshold) and some for being easy-going (low threshold). Again, these thresholds vary over time and by context. For example, when evaluating a workshop paper presenting preliminary results, we may be comfortable overlooking some of the flaws of the presentation style or research design in favour of encouraging what seems like a good topic and promising initial findings. We can ask ourselves: Will the authors benefit from attending the workshop to receive feedback and community support? Will the community benefit from a discussion on this topic or method? On the other hand, while reviewing a top conference or journal paper, we may apply a higher acceptance threshold, suited to the average submission quality of that journal.

13.1.4 Cultivating a Constructive Feedback Style

A review is not only an entry pass to getting a paper published or a presentation accepted, but it's also an opportunity to gain guidance and support from the wider community. Most software engineering journals practice single-anonymous reviewing where the author's identity is known to the reviewers but the reviewer's identity is not shared with the authors. Many software engineering conferences practice double-anonymous reviewing where both author's and reviewer's identities are concealed from each other. In most cases, the reviewer's identity is concealed. It is easy to become overly critical or negative when we are not "seen". How can we cultivate a constructive feedback style, especially when we are acting from behind a wall? Empathy is the key. Aim to write reviews that we would like to receive. That is not to say accept all papers! Rather, keep the words, tone, critiques, questions, recommendations, and suggestions professional, respectful, constructive, and helpful to the authors. For example, we can choose our words carefully in a way that makes it clear that we are evaluating the work, not the authors. This is an important distinction, especially for new authors who may very well be conflating the two themselves. Similarly, highlighting areas of improvement and providing clear and actionable recommendations also make the review constructive. Furthermore, we can choose to identify ourselves if the conference or journal allows it or write our feedback imagining that we are talking to the authors face to face or imagining we are the ones receiving the review. This is likely to induce more empathy in our feedback style.

13.2 Evaluation Criteria

Evaluating STGT consists of evaluating the research method application and evaluating the outcomes of the study. The following sections present separate set of criteria for evaluating:

- *The method application*
- *The outcomes*

Here, the focus is on criteria that are especially relevant for STGT studies. Other general criteria expected of good quality research, such as ethical conduct, sufficient evidence and details, good presentation, and so on, still apply.

The STGT evaluation criteria are deliberately designed to be nuanced, distinguishing between method application and outcomes, and further between preliminary outcomes and mature outcomes. These criteria will be useful for reviewers assessing STGT-based work, whether as *full STGT studies* or the limited application as *STGT for data analysis* with other methods. They will also be beneficial to guide authors towards strong STGT applications and presentations. Table 13.1 summarises the evaluation criteria for the method application and outcomes.

Table 13.1 Socio-technical grounded theory evaluation criteria—for evaluating application and outcomes

Application	Preliminary or interim outcomes	Mature outcomes
Credibility, rigour	Originality, relevance, density	Novelty, usefulness, parsimony, modifiability

13.3 Evaluating STGT Application

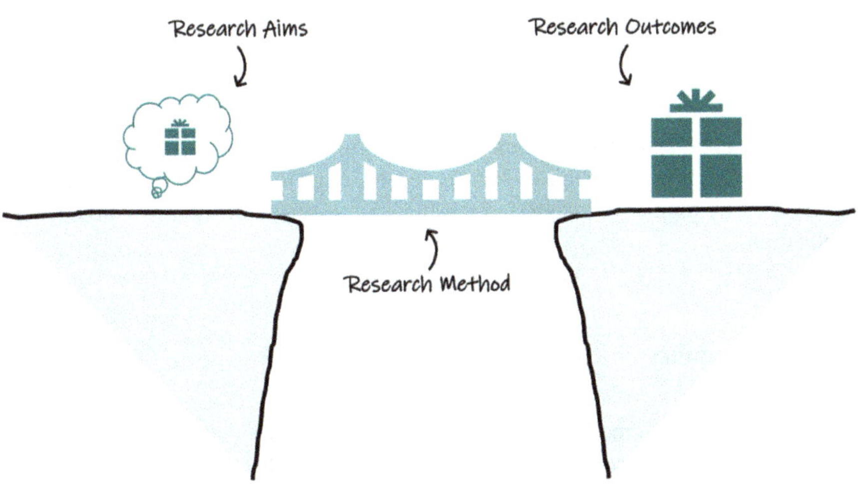

Fig. 13.1 Research method is the bridge that connects the research aims to the research outcomes

> The research method is the bridge that connects the research aims to the research outcomes (Hoda, 2022). The researcher has to build that bridge, i.e. apply the method, in order to go from formulating the aims to achieving the outcomes. In turn, the reviewer has to cross that bridge to go from understanding the aims to accepting the outcomes. If the methodology bridge is assessed to be unstable, it will instil mistrust in the reviewer's mind. On the other hand, if the bridge is assessed to be stable, it will instil confidence in the reviewer's mind and make it easier for them to "cross over" to accepting the outcomes. It is the researcher's job to build a strong bridge and share enough details of its building process to enable the reviewer to assess and cross it (Fig. 13.1).

Treat the research methodology section as a *first-class citizen* in the paper. Research papers we consider to be exemplar typically offer a stable and secure bridge in the form of comprehensive details of the research method application. They do so not just by listing how the method is meant to be applied or repeating the definitions but also by describing concrete details of how the method was applied in their specific study. Some also include details of adaptations made. Methodology details serve to guide other researchers interested in conducting similar research.

However, many manuscripts do not provide sufficient details of the research method application, citing the lack of space as a justification. Reserve enough space for research methodology details. Where necessary, balance it with the space used for findings, discussions, and other sections of the paper. Supplementary materials, archives, or online repositories can also be used to cover additional methodology details. However, keep the paper as standalone as possible in terms of including all the necessary details of method application.

The two criteria for assessing STGT application are *credibility* and *rigour*. Credibility is achieved when it is clear that the research work was in fact done, as per the relevant guidelines. Rigour is achieved when it is clear that the research work was done well. These criteria can be used by authors to guide the building of a strong STGT bridge, i.e. achieve and demonstrate quality STGT application. They can be used by reviewers to assess the bridge, i.e. evaluate the quality of the STGT application.

13.3.1 Credibility

In order to establish credibility, the concrete details of the method application are made available by the researchers and are evaluated by the reviewers, considering the following key aspects:

- *How the participants were recruited*
- *What initial sampling technique was applied*
- *How the iterative and interleaved data collection and analysis occurred*
- *How memos were written*

For mature outcomes, additional information is considered, including:

- *How theoretical sampling was applied*
- *Which mode of theory development—emergent or structured—was used*
- *Whether theoretical structuring or theoretical integration was applied*
- *How the research protocols were refined*
- *How advanced memoing was leveraged*
- *How was theoretical saturation achieved*

Furthermore, manuscripts presenting mature outcomes will benefit from stating the research paradigm applied, including ontology and epistemology. Where a positivist paradigm is applied, credibility can be further assessed through criteria such as replicability, reproducibility, and generalisability. However, these additional criteria are not relevant for a majority of STGT studies that will typically leverage the constructivist paradigm (see Chap. 5 Research Philosophy).

13.3.2 Rigour

For researchers to demonstrate and for reviewers to assess rigour, it is important that sufficient and strong evidence is available. Examples of underlying raw data, coding procedures, and memos help establish credibility and rigour. Some examples of how rigour can be demonstrated and assessed include the following:

- *Sharing sanitised evidence.* While research ethics and participant confidentiality may prevent the full set of raw data to be shared outside of the core research team, it is usually possible to share some examples of sanitised raw data such as interview quotes, snippets from repositories and discussion forums, photos from observations, and links to public documents. These selections of evidences can be sanitised in a way that removes or obfuscates all identifying details. For example, photos can be sanitised by blurring out faces of people, company logos, and other identifying details. Including such examples throughout the findings not only adds strength of evidence, but it also adds to the pleasure of reading a qualitative research paper, as shared in Chap. 12: Theory Development.

- *Sharing coding examples.* Include at least one working example of how coding procedures such as open coding and constant comparison were applied to derive codes, concepts, and categories, such as in Madampe et al. (2021, 2023), Graetsch et al. (2023); Hidellaarachchi et al. (2023).

- *Sharing details of theory development.* In case of researchers presenting, and reviewers evaluating, mature outcomes from the application of a *full STGT study*, examples of applying the advanced stage of theory development will help. Sharing examples of memos and targeted or structured coding (depending on the mode selected) as well as how the theory was structured or integrated allows the reviewers to better understand how the theory was developed.

When sharing sanitised evidence, carefully assess all relevant ethical considerations as discussed in Chap. 7: Basics of Qualitative Data Collection. When reporting qualitative findings, researchers can err on the side of withholding all evidence and examples in an effort to preserve research ethics and confidentiality. However, such extreme withholding is usually unnecessary. As described above, some sanitised evidence can usually be shared within the manuscript itself and as supplementary materials by obfuscating identifying details. Applying such a balanced approach to sharing of evidence in qualitative research is both practical and desirable from an evaluation perspective and for the pleasure of reading.

13.4 Evaluating STGT Outcomes

Depending on the level of STGT application, the research outcomes will vary. When the *full STGT method* is applied, including both the basic stage of data analysis and advanced stage of theory development, the expected outcomes are a mature theory, theoretical model, framework, or rich taxonomies. When STGT is applied in a limited capacity, as *STGT for data analysis* typically with another research method, the expected outcomes are descriptive concepts and categories and emerging hypotheses, propositions, models, frameworks, or taxonomies, all of which can be reported in publications. Details of the various types of outcomes expected from the two levels of application of STGT and how to report them are described in Chap. 12: Theory Development. Evaluating these different outcomes using the same set of criteria is not reasonable. They need to be evaluated differently, using appropriate criteria as described in this section.

13.4.1 Evaluating Outcomes from STGT for Data Analysis

> "The application of STGT's basic stage or the basic data analysis procedures of open coding, constant comparison, and memoing can result in some strong concepts and categories and emerging hypotheses, propositions, models, frameworks, or taxonomies, which can be reported in publications. These outcomes are meant to exhibit *originality*, *relevance*, and *density*."

Originality

STGT studies are typically purpose designed and are highly likely to produce original findings. In this sense, originality can be assumed as a given, unless it is challenged. For example, when evaluating the findings, the reviewer may feel that the findings resemble some existing theory or model from research literature or practitioner sources. In this case, they can inquire about the similarities, if not already explained. The researchers can explain such similarities by describing whether or not they were aware of the existing work and how that may have influenced their study findings.

If the researchers are applying a positivist research worldview, they can explain how they ensured the existing work did not influence their study findings. If they are applying a constructivist research worldview, as is more common for STGT studies, they can explain the role of the existing work in the development of their original study findings. For example, researchers may have used the *theoretical structure* of an existing theory or model, because it was found to be a good fit for their own original findings. Explaining such *theoretical structuring* explicitly will help reviewers not conflate this with lack of originality. For details, refer to Chap. 12: Theory Development.

In other cases, original STGT findings may resemble an existing model or framework that the reviewers are familiar with but the researchers were not aware of. Such coincidences can be explained by the authors by comparing their STGT findings with the (now known) related works. Finally, a rare case is that the reviewers are convinced the findings are not original. Such cases of suspected plagiarism can be handled as per the standard protocols of professional research applied by the journal or conference, irrespective of the research method applied.

Relevance

There are several ways to ascertain relevance. STGT studies are empirically based, that is, they are drawn from the practice of the topic being studied. If the findings "ring true" to the practitioners in the field, it is a good sign that the outcomes are not only credible but also relevant.

One way to check for relevance is to share the findings with the practitioners who participated in the research. This is referred to as member checking (Lincoln & Guba, 1985), often executed in the form of participant focus groups or through sharing of raw data and researcher notes with participants for their feedback and inputs (Creswell & Miller, 2000). The latter is limited to individuals as only their own raw data may be shared with them to provide feedback on the accuracy of the transcription or agreement with the interpretations of what they shared. The former is becoming less of a concern with the improved accuracy of auto-transcription tools and may only require correction of a few words or phrases.

To gain feedback from participants on the wider research findings beyond the data they shared, researchers can share emerging findings, as opposed to raw data, in sensible ways that do not reveal the identity of the participants to each other. Since the findings are drawn from analysing a number of sources, not every participant will relate to every concept or example. However, they will be able to suggest if the overall findings are in line with what they have experienced or have seen others experience in practice. However, there are contexts where member checking is not feasible. If the study relies on data that is anonymous (e.g. from a survey) or coming from sources where reaching back to the original sources is not easy (e.g. forum posts on Stack Overflow), it may become impossible to perform member checking.

Another way to establish relevance is to share the findings with practitioners in the field who were not participants in the research. This can be done by sharing findings in practitioner-friendly formats, e.g. as-one page summaries, posters, or short videos, typically on platforms that are frequented by practitioners, e.g. LinkedIn. Taking the opportunity to present our findings at practitioner-based events and conferences is a great way to check for relevance from the wider community of practice. In doing so, we "give back" to the practitioner community so they can benefit from the research findings which may otherwise not be as easily accessible for them.

Accounts of member checking and presentation of findings to practitioners and the feedback received can be shared as evidence of establishing relevance, either within manuscripts where space allows for it or with reviewers through the response letters or as supplementary materials where possible. Relevance can also be evaluated by reviewers independently based on their knowledge of the practice domain. However, this may be difficult for reviewers whose work in the area is not as practice-based or who have been removed from the field for a while.

A common side effect of achieving relevance is that the findings can come across as *unsurprising* or *intuitive* to the experienced reader (Hoda, 2022). Applying STGT for data analysis rigorously will ensure that while the outcomes may appear intuitive to the experienced reader, they are never trivial or lacking in depth.

Density

When the data analysis procedures of open coding, constant comparison, and memoing are applied rigorously, we can expect outcomes that are dense. In qualitative research, density can be described as the depth or richness of the findings (Hoda, 2022). When STGT data analysis procedures are applied rigorously, they will yield findings that have depth as demonstrated by layers of codes and concepts sitting underneath each category. They will also come through as nuanced when effort is made to explore the topic from multiple perspectives, multiple data sources, and data collection methods. The role of memoing is critical in achieving dense results as the analyst takes a "deep dive" into the topic, instead of simply reporting what is easily accessible on the surface. Examples of dense findings from the application of *STGT for data analysis* can be found in Graetsch et al. (2023), Hidellaarachchi et al. (2023), Madampe et al. (2021, 2022) which present layered, nuanced, and faceted findings.

13.4.2 Evaluating Outcomes from Full STGT Studies

> "The application of the *full STGT method*, including its basic and advanced stages, results in outcomes such as mature theories, theoretical models, frameworks, and taxonomies. The mature outcomes from the full STGT method application need to be evaluated to higher standards than preliminary outcomes. They are meant to demonstrate the characteristics of *novelty*, *usefulness*, *parsimony*, and *modifiability*."

An outcome of the full STGT method is considered mature once it comprises of well-supported categories and relationships. For example, a "lightweight" taxonomy that serves as a high-level classification of a topic of interest can result from the limited application of STGT, i.e. the basic stage of data analysis. On the other hand, a taxonomy resulting from the full application of the STGT method, including the basic and advanced stages, can be expected to be more dense, nuanced, and generally more comprehensive.

The maturity of the outcome needs to be considered relative to the context of the research topic studied. For example, a theory developed on the role of emojis in workplace communication in software teams studied in Brazil needs to be assessed relative to the context studied, i.e. how work teams in a specific domain in a specific country use a specific tool for a specific purpose. Such a theory represents a narrow phenomenon and context. It cannot be compared to, say, the traditional theory of scientific management proposed by Frederick Taylor, which was studied as a broader phenomenon and later applied in a much broader context. Chapter 12: Theory Development provides more details and examples of the different types of theories that can be generated.

The term "mature" does not mean the outcomes are expected to be universally applicable nor that they represent a "final" immutable theory, model, or taxonomy. In fact, one of the key characteristics of a mature outcome is *modifiability*. Others are *novelty*, *usefulness*, and *parsimony*.

Novelty

A key motivation for conducting a full STGT study is to develop new theoretical outcomes, as opposed to verifying or applying existing theories. Novelty is therefore a key evaluation criteria for mature outcomes resulting from full STGT studies. Novelty is said to be achieved when the outcome presents unprecedented insights on a relatively under-researched phenomenon or a fresh approach to understanding a well-studied phenomenon (Hoda, 2022).

Since an STGT study is conducted on an under-researched topic or with a fresh approach to understanding a well-studied topic, the outcomes are naturally likely to be novel. Purposeful collection of data guided by the emerging outcomes and rigorous application of the analysis procedures further ensure that the insights generated present a novel view. In other words, it is highly unlikely for an STGT study to produce the same or very similar outcomes as from another study. If a mature outcome of a full STGT study resembles other existing theories or models, its novelty can be further scrutinised, and the researchers may need to explain the role or influence of the existing theories or models on their original findings.

Usefulness

Mature outcomes go beyond achieving relevance and resonating with practice. Mature outcomes are additionally *useful*, especially to the domain actors where the phenomenon occurs. Usefulness is said to be achieved when the possible applications and implications for research and practice are shared (Hoda, 2022). For example, a full STGT study that explores the views and experiences of AI practitioners on developing ethical AI systems will produce outcomes that will not only "ring true" with AI practitioners but also provide them with practical guidance and recommendations that they can use to improve their practice.

Usefulness also includes explaining the contexts in which the outcomes apply and those where they possibly may not. This will help practitioners understand when and where to apply the recommendations. Similarly, it will help researchers better understand aspects that are covered by the research and those that can be addressed through future work. Sharing the implications for future research improves the overall usefulness of the research. The role of advanced memoing is key in deriving actionable guidelines and recommendations, as memos help draw insights from across entire datasets.

Parsimony

Parsimony refers to the compactness of the theoretical outcomes such that they exhibit conceptual density and explain potentially complex phenomenon in simple and elegant ways (Hoda, 2022). Parsimony can be demonstrated by describing the overall theoretical outcomes in compact ways, e.g. in a few sentences or a small paragraph that succinctly capture the key categories and relationships between them. Examples of theory statements can be found in Chap. 12: Theory Development. Similarly, parsimony can be demonstrated through visualising mature theoretical outcomes as diagrams and figures. An example of a diagrammatic representation of a mature theory resulting from the application of the full STGT method can be found in Graetsch et al. (2023) and more can be seen in Chap. 12.

Parsimony is highly desirable because it shows that the outcome has reached a level of maturity and clarity where it can be expounded in succinct and elegant ways. It also shows the underlying concepts and categories are cohesive, integrated, and structured. Advanced procedures such as theoretical structuring and integration are key to achieving parsimony. Another advantage of presenting the theoretical outcomes in simple, succinct, and elegant ways is that it makes it easily accessible for the practitioners and researchers to consume, discuss, and share. Popular models such as *the stages of small group development* (Tuckman & Jensen, 1977) and the Scrum software development model are accompanied by elegant visual diagrams that explain complex underlying processes in simple ways, ultimately making it easier to impact practice.

Modifiability

Modifiability is the ability of a theoretical outcome to be adapted to new and changing evidences and contexts over time. Contrary to popular belief, mature theoretical outcomes are not meant to be "final" or immutable. Rather, a quality attribute of a mature theoretical outcome is its modifiability.

When it comes to qualitative research, the saying "*you never step in the same river twice*" is highly applicable. Mature outcomes of full STGT studies represent the results of painstaking work into understanding a socio-technical topic, as it stood at the time when they were studied. As the world evolves, the socio-technical aspects associated with a phenomena also evolve. Modifiability represents the flexibility of the theoretical outcome to stand the test of time by adapting to the changing landscape. It can be thought of as the elasticity of the outcome, its ability to stretch and encompass other similar contexts. For example, a hypothetical empirically derived theory of how friendships developed in school years in metropolitan Australian public schools in the mid-1990s can be considered modifiable if its core categories and relationships can be refined in response to new data, e.g. to account for the use of social media in today's times.

Researchers using the positivist paradigm for their STGT study can understand modifiability in terms of improving the generalisability of their outcomes beyond the research participant base to other similar contexts. Generalisability here does not refer to universality as may apply to *hard* scientific theories and laws. Rather, it refers to the stretch value of the *soft* grounded theories, such that it is not strictly limited to the data analysed or the participants studied but can also apply to similar contexts. See Chap. 11: What Is Theory? for more on *hard* and *soft* theories. Researchers using the constructivist paradigm can understand this in terms of capturing the evolving nature of the world around them while also accounting for the evolution of the researchers themselves as they gain experience in the field.

Developing mature theoretical outcomes is a non-trivial pursuit. Expecting the same research team to demonstrate evidence of modifiability by conducting a similar study in another context is not practical. This can be left to be pursued in future studies by the same or a different research team. To demonstrate modifiability, researchers can suggest how their theoretical outcomes can be modified to account for new contexts. Reviewers will have to assess how practical or grandiose these thought experiments are and steer the research team towards practicality if they are inclined to the latter.

There will be a point beyond which an empirically derived grounded theory will not stretch and a new study may be required to understand the new context. For example, it may be difficult to modify the previously mentioned hypothetical theory of how friendships developed in school years in metropolitan Australian public schools in the 1990s to account for the evolving concept of friendship in the age of AI-based chatbots. A fresh study may be required with new empirical data and observations to understand this modern phenomenon of human-AI friendship development during school years in metropolitan Australian public schools or any given region, country, or classification of school for that matter.

Those who subscribe to Karl Popper's school of thought may bring up *falsifiability*, when referring to the underlying logic, or falsification, when referring to the methodology, and use it to challenge the scientific basis of induction (Popper, 2005) and, by extension, the scientific basis of empirically based theories. However, this is a non-issue since empirically grounded theoretical outcomes derived from the application of STGT (and traditional GT methods) do not claim to be universal in nature. They are mid-ranged theories and theoretical outcomes whose applications are limited to the context studied and, by some extension, to similar contexts. For example, if a metropolitan Australian public school is found where the original theory does not serve to explain how friendships develop in that school, the researchers can attempt to modify the original theory to account for the specific differences observed at the new school, adding to the breadth and richness of the theory. However, how friendship develops during school years in metropolitan Australian public schools may be very different to how it develops in private girls schools in Malaysian villages. In this case, it makes little sense to say that the latter serves as empirical evidence of a contradiction to the original theory because the original theory never claimed to be universal nor does its modifiability stretch to the latter context.

13.5 Summary

In this chapter, we learned about the *evaluation approach* applied when assessing socio-technical grounded theory (STGT) but also, more generally, any research. The evaluation approach includes assessing reviewer suitability, acknowledging default review position, establishing an acceptance threshold, and cultivating a constructive review style. Next, we learned about the two sets of *evaluation criteria* for STGT, one for *evaluating the method application* and the other for *evaluating the outcomes*. This was followed by explaining the details of the evaluation criteria for the method application, namely, credibility and rigour. Next, we learned about the details of the criteria for evaluating the outcomes of applying *STGT for data analysis*: originality, relevance, and density. Finally, we covered the criteria for evaluating the outcomes of applying *a full STGT study* to produce mature theoretical outcomes: novelty, usefulness, parsimony, and modifiability.

References

Creswell, J. W., & Miller, D. L. (2000). Determining validity in qualitative inquiry, *Theory into Practice, 39*(3), 124–130.

Graetsch, U. M., Khalajzadeh, H., Shahin, M., Hoda, R., & Grundy, J. (2023). Dealing with data challenges when delivering data-intensive software solutions, *IEEE Transactions on Software Engineering, 49*, 4349–4370. https://doi.org/10.1109/TSE.2023.3291003

Hidellaarachchi, D., Grundy, J., Hoda, R., & Mueller, I. (2023). The influence of human aspects on requirements engineering-related activities: Software practitioners' perspective. *ACM Transactions on Software Engineering and Methodology, 32*(5), 1–37.

Hoda, R. (2022). Socio-technical grounded theory for software engineering. *IEEE Transactions on Software Engineering, 48*(10), 3808–3832.

Lincoln, Y. S., & Guba, E. G. (1985). *Naturalistic inquiry*. Sage.

Madampe, K., Hoda, R., & Grundy, J. (2021). A faceted taxonomy of requirements changes in agile contexts, *IEEE Transactions on Software Engineering, 48*(10), 3737–3752.

Madampe, K., Hoda, R., & Grundy, J. (2022). The emotional roller coaster of responding to requirements changes in software engineering, *IEEE Transactions on Software Engineering, 49*(3), 1171–1187.

Madampe, K., Hoda, R., & Grundy, J. (2023). A framework for emotion-oriented requirements change handling in agile software engineering, *IEEE Transactions on Software Engineering, 49*, 3325–3343 . https://doi.org/10.1109/TSE.2023.3253145

Popper, K. (2005). *The logic of scientific discovery*. Routledge.

Tuckman, B. W., & Jensen, M. A. C. (1977). Stages of small-group development revisited, *Group & Organization Studies, 2*(4), 419–427.

14 Future Directions in Qualitative Research

Abstract In this chapter, we will explore possible future directions in qualitative research. First, we will consider an overview of the opportunities, risks, and limitations associated with the possible use of large language models (LLMs) in qualitative research. Next, we will explore capabilities of ChatGPT in analysing qualitative data and formulating theory. Finally, we will conclude by considering some further applications of the socio-technical research framework beyond grounded theory and of socio-technical grounded theory beyond the software engineering discipline.

14.1 Qualitative Research with LLMs

In my TSE paper (Hoda, 2022) introducing socio-technical grounded theory (STGT) for software engineering (early access August 2021, published 2022), I had shared a vision for the future: "Further advancements in technology and artificial intelligence offer unexplored potential in supplementing, augmenting, and automating parts of qualitative data analysis to ease human effort and improve both the quality and the

R. Hoda, *Qualitative Research with Socio-Technical Grounded Theory*,
https://doi.org/10.1007/978-3-031-60533-8_14

scale of theory development". What I did not anticipate was how soon this vision would come to pass.

When Open AI released ChatGPT in November 2022, it ushered in the use of large language models (LLMs) in the public realm. Since then, there has been much speculation and debate on the risks posed by LLMs, including ethical considerations. Yet, most domains are being rapidly influenced by LLMs, including software engineering. A recent systematic literature review of LLMs in software engineering presents a roadmap of practical applications and future research (Hou et al., 2023).

Research is not immune to the LLM revolution. Researchers are exploring the opportunities and risks of LLMs in qualitative research (Siiman et al., 2023; Bano et al., 2024). Given their extensive linguistic capabilities, it is easy to imagine LLMs as a silver bullet to resolve many challenges traditionally associated with qualitative research such as time-intensive work, consistency, subjectivity, and generalisability. While subjectivity and generalisability may be non-issues in constructivist research approaches, advanced AI techniques promise to ease human effort and expand the scale of theory development beyond what is typically achievable by human research teams. Some researchers suggest LLMs offer enhanced transparency in research (Siiman et al., 2023). Others go as far as suggesting that LLMs such as GPT-3 can augment and potentially replace human analysis in human-computer interaction research (Byun et al., 2023).

While some researchers enumerate the opportunities offered by LLMs, others highlight the associated challenges such as ethical and privacy concerns, biases in the underlying model, model drift, and lack of contextual and philosophical understanding among others (Bano et al., 2024). Intellectual property concerns are also raised when it comes to the use of LLMs in research (Balel, 2023). The risk of biased interpretation is seen to arise from biased training data (Siiman et al., 2023). At the same time, LLMs are also seen to pose the threat of over-dependence on technology, especially for novice researchers (Bano et al., 2024). Overall, studies have begun to scratch what is undeniably only the surface of all the possibilities of using LLMs in qualitative research.

14.2 Exploring ChatGPT for Qualitative Data Analysis

Qualitative data analysis (QDA) is a foundational step in qualitative research. It is also one of the most rigorous and tedious. If LLMs could help improve the quality, speed, and effectiveness of QDA, it would be a big win for researchers engaging in qualitative and mixed methods research. Recently, attempts have been made to assess the use of LLMs for content analysis (Chew et al., 2023), thematic analysis (Dai et al., 2023), and deductive coding in general (Xiao et al., 2023). Gains from the use of LLMs have been reported in the form of improved speed, promising quality, discernible effectiveness for deductive coding (Chew et al., 2023), and *almost perfect agreement* between human coder and machine coder (Dai et al., 2023). For inductive coding, a study of interaction techniques and controls is recommended to support researchers in effective use of LLMs (Xiao et al., 2023).

I wanted to explore ChatGPT's capabilities for inductive QDA. To do this, I explored its capabilities in qualitative data analysis using open coding, in reviewing human coding, and in theory development. Here are my experiences.

14.2.1 Can ChatGPT Perform Qualitative Data Analysis?

I asked ChatGPT to perform open coding on a very short interview transcript excerpt. Figure 14.1 shows my query and ChatGPT's response. Figure 14.2 shows my manual open coding of the same excerpt. Detailed description of the manual analysis can be found in Chap. 10: STGT for Qualitative Data Analysis.

Comparing the two, it can be seen that some codes are similar. For example, customer-driven changes suggested by ChatGPT map to #customerDemand as I coded it. External influences map to #forcedExternalCircumstances. However, the code-name selected in manual coding captured the additional aspect of the external circumstances (or influences) being *forced* on the participant, while ChatGPT seems to have missed this aspect. It does, however, pick up words such as forced and compelled when describing other codes. While this may appear to be a minor issue, the loss of the word *forced* in the code-name at this stage can easily be carried through to the next levels of analysis as similar codes are meant to be combined to create concepts and similar concepts are meant to be combined to create categories. How such multiple levels of analysis can be done with LLMs through multiple prompts without losing the context or level information (code versus concept versus category) needs to be explored in the future.

Next, we note that ChatGPT's description of external influences includes several examples such as regulatory requirements. It is unclear where these examples come from as no such information was present in the two-sentence excerpt given as input for analysis. This is an example of ChatGPT drawing on its extensive database to bring depth to its responses. If a human analyst introduces such examples, say, based on their wider professional experience, it would still be considered inaccurate as they are meant to analyse only the empirical data that is part of the study and not combine it with their own experiences.[1] With further prompt engineering asking ChatGPT to restrict itself to the information available in the excerpt, a revised response was presented which contained the same codes but no additional examples beyond what was present in the given excerpt. Again, this points to the human analysts needing to be well versed in anticipating and designing prompts that eliminate such issues.

[1] Research techniques such as participatory research provide strategies to systematically include participant-researcher experiences as evidence in the study.

You

Perform open coding on following Interview Transcript Excerpt. Do not repeat the excerpt.

Interviewer: In your words, what is requirements change?

Participant: Well, two parts, anything the customer wants and anything that's forced by external circumstances.

ChatGPT

Based on the provided interview transcript excerpt, here's an example of open coding:

Open Coding:

1. **Customer-Driven Changes:** The participant highlights changes in requirements that originate from the desires, needs, or requests of the customer. These changes are initiated by the customer and reflect their preferences, feedback, or evolving understanding of the project.
2. **External Influences:** The participant mentions changes in requirements that are influenced by external circumstances beyond the control of the customer or the development team. These changes may be prompted by factors such as regulatory requirements, market conditions, technological advancements, or other external pressures.
3. **Dual Nature of Requirements Change:** The participant characterizes requirements change as having two distinct components: those driven by customer preferences and those compelled by external factors. This suggests that requirements change can result from a combination of customer-driven demands and external constraints.
4. **Definition of Requirements Change:** The participant provides a definition of requirements change as comprising both customer-requested changes and changes forced by external circumstances. This definition underscores the multifaceted nature of requirements change in software development projects.

These codes represent initial interpretations and conceptualizations of the qualitative data. In grounded theory methodology, the coding process would continue iteratively, with additional segments of data being coded and compared to identify broader patterns, themes, and categories related to requirements change. Through constant comparison, memoing, and reflexivity, researchers would refine and develop these initial codes into a comprehensive coding framework that forms the basis for further analysis.

Fig. 14.1 ChatGPT's attempt to perform open coding on a short interview transcript excerpt

Both human and AI analysis picked up on the presence of *two parts*. ChatGPT coded this as dual nature of requirements change. Human analysis interpreted this as two distinct reasons why requirements changes arise. However, with the knowledge of the wider empirical dataset and anticipation of other possible reasons to be discovered in future interviews, the human analyst coded this as #Reasons4RCs or reasons for requirements change. More experimentation is required before it becomes clear how ChatGPT's knowledge base can be controlled to not invoke its full underlying training dataset but at the same time consider the full empirical dataset that is part of the research study.

Another nuanced point worth noting about the excerpt is that while the interviewer had asked the participant about their definition of requirements change, the participant did not really provide a definition. Rather, the participant described two aspects behind why requirements changes arise. ChatGPT created the code *definition*

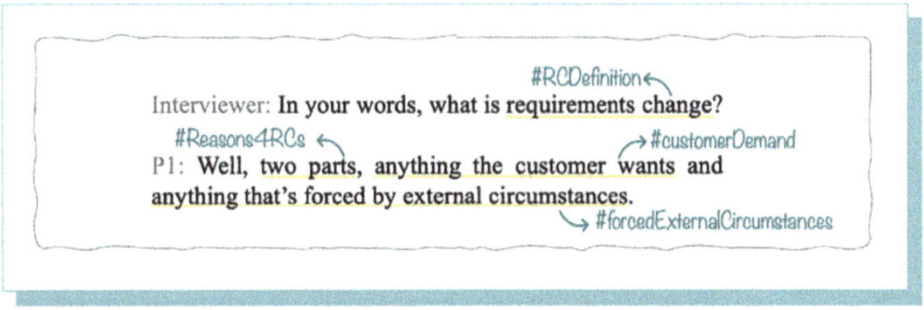

Fig. 14.2 Human open coding with hashtags on the same excerpt

of requirements change and explained it as "*...having two distinct components: those driven by customer preferences and those compelled by external factors.*" This is an attempt at simple classification that can give rise to a high-level taxonomy of the types of RCs. However, the human analyst acknowledges that the participant did not really answer the question as they did not define what they consider to be a requirements change. Instead, the participant highlighted the #Reasons4RCs, i.e. aspects that lead to requirements changes arising. This serves to highlight the unpredictable nature of human-based data and the need to stay critical and open during analysis. ChatGPT generated the code—definition of RC—because the interviewer had asked about it rather than critically assessing the answer to see whether the participant's answer had in fact addressed the question.

14.2.2 Can ChatGPT Review Qualitative Data Analysis?

Next, I went about testing the capabilities of ChatGPT to evaluate my coding. I shared the same interview transcript as before along with the manual codes I had generated and asked ChatGPT to check if my open coding was correct. Figure 14.3 shows my query and ChatGPT's response. It tells me I am on the right track. Then it goes on to describe what my codes mean.

I found this interesting for several reasons: First, it picked up on the hashtags and code-naming conventions without me explaining them. Second, it offered explanations of the code back to me even though I hadn't asked for them. Third, it was able to discern that #customerDemand and #forcedExternalCircumstances are *sub-categories* within the *broader theme* of reasons for requirements change. It is impressive that it was able to pick up on the multilayered grouping. However, using the term *sub-categories* may be premature at this point since we are working at the lowest level of analysis, with the codes. Similar codes combine to form concepts. Similar concepts combine to form categories, and there may be sub-categories arising in some cases. With this small amount of data, it is too early to suggest *sub-categories*. It may have used the term in a more general sense, something I caution against as it can confuse analysts going forward. Interestingly, it also used the term *theme* which

You

I analysed this interview transcript excerpt:
"Interviewer: In your words, what is requirements change?
Participant: Well, two parts, anything that the customer wants and anything that is forced by external circumstances"
I derived the following codes: #RCDefinition, #Reasons4RCs, #customerDemand, #forcedExternalCircumstances. Am I open coding correctly?

ChatGPT

Yes, your open coding appears to be on the right track based on the provided interview transcript excerpt. Let's review your codes in relation to the content of the excerpt:

1. **#RCDefinition:** This code captures the participant's definition or understanding of requirements change (RC). It reflects the participant's explanation of what constitutes requirements change, which aligns with the objective of defining key concepts in open coding.
2. **#Reasons4RCs:** This code indicates the participant's reasons or motivations for requirements change. It encompasses the two aspects mentioned by the participant: customer demands and external circumstances. This code demonstrates your ability to identify broader themes and categorize them accordingly.
3. **#customerDemand:** This code specifically focuses on requirements changes driven by customer demands. It's a relevant subcategory within the broader theme of reasons for requirements change, aligning with the participant's mention of "anything that the customer wants."
4. **#forcedExternalCircumstances:** This code refers to requirements changes that are forced by external circumstances, as mentioned by the participant. It's another relevant subcategory within the broader theme of reasons for requirements change, capturing the participant's reference to changes imposed by external factors.

Overall, your open coding process effectively captures the key concepts and themes present in the interview transcript excerpt. Your codes reflect an understanding of the content and allow for categorization and organization of the data into meaningful units for further analysis. Well done!

Fig. 14.3 ChatGPT evaluating human open coding and providing feedback

may be misleading in an open coding context as novice researchers can confuse this with thematic analysis. Finally, it also commented on how my coding aligned with the basics and objectives of the open coding procedure. Such validation can be useful for novice coders. Overall, it evaluated my coding as *effective* and gave me a *well done*.

Next, I asked it to code the same text on its own. It went on to identify three codes: #RCDefinition, #CustomerDemands, and #ExternalForces. Interestingly, it picked up on my hashtags and code-naming conventions and started using them even though I had provided no such instruction. When I asked it to compare my codes with the codes it had derived, it concluded that "*Both sets of codes adequately capture the participant's discussion of requirements change and provide a structured framework for organizing and analyzing the data.*"

I then asked why its coding did not include #Reasons4RCs as a code. It acknowledged that was missing and explained that it had not grouped its codes: "*However, if you prefer to include a broader code encompassing all reasons for requirements change, such as "Reasons4RCs," it can certainly be added to the coding scheme.*"

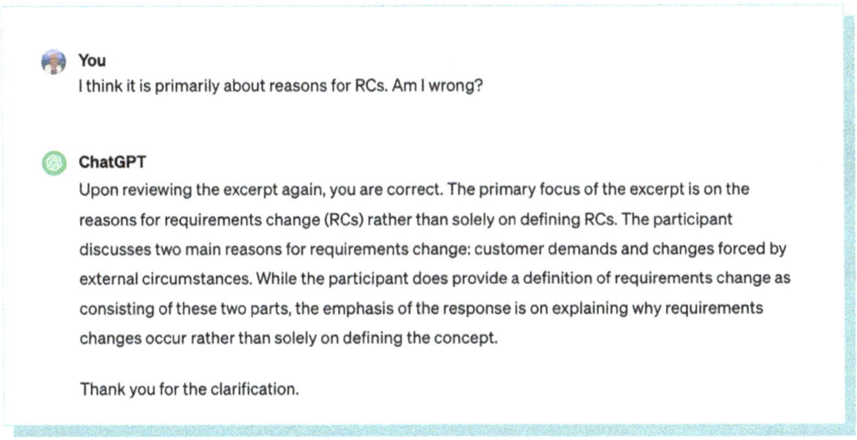

You
I think it is primarily about reasons for RCs. Am I wrong?

ChatGPT
Upon reviewing the excerpt again, you are correct. The primary focus of the excerpt is on the reasons for requirements change (RCs) rather than solely on defining RCs. The participant discusses two main reasons for requirements change: customer demands and changes forced by external circumstances. While the participant does provide a definition of requirements change as consisting of these two parts, the emphasis of the response is on explaining why requirements changes occur rather than solely on defining the concept.

Thank you for the clarification.

Fig. 14.4 ChatGPT revising its coding in response to human discussion

Then I probed it some more on what the excerpt was about: defining RCs or reasons why RCs occur. It defended by saying it was about both. I asked what it was *primarily* about. It explained why it's primarily about defining RCs. Next, I decided to share my view and said "*I think it is primarily about reasons for RCs. Am I wrong?*" In response, it changed its original position. Figure 14.4 shows my query and ChatGPT's response. Here, it reconsidered its original position—as if attempting not to displease me and avoid confrontation, possibly because I asked if I was wrong—and agreed with my interpretation that the excerpt was mainly about reasons why RCs occur. I asked why it changed its mind, to which it provided a reasonably good explanation of why it agreed with my view. I decided to challenge it again by saying "*I may be wrong. Maybe it is not about reasons?*" Again, it changed its position, possibly with my use of the word *wrong*. It tried to find a middle ground and suggested the excerpt is about both aspects. It ended by thanking me for informing it and for my patience. This continued as I kept giving it different prompts about what I thought the excerpt was about. So long as I was sufficiently vague but somehow related to the topic, it tended to agree with me. Each time, it presented an explanation on how what I was suggesting could be seen in the text. When I asked about an aspect that was clearly not relevant, it informed me it was not part of the excerpt and offered to discuss that topic.

These set of prompt experiments point to the fact that ChatGPT can be used to confirm what is clearly out of scope and inform the human analyst when they are clearly off the mark. However, when it comes to assisting with analysis of what is within the parameters of being considered relevant, it is unable to offer reliable and consistent advice and tends to agree with the human analyst's perspective.

From these handful of interactions, it seems that ChatGPT can be useful for novice researchers who need to steer clear from clearly wrong interpretations. It does not seem to be of much use when it comes to discerning between a few different appealing codes and explanations. The role of an experienced (human) analyst becomes vital in this case to review the candidate codes, provide more concrete guidance, and help the novice researcher take final decisions on the prominence of certain interpretations over others based on a variety factors. Future explorations with ChatGPT and other emerging LLMs can assess their ability to take on more of an expert role and provide more direct guidance and help with decision-making.

14.2.3 Can ChatGPT Generate Theories?

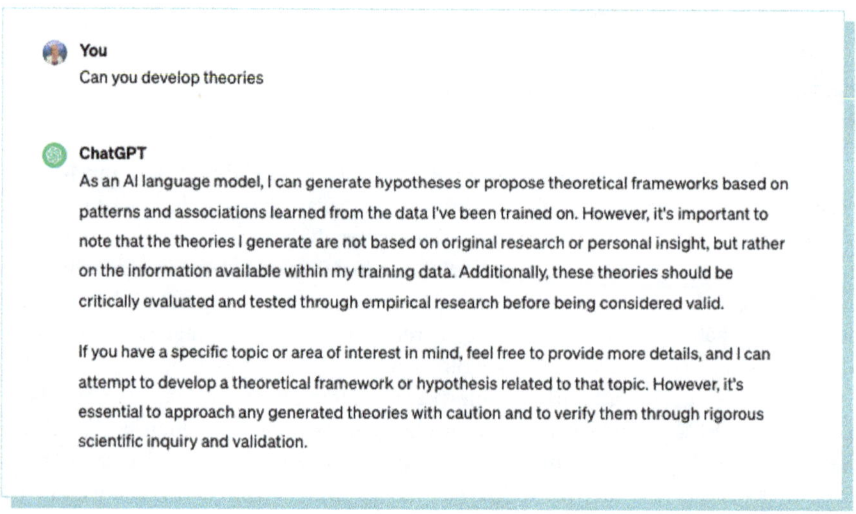

Fig. 14.5 ChatGPT's response to being asked if it can generate a theory

ChatGPT's basic approach of finding patterns across extremely large qualitative datasets sounds akin to STGT's inductive data analysis approach unleashed at scale and on boosters! In playing with the capabilities of ChatGPT 3.5, I queried if it can develop theories. In response, besides including the typical disclaimer statements about its limitations and need for scientific inquiry and validation, it offered to generate hypotheses and theoretical frameworks on specific topics (see Fig. 14.5).

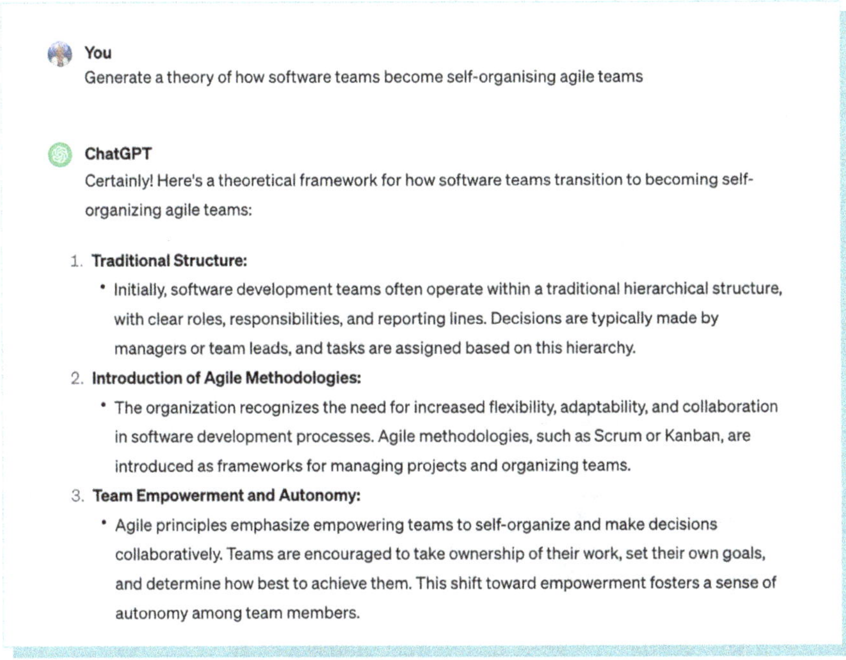

Fig. 14.6 Part of ChatGPT's attempt to generate a specific theory

So, I asked ChatGPT to generate a theory on how software teams become self-organising agile teams. The response generated nine categories: traditional hierarchical structure, introduction of agile methodologies, team empowerment and autonomy, clear vision and goals, iterative development, collaborative culture, servant leadership, continuous learning and adaptation, and organisational support and alignment. Figure 14.6 shows the query and part of the response.

Let us compare the theoretical framework that ChatGPT developed to the *theory of becoming agile* developed from empirical evidence (Hoda & Noble, 2017). The theory of becoming agile explains transitions across five dimensions: software development practices, team practices, management approach, reflective practices, and culture. Comparing ChatGPT's categories to the empirically derived theory:

- *Traditional structure* present at the beginning of an agile transition is most closely captured in the dimension *culture* but also relates to how *management approach* and *team practices* typically start off. ChatGPT's sixth category *collaborative culture* is seen as a desired end goal of the dimensions of the empirical theory.
- Introduction of agile methodologies captures the context in which the transition takes place, captured across multiple dimensions.

- ChatGPT's categories of *team empowerment and autonomy* and *clear vision and goals* can be seen to be present in the dimensions of *team practices* and *management approach*.
- *Iterative development* is captured in the dimension of *software development practices*.
- *Servant leadership* closely matches the mature version of the *management approach*.
- *Continuous learning and adaptation* can be seen to map to the dimension of *reflective practices*.
- *Organisational support and alignment* is covered under the dimensions of *culture* and *management approach*.

There was reasonably good mapping between the categories ChatGPT listed and the five dimensions of the empirical theory. Such alignment can serve to demonstrate the *stretch value* of the theory derived by humans from limited contexts as it maps to theoretical framework derived from the analysis of extremely large amounts and variety of datasets by the LLMs.

However, the empirically grounded theory included several nuanced aspects that the ChatGPT response lacked. For example, the grounded theory explained that software teams could be at low, medium, or high levels of maturity on a given dimension and that their progress on different dimensions can vary. No such ideas were included in the ChatGPT response, pointing to missing elements or the need for further prompt engineering.

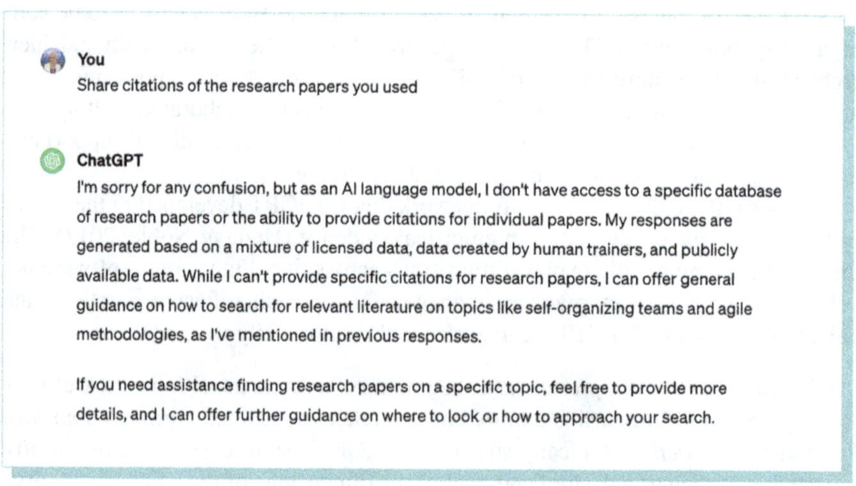

Fig. 14.7 ChatGPT unable to share its exact source of information, citations, and references

The ChatGPT response also exhibited an impressive interdisciplinary approach tapping into multiple disciplines of organizational psychology, systems theory, and agile methodologies. On the other hand, there are known issues of transparency where currently ChatGPT does not share the sources of information, even when asked, which makes for a poor chain of evidence in qualitative research in general and in theory development in particular (see Fig. 14.7).

Another key aspect related to theory development is the idea of *theoretical saturation* applied as an indicator to stop data collection. I quizzed ChatGPT how can we ensure theoretical saturation has been reached. In response, it suggested strategies such as diverse sampling, ongoing data analysis, theoretical sampling, triangulation, peer debriefing, member checking, and reflexivity, along with short descriptions of each.

Next, I made my query more concrete and asked *suppose you have collected data from 1000 twitter posts. When is theoretical saturation reached?* To this, it responded by saying a number of aspects needed to be considered, including variety of themes and perspectives identified, diminishing returns, theoretical sampling, peer review and member checking, reflexivity, and contextual factors.

I used other prompts to try and get more direct guidance around the quantity of data needed for theoretical saturation—this is a common question I get asked by researchers new to theory development. First, I asked "*If I am consistently encountering the same themes without significant variation or new insights should I stop collecting data?*" In response, it said that is a strong indication of theoretical saturation; however, I should still consider several other factors and went on to enumerate the previous and some new ones. Then I asked "*How much data is enough? is 10,000 twitter posts enough?* In response, it said that this question does not have a straightforward answer and went on to list several factors again. After a few other attempts, I asked "*Are 1000 twitter posts better or 10,000 for reaching theoretical saturation?*" This was an attempt to see if it would offer preference for greater quantity of data or share an acceptable range. It responded by saying "*There isn't a fixed number of Twitter posts that guarantees theoretical saturation, as it ultimately depends on the richness and variability of insights gleaned from the data.*" I would agree with this answer in principle. For researchers who need more concrete guidance, however, this conversation was not helping beyond establishing what factors need to be considered when gauging theoretical saturation. Figure 14.8 shows one of my final prompts in an attempt to extract concrete guidance from ChatGPT on theoretical saturation. In response, it acknowledged its data analysis limitations and reminded me that access to data is not enough to establish saturation; other aspects also need to be considered.

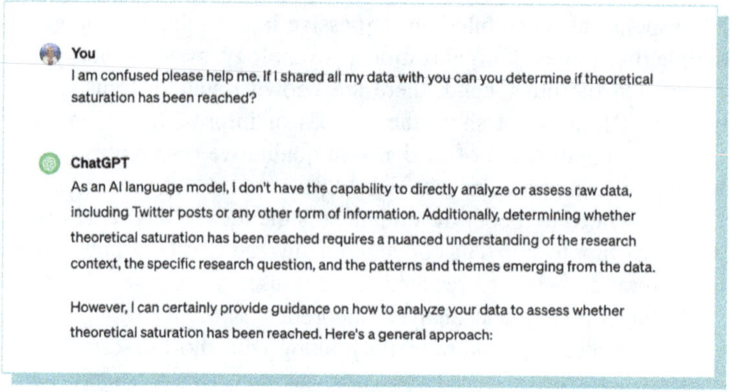

Fig. 14.8 ChatGPT provides guidance on how to go about assessing theoretical saturation but cannot help assess if saturation has been reached

Reasoning or logic is another key aspect of theory development. See Chap. 5: Research Philosophy for more on types of reasoning. I queried ChatGPT about the different types of reasoning in theory development over a series of prompts. It identified induction as the key approach while acknowledging a limited role of deduction and some role of abduction. It presented summarised information that described these aspects. When I asked for a concrete example, it responded by suggesting a hypothetical grounded theory study on exploring the experiences of individuals transitioning to remote work during the COVID-19 pandemic. It used that context to share some examples of what it again called *themes*, such as *work-life balance challenges* and *lack of social interaction*, to explain how abduction can be used in generating initial ideas, identifying patterns and relationships, refining and testing hypotheses, and generating alternative explanations. Again, these are useful pointers. How well ChatGPT and other LLMs can support researchers to attempt each of these steps and procedures in real-world research contexts will need to be tested in the future. Critically, how human anticipation and intuition, which are part of abductive reasoning in theory development, can possibly be mimicked by LLMs will also be interesting to explore.

14.2.4 LLM-Assisted Qualitative Research

To draw robust conclusions about LLMs such as ChatGPT, carefully designed experimentation will need to be conducted to systematically and thoroughly test out their analysis capability, reliability, and consistency with multiple scenarios, datasets, roles played, and prompts. In the meantime, based on my *fun explorations* with ChatGPT and its current capabilities, which are fast evolving, I share the following observations:

There is scope for engaging with ChatGPT during qualitative research. It can be leveraged as an extensive, multidisciplinary, and rather comprehensive *information base* to easily access summarised information on method guidelines, definition of research procedures and concepts, and to provide guidance on how to go about applying certain procedures with examples. However, the ethical risks of taking ChatGPT responses on face value cannot be ignored. ChatGPT relies on the data it was trained on. It's current inability to isolate specific sources of data it draws on for responses combined with its current inability to be able to satisfactorily explain the process by which it derives conclusions poses threats to the credibility and validity of its conclusions.

When it comes to helping human researchers conduct actual research tasks and procedures—as a human research assistant would do—there does not seem to be fast and easy ways to get it to do research tasks for human researchers. Getting ChatGPT to assist with research tasks will likely take the form of a series of interactions. Prompt engineering will play an important role in identifying the most effective prompts to use for achieving good outcomes with specific research tasks. Even so, prompts will need to be customised to specific project needs and constraints.

With its current capabilities, ChatGPT is far from enabling reliable theory development or automated analysis or even semi-automated analysis. With rapid improvements in its capabilities and the right level of access, LLMs such as ChatGPT can possibly be trained to understand qualitative research tasks better and to perform them well with relatively reduced human intervention beyond the initial prompts. Currently, what it does reasonably well is to play the role of a *novice research assistant* who needs to be instructed exactly what to do with clear boundary parameters, working on small units of the research tasks. It also needs to be carefully managed—through prompts—to not overstep the boundaries of the research context, its own role, and to avoid conjectures based on wider datasets beyond what is available in the research study.

My preliminary explorations also point to ChatGPT's potential role as a *gentle peer reviewer* to human researchers that can serve to provide second opinions on emerging categories and findings. This can be especially useful for novice researchers who need to know if they are off-track. By comparing emerging findings with its responses, researchers can identify possible theoretical gaps and drive theoretical sampling. With its default configurations, it serves as a gentle peer, inclined to agree with and looking to please the human analyst. It is neither very critical nor decisive in nature. The indecisiveness is a cause for concern, especially for novice researchers who can easily be confused by its changing positions. Its ability to role-play as a *critical expert reviewer* or *advisor* can be explored in the future.

Overall, how generative AI and their underlying large language models evolve over time to possibly address current limitations remains to be seen. In the meantime, researchers can explore its capabilities but not rely on it.

14.3 Further Applications

In addition to exploring LLMs in qualitative research, there are further applications of the socio-technical framework and the STGT method and techniques.

14.3.1 Beyond Grounded Theory

The socio-technical research framework described in Chap. 3: STGT Overview lays a foundation for what it means (and takes) to conduct research in socio-technical contexts, say, as opposed to social science research. STGT applies the socio-technical framework, along with other adaptations, to define a socio-technical version of traditional grounded theory. Similarly, other research methods originating from the social sciences that are popular in SE research can also formally acknowledge and apply the socio-technical framework. For example, applying the ST framework can enable socio-technical case studies, socio-technical ethnography, and more.

14.3.2 Beyond Software Engineering

STGT is a natural choice of research method to conduct studies that are exclusively qualitative in nature as well as for the qualitative components of mixed methods studies in SE due to its inherently socio-technical context. However, STGT can be applied in not only SE but other disciplines where socio-technical contexts abound. For example, a study of human-robot interaction applied STGT to study incidental encounters between humans and autonomous quadruped robots (Chan & Hauser, 2023). They applied STGT in a mixed methods research context including conducting a lean literature review, a lab-based experiment, a survey, a free-form interaction session with the robot, and an interview with 21 participants. The research team applied the data analysis procedures of coding, constant comparison, and memoing and presented their emerging theory of human reactions in encountering an autonomous quadruped robot where they found the reactions to be influenced by familiarity, certainty, and confidence. This study serves to demonstrate the application of STGT in areas outside SE, where the human/social and technical aspects of a phenomenon are worth studying.

Other avenues for applying STGT to leverage its robust qualitative research procedures include human-computer interaction (HCI) and human-AI interaction (HAI). For example, STGT can be a useful approach to analysing the DevGPT datasets which capture interactions between human developers and ChatGPT to answer a range of open research questions as part of the MSR challenge.[2]

[2] https://2024.msrconf.org/track/msr-2024-mining-challenge.

When we consider the increasing digitisation of domains such as banking, retail, education, medicine, and health, it is not a stretch to imagine the use of STGT in these areas to study increasing socio-technical phenomena. Particularly, with the advent and proliferation of AI across all domains, the role of STGT as a customised research method to study human and socio-technical topics becomes more promising.

14.4 Summary

In this chapter, we gained an overview of the opportunities, risks, and limitations of large language models in qualitative research. Next, we learned about ChatGPT's apparent capabilities and limitations in assisting with qualitative data analysis, reviewing, and theory development. Finally, we learned about how the socio-technical framework can be applied to other research methods arising from social sciences and how STGT can be applied to study topics beyond software engineering in other socio-technical domains.

References

Balel, Y. (2023). The role of artificial intelligence in academic paper writing and its potential as a co-author, *European Journal of Therapeutics, 29*(4): 984–985.

Bano, M., Hoda, R., Zowghi, D., & Treude, C. (2024). Large language models for qualitative research in software engineering: Exploring opportunities and challenges, *Automated Software Engineering, 31*(1): 8.

Byun, C., Vasicek, P., & Seppi, K. (2023). Dispensing with humans in human-computer interaction research, *Extended Abstracts of the 2023 CHI Conference on Human Factors in Computing Systems* (pp. 1–26).

Chan, Y.-C., & Hauser, E. (2023). Understanding reactions in human-robot encounters with autonomous quadruped robots, *Proceedings of the Association for Information Science and Technology, 60*(1): 86–97.

Chew, R., Bollenbacher, J., Wenger, M., Speer, J., & Kim, A. (2023). LLM-assisted content analysis: Using large language models to support deductive coding. arXiv preprint arXiv:2306.14924.

Dai, S.-C., Xiong, A., & Ku, L.-W. (2023). LLM-in-the-loop: Leveraging large language model for thematic analysis. arXiv preprint arXiv:2310.15100.

Hoda, R., & Noble, J. (2017). Becoming agile: A grounded theory of agile transitions in practice. In *2017 IEEE/ACM 39th International Conference on Software Engineering (ICSE)* (pp. 141–151). IEEE.

Hoda, R. (2022). Socio-technical grounded theory for software engineering. *IEEE Transactions on Software Engineering, 48*(10), 3808–3832.

Hou, X., Zhao, Y., Liu, Y., Yang, Z., Wang, K., Li, L., Luo, X., Lo, D., Grundy, J., & Wang, H. (2023). Large language models for software engineering: A systematic literature review. arXiv preprint arXiv:2308.10620.

Siiman, L. A., Rannastu-Avalos, M., Pöysä-Tarhonen, J., Häkkinen, P., & Pedaste, M. (2023). Opportunities and challenges for ai-assisted qualitative data analysis: An example from collaborative problem-solving discourse data. In *International Conference on Innovative Technologies and Learning* (pp. 87–96). Springer.

Xiao, Z., Yuan, X., Liao, Q. V., Abdelghani, R., & Oudeyer, P.-Y. (2023). Supporting qualitative analysis with large language models: Combining codebook with gpt-3 for deductive coding. In *Companion Proceedings of the 28th International Conference on Intelligent User Interfaces* (pp. 75–78).

Index

R. Hoda, *Qualitative Research with Socio-Technical Grounded Theory*,
https://doi.org/10.1007/978-3-031-60533-8

www.ingramcontent.com/pod-product-compliance
Lightning Source LLC
Chambersburg PA
CBHW070758220126
38433CB00024B/380
* 9 7 8 3 0 3 1 6 0 5 3 2 1 *